LAW AND ETHICS IN GLOBAL BUSINESS

In my career I have had the task of teaching business ethics to lawyers and teaching introductory business law to MBA students. Brian Nelson's *Law and Ethics in Global Business* would have helped considerably in both courses, and I would have no hesitation in recommending it to students in future. This interface of business ethics, business law and business practice is becoming a key focus for both business schools and law schools.
Professor Thomas Clarke, *Director, Centre for Corporate Governance, UTS Sydney*

A very valuable new text, currently adopted onto our distance learning programmes as a core text. The law and ethics issues are a "must" for business students, and are delivered here in a user friendly, but challenging, fashion.
Dr Alistair Benson, *Academic Director, Manchester Business School Worldwide*

A helpful book for introducing business students to essential issues in law and ethics. The text provides basic, easily-understood information for students. Nelson's approach permits instructors to supplement in a wide variety of ways, depending upon their course objectives.
Kathleen Getz, *Associate Professor of Global Corporate Citizenship, Kogod School of Business, American University, USA*

Law and Ethics in Global Business made business law straight forward and understandable. It is more than a good text book; I continue to use it regularly as reference in managing my farm supply and marketing cooperative.
George Green, *General Manager, Excel Co-op, Inc.*

An understanding of the legal context of business is a prerequisite of all business studies courses. At MBA level it is an essential aspect of the potential executive knowledge, yet too often it is poorly understood and even more poorly applied to business decisions.

This book provides comprehensive and, above all, business-focused guidance on the fundamentals of business law and how they should be integrated into ethical and effective business decisions. It concentrates on legal principles and thereby is able to articulate the impact of global business law and its international applications. This is an ambitious project, yet arguably no more ambitious than the projects undertaken by global business leaders making business decisions around the world. This book provides a comprehensive overview of the legal and ethical principles which both facilitate and regulate corporate business.

Courses, modules and electives on this topic are taught in almost every MBA, and the author personally teaches courses in the USA, UK, The Netherlands, France, Germany, Hungary, Australia and Singapore. Similar courses are offered at business schools in North America, Europe and the Far East. This book will act as a course book and a business reference source suitable for executives. The author combines the expertise of a law background with the insights of an experienced business educator.

Brian Nelson teaches courses in executive leadership in the USA, UK, Europe and Asia-Pacific. He has handled worldwide corporate legal matters for over 20 years in both corporate and private legal practice. His clients include General Motors, Goldman Sachs, United Airlines and Natwest USA. He has taught at Purdue, RSM-Erasmus, MBS, ESSEC, ESCP-EAP and the Australian National University amongst others.

D0024255

Law and Ethics in Global Business

How to Integrate Law and Ethics into Corporate Governance around the World

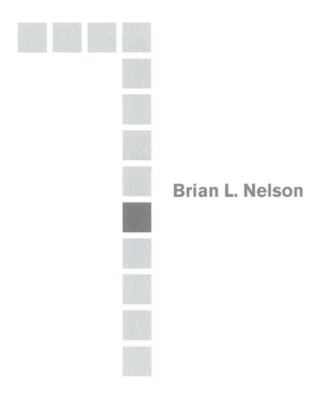

Brian L. Nelson

 Routledge
Taylor & Francis Group

LONDON AND NEW YORK

First published 2006
by Routledge
2 Park Square, Milton Park, Abingdon, Oxon OX14 4RN

Simultaneously published in the USA and Canada
by Routledge
270 Madison Ave, New York, NY 10016

Routledge is an imprint of the Taylor & Francis Group

© 2005 Brian L. Nelson

Typeset in Amasis MT and Akzidenz Grotesk by
Taylor & Francis Books
Printed and bound in Great Britain by
MPG Books Ltd, Bodmin

British Library Cataloguing in Publication Data
A catalogue record for this book is available from the British Library

Library of Congress Cataloging in Publication Data
A catalog record for this book has been requested

ISBN10: 0-415-37778-1 (hbk)
ISBN10: 0-415-37779-X (pbk)

ISBN13: 978-0-415-37778-2 (hbk)
ISBN13: 978-0-415-37779-9 (pbk)

Taylor & Francis Group is the Academic Division of T&F Informa plc.

Contents

PART 5   OTHER LEGAL FACILITIES

List of Contributors

Brian L. Nelson teaches "Law and Ethics in Global Business," a course in corporate leadership. Prof. Nelson's course is based on over twenty years of practicing international corporate law and six years of teaching at top business schools in Europe and the United States. In addition to this text, he has developed his own course materials, focusing on integrating legal and ethical issues into corporate governance around the world. Among other appointments, he has taught for four years at Purdue University's Krannert Center for Executive Education and Research. During the 2005–2006 academic year Prof. Nelson is serving as an Executive-in-Residence at American University's Kogod School of Business in Washington, D.C.

Prof. Nelson's course has been offered as part of undergraduate MBA, executive MBA and in-company MBA programs at Purdue University (USA), Rotterdam School of Management (The Netherlands), Manchester Business School (UK), ESSEC (France), ESCP-EAP (France), University of Tilburg (The Netherlands), GISMA (Germany) and Central European University (Hungary). His students include corporate executives, mid-level managers, consultants and entrepreneurs from the United States, Latin America, the Far East and every country in Europe (including the former members of the Warsaw Pact and the Soviet Union). He has also taught courses on "effective legal counseling for global corporations" as part of accredited post-graduate programs (LLM) in international business law for law schools in the United States and France.

Prof. Nelson graduated with honors in international and comparative law from Columbia Law School in 1981. Since then, he has practiced international corporate law for over twenty years: eight years at the world headquarters of two multinational corporations, where he held various positions of increasing responsibility; and over twelve years in private practice in Brussels, New York and Chicago, where he maintains his office. Throughout Prof. Nelson's career, he has provided multinational corporations with general counseling for their global, regional, national and local business operations, including governance issues and compliance programs. His regional assignments have included managing corporate legal affairs in Europe, North America and South America. In addition, Prof. Nelson has handled transactions spanning the globe: acquisitions and joint ventures in Europe, North and South America, the Middle East and the Far East; structuring European operations for various US companies; structuring US operations for two French companies; global patent and other intellectual property programs; litigation management, including European patent litigation; and representing various money center banks in their corporate credit facilities.

Prof. Nelson's corporate clients have included United Airlines, Inc., General Motors Corporation, FMC Corporation, Abbott Laboratories, Inc., National Medical Care, W. R. Grace & Co., Great Lakes Chemical Corp., Beatrice Companies, Inc., AL Laboratories AB, Grundig AG, and two French multinational groups (Hutchinson SA and SASM SA). His banking clients have included Goldman Sachs, National Westminster Bank USA, ABN AMRO, Westpac Banking Corporation, The Fuji Bank, Heller Financial Corporation (US subsidiary of Fuji Bank) and Harris Bank (US subsidiary of Bank of Montreal). Prof. Nelson has also conducted comparative law studies for the Commission of the European Union, the Republic of Mexico and the Kingdom of Belgium.

Brian L. Nelson, Member of the Bar: New York (1982), Illinois (1984). Education: Harvard University B.A. 1976, Columbia University J.D. 1981. Contact: 203 North LaSalle Street, Suite 2100, Chicago, Illinois 60601 USA; telephone: (1) (312) 320 7972; e-mail: brianlnelson@hotmail.com; Languages: English, German, French and Spanish.

Estelle J. Tsevdos (Chapter 18: Intellectual property rights) has many years of experience in all areas of intellectual property law, with particular emphasis on patents in the areas of biotechnology, organic chemistry and all life sciences. This experience includes client counseling, transactional licensing, mergers and acquisitions, patent prosecution and litigation.

Dr Tsevdos has accumulated first-hand knowledge into the intellectual property needs of corporate clients based on her in-house experience as Manager of a Biotechnology Section within a corporate environment. This forms the cornerstone of Dr Tsevdos' extensive experience not only in licensing and mergers and acquisitions, but in building meaningful patent protection for inventions, guiding clients to avoid any potential infringement of third party patents, enforcing patents and defending against allegations of patent infringement.

Estelle Tsevdos JD, Member of the Bar: Ohio, US Patent and Trademark Office, Registered Patent Attorney. Education: Case Western Reserve University School of Law, 1981; PhD, Ohio State University, Graduate School of Medicine, 1978; Pharmacology, BA, Ohio Wesleyan University, Pre-med and Zoology, 1973; Contact: Partner, Hunton & Williams, 200 Park Avenue, New York, NY 10166-0136, tel: (1) (212) 309-1021.

Bernd C. Janssen (Chapter 19: International and European patents) is a German and European patent attorney active in the areas of trademark law and patent law, especially in the areas of chemistry and pharmacology. He concentrates mainly on conducting opposition proceedings and opposition appeal proceedings before the European Patent Office, and on trademark prosecution and oppositions before the German Patent and Trademark Office.

Bernd Janssen PhD, Member of the bar of German Patent Attorneys and the EPI, received his PhD in organometal chemistry from the University of Heidelberg, Germany. He became a German Patent Attorney in 1997 and a European Patent Attorney in 1998, and gained experience in US patent practice by working at a patent law firm in Chicago, IL and at the patent departments of ExxonMobil in Florham Park, NJ and Baytown, TX.

Contact: Uexküll & Stolberg, Beselerstr. 4, Hamburg, 22607, Germany, telephone: (49) (40) 899–6540, email: janssen@uex.de.

Preface

This book embodies an ambitious project: articulating techniques and principles useful for integrating law and ethics into corporate governance around the world. At the same time, this book is no more ambitious than the opportunities and challenges facing global corporate leaders: making business decisions around the world and implementing those decisions in and through the global organizations they lead.

Businesses everywhere are founded on legal institutions, e.g., private property rights, contracts, markets and corporations. A better understanding of those legal institutions facilitates business operations everywhere. Businesses everywhere are subject to legal and ethical principles, e.g., general obligations law, competition law, agency law and the ethical norms of the communities where they operate. A better understanding of those legal and ethical principles enables corporations to conduct business faithfully and diligently in pursuit of their missions. Many corporations conduct business globally – or aspire to do so. Accordingly, corporate leaders would benefit from a better understanding of the legal and ethical aspects of the opportunities and challenges they face around the world. This book provides that understanding.

Several books intended for corporate leaders address "international business law." Some of those books are based upon "international public law," i.e., the treaties governing the conduct of nations – not the conduct of business. These books provide isolated chapters on national business laws, but only to the extent that those national laws are dictated by international treaty obligations, e.g., tariffs and the international sale of goods. Other books on international business law consist primarily of detailed descriptions on the business laws of one country, such as the United States or France. These books provide occasional supplementary material on foreign laws, international treaty obligations or laws specifically applicable to business abroad, e.g., trade embargoes. (Of course, books on international business law intended for lawyers typically simply select and describe in detail a limited range of business laws from one or more countries, e.g., contract or competition law.)

None of the currently published books on international business law is written from the perspective of a corporate leader. None of those books provides techniques for integrating laws and ethics into business decisions and corporate organizations around the world in a manner which is effective, efficient and consistent with other business concerns such as commercial interests and financial returns. None of those books provides a comprehensive overview of the legal and ethical principles which facilitate and regulate business around the world. This book provides those techniques and principles, all from the perspective of corporate leaders and all in a manner which is easy to understand and to apply.

Finally, the insights offered in this book are intended to survive specific changes in the laws and in the community ethical norms applicable to global business. In other words, this book's insights are intended to assist global corporations to adapt to the varied and changing legal and ethical climates in which they operate.

Brian L. Nelson
28 February 2005

PART ONE

Introduction

Integrating law and ethics into corporate governance

1

A Global Framework

A GLOBAL FRAMEWORK FOR INTEGRATING LAW AND ETHICS INTO BUSINESS CONDUCT

This book provides corporate executives with a comprehensive framework for integrating law and ethics into business conduct. Integrating applicable law and community ethical norms into business conduct enables executives

1 to take fuller advantage of the opportunities available to their businesses, and
2 to manage the risks inherent in pursuing those opportunities.

The framework provided in this book consists of both

(a) techniques for making and implementing business decisions which give due consideration to legal and ethical concerns, and
(b) an overview of the legal principles and ethical norms applicable to business.

The techniques, principles and norms are all explained in terms generally applicable around the world.

Having such a framework is desirable

Obviously, it would be useful for every corporation to have a single framework for integrating law and ethics into all of its decisions and operations. Such a framework for legal principles would be useful because the law provides the fundamental institutions making business possible: private property, contracts, markets and corporations. In addition, such a framework for ethical norms would be useful because corporations can promote their business goals by observing the ethical norms of the many communities in which they operate. Violating legal and ethical norms, on the other hand, can have significant negative consequences for businesses.

Moreover, it is useful for corporations conducting business internationally to have such a framework on a global basis. Giving managers throughout a corporation a common understanding of legal principles and ethical norms in terms generally applicable around the world provides those corporations with a single starting point for integrating law and ethics into their worldwide business operations, thereby enhancing the quality of decisions made and implemented throughout the corporation.

Finally, such a framework is feasible because managers in corporations around the world are similarly situated. Corporate managers around the world make and implement decisions on behalf of corporations. They all seek to provide goods and services in return for revenues which exceed costs. They are all faced with the challenge of obtaining those returns while giving due consideration to legal principles and community ethical norms.

Having such a framework is feasible

Providing corporations with a single framework for integrating law and ethics into business conduct is an ambitious challenge, but providing such a framework is no more ambitious than the challenges facing corporate leaders every day. After all, legal and ethical considerations are only two aspects of the multi-faceted decisions corporate leaders regularly make and implement.

Providing such a framework on a global basis is feasible because there are significant commonalities among legal principles and ethical norms applicable to business around the world. The commonalities are significant because, even in the absence of contact between separate markets in different parts of the world, all markets were – with some exceptions – conducted for centuries on the basis of the same fundamental legal institutions, i.e., private property rights and contracts, and on the basis of common customs and conventions among merchants. The commonalities are significant also because, from an early date, markets were "international," with merchants from different parts of the world relying on private property rights, contracts and a single set of customs and conventions to conduct business. With the rise of the modern era, national governments have slowly and surely, but – to a surprising extent – simply incorporated those common customs and conventions into their business laws. As a result, the business laws of the various nations are surprisingly homogeneous. In fact, business laws around the world were, to a great extent, specifically intended to be similar so as to facilitate trade.

CORPORATE GOVERNANCE

Structures and procedures

For the purposes of this book, corporate governance shall mean the internal structures and procedures within a corporation intended to provide reasonable assurances that corporate directors, officers and employees make and implement decisions in accordance with their duties of care and loyalty to their corporations.

The term "internal controls" is sometimes used by some persons for some purposes to refer to the internal structures and procedures encompassed by the term "corporate governance" as used in this book. For example, the United States' Sarbanes-Oxley Act of 2002 ("Sarbanes-Oxley") uses the term "internal controls" in its Section 404 to designate corporate governance structures and procedures for the limited purpose of reliable financial reporting.

Governance structures: who makes and implements decisions?

The "structures" comprising one aspect of corporate governance systems are the formal delegations of authority within a corporation for making and implementing decisions. Generally speaking, the formal structures prescribe "who" makes and implements decisions. The authority to make and implement decisions is delegated among individuals organized, for example, as shareholders, boards of directors, corporate officers, other employees and other positions. This definition of "structures" obviously excludes entities from outside the corporation. Accordingly, the role of market intermediaries such as stock market analysts and rating agencies is excluded from this definition of corporate governance. The term "structures" within the definition of corporate governance is roughly analogous to the term "constitution" in the governmental sphere.

Governance procedures: how are decisions made and implemented?

"Procedures," comprising the other element of corporate governance systems, is quite simply the supervision of individuals who have been delegated authority for making and implementing decisions. Generally speaking, procedures prescribe "how" decisions are made and implemented. Procedures consist of direction, instruction, ongoing assistance and monitoring for individuals within a corporation as they exercise their delegated authorities. Procedures can take the form of, for example, corporate mission statements, statements of business principles, codes of conduct, announcements about corporate goals, reviews and approvals. Procedures can include general instructions concerning the factors and criteria to be considered in making and implementing decisions. In addition, procedures include the arrangements for communicating those general instructions and to monitor and enforce compliance with them. The term "procedures" does not, of course, include the specific decisions made and implemented pursuant to such supervision. The term "procedures" included within the definition of corporate governance is roughly analogous to the two terms, "substantive law" and "procedural rules," in the governmental sphere.

OPPORTUNITY AND RISK MANAGEMENT

Workable procedures for corporate governance systems

In order to provide workable procedures, corporate governance systems need more than a framework for reconciling law and ethics with decisions previously made on the basis of commercial and financial considerations. Corporate executives need a single framework for making and implementing business decisions which include due consideration for all relevant factors, including legal principles and ethics norms as well as commercial interests and financial returns. "Opportunity and risk management" provides such a framework.

The key to ORM is to view all factors affecting business conduct, including legal principles and community ethical norms, from the perspective of opportunities and risks to corporations as they select and pursue goals to fulfill their corporate missions. "Opportunities" are possible future events – both events brought about by corporations themselves and events brought about by other actors – which potentially contribute to fulfilling a corporation's mission. "Risks" are possible future events – again brought about by corporations themselves or by other actors – which potentially constitute impediments to fulfilling a corporate mission. "Goals" are the opportunities management decides to pursue from among the available opportunities for the purpose of fulfilling a corporate mission. "Missions" are the reason for the corporations' existence. For business corporations, the reason for existence – and, therefore, their "mission" – is enhancing stakeholder value.

Various opportunities need to be evaluated in terms of their inherent risks before one or more of the opportunities can be selected as goals. After senior management selects goals, the risks inherent in achieving them need to be managed at all corporate levels (i.e., avoided, reduced, shared or accepted). Within the ORM framework, the role of corporate executives can be defined as setting corporate goals consistent with their corporations' missions in light of the opportunities and risks presented by possible future events and managing the risks inherent in pursuing those goals.

Existing law and ethics present opportunities and risks

Even if there are no changes in the factors relevant to a corporation's operations, its executives can select new corporate goals and the means to achieve them from among existing opportunities. Selecting a new goal or instrumentality from among available opportunities necessarily leads to a reassessment of the entire range of factors affecting business operations in terms of the opportunities and risks they present for achieving the new goal or for achieving existing goals in better ways.

Existing laws clearly present opportunities for business. After all, the facilities most fundamental to business (private property, contracts and markets and corporations) are also fundamental legal institutions. Accordingly, the correct understanding and proper use of basic business laws (and other laws facilitating business) creates business opportunities. As an illustration, the success of companies such as Microsoft Corporation – indeed, the structure of the entire software industry – would be very different if Microsoft had used purchase-and-sales contracts for the purpose of commercializing its software programs rather than seizing the opportunity presented by licensing contracts.

Existing laws, on the other hand, clearly present risks for business. No one can doubt that violating other persons' legal rights and violating government regulations typically constitute ongoing risks in doing business. Again using Microsoft as an example, violating the various official interpretations of "antitrust law" in the United States – and of "competition law" in the European Union – has clearly constituted a significant risk over a long period of time for Microsoft. More precisely, governmental interpretations of applicable antitrust in the United States and competition law in the European Union have constituted a risk for Microsoft's commercial policies regarding source codes and product bundling.

Similarly, as illustrated by companies such as the Body Works and Shell Oil Company, respecting community ethical norms can create business opportunities, while offending community ethical norms can constitute risks to achieving business goals.

Changes in law and ethics present opportunities and risks

Of course, changes in the factors relevant to business operations also present corporations with opportunities and risks. Such changes can, of course, include modifications in legal principles and in community ethical norms, just as those events can include technical innovation, evolutions in consumer tastes and fluctuations in available supplies (i.e., labor, raw materials or capital). All of these possible modifications, innovations, evolutions and fluctuations can be viewed as future events having potentially positive and negative effects on fulfilling a corporation's mission. In other words, all of these possible changes, including modifications in law and ethics, can all be understood in terms of opportunities and risks.

Corporate executives cannot effectively manage the opportunities and risks entailed by changes in any one of those factors (e.g., technical, supply or demand) without considering all of the other factors (e.g., legal and ethical). For example, setting corporate goals (i.e., deciding to pursue certain opportunities) made available by changes in technology, supply or demand typically can entail legal and ethical risks. Conversely, setting corporate goals made available by changes in applicable laws and ethical norms typically entails risks concerning redeployment of a corporation's employees and assets, as well as a rearrangement of its ongoing relationships with suppliers, customers and users.

Opportunities and risks created by third-party actions

As previously noted, possible future events constituting opportunities and risks for corporations often take the form of – and so can often be understood as – possible future actions by persons other than the corporation. For example, the possibility of competitors entering a market constitutes a "supply side" risk for other suppliers already in the market. Similarly, buyers' price sensitivities obviously constitute fundamental "buy side" risk for all suppliers.

Legal and ethical risks created by governments and media

Legal and ethical opportunities and risks can be understood in the same way. In fact, legal and ethical opportunities and risks often take the form of – and so can often be understood as – possible future actions by governments and media. Legal and ethical risks, for example, often take the form of governmental and media responses to business conduct, especially business conduct which threatens to violate legal principles or which offends community ethical norms.

No business plan is complete without considering the opportunities and risks presented by possible future actions of governments and media in light of applicable legal principles and ethical norms, just as no business plan is complete without considering the opportunities and risks presented by possible competitor and consumer reactions in light of their commercial interests.

Legal and ethical risks created by corporate constituencies

In fact, legal principles and ethical norms can be the basis of possible future actions by any and all "corporate constituencies," i.e., the individuals and groups who contribute to business operations: such as customers, employees and shareholders. In general, corporate constituencies have the ability to terminate, suspend or withhold their contributions to corporate operations in light of commercial interests, legal rights or ethical concerns.

Consumers, employees and shareholders are usually motivated primarily by commercial interests, but legal rights provide the basis for all those business relationships, while ethical norms can become overriding concerns for any of them. Accordingly, the actions of corporate constituencies can also be motivated by legal rights and ethical concerns, especially in those instances when business conduct threatens to violate those legal rights or ethical norms.

Just as no business plan is complete without considering the possible actions of corporate constituencies in light of their commercial interests, so no business plan is complete without considering the possible actions of those same corporate constituencies in light of applicable legal principles and ethical norms.

Legal and ethical risks created by affected and concerned persons

Finally, legal principles and ethical norms can be the basis of possible future actions by parties other than corporate constituencies, if those other parties are affected by business conduct or simply concerned about it.

Parties affected by business conduct other than corporate constituencies do not have the ability to terminate, suspend or withhold their contributions to corporate operations, but they can seek compensation in courts of law for personal injury and property damage they have suffered as the result of past business conduct.

In addition, business conduct can offend the ethical norms of persons affected by business conduct or simply concerned about it. In these instances, such persons can seek to rally governments, media and corporate constituencies to take actions within their power in respect of that business conduct.

CORPORATE GOVERNANCE IN THE UNITED STATES

Sarbanes-Oxley Act of 2002

In 2002, the United States' Congress enacted the Sarbanes-Oxley Act of 2002 ("Sarbanes-Oxley") for the purpose of protecting investors in corporations listed on public stock exchanges in the United States by improving the accuracy and reliability of corporate disclosures made pursuant to securities regulations.

Pursuant to Section 404 of Sarbanes-Oxley, corporations publicly traded in the United States are effectively required to establish and maintain "an adequate internal control structure and procedures for financial reporting." In addition, the management of each publicly-traded corporation is required to provide its own assessment to shareholders of the effectiveness of that corporation's financial reporting controls. Finally, the corporation's auditors shall attest to and report on management's assessment of financial reporting controls.

COSO's 1992 integrated framework – internal controls

In September 1992, a report entitled "Internal Control – Integrated Framework" was published by COSO (i.e., "The Committee of Sponsoring Organizations of the Treadway Commission"). The Treadway Commission was formed in the United States in 1985 to study the financial reporting system in the United States. The Treadway Commission recommended that its sponsoring organizations form a committee to develop a common understanding of corporate internal controls. From that early date, the understanding of corporate governance issues in the United States has included:

1 legal compliance; together with
2 effective and efficient operation; and
3 reliable financial reporting as the three fundamental objectives of corporate governance.

(By the way, the members of COSO are (a) the American Accounting Association, (b) the American Institute of Certified Public Accountants, (c) Financial Executives International, (d) the Institute of Management Accountants, and (e) the Institute of Internal Auditors, arguably the five top professional associations of accounting and financial professionals in the United States.)

COSO's 1992 integrated framework is important because on 5 June 2003, the United States' Securities and Exchange Commission (the "SEC") officially recognized COSO's framework of internal controls as an effective system for corporate governance. In fact, COSO's framework is the only system recognized by the SEC as an effective system for the purposes of public financial disclosure. Even though the SEC's recognition of COSO's integrated framework is limited to the risk of inadequate public financial reporting, the SECs acknowledges that COSO's framework offers corporate governance procedures for managing various aspects of business operations, including legal compliance and effective and efficient operation.

COSO's 2004 integrated framework – enterprise risk management

In September 2004, after a lengthy period for public comment, COSO published an updated framework addressing issues of corporate governance. This framework is entitled, "Enterprise Risk Management –Integrated Framework." As stated by the COSO, the updated system of enterprise risk management subsumes rather than replaces COSO's internal control framework:

> This Enterprise Risk Management – Integrated Framework expands on internal control, providing a more robust and extensive focus on the broader subject of enterprise risk management. While it is not intended to and does not replace the internal control framework, but rather incorporated the internal control framework within it, companies may decide to look to this enterprise risk management system both to satisfy their internal control needs and to move toward a fuller risk management process.
>
> (Committee of Sponsoring Organizations of the Treadway Commission (2004), p. V (Executive Summary))

Like the ORM system outlined above, COSO's framework invites corporate executives to view all factors affecting business conduct from the perspective of opportunities and risks to corporations as they select and pursue goals to fulfill their corporate missions. In fact, the ORM system described above is based in large part on COSO's "Enterprise Risk Management – Integrated Framework."

COSO's four "categories" for all risk management

In particular, COSO's framework identifies legal matters as one of the four fundamental dimensions for corporate governance, with the other three fundamental dimensions being: strategic, operational and financial reporting.

More generally, COSO outlines four "categories of objectives" which all corporate executives can use for making and implementing business decisions. These categories are:

1 "strategic" – i.e., pursuing the high-level goals in fulfillment of the corporate mission;
2 "operations" – i.e., using resources effectively and efficiently in pursuit of those goals;
3 "legal compliance" – i.e., complying with applicable law and regulations; and

4 i.e., "reporting" – i.e., reporting reliably on the returns from operations.

In effect, COSO's integrated framework suggests that these four "categories" provide a complete set of criteria for assessing all planned and ongoing corporate activity. For example, the planned activities of a corporation's worldwide business unit can be comprehensively assessed, according to COSO, by inquiring:

1 whether the business unit has arranged for its planned activities to be conducted in line with the corporation's mission and the high-level goals set by senior management;
2 whether the unit has arranged for its planned activities to be conducted effectively and efficiently, i.e., whether they will yield highest revenue at lowest cost;
3 whether the business unit has arranged for the planned activities to be conducted in compliance with applicable laws and regulations; and
4 whether the business unit has made arrangements to report reliably on the financial returns from its planned activities.

Obviously, the business unit's activities can be managed on an ongoing basis using the same criteria, focusing on past and ongoing activities instead of future plans.

COSO's high standard for legal compliance

COSO has effectively cast its four "categories of objectives" within an ORM framework. Accordingly, COSO sets performance standards in part on the basis of corporate executives' ability to manage risk within each category. COSO sets a higher standard for legal compliance than for strategic and operational objectives because there are fewer risks involved in achieving legal compliance than in achieving strategic and operational objectives:

> Because objectives related to ... compliance with laws and regulations are within the entity's control, enterprise risk management can be expected to provide reasonable assurances of achieving those objectives. Achievement of strategic objectives and operations objectives, however, is subject to

external events not always within the entity's control; accordingly, for these objectives enterprise risk management can [only] provide reasonable assurance that management, and the board in its oversight role, are made aware, in a timely manner, of the extent which the entity is moving toward achievement of the objectives.

(Executive Summary, p. 5)

In other words, corporate executives are expected, within reason, to achieve legal compliance in all business activities because legal compliance is within their control. By way of contrast, corporate executives are expected merely to monitor and report to directors and shareholders on the degree to which operations achieve strategic and operational objectives. Strategic and operational objectives are subject to a lower performance standard because achievement of those objectives is subject to risks beyond corporate executives' control.

COSO's framework includes ethical values

Pursuant to Section 406 of Sarbanes-Oxley, the SEC currently requires corporations whose shares are publicly-traded in the United States to disclose whether they have adopted a "code of ethics" applicable to their principal executive officer, principal financial officer, principal accounting officer or controller, or persons performing similar functions (17 CFR Section 229.406. Item 406). Sarbanes-Oxley defines "codes of ethics" to mean "such standards as are reasonably necessary to promote," at a minimum:

1　"honest and ethical conduct …;
2　full, fair, accurate, timely and understandable [public disclosures], and
3　compliance with applicable governmental rules and regulations."

Sarbanes-Oxley does not define the term "ethical conduct" (Section 406 (c) of Sarbanes-Oxley).

Consistent with Sarbanes-Oxley, COSO includes ethics in as an essential element of the corporate "mission," to be defined by senior management. Incorporating ethics as an essential element of a corporate mission is, in effect, equivalent to including ethics as a fundamental corporate objective. In other words, COSO intends for ethics to become a standard for judging all corporate behavior:

An entity's strategy and [goals] and the way they are implemented are based on preferences, value judgments and managerial styles. Management's integrity and commitment to ethical values influence these preferences and judgments and are translated into standards of behavior. Because an entity's good reputation is so valuable, the standards of behavior must go beyond compliance with law. Managers of well-run enterprises increasingly have accepted the view that ethics pays and ethical behavior is good business.

(Executive Summary, p. 29)

The definition of management's "integrity," in turn, includes "the desire to do the right thing; to profess and live up to a set of values and expectations" (Executive Summary, p. 122.) While COSO also does not define the term "ethics" or "ethical values," COSO requires that management both make outline ethical values applicable to actions on behalf of the corporation and that they act in accordance with those values, whatever those values might be.

WHAT IS BUSINESS LAW?

Very generally, the law is a set of expectations concerning acceptable and unacceptable human interactions which are formulated, interpreted and enforced by governments. Applying this definition, "business laws" are – quite simply – expectations concerning acceptable and unacceptable business conduct which are formulated, interpreted and enforced by governments. The law classifies unacceptable conduct as 'illegal,' while acceptable conduct is classified as "legal" (or, at least, not illegal).

Of course, the laws of concern in this book are the laws applicable to business conduct, such as the laws of: private property, contracts, competition and corporations. Each of these laws creates an institution fundamental to business conduct. At the same time, each of these laws defines fundamental business relationships, such as: landlord, tenant, seller, buyer, competitor, director, officer and employee. The legal expectations comprising these relationships, i.e., the expectations enforced by governments, are usually referred to as "legal rights" and "legal obligations."

Categorical imperatives formulated by governments

Business laws, like all other laws, tend to be formulated as "categorical imperatives," such as the following statement: "All persons – including corporations – should be free to use and dispose of their private property as they see fit, provided they do not cause injury to other persons or damage to their property." Under governments with separate legislative, judicial and executive branches, new laws are written by the legislative branch.

Courts apply business law to past business conduct

With respect to conduct which has already occurred – including past business conduct – laws are interpreted and enforced by courts. Court judgments are generally available for any conduct – including business conduct – which results in injury to persons or damage to their property. Under governments with separate legislative, judicial and executive branches powers (i.e., a separation of powers), court judgments are rendered by the judicial branch of government.

Executive agencies apply business law to ongoing business conduct

With respect to current conduct – including ongoing business conduct – laws are interpreted and enforced by government agencies. These agencies act pursuant to the "police powers" inherent in all governments. In general, government agencies act to prevent conduct – including business conduct – which, according to the applicable government regulation, entails an unreasonable risk of harm or injury to persons or damage to their property. Under governments with separate legislative, judicial and executive branches powers (i.e., a separation of powers), agency actions are undertaken by the executive branch of government.

WHAT IS BUSINESS ETHICS?

Very generally, ethics are expectations – other than laws – regarding acceptable and unacceptable human interactions. Applying this definition, business ethics are expectations – other than business laws – regarding acceptable and unacceptable business conduct. In light of business ethics, each individual classifies unacceptable business conduct as "bad," while acceptable conduct is "good" (or, at least, not bad).

Business ethics distinguished from business law

As with business law, business ethics apply to the way in which persons behave in their business dealings. However, business ethics are not formulated and interpreted by governments. Instead, business ethics are formulated and interpreted by various "members of civil society," i.e., individuals and groups not acting in the government's name and pursuant to government powers. (Collectively, such non-governmental individuals and groups – including businesses – and their interactions are sometimes referred to as "civil society.")

Categorical imperatives formulated and interpreted by civil society

Even though business ethics are formulated and interpreted by members of civil society rather than by governments, business ethics (and, indeed, all ethical principles) tend to be formulated as "categorical imperatives," i.e., in the same terms as laws formulated by governments. Accordingly, an example of such an ethical norm applicable to business might be the following statement: "Persons should be free to use and dispose of their private property as they see fit, provided they do not cause personal injury to other persons or damage to their property." (As you can see by comparing this ethical expectation with the business law cited above, an ethical principle is formulated in the same manner as a law.)

Various individuals and groups in civil society play important roles in formulating and interpreting ethical norms applicable to business. For example, families, religions, schools, the media, local communities and individual members of those various groups all formulate ethical norms, some of which are applicable to business. In addition, each of these groups (and their individual members) develops its own formulations and interpretations of ethics in response to business practices as those practices evolve and become known to those groups (and individuals).

These groups may not have any direct involvement in business processes. None the less, their ethical expectations can have an independent significance, in part because their expectations can lead to new business laws and in part because their expectations can influence the expectations of "corporate constituencies" important to management, i.e., groups contributing directly to ongoing or planned business processes. Management's corporate constituencies include customers, shareholders and employees.

Categorical imperatives enforced by civil society

Ethical norms are not enforced by governments (unless governments adopt them as laws). This does not mean, however, that individuals and groups – including businesses – are not subject to negative consequences for violating ethical norms. Prison terms and court judgments might not be available to various members of civil society to sanction violations of their business ethics, but members of civil society have other means for sanctioning behavior which violate their business ethics.

Most importantly, corporate constituencies other than management (e.g., customers, shareholders and employees) and potential constituents whose ethical expectations are offended can, and often do:

(a) terminate or withhold future dealings with businesses they consider to be unethical; or
(b) seek further assurances in those future business dealings.

For example, buyers can and do respond to suppliers engaging in unethical conduct by taking their business elsewhere or by demanding more assurances that the suppliers will not engage in the conduct which the buyers consider to be unethical.

Considered in light of responses, the business ethics formulated by corporate constituencies are at least as important as – and arguably more important than – the business ethics which management formulates concerning their own business conduct. This is true because businesses' responses to violations of their own ethical norms are entirely within their discretion. Following the example given above, man-

agers' responses to their own unethical selling practices are likely to be less significant than the responses of either buyers or other corporate constituencies.

The implication for business executives is clear. From the corporate perspective, the ethical expectations of customers, shareholders, employees and other corporate constituencies such as the communities in which businesses operate have a significance, independent and apart from the validity which management might ascribe to those ethical expectations. This does not mean that business executives should disregard or minimize their own ethical perspectives in making and implementing decisions on behalf of the corporations they lead. Instead, business executives are well advised to identify and consider the ethical perspectives of corporate constituencies in addition to their own ethics in determining business conduct.

Business ethics distinguished from commercial expectations

In addition to distinguishing business ethics from business law, business ethics need to be distinguished from commercial expectations. Both business ethics and commercial expectations are formulated and interpreted by members of civil society (not by governments), but commercial expectations apply to the way in which each individual expects businesses to behave in their dealings with that individual. Business ethics, in contrast, apply to the way in which each individual expects businesses to behave in their dealings with other individuals. More precisely, commercial expectations apply to the material benefits each individual expects to obtain personally from his or her own business dealings. Business ethics can include the material benefits each individual expects others to obtain in their business dealings. While business ethics – like business laws – are formulated in terms of categorical imperatives, commercial interests are formulated in terms of preferences. In light of business ethics, each individual classifies business conduct as good or bad. In light of commercial expectations, each individual classifies acceptable business conduct as "the best available," while unacceptable business conduct is classified as not "the best available."

Since each individual applies commercial expectations exclusively to his or her own business dealings, business executives need consider only whether and how their dealings with each individual affects that individual's commercial interests. As regards ethical concerns, on the other hand, business executives need to consider whether and how their dealings with any one individual violates the ethical principles, and therefore their dealings, with other individuals who are members of the different or the same corporate constituencies.

This last point merits further consideration. Each individual's business ethics cover his or her expectations about how businesses should behave in their business dealings with individuals who are members of different corporate constituencies. For example, a buyer's business ethics can cover his or her reaction to how businesses behave in their dealings with employees. This ethical perspective is sometimes referred to as a "sympathetic" reaction and includes the emotion of pity but not the emotion of fear. Fear is not a part of this ethical perspective because the individuals formulating the response do not see themselves in the same situation as the person who has been the subject of the unethical behavior. For example, buyers might pity employees who are the object of unethical treatment but buyers typically do not fear that they will be the object of the same unethical treatment.

In addition, each individual's business ethics cover his or her reactions to how businesses behave in their dealings with other individuals who are members of the same corporate constituency. Following the example of buyers, one buyer's business ethics can cover his or her reaction to how businesses behave in their dealing with other buyers. This ethical perspec-

tive is sometimes classified as an "empathetic" reaction and includes the emotions of both pity and fear. Fear is included in this ethical perspective because the individual formulating the response can see himself or herself in the same situation as the person who has been the subject of the unethical behavior. For example, buyers both can pity other buyers who are the object of unethical treatment and fear that they will be the object of the same unethical treatment.

The implication for business executives is clear. Managers are well advised to give due consideration to the ethical perspectives of each corporate constituency not only:

1 to the extent that the constituency is directly affected by its dealings with the corporation, but also
2 to the extent that all constituencies are generally concerned about the conduct of the corporations with which they deal.

Indeed, this second category, i.e., the "general concerns" of unaffected corporate constituencies, clearly distinguishes the consideration of ethical norms from the consideration of commercial interests in a business context.

REFERENCES

Committee of Sponsoring Organizations of the Treadway Commission (2004) *Enterprise Risk Management – Integrated Framework*, New York: AICPA.

2

Making Business Decisions

Integrating law and ethics

INTRODUCTION

The best business decision-makers are aware of more than the benefits they intend for themselves. The best decision-makers are also aware of the costs, delays and uncertainties associated with obtaining those intended benefits. In addition, the best decision-makers are aware of the manner and extent to which their decisions can unintentionally affect other parties' interests. Finally, the best decision-makers are aware of the way in which their decisions are perceived by constituencies important to their business (often called "stakeholders"), shareholders, customers, employees, governments, media and the communities where the business operates. The best decision-makers integrate all of these factors, both intended results and unintended consequences, into sound business decisions.

Accordingly, the best decision-makers necessarily integrate law and ethics into their business decisions. They necessarily integrate law because the individual interests of parties affected by their decisions are often protected as "legal rights," subjecting the decision-maker to civil liability and even criminal guilt for violating them. The best decision-makers also necessarily integrate ethics into their decisions, because the perceptions of important constituencies are often shaped by community ethical norms.

Failing to give due consideration to the law can require businesses to pay compensation and penalties for the harm caused by past business activities. Failing to give due consideration to community ethical norms can decrease future revenues and other support, both from affected parties and from constituencies offended by a business decision.

In this chapter, I will begin to show you how to balance intended results, unintended consequences, conflicting interests, differing ethical perceptions and various time frames in order to make sound business decisions.

UNDERSTANDING "COMMUNITY ETHICAL NORMS"

First, I outline five different ethical perspectives often relevant to business. These five perspectives are not the only ethical norms possibly applicable to business decisions, but they are good illustrations. The community ethical norms – and other norms like them – are significant to businesses described below if they are significant to the businesses' constituencies.

Self- interested decision-making

Self-interested decision-makers decide in favor of actions which are expected to maximize their own estimated welfare. Self-interested decision-makers consider only their own interests (i.e., all foreseeable results for the decision-maker at the time that the decision is made, having due regard for issues of time and probability). This is the stereotypically classical approach taken by many businesses. Adam Smith's "rational man" and "invisible hand" are most often cited as the philosophical justification for this approach.

Utilitarianism

Under the "utilitarian" approach, decision-makers decide in favor of actions which are expected to maximize the welfare of all of the parties affected by the decision including but not limited to the decision-maker. Unlike self-interested decision-makers (who take only their own interests into account), the utilitarian takes into account all of the advantages and disadvantages for all affected parties. Jeremy Bentham and John Stuart Mill are most often cited as the philosophical justification for this approach.

Individual rights

Under the "individual rights" approach, decision-makers decide in favor of actions which respect all affected parties' legitimate rights. If an individual need is generally recognized as legitimate (e.g., food, clothing or shelter), then meeting that need is usually considered to be a "right." Unfortunately, beyond the basic requirements for survival, the term "individual need" is very vague. Therefore, legitimizing rights on the basis of individual needs, in practice, has always been debatable.

The term "individual rights" embraces other ambiguities. For example, is a specific "individual right" an authorization for a person to do something (i.e., the right to meet your personal needs and pursue your personal goals), or is an "individual right" an entitlement to have someone else do something for a person (i.e., the right to have someone else meet your personal needs or assist you in pursuing your personal goal). There is, I believe, a general political consensus in support of "authorizations," provided that you do not interfere with the similar authorizations in favor of other persons. There is less consensus on the "entitlements." Most people probably agree that people are "entitled" to have other persons meet their "needs":

(i) to the extent that those other persons have agreed to do so, or
(ii) to the extent that the people in need cannot meet those needs for reasons beyond their control.

Even within the scope of this limited consensus on entitlements, there is disagreement on what constitutes "needs" for people who cannot provide for themselves. One way to determine more generally the people's need is to ask yourself: What are my own needs? What have been my own needs?

Pursuant to another perspective, in order to be recognized as legitimate, a right must generally be:

(i) universal (i.e., it must exist, at least in theory, for all individuals), and
(ii) reciprocal (i.e., consistent with the same rights for all other individuals).

Immanuel Kant is often cited as providing, with his first formulation of the "categorical imperative," the philosophical justification for the universal and reciprocal nature of individual rights. Immanuel Kant's first formulation of the "categorical imperative" can be paraphrased as follows: "do unto others as you would have them do unto you." It might make sense to apply all three standards (needs, universal and reciprocal), together with "legitimate means," in determining the scope of legitimate rights.

Private property

Individual rights are generally understood to include "private property." Private property consists of an individual's right to exclude others from possessing, occupying, using and consuming clearly identified tangible or intangible assets, and – by implication – that individual's "exclusive" right to possess, occupy, use and consume those assets. Private property rights also include an individual's right to transfer some or all of those rights to other individuals (i.e., with the transferring individual retaining some or none of those rights). Whether the concept of private property rights satisfies the criteria of "universality" and "reciprocity" is often debated.

The institution of private property satisfies the criterion of "universality," at least in theory, to the extent that each person has the right to own private property. Because of the exclusionary nature of private property rights, however, private property arguably does not satisfy the criterion of "universality" as to any particular tangible or intangible asset. Moreover, private property arguably satisfies the criterion of "universality" only in theory to the extent that some people own property (e.g., real estate) while others – who would like to own property (e.g., real estate) – own none. Private property satisfies the criterion of "reciprocity" among owners of private property (i.e., "I will respect your property if you respect mine"). Again because of its exclusionary nature, private property is not a reciprocal arrangement as to any particular tangible or intangible asset or, more generally, between those who own property and those who do not.

Freedom of contract

Individual rights are also generally understood to include "freedom of contract." Generally, a contract is promise to another person to do a particular thing (e.g., to pay money, transfer property rights, provide personal services or refrain from doing any of those things), in exchange for a promise from that person to do a particular thing. Accordingly, contract rights for one person generally consist of another person's obligation to do something, but only if, in exchange for that obligation, the holder of the contract right has given to the obligated person something he or she values (usually a reciprocal promise). The concept of contract rights satisfies the criteria of "universality" and "reciprocity" more readily than private property rights. The institution of contract rights satisfies the criterion of "universality" to the extent that each person has the right to enter into contracts and to enforce them. Because of the mutual exchange of contract rights for contract obligations, contracts generally do satisfy the criterion of "reciprocity," at least as between the parties to the contract.

General obligations

Finally, individual rights are generally understood to include "freedom from physical injury" and "freedom from property damage." These rights operate as general obligations for persons exercising property and contract rights. These general obligations state, in effect, that "you cannot use your property and contract rights to injure me physically or to damage my property."

More generally, individual property and contract rights arguably can be exercised only to the extent that the exercise of those rights fulfills the criteria of universality and reciprocity. This concept is expressed very eloquently in the 1789 Universal Declaration of the Rights of Man by the First French Republic:

Article 4. – Liberty consists in being able to do anything that does not harm others: thus, the exercise of the natural rights of every man has no bounds other than those that ensure to the other members of society the enjoyment of these same rights. These bounds may be determined only by Law.
(1789 Universal Declaration of the Rights of Man by the First French Republic)

The 1789 French Declaration of the Rights of Man is an expression of enlightenment philosophy, including a belief in "the natural rights of every man." Those natural rights include the right to own property and the right to enter into contracts, two fundamental legal institutions facilitating the conduct of business.

Both the American Declaration of Independence in 1776 and the French Declaration of the Rights of Man in 1789 are expressions of enlightenment philosophy, including a belief in natural rights such as property and contract. At the same time, there are important differences: Generally, the American Revolution focused on "public society," i.e., the relationship between citizens and government (e.g., no taxation without representation, the Bill of Rights and the US Constitution's separation and balance of powers). The French Revolution focused both on "public society" and on "civil society," i.e., the relationships directly amongst individual citizens. Since most modern business relationships fall squarely within "civil society," as articulated in the 1789 French Declaration of the Rights of Man, this brief document is very interesting to study to understand the social foundations for modern business affairs.

Trust and caring

Under the "caring" approach, decision-makers are concerned about respecting the trust placed in them by all parties affected by their decisions. All individuals arguably have the right to know all relevant facts in respect of all transactions and relationships involving or affecting them. In practice, however, individuals often forgo this "right to know" everything about such transactions and relationships.

Individuals often forgo the "right to know," either knowingly or unknowingly, because of the time, effort and expertise required to know and understand all of the relevant facts. To the extent that individuals, either intentionally or in effect, forgo their right to know all relevant information in connection with business dealings, they are placing "trust" in the decision-makers with whom they are dealing or whose decisions can affect them.

Under the "caring" approach, businesses attempt to reciprocate this trust by making decisions affecting other parties as if the affected parties were involved in making the decision and knew all of the relevant facts. The caring approach emphasizes maximizing the return from continuing relationships rather than maximizing the return from isolated transactions. Carol Gilligan is most associated with the "caring" approach.

Trust is an incidental aspect to most commercial transactions involving the purchase and sale of goods and services. Each of the parties (buyer and seller) attempts to obtain sufficient material information before they make decisions. Trust is an essential aspect of most corporate relationships. For example, shareholders in publicly traded companies do not attempt to obtain any material information before management makes decisions on their behalf. In other words, they trust management.

Justice

Under the "justice" approach, decision-makers decide in favor of actions which distribute costs and benefits equally, or as equally as possible, among all affected parties. Justice, i.e., treating similarly situated persons in a similar fashion, is a practically universal human expectation. Of course, as with "individual rights," there are many different classifications and descriptions of the concept of justice. The various definitions tend to focus on the different contexts in which concepts of justice are applicable.

Justice is imposed as a separate standard on behavior where one person has "power" over another person, i.e., the ability to treat others unequally with impunity. For example, concepts of justice are imposed as a discipline on government action because governments have the ability to treat their citizens unequally. The market itself imposes "justice" (i.e., equal treatment) as a discipline on business dealings to the extent that market forces predominate. Accordingly, it is typically not useful to apply concepts of justice to business dealings governed by market forces. Concepts of justice

are applicable to business dealings, however, to the extent that there is some inefficiency in markets (i.e., the absence of alternatives, hidden costs or transactional costs). Market inefficiencies give one party to a transaction or relationship power over another party. The ethical norm of "justice" is applicable to such transactions and relationships because the exercise of power can result in unequal treatment.

Moreover, concepts of justice are generally applied separately to business dealings only to the extent that individuals are treated differently in respect of their needs (and, thus, their rights). Many philosophers and commentators through the ages have expounded on justice. John Rawls is often cited as a modern philosopher who has stated a comprehensive theory of justice. John Rawls' theory of justice can be summarized as follows: Each person has an equal right to the most extensive personal liberties which are compatible with personal liberties for all ("equal political liberties'); and economic inequalities should:

(a) arise only out of offices and positions which are open to all under conditions of equal opportunity ("equal economic opportunity"); and
(b) be arranged so as to maximize the welfare of the least advantaged person ("greatest minimum welfare").

Other ethical norms

Other ethical norms include:

1 social contracts, and
2 survival of the fittest.

Social contracts have been famously applied in a purely political context (Jean-Jacques Rousseau) but can also be applied in an economic context. For example, individuals enter into a "social contract" when they – or their ancestors – abandon their means of subsistence in exchange for participation in the market economy. Most people believe that "survival of the fittest" was first applied to explain the theory of biological evolution (Charles Darwin). It can also be applied to explain the outcome of combative and competitive activities (Herbert Spencer).

UNDERSTANDING "LEGAL RIGHTS"

Individual rights, one of the ethical perspectives described above, have been classified – and justified – in various ways. For example, property and contracts have been described as "natural rights," pertaining to all men and women by virtue of their nature as individuals. At the same time, property and contract rights have been described as "positive rights" because they permit rather than prohibit certain actions. Freedom from personal injury and freedom from property damage are also considered examples of "natural rights" but have been classified as "negative rights" – because they prohibit rather than permit certain actions.

Generally, if individual rights are enforceable only pursuant to community ethical norms, then most people refer to those rights as "moral rights." If individual rights are enforceable by individuals through their governments pursuant to laws, then most people refer to them as "legal rights." Law in turn is typically justified as emanating from a legitimate source, whether this be God, nature, reason, the will of the people or a combination of those sources. Such sources – or their representatives – are considered to be the "sovereigns" of the political state. Individual rights granted by governments but not pursuant to law (e.g., pursuant to arbitrary actions of tyrants) are probably not "legal rights" because the ability to have the government enforce those rights is uncertain.

Moral rights and legal rights are not always identical

Sometimes, the exercise of rights considered moral under community ethical norms (or the exercise of rights for which there is no clear community norm) is nonetheless illegal under applicable government regulation (e.g., outlawing trade with certain countries for political reasons). Sometimes, actions generally considered to be immoral under community ethical norms are nonetheless legal under applicable law (e.g., distributing some types of pornography). More often, actions violating community ethical norms are considered to be illegal (e.g., theft and embezzlement). Moreover, committing illegal acts is usually considered to violate community ethical norms (even if there is no independent basis for condemning the illegal act as "immoral" under ethical norms).

Property and contracts are often both moral and legal rights

Sometimes, but not always, the same individual right is considered to be both a moral right and a legal right. For example, private property and freedom of contract are generally considered to be both moral rights (as discussed above) and legal rights because they are enforceable by individuals through governments pursuant to laws. Contract rights are enforceable against certain individuals because of their prior consent. Property rights are enforceable against all individuals without their consent (e.g., I do not need your consent to keep you out of my home). Under the law of contract and property law, violating other persons' rights (for example, failing to keep your bargain or infringing on property rights) gives rise to the payment of monetary compensation to the person whose contract or property rights are violated.

General obligations are usually both moral and legal rights

Freedom from personal injury and freedom from property damage are also both moral rights (as discussed above) and legal rights. For example, if one person's use of his or her property injures another person, then the person who caused the injury has violated the injured person's legal rights as well as moral rights. Viewed from the perspective of the actor's obligations, the person who caused the injury has violated his or her "general obligations" to the injured person. As with property rights, general obligations are enforceable by governments against all individuals without their consent. In fact, general obligations are the complement to private property rights, just as contract obligations are the complement to contract rights.

In common law countries (such as England, Canada, Australia and the United States), breaches of general obligations are called "torts." In common law countries, the law of general obligations is called "tort law." Under the law of general obligations, as under the law of contract, violating another persons' rights gives rise to the payment of monetary compensation in an amount estimated to compensate for the injury or harm.

PUTTING IT ALL TOGETHER

Within a corporate context, all of the ethical approaches need to be understood and explained in terms of their significance for the corporation. By considering all of the ethical approaches, including individual legal rights, managers will develop a more "enlightened" understanding of their corporations' self-interests. In other words, managers will understand both:

1 the intended, immediate results of their decisions on current income statements and balance sheets and
2 the impact of unintended, long-term consequences on their future financial statements.

The self-interested decision-maker

The strictly self-interested perspective is a good starting point for making business decisions but often not a good finish line. As a starting point, managers can take advantage of powerful quantitative tools available through the financial reporting system to understand a decision's probable effect on immediate revenues and costs. As a finish line, the strictly self-interested approach leaves management vulnerable to claims that it violated other people's legal rights or offended community ethical norms.

The self-interested approach does not need to be abandoned. Instead, other persons' interests and perceptions need to be understood and explained in terms of their significance for the corporation. The various ethical perspectives outlined in this chapter are useful in obtaining those understandings and in formulating those explanations. The ethical perspectives outlined in this chapter are not intended, however, to be exclusive. They merely indicate the perspectives important corporate constituencies sometimes use in evaluating corporate conduct. The outlined ethical perspectives, and other ethical perspectives, have significance to the extent they constitute applicable community ethical norms – or to the extent corporate management endorses them.

Corporate management sometimes overlooks that community ethical norms have an independent significance even if management does not endorse them.

Utilitarianism

This is a good adjunct to a decision-maker's consideration of his/her own self-interests. Utilitarianism is a useful discipline for identifying all parties affected by a decision and for estimating the costs and benefits for each of them. Please note that a utilitarian analysis differs from the self-interested approach in that the self-interested decision-maker considers neither the benefits obtained by others nor the losses which they incur.

Utilitarian analysis, including the application of quantitative techniques to costs incurred and losses suffered by affected parties other than the corporation, is useful to the purely self-interested decision-maker. It is useful because, assuming that the legal rights of affected parties are violated, courts (using principles of "compensatory justice") can impose on decision-makers the costs incurred and losses suffered by others as a result of their decisions. It is also useful because ethical responses to business conduct are often based on the amount of costs and losses imposed on parties other than the corporation.

Individual rights

"Individual rights" should always be considered in making business decisions. In an important way, they are part of the "rules of the game" in business. Sometimes respecting individual rights renders a certain decision impracticable. More often, however, accommodating individual rights takes the form of conditions or qualifications on business decisions. (Generally, "I will operate efficiently and effectively in line with my corporation's mission and values as defined by directors and senior management, provided that I give due consideration to all affected parties' moral rights and that I do not violate anyone's legal rights.")

Legal rights always include freedom from personal injury and property damage. To the extent that your company's activities cause personal injury or property damage to other persons, your company can be liable to pay monetary compensation in an amount equivalent to the value of the injury or damage, plus a punitive amount considered sufficient to discourage further such activities.

Legal rights also often include the "right to know." Accordingly, respecting the right to know with adequate disclosures can often protect a corporate decision-maker from violations of others' legal rights because parties who enter into dealings on the basis of prior knowledge are often considered to have "assumed the risks" inherent in the disclosures.

Caring and trust

Trust is obviously a vital commodity in business: a competitive advantage for those businesses which possess it – and the downfall for those businesses which do not. Caring and trust are important because most business successes are based on continuing relationships – not isolated transactions.

Caring and trust are very important also because a corporation's attitude toward each relationship is magnified through its reputation. In the case of the Pinto, preserving the trust of Ford's customers probably should have been an important consideration, possibly prompting Ford to redesign the gas tank while managing the increased cost and delay in production. In this way, Ford would have preserved both its relationships and reputations while avoiding violations of its customers' legal rights.

Justice

It is often useful to consider whether the costs entailed in a corporate decision can be shared by affected parties. With limited exceptions, businesses are not subject to paying legal compensation for failing to treat customers equally. However, as illustrated by the case of the Ford Pinto, "distributive justice" can sometimes offer a possible solution to problems which otherwise could result in the obligation to pay legal compensation. In addition, even though there are no legal consequences for failing to treat customers equally, there is strong support for concepts of justice in the general population. Failing to treat customers fairly can easily adversely affect relationships, reputation and, in this way, future revenues.

WHICH IS THE "RIGHT" DECISION?

The short answer is that corporate management does not have to choose amongst the various ethical perspectives in making a decision. The five perspectives outlined in this chapter are not mutually exclusive. In fact, there may even be other community ethical norms prevalent among corporate constituencies – or endorsed by management. You should consider all of them. Each of them can be used as a tool to identify parties affected by business decisions and to evaluate their interests and perceptions. It is most important to capture all of the various interests and perspectives within a single analytical framework, so that conflicts can be reconciled and accommodated.

Of course, identifying affected parties and community ethical norms does not reconcile and accommodate conflicting interests and perceptions. In each case, management must develop the alternatives which best reflect their evaluation of all applicable interests and perceptions (including their own corporate interests and values). Nonetheless, I believe that there are several overriding considerations management should keep in mind. Those considerations are listed and explained below.

Have you considered all affected parties and corporate constituencies?

Have you considered the perceptions of constituencies important to your business? More and more, customers, shareholders and employees are concerned not only about their own interests but also about the interests of other stakeholders. Injury to the interests of one type of stakeholder can be offensive to other stakeholders. As a result, affinities and coalitions amongst different stakeholder groups are developing, magnifying the adverse impact on corporations from injuries to any one group of stakeholders.

Have you considered various points in time over the long run?

Have you evaluated the probable results and effects of your decision at various points of time in the future? I suggest that decision-makers consider the extent to which they would be as satisfied with the decision at various moments in the future. In fact, once the parties involved have been identified, I believe that the single most important consideration in making a valid decision is considering events and identifying their consequences over the appropriate time frames. In addition, more alternatives will suggest themselves as you introduce timing into your deliberations. Accordingly, identifying and evaluating available alternatives and their effects over time, as well as immediate alternatives and effects, is an important step in making decisions. A decision justified over a period of one year may not be justified when considered over a period of five years.

Have you understood the assumptions of generally accepted accounting principles?

Generally accepted accounting principles and the accounting systems used to apply them to corporate operations are powerful tools for fairly reflecting both corporate performance and corporate condition from a financial perspective. At the same time, there are important assumptions built into accounting principles making them particularly useful for reporting to shareholders about historical performance and conditions. These assumptions can limit the ability of corporate decision-makers to rely on accounting principles in integrating law and ethics into business decisions.

For example, revenues and expenses are generally not included in financial statements if they are too remote in the future, too uncertain to occur or too difficult to quantify. Leaders' vision depends in part on their ability to see through the assumptions made in accounting principles for the purpose of anticipating future revenues and expenses, even though they are uncertain and difficult to quantify. Ethical and legal issues in particular are important considerations in corporate decisions even though their consequences are sometimes difficult to capture in accounting terms

Have you understood the limitations of probability theories?

Have you avoided all catastrophic contingencies even if they appear to lie relatively far in the future and to be very uncertain to occur? Obviously, the present monetary value of any given event is reduced as it becomes more remote in time. The present value of any given event is further reduced by the uncertainty

which often accompanies their occurrence. Still, the costs of some remote, uncertain contingencies would be so catastrophic that it would be unreasonable to accept any significant risk that they will occur. (Litigation is often such a risk.)

Have you assumed that all information will be public?

Have you assumed that all information available to you will eventually be available to all affected parties? There are at least three reasons making this a valid operating assumption. First, much corporate information is disclosed to the public pursuant to the securities laws. Second, even more information becomes available to affected parties as part of the normal course of business – even in the absence of formal disclosure. Finally, in the US and some other jurisdictions, the law typically gives persons whose legal rights are violated by business decisions (or, in their behalf, the government) the ability to discover practically all of the facts surrounding those decisions.

Even if you conclude that all information available to you will not in fact eventually be available to others, it is useful to assume that all information will be available to the extent that the other parties are trusting you to make the "right" decision (i.e., the decision they would have made with the information available to you). The trust others place in you can be inferred from the facts of the situation: Consumers trust makers of sophisticated and complex products. Shareholders, employees and other corporate constituencies trust management.

Have you involved all responsible corporate officers?

Did you involve as many affected parties as possible (or their representatives) in the decision-making process? Involving affected parties (or their representatives) overcomes errors that can be made in valuing their interests. Obviously not every affected party can be involved. In fact, in many business decisions most of the affected parties cannot be (and in fact are not) directly involved in making decisions affecting them.

There are, however, members of a corporate management and staff who are sensitive to the interests of groups of affected parties and the perceptions of each important corporate constituency. These individuals are the vice-presidents in charge of various regions, staff functions and line operations. They should be informed of all pending decisions within their areas of competence and included as appropriate in the decision-making process.

It is often the case that a chief financial officer, a chief human resources officer and a chief legal officer (to name a few) can help to optimize corporate decisions

(a) by identifying various parties' conflicting interests and differing perceptions, and
(b) by helping to accommodate them.

AN ILLUSTRATION: THE FORD PINTO CASE

In the early 1960s, Japanese automobile manufacturers were establishing themselves in the North American market by selling cars for less than $2,000. Various North American manufacturers were developing and implementing responses to the competitive threat posed by the inexpensive Japanese cars.

One of the North American manufacturers, Ford Motor Company, decided to manufacture the "Pinto" automobile. Unfortunately, as initially designed, the Pinto had a gas tank which, as known to Ford on the basis of pre-production crash tests, "regularly ruptured" when the Pinto was struck from the rear at 20 miles per hour. At the same time, as a result of the rupture, gasoline could spray into the passenger compartment, often igniting and possibly seriously injuring the driver and any Pinto occupants. Although these test results were troubling, they were in compliance with the then-applicable governmental regulatory safety standards.

Ford's departmental recommendations

Ford's Engineering Department concluded that it would have cost the Ford Motor Company $121 million (about $11 per car) to redesign the gas tank before beginning production. This extra expense would have put the price of the Pinto above $2,000. In addition, Engineering concluded that correcting the defect would delay production for about six months, enabling competing North American manufacturers

to introduce their inexpensive models months before Ford would be able to launch its Pinto.

The Marketing Department concluded that an increase in Pinto's price above $2,000 would jeopardize the Pinto's ability to compete effectively with Japanese imports and other inexpensive North American models. The most difficult fact was presented by the Safety Department: approximately 180 persons would die as a result of the defect if the gas tank was not redesigned. At the time of these deliberations, the US Federal Government valued a human life at $200,000 for the purposes of traffic-safety engineering.

Ford's decision and its consequences

Ford decided to proceed with making Pinto automobiles without redesigning the defective gas tanks because the amount of money Ford saved from foregoing the repairs ($121 million) exceeded Ford's estimate of the legal claims arising from the defect ($36 million). Ford decided to forgo the repair of the gas tank also because doing so enabled it to meet its price and timing targets, thereby preserving an uncertain but significant amount of revenue from Pinto sales.

After the defects became known, Pinto sales suffered dramatically and never recovered. Ford discontinued the manufacture of the Pinto within a few years. In addition, Ford's total sales revenues from all of its models suffered for several years – even after the Pinto was discontinued. In addition, Ford was subject to several lawsuits on behalf of Pinto occupants who died or were injured when the gas tanks of their Pintos exploded in the course of accidents. Ford settled the lawsuits by making confidential payments to plaintiffs. While the amount of the settlements is confidential and therefore unknown, it is estimated that Ford's settlement payment for each Pinto victim was well over $2,000,000 and, in the aggregate, that Ford's settlement payments were well over the $121 million savings estimated from forgoing correction of the defective gas tank.

Discussion of Ford's decision

Ford had incorrectly concluded that compliance with applicable government safety regulations would exonerate Ford from liability under the law of general obligations. In fact, government regulations and the law of general obligations are largely completely independent from each other. While a court might conclude that an automobile manufacturer such as Ford does not breach its general obligations when it builds an automobile complying with the governmental safety standards, a court certainly is not bound to make such a determination. On the contrary, manufacturers and distributors are often held liable under the law of general obligations for injuries and deaths caused by products and services complying with all applicable governmental safety regulations.

Ford also probably failed to give appropriate consideration to the interests of parties affected by its decision. In particular, Ford had reduced its general obligations under law to a monetary amount, thereby failing to capture the entire significance for Ford of complying with those legal obligations. In addition, Ford had grossly underestimated the value of a human life in the context of lawsuits for personal injury and wrongful death. In fact, the US government used the figure of $200,000 to calculate the value of design enhancements in road construction. There was and is no governmentally sanctioned value in the United States for the value of human life in the context of claims for personal injury and wrongful death.

Ford also appears to have completely ignored the importance of community ethical norms. In fact, Ford's decision raised concerns not only for the 180 persons injured or killed in defect-related explosions. Ford's decision also raised concerns for all purchasers of Ford Pintos and, in fact, for purchasers of all Ford models. All of Ford's potential customers apparently concluded that Ford had violated the trust they placed in Ford when it manufactured an automobile with a known, lethal and repairable defect in its gas tank.

PART TWO

Basic Business Laws

3

Business Regulation in General

INTRODUCTION

Businesses are "regulated" when, in addition to the returns they intend to realize immediately from their decisions, they give due consideration:

1 to interests of parties affected by their actions, including those parties' individual legal rights;
2 to the perceptions of parties concerned about their actions; and
3 to time frames other than the immediate future.

The rights, interests and perceptions of third parties (i.e., in this context: persons other than the decision-maker) are often overlooked in business because they are considered to be unintended consequences, merely collateral effects, too contingent and too remote to be real concerns. Losses and costs are considered to be merely collateral if they are borne by third parties. Third-party losses and costs are considered to be too contingent if they are not certain to occur and too remote if they risk occurring only in a relatively distant future.

As I illustrated in Chapter 2 (Ford Pinto Case), the impact of these unintended consequences is often underestimated and should not be overlooked. At the same time, they can usually be adequately identified and understood, at least for the purpose of incorporating them into sound business decisions. In Chapter 2, I also described five different ethical perspectives and gave you an initial understanding of legal rights, one sort of personal interest potentially affected by business decisions. In Chapter 2, I outlined a method for balancing intended results and unintended consequences by focusing on conflicting interests (including a business' self-interests)[1] and differing ethical perceptions over various time frames.

In this chapter, I explain why and how government regulates business activities. Generally, governments regulate businesses:

1 by providing compensation whenever past business activity results in personal injury, property damage, contract breaches or other violations of their individual legal rights, and
2 by giving choice and information to buyers so that they can prevent future violations of their individual legal rights without further government involvement, and
3 finally, when buyers cannot protect their own interests through informed choice, by establishing mandatory minimum quality standards.

I also explain in this chapter how, in addition to government regulation, businesses regulate themselves

4 by taking into account important future relationships and their own reputations.

In addition, I examine the very different economic impact of these three types of business regulation on individual businesses.

Finally, I explain that corporations have three opportunities for avoiding judicial remedies and precluding government regulation while promoting important future relationships and their own reputations. Those opportunities exist:

(a) within corporations;

(b) in contract negotiation and performance; and

(c) through industry associations.

JUDICIAL REMEDIES

Deterrence through compensation

From a legal perspective, business conduct is based on the exercise of private property and contract rights. Those rights are usually classified as "individual legal rights" because they are exercised in the first instance by individuals (thus, individual) but ultimately dependent upon government enforcement (thus, legal). At the same time, property and contract rights are subject to limitations maintained by judicial remedies.

Breaches of general obligations (torts)

Property rights are limited, as explained in the 1789 French Declaration of the Rights of Man and Citizen, because one individual's use of private property should not be allowed to injure other individuals or damage their property.[2] In fact, personal injury and property damage are violations of legal rights around the world. Such violations are called "torts" in common law countries. In civil law countries, causing personal injury or property damage is referred to as a violation of "general obligations."[3]

General obligations and torts need to be distinguished from crimes: Persons commit "crimes" when they *intentionally* use their property to injure other persons or to damage their property. Crimes are considered to be acts against governments.[4] When individuals are injured or their property damaged *unintentionally* by another individual, such injury or damage can constitute tort (i.e., a breach of the second individual's general obligations). In other words, in the absence of the intent to cause personal injury or property damage, causing personal injury or property damage cannot constitute crimes.[5]

In order to enforce the law of general obligations (or "the law of torts"), individuals who have suffered personal injury or property damage have recourse to courts for the purpose of obtaining monetary compensation.[6] Individuals whose general legal rights have been violated (i.e., who have suffered a tort) can obtain monetary damages in court to the extent that

the violation (or tort) caused them to suffer losses and incur costs (measured in terms of their personal well-being and property values before and after the tort, i.e., before and after the breach of general obligations). The measure of damages is intended to compensate the victims for the costs and losses they suffer as a result of the past violation of their individual legal rights. In effect, paying compensatory damages reallocates the losses and costs borne in the normal course of past business by "third parties" (i.e., persons other than the business engaged in the activity) in violation of their general legal rights. Compensatory damages reallocate those losses and costs away from those third parties and on to the businesses which violated their general obligations and, in so doing, caused harm. The possibility of having to pay compensation also acts as a deterrent to businesses. Businesses use due care to avoid personal injury and property damage to others because of the possibility of having to pay compensation.

Breaches of contract obligations

Rights protected by recourse to courts are not limited to personal injury and property damage. As already indicated, such rights include the enforcement of contract rights. Individuals whose contract rights have been violated can obtain monetary damages in court to the extent that the violation of their contract rights caused them to suffer losses and incur costs (measured in terms of their reasonable expectations pursuant to the contract). As with tort law, paying compensatory damages for contract breaches reallocates the losses and costs for past business conduct. The measure of damages for contract breaches is intended, at least financially, to give the parties the benefits – and burdens – they would have been given had the contract been formed and fully performed. In effect, paying damages in such circumstances gives persons whose contract rights are violated the value of the rights for which they bargained, while imposing a corresponding burden on the breaching contract party. Compensatory damages reallocate those losses and costs away from the contract parties who suffered and incurred them and on to the businesses which breached their contract obligations and, in doing so, caused harm. As with tort law, the possibility of having to pay compensation acts as a deterrent to businesses to breach their contracts.

Punitive damages

As mentioned above, the possibility of paying compensation for causing personal injury and property damage or for breaching contracts is intended to deter similar violations of personal, property and contract rights in the future. Sometimes, however, the possibility of paying such compensation is not a sufficient deterrent. In such cases, courts also typically have the ability to require businesses violating their general or contract obligations to pay "punitive damages." Punitive damages are amounts above and beyond the amount necessary to compensate the victims for the costs and losses they suffered as a result of the violation of their rights.[7] The circumstances in which punitive damages can be imposed differ between cases involving breaches of general obligations and those involving breaches of contract obligations. In each case, however, the possibility of punitive damages is greater if general or contract obligations are breached intentionally, as opposed to unintentionally (i.e., negligently).[8]

GOVERNMENT REGULATION

Prevention through penalties

Judicial remedies are court decisions, typically ordering the payment of compensation for harm caused *in the past* by violations of individual legal rights, especially past personal injury, property damage and contract breaches. Government regulations take the form of statutes adopted by legislatures and rules adopted by government agencies created pursuant to statute. Both statutes and agency rules are intended to prevent violations of individual legal rights *in the future*, including future personal injury, property damage and contract breaches.

The possibility of having to pay compensatory and even punitive damages obviously *deters* breaches of general and contract obligations. The payment of damages in courts of law does not, however, prevent such breaches. In order to *prevent* personal injury, property damage and breaches of contract obligations, legislatures (e.g., parliaments and congresses) enact statutes and agencies adopt rules applicable to business conduct.

In order to protect buyers from future harm, in the first instance, most governments attempt to give buy-

ers real choices whenever possible. With real choice, buyers can protect themselves from future harm without more intrusive government regulation. In order to give buyers real choices, most governments rely on competition amongst sellers in the market place. By enforcing competition, governments have effectively elevated buyers' economic interest in real choice to the status of a legal right instrumental in protecting their general and contract rights. (In this context, "real choice" means choices not subject to substantial transactional or other collateral costs.)

To the extent that governments are successful in providing buyers with real choice through competition, governments do not need to intervene further in business conduct:

1 unless competition does not provide buyers with adequate information to make informed choices; or
2 informed choices do not enable buyers to avoid personal injury, property damage or other violations of their general or contract rights.

With the spread of private property and freedom of contract as the two fundamental business facilities, more and more governments are using competition law, to the extent applicable, as their first attempt to prevent breaches of general and contract obligations.

Giving choice to buyers

Participants in market transactions are assumed to be "on equal footing" where there is perfect competition (i.e., where each of them has complete freedom of choice). Where there is perfect competition, buyers can negotiate for the necessary information, terms and conditions from among competing sellers for the purpose of making prudent buying decisions.

In this way, buyers can avoid many or most violations of their general and contract rights. Each buyer can, moreover, promote his or her other interests in the manner and to the extent he or she deems appropriate. In effect, protecting the buyers' right to informed choice is a very flexible form of government regulation. Giving buyers informed choices is also a relatively inexpensive form of government regulation because buyers do not rely on government agencies to protect and promote their interests. Instead, buyers protect and promote their own rights and other interests in the manner and to the extent they see fit.

As a result, competition law is probably the most fundamental form of government regulation and is becoming increasingly popular around the world. Governments prefer enforcing competition as a method of business regulation because it is unobtrusive and generally inexpensive. For both of these reasons, enforcing competition is a method for government regulation also generally preferred by businesses over the other methods described below (giving information to buyers and establishing quality standards).

In the United States, competition law is called "anti-trust law," because one of the first techniques businesses used to eliminate competition in the early twentieth century was called a "trust." Since competition law in the United States prohibited the creation of trusts in order to preserve competition, US competition law has been called "anti-trust law" since that early date.

Giving information to buyers

In the absence of all relevant information, participants in business transactions cannot effectively promote their own interests.[9] Moreover, even though all relevant information is necessary for markets to allocate goods and services efficiently, historically, general principles of law have not required sellers to disclose all relevant information about their goods and services. On the contrary, in the absence of specific government regulation, sellers are generally allowed to keep secrets about their goods and services. They simply are not allowed to tell lies about their goods and services.

Enforcing competition is frequently sufficient to ensure adequate information. In competitive markets, sellers frequently volunteer information adequate for buyers to make effective choices because, in competitive markets, sellers who do not disclose adequate information are at a disadvantage. Experience shows, however, that competition alone does not always lead to sellers' disclosure of all relevant information.[10]

Accordingly, in addition to enforcing competition, government regulators sometimes take the step of creating and enforcing a "right to know" in favor of buyers. In general, "right to know" regulations make it illegal for sellers to keep secrets about

their goods and services. The "right to know" can take the form of various disclosure obligations, such as labelling requirements and fair dealing regulations. Enforcing disclosure requirements typically leads to government regulations which are less flexible and more expensive to implement than competition law. While competition law is usually based on relatively broad principles and enforced through occasional, selective agency action, disclosure requirements are usually based on relatively detailed regulations and enforced through frequent or even continuous agency review.

Establishing quality standards

Finally, sometimes both competition regulation and disclosure requirements, taken together, are not sufficient to enable buyers to avoid personal injury and property damage and to promote their other interests. In such instances, governments intervene in business by imposing quality standards on suppliers, on their procedures, and on the goods and services they deliver. By imposing these quality standards, governments attempt to protect buyers from future violations of their individual rights (both general and contract rights) rather than allowing buyers to protect themselves.[11] The protected class of buyers is often, but not always, limited to individual retail consumers.

Such government regulation can take the form of:

1 minimum educational requirements and professional licensing for suppliers;
2 standards for procedures and practices of all sorts; and
3 quality specifications for goods and services or any combination of the foregoing regulations, all prescribed in a relatively detailed fashion.

Governments attempt to enforce these various quality standards by licensing, by inspections, by reviews and by approvals of final products, all on a relatively regular basis.

Important differences from judicial remedies

There are important differences between, on the one hand, judicial remedies for breaches of general and contract obligations and, on the other hand, government regulation of competition, disclosures and quality.

First, the law of general obligations and contracts is based upon very general principles of law,[12] while government regulation of competition, disclosures and quality are based upon more or less specific government statutes and regulations adopted by legislatures and executive agencies. Accordingly, the laws of general obligations and contract are more generally (although not universally) known and understood by the public and within the business communities to which they apply. Government regulation is generally less known and understood by the general public and even by the business communities to which they apply.

Second, the compensatory damages available for breaches of general or contract obligations are specifically intended to compensate individuals for the harm they suffer personally as a result of the breaches. In the absence of punitive damages and class actions,[13] the amount of compensatory damages is limited to the amount of harm actually suffered by the individual claiming compensation.[14] The penalties imposed for violations of government regulation, on the other hand, are specifically intended to prevent future harm.[15] Accordingly, the amount of penalties for violations of government regulations is not limited to the harm actually suffered by any one individual. In fact, the amount of penalties is not limited to the harm actually suffered in the past or even potentially suffered in the future by any one or more individuals. Instead, in order to be effective, the amount of the penalty arguably should exceed the amount of harm actually or potentially suffered by all individuals as a result of the violation of the government regulation.[16]

Third, it is possible to obtain remedies in court other than (or in addition to) compensatory damages, but such remedies are generally considered to be extraordinary remedies. In addition to punitive damages, such extraordinary remedies include negative injunctions and affirmative injunctions (i.e., court orders instructing individuals, under threat of police action, *not* to undertake actions specified by the court – "negative injunctions" – or to undertake court-specified actions – "affirmative injunctions"). Courts grant injunctions generally only if courts consider them to be reasonably necessary to prevent future harm. Compensating for past harm, not preventing future harm, is the purpose of court actions.

Government regulation, on the other hand, is specifically intended to prevent future harm. Accordingly, remedies precluding future harm are not considered extraordinary by government agencies charged with enforcing them. Plant closures, seizures of goods and even incarceration of suppliers are remedies commonly within the scope of government agency authority.

Fourth, the laws of general obligations and contracts are enforced by harmed individuals while government regulations are enforced by government agencies. As a result, breaches of general obligations and contracts – enforced by harmed individuals – are often enforced only if the breaches result in significant harm to specific individuals. Generally, the amount of harm to any one individual needs to be sufficient to prompt the individual harmed to initiate a complaint in court.[17] The amount of harm caused to specific individuals is not a barrier, however, to actions by government agencies. Instead, government agencies tend to focus on the amount of harm potentially caused in the aggregate by specific practices. As a result, actions by government agencies are economically justified in instances where court actions by individuals might not be justified.[18]

Fifth, procedures in courts are sometimes significantly different from procedures before government agencies. In court, for example, one business or individual commences a complaint against another business or individual – and each presents its case to the judge. The judge is a government appointee with no connection to the businesses or individuals involved in the dispute. At government agencies, the agency itself commences an action against a business or individual – and, in the first instance, makes its case at an administrative hearing, presided over by a government appointee affiliated with the government agency. Agency appointees are usually more competent in specific areas of law than judges in courts. At the same time, agency appointees are generally considered to be less neutral than judges in courts. While agencies typically maintain procedural safeguards for their hearings similar to the safeguards available in court trials, a business subject to a claim by an administrative agency often does not have access to a judge (i.e., a neutral decision-maker) until the proceedings at the agency are complete and the business appeals the agency action to a court of law. Moreover, depending upon the statute establishing the agency, the review by the court may be limited, as regards its review of either or both the facts and the law.

INTERNATIONAL GOVERNMENTAL REGULATION

Enactment, coordination, cooperation, treaties

Throughout history, each state (e.g., duchies, kingdoms, empires, city-states and nation-states) has adopted and enforced with relative ease regulations concerning commercial conduct within its boundaries. At the same time, it has been more difficult for states to adopt and enforce regulations concerning commercial conduct occurring outside of their boundaries. Each state has been interested in regulating business conduct both when such conduct occurs within its borders and when it occurs abroad but has intended results or unintended consequences within its borders or on its subjects or citizens. To deal with these difficulties, states have developed legal principles and practices concerning the enactment and enforcement of regulations concerning international business, including arrangements for coordination of enactments and cooperation in enforcement. The coordination and cooperation are often embodied in treaties between countries. Recent multilateral treaties have created "regional organizations" for the purpose of interpreting and enforcing treaty obligations.

Enactments by individual countries

Many states have developed legal principles to enact regulations concerning commercial conduct abroad if the conduct has its results or effects within their boundaries. This legal principle is called the "effects doctrine" and is widely accepted as a legitimate form of jurisdiction. The best known example of the effects doctrine is competition law (called "antitrust law" in the United States). If commercial conduct in one state restricts or distorts competition within a second state, then the second state claims the right to regulate that foreign commercial conduct. (There are legal concepts in addition to the "effects doctrine," which allow states to govern conduct abroad. For example, under the "citizenship doctrine," states claim the right to regulate conduct affecting its citizens.)

Coordination of enactments

International business can suffer if the same conduct is subject to inconsistent government regulation by two states. In order to address this problem, states sometimes agree to coordinate their government regulation. Two common mechanisms for achieving consistent regulations are:

1 mutual recognition; and
2 harmonization.

If two states agree on "mutual recognition," then each state agrees – usually in a very limited context – to give effect within its own legal system to the other state's laws. For example, a bank established in one state might be recognized as a bank in a second state even though the bank does not have a separate legal existence in the second state. Mutual recognition is used frequently – but certainly not always – to address issues such as the safety of products made in one country and sold in another. An importing country's recognition of an exporting country's laws for the purpose of determining food safety is usually considered to facilitate the export of those food products. The importing country usually gives such a concession only if the exporting country agrees to recognize the importing country's food safety regulations, thus: "mutual recognition."

"Harmonization" is another form of international legal coordination. If two states agree to harmonize their laws, each agrees to adopt and enforce substantially the same laws. Harmonization is generally considered to go beyond mutual recognition because it implies some coordination of the legislative process in two different countries. At the same time, harmonization is not a complete unification. Unless there is a single body with final authority to enforce the harmonized laws (i.e., a single executive) and a single court system to interpret the harmonized legislation, differences can arise between or among different states as regards their "harmonized" laws.

Cooperation in enforcement

In addition to principles used by states to enact regulation of business conduct occurring abroad, and to coordinate their regulations (i.e., through mutual recognition or harmonization), states have developed cooperative practices to facilitate enforcement of their laws, whether those laws apply to conduct within their boundaries or abroad. Pursuant to these cooperative enforcement arrangements, one state agrees to assist another state (the "second state") in the second state's enforcement of its own laws within the second state's legal system (i.e., enforcement within the territory of the second state). At the level of cooperation in enforcement, there is no attempt to coordinate the laws adopted by each state within its own boundaries.

Such cooperation can take the form, for example, of assistance in criminal investigations or, less often, enforcement of final judgments. In order to achieve some level of cooperation, it is necessary that one state agree to respect the laws of another country. At the level of cooperation, the respect typically takes the form "reciprocity." In other words, if you will help me to enforce my laws, then I will help you to enforce your laws. For example, one state might agree to assist another state in investigating crimes provided that the other state agrees to do the same.

Treaties

Treaties between or among states (i.e., bilateral or multilateral) are often used to embody agreements on international cooperation and coordination. Traditionally, each state assumes ultimate responsibility for respecting its treaty obligations, refusing to surrender "sovereignty" to any international forum. More recently, various multilateral treaties – such as the ones establishing the European Union or the North American Free Trade Agreement – have established institutions and procedures to provide interpretations and enforcement of treaty obligations.

BUSINESS SELF-REGULATION

Deterrence through loss of future revenue

Businesses regulate themselves when, in the absence of possible judicial remedies and actual government regulation, they give due consideration:

1 to interests of parties affected by their actions, including those parties' individual legal rights;

2 to the perceptions of parties concerned about their actions; and

3 to time frames other than the immediate future.[19]

Clearly, judicial remedies and government regulation can be very burdensome for business. This does not mean, however, that there are no constraints on business conduct in the absence of judicial remedies and government regulation. In addition to judicial remedies and government regulation, two important non-governmental constraints on business conduct are:

1 commercial relationships; and

2 corporate reputations.

Failing to take these constraints into account in making business decisions can have significant adverse consequences.

Commercial relationships

Most students have heard of the "prisoners' dilemma" problem and are aware of one or more of its versions.[20] In one version of the "dilemma," both prisoners would serve a relatively moderate sentence (e.g., ten years) if neither prisoner testifies against the other (effectively cooperating). On the other hand, each prisoner can avoid sentencing entirely by being the first to agree to testify against the other, thereby condemning the other prisoner to a long prison sentence (e.g., twenty-five years). In these circumstances, there is a significant reward for each prisoner if the other prisoner cooperates with him or her (by not testifying). There is an even greater reward for each prisoner if he or she is the first to agree to testify against the other (effectively betraying his or her colleague).

In these circumstances (i.e., freedom from prison in exchange for testifying), I believe that each prisoner would be sorely tempted to testify against the other in exchange for his freedom. If the circumstances were altered such that the prisoner agreeing to testify were subject to a shorter sentence (e.g., five years) instead of being set free, I believe that the outcome could be different. In the context of a continuing relationship over the next five years in prison, each prisoner might consider it prudent to accept the relatively moderate sentence (i.e., ten years) rather than the shorter sentence (i.e., five years) with the constant threat of retribution for the betrayal.

I believe that there is a similar dilemma for merchants in respect of ongoing commercial relationships. A business can be sorely tempted to maximize its return on a single transaction, sometimes through misrepresentations and other unfair dealing, if there is no prospect of a long-term relationship. Conversely, the promise of even greater future returns over the course of an ongoing commercial relationship serves as a moderating influence, discouraging businesses from seeking the highest immediate returns through misrepresentation and other unfair dealing. Here is an example which raises these issues. If you were Woody, what would you do?

Miraculous Hardwood, Inc. ("MH") is a furniture manufacturer in Georgia, with its headquarters in Atlanta. Sitting Pretty & Co. ("SP") is a chain of furniture stores throughout the north-central United States (i.e., Montana, Wyoming, North Dakota and South Dakota) with its headquarters in Fargo, North Dakota. Over the past twenty years, in terms of volume SP has usually ranked between eighth and twelfth among MH's 120 purchasers, with no foreseeable change. In other words, SP has been (and presumably will remain) a relatively small but steady customer. In fact, SP is one of the accounts handled personally by William "Woody" Sellers, MH's national sales manager. On 17 April, MH's CEO, Mr Michael Oakes, informed Woody that due to an oversight in quality control, eighty (80) sets of dining-room furniture were recently manufactured using sub-quality wood to make the joints in the chairs (maple instead of ash). All of the defective chairs are still in inventory. While the defect is not immediately apparent, stress tests by MH's production staff show that the defect will eventually lead to loose backs in many chairs. The production staff estimates that the defects will become apparent in a significant number of chairs (more than 20%) after about one year of normal usage. On the other hand, the production staff believes that the defects will never manifest themselves in more than one-half (50%) of the chairs – again assuming normal usage. At the same time, Mr Oakes – who has announced that he will retire at the end of this calendar year – informed Woody that, since revenues for the calendar year have been down, MH needs to sell the eighty dining-room sets quickly in the normal course of business. Mr Oakes also insists that the chairs be sold at list price, without disclosing the defect and without an extended warranty or other promotional consideration. (Mr Oakes' retirement package will be calculated in part on the basis of the current calendar year's total sales revenues.) Woody knows that Mr Oakes and his heir apparent, Mr Thomas Birch, hold Woody personally responsible for the recent drop in sales. Unless Woody turns sales around in the second quarter, it is possible that, at the request of Mr Birch, Mr Oakes will replace Woody as early as the beginning of the third quarter. Woody holds an order from SP for the delivery of 100 dining-room sets during May and June. Accepting this single purchase order would go a long way in satisfying Mr Oakes and relieving the pressure on Woody. Under MH's standard warranty, MH will fully reimburse a furniture store's repair costs arising out of any defects in materials or workmanship, but only under conditions of normal customer usage and only for a period of one year after the furniture is delivered by MH to the furniture store.

In the absence of the ongoing commercial relationship between MH and SP, I believe that Woody would be sorely tempted to sell the dining-room sets, including the defective chairs, to SP in the manner stated by Mr Oakes (i.e., "at list price, without disclosing the defect and without an extended warranty or other promotional consideration"). At the same time, the promise of even greater future returns over the course of the ongoing relationship with SP probably serves as a moderating influence on Woody, discouraging him from making the sale while failing to disclose the defect.

As illustrated by the foregoing example, ongoing commercial relationships generally discourage concealment and other unfair dealing.[21] The deterrent effect of ongoing commercial relationships can be understood by asking three questions about any concealment or other unfair dealing: Will other person(s) eventually know about the unfair dealing? Will other person(s) be concerned about the unfair dealing? What are the consequences of their knowledge and concern?

As regards commercial relationships, the "other person(s)" are the persons directly involved in the underlying commercial transaction (e.g., buyers of goods or services). In my example, Sitting Pretty & Co. (SP) is the "other person."[22]

In response to the first question: it is fair to assume that such persons (e.g., the buyers such as SP) will *eventually* know all of the facts relevant to each transaction in which they are involved, even if they do not know all of the relevant facts at the time they enter into each transaction.

In response to the second question: it is fair to assume that such persons (e.g., buyers) will be concerned if, at the time they enter into transactions, sellers know – but do not disclose – facts potentially detrimental to the buyers.

In response to the third question: even if the transaction is isolated (i.e., not part of an ongoing commercial relationship), the person(s) directly involved would be able to seek a judicial remedy on the basis of undisclosed detrimental facts. In further response to the third question: if the transaction is part of an ongoing commercial relationship, then the person(s) directly involved would be able to terminate the ongoing commercial relationship in addition to seeking a judicial remedy.

As explained by the foregoing discussion, ongoing commercial relationships can be an effective non-governmental constraint on business conduct because the threat of terminated relationships can be a credible deterrent to concealment and other unfair practices. In fact, the threat of terminated commercial relationships can be a more significant deterrent than the threat of judicial remedies, in part because termination is sometimes available in cases where judicial remedies would be difficult to obtain. In the case of Miraculous Hardwoods, for example, it is not clear that a judicial remedy would be available to SP on the basis of MH's conduct in that case. The availability of such a remedy would depend on the terms and conditions of the contract between MH and SP.[23]

As illustrated by MH–SP, the prospect of maximum aggregate returns on the basis of long-term relationships serves to moderate the impulse to seek the highest possible returns from each transaction. Conversely, the pressure for the highest possible immediate gain from a single transaction is often at odds with the prospect of maximum aggregate gains over the lifetime of an ongoing long-term commercial relationship.

If you agree with the premise that the prospect of long-term commercial relationships serves to moderate business behavior, then you should also agree that the absence of such a prospect eliminates an important constraint on business behavior. Accordingly, if you are entering into an isolated commercial transaction, i.e., a commercial transaction without the prospect of a continuing relationship, you should exercise caution. Similarly, you should exercise caution if you are entering into the last of many transac-tions based upon a past commercial relationship, if the relationship has no prospect of continuing.

Corporate reputations

In addition to the prospect of ongoing commercial relationships, there is another important non-governmental constraint on business conduct: the existence of corporate reputations. As with ongoing commercial relationships, corporate reputations discourage concealment and other unfair dealing.

To understand the deterrent effect of corporate reputations, we can again ask the three questions we asked about the deterrent effect of commercial relationships: Will other person(s) eventually know about the unfair dealing? Will other person(s) be concerned about the unfair dealing? What are the consequences of their knowledge and concern?

As regards corporate reputations, the "other person(s)" are not, as with commercial relationships, necessarily directly involved in the underlying commercial transactions. Those persons usually include:

(a) shareholders;
(b) employees;
(c) customers in addition to the one(s) directly involved in the unfair dealing;
(d) the various communities in which corporations source materials, maintain production or market their goods and services; and
(d) governments with jurisdiction over a corporation's various activities.

In response to the first question: it is *less likely* that such persons will eventually know all of the facts relevant to a transaction. It is less likely simply because they are not involved (e.g., they were not the actual buyers). At the same time, it is quite possible that such "other person(s)" could learn the facts. They could learn the facts:

(a) in the normal course of business (e.g., discussions with the buyers or through press reports);
(b) through litigation (e.g., lawsuits filed by the buyers and resulting press coverage); or
(c) through public disclosures pursuant to securities law regulations if the transaction is material for a publicly-traded corporation (and resulting press coverage).

In response to the second question: it is also *less likely* that persons not directly involved in a transaction will be concerned if other persons directly involved (e.g., the actual buyers) are the victims of concealment or some other unfair practice. At the same time, it is possible that such other persons (e.g., persons other than actual buyers) would be concerned, especially if they were members of the same "category" of persons (e.g., other buyers from the same seller on other occasions or other buyers from the same type of seller).

In further response to the second question: The "other person(s)" may be concerned even if they are not in the same category as the persons involved in the transaction (e.g., even if they are not buyers from the same seller or from the same type of seller). Shareholders and employees, for example, are obviously concerned about unfair treatment of customers. Increasingly, customers are concerned about unfair treatment of employees. Each community where businesses operate are concerned about environmental and worker health-and-safety issues, both within their own communities and, increasingly, within other communities. Shareholders and consumers, moreover, frequently share the concerns of local communities. Consistently unfair treatment of any sort can also attract the attention of the press, the general public and governments.

In response to the third question: person(s) not directly involved in an unfair transaction would not be able to seek a judicial remedy. On the other hand, persons who are not victims of an unfair transaction, but who are members of the same category (e.g., certainly purchasers from the same seller and, even possibly, purchasers from the same type of seller), could be tempted to terminate – or at least to diversify – their ongoing commercial relationships on the basis of a declining corporate reputation. (Such a reaction can compound the deterrent effect of ongoing commercial relationships on unfair business practices.)

In further response to the third question: "other person(s)" concerned about a corporate reputation may be less likely to terminate ongoing relationships if they are not members of the category of persons victimized by an unfair practice (e.g., they were not buyers in similar transactions). At the same time, a corporate reputation for unfair dealing can have a detrimental effect on relationships with all important corporate constituencies, as members of each constituency react – both individually and as groups – in

the manner they consider appropriate. Such constituencies commonly include shareholders, employees, customers, various communities, the press, the general public and governments.[24]

Persons not victimized by unfair business practices are less likely to know and to care about them. Nonetheless, the deterrent effect of corporate reputations is considerable. It is considerable because of the large number of persons included in the various constituencies important to corporations. In fact, the number of persons potentially concerned about an unfair practice is generally much larger than the number of persons directly victimized. The persons directly victimized can usually be identified individually, while the persons included in various concerned corporate constituencies are usually innumerable, and so can be discussed meaningfully only as various "groups."[25]

Community ethical norms

The impact of non-governmental constraints on business conduct is always potentially significant. I believe that you cannot make sound business decisions without taking them into account. As illustrated by Miraculous Hardwoods, the prospect of ongoing commercial relationships and the existence of corporate reputations come into play, together with judicial remedies, if proposed business practices could result in personal injury, property damages or contract breaches. Similarly, those non-governmental constraints can come into play, together with governmental regulation, where proposed business practices fail to give buyers real choice, adequate information or other protections from breaches of general and contract violations.

The ongoing commercial relationships and corporate reputations compound consequences for business which commit breaches of their general obligations, contract obligations or applicable government regulations. Relationships and reputations compound the consequences of such breaches because such breaches generally offend community ethical norms, even if the practices constituting the breach would not be offensive to community ethical norms in the absence of general obligation, contract obligation or government regulation.[26]

Finally, ongoing commercial relationships and corporate reputations often come into play even if judicial remedies are not available and government regulations do not apply. Relationships and reputations come into play in such circumstances because community ethical norms often apply to practices which do not violate individual legal rights or government regulations.

Two points should be clear from the foregoing discussion. First, the scope of community ethical norms often determines the scope of business practices with adverse consequences for commercial relationships and corporate reputations.[27] Second, the significance of community ethical norms for specific business practices is determined at least in part by the potential impact of such practices on commercial relationships and corporate reputations. Third, based on the other two points, community ethical norms have significance for making sound business decisions independent from management's own ethical perceptions.[28]

ECONOMIC IMPACT OF REGULATION ON BUSINESS

As summarized below, judicial remedies, government regulation and self-regulation all have significant, but very different, economic impacts on individual businesses. It is most important to remember that the economic impact of all three can apply cumulatively to the same business practice.

Judicial remedies

As already explained, judicial remedies require businesses to pay compensation for harm others suffer as a result of past business practices if the practices constitute breaches of general or contract obligations. Compensatory damages are specifically intended to reallocate losses away from those who suffer harm and on to the businesses causing harm in breach of their general and contract obligations. At the same time, the possibility of paying compensation has the effect of deterring future breaches of general and contract obligations as businesses modify their practices to avoid future breaches. In those instances where the possibility of paying compensation is not sufficient to deter future breaches (as illustrated by the Ford Pinto Case), courts also frequently have the ability to require businesses to pay "punitive damages." In either case, it is usually reasonable for

businesses to modify practices to avoid personal injury, property damages and contract breaches because doing so can effectively avoid future payments of compensatory and punitive damages.[29]

Government regulation

As previously outlined, the law of general obligations (or tort law) often effectively *deters* personal injury and property damage by *prompting* businesses to modify their practices. The law of general obligations (or tort law) does not, however, prevent personal injury or property damage. Government regulation is specifically intended to *prevent* personal injury and property damage by *requiring* businesses to modify their practices. In order to compel businesses to comply with regulatory requirements, governments tend to impose penalties for non-compliance (i.e., fines and other sanctions). To have their intended effect (i.e., compelling businesses to adopt modifications in their practices), those penalties tend to exceed both

1 the compensation potentially due and owing in the future by business on the basis of the harmful business practice; and
2 the cost of making the required modification.[30]

Accordingly, it is usually reasonable for businesses to comply with government regulations because:

1 incurring penalties does not relieve businesses from the requirement to modify their practices (i.e., it is possible for businesses to pay both for the penalty and for making modifications); and
2 making the required modifications can, on occasion, excuse businesses from paying compensation for future personal injury and property damage they cause after (and even though) the business practice is modified.[31]

Self-regulation

The economic impact of self-regulation differs significantly from the economic impact of judicial remedies and government regulation. Judicial remedies reallocate the costs for past injury and damage. Government regulation increases the cost of current operations in an attempt to prevent future injury and damage. Breaching community ethical norms can undermine future relationships and corporate reputations, thereby decreasing future revenues and increasing costs. Businesses' revenues can decrease as constituencies purchasing goods and services perceive a potential harm to themselves through continued dealings with the businesses engaged in conduct offending community ethical norms. Revenues can also decrease as other purchasers simply give expression to the offence they perceive by distancing themselves from the businesses engaged in the offensive practice(s). Similarly, costs can increase as constituencies supplying resources react to the potential of future harm or perceived offenses.

A significant cumulative impact

Of course, business practices breaching general, contract obligations or government regulations also often offend community ethical norms. Accordingly, violations of law can undermine a corporation's relationships and reputation Accordingly, the various economic impacts of judicial remedies, government regulation and community ethical norms are not mutually exclusive. In other words, the same business conduct can lead to the payment of compensatory and punitive damages, the payment of penalties to the government (without avoiding the cost of making required modifications to business practices) and, by undermining commercial relationships and corporate reputations, losses of future revenue and increases of future costs.

THREE OPPORTUNITIES FOR SELF-REGULATION

Businesses engage in self-regulation when, in the absence of possible judicial remedies and actual government regulation, they give due consideration:

1   to interests of parties affected by their actions, including those parties' individual legal rights;
2   to the perceptions of parties concerned about their actions; and
3   to time frames other than the immediate future.

Conversely, judicial remedies are available and government regulations are enacted when businesses fail to engage in self-regulation.

Corporations have three opportunities for avoiding judicial remedies and government regulation. Those opportunities exist:

(a) within individual corporations;
(b) in contract negotiation and performance; and
(c) through industry associations.

Before explaining those three opportunities, I need to discuss briefly private property and contracts, reminding you that:

1   private property and contracts are, in the first instance, individual rights, and explaining that
2   private property and contracts are fundamental business facilities.

Indeed, far from constituting forms of government regulation, they provide opportunities for business to regulate itself.

As discussed in Chapter 2, private property rights entail each owner's right to have the government physically exclude others from occupying or possessing certain assets. Private property rights also include *the owners' right to use assets "freely"*, i.e., as the owners see fit (not imposed by government). Freedom of contract gives individual owners additional rights concerning those assets. Most importantly, freedom of contract includes *the owners' right to transfer assets "freely"*, i.e., on terms owners agree with transferees (not imposed by the government).

Private property and contracts are also fundamental business facilities because, around the world, they are the basis for commercial and industrial activity.[32] Expressed in the simplest legal terms, commercial activity consists of contracts whereby sellers exchange their private property (typically: final goods or services) for buyers' private property (typically: money). Again expressed in the simplest legal terms, industrial activity consists of sellers using some of their assets (i.e., fixed assets and raw materials) to make other assets intended for commercial activity (i.e., final goods and services).[33]

Private property and contracts are individual rights because individuals decide in the first instance whether and how to obtain, exercise and enforce those rights.[34] In the same way, private property and contracts offer the first two opportunities for business self-regulation:

1 within individual corporations; and
2 in negotiating and performing contracts.

Within corporations

Private property rights effectively allow individual corporations to decide how to use their business assets. Accordingly, the first opportunity for self-regulation exists within each corporation. In other words, in the first instance, individual corporations are free to regulate themselves, even in the absence of government regulation, by giving due consideration not only to:

1 the returns they intend to realize immediately from their decisions (including inherent costs, delays and uncertainties); but also
2 to interests of parties affected by their actions, including those parties' individual legal rights;
3 to the perceptions of parties concerned about their actions; and
4 to time frames other than the immediate future.

Of course, owners (usually, shareholders) have already committed corporate assets to commercial or industrial activity – as opposed to using such assets for consumption or savings. Shareholders, moreover, typically entrust those corporate assets to managers. (Sometimes, especially in smaller corporations, one or more of the shareholders are also managers.) Corporate management, in turn, agrees to use the corporate assets – in accordance with the terms of that trust – for commercial and industrial purposes. Subject to those duties of trust, management is free to use the shareholders' corporate assets entirely as management sees fit. Management is free to do so because management is exercising the shareholders' private property rights on their behalf and, as you may recall, individuals (in this case, shareholders or their corporation) can exercise their private property rights without the consent of any third party.

Management is free to use corporate assets in a manner which:

(a) respects the legal rights of those persons with whom its corporations deal;
(b) promotes those persons' other interests; and
(c) respects community ethical norms. (On the other hand, at least in the first instance, management is effectively free not to do so.[35])

In contract negotiation and performance

Contract rights, like private property rights, are fundamental business facilities. Like private property rights, contracts are individual legal rights, i.e., ultimately enforceable by individuals through their governments, but are exercised in the first instance by the individuals holding them. Accordingly, like private property rights, contracts are opportunities for businesses to self-regulate; both in their dealings with the persons who are parties to their contracts and in respect of those persons affected by their contracts but not party to them.

Businesses self-regulate regarding their contract parties both when they negotiate their contracts and when businesses perform their contracts. Sellers in particular engage in self-regulation when they disclose all information relevant for buyers to make informed decisions. Sellers also self-regulate when, after negotiating contracts, they perform the contracts in good faith, having due regard for their contract parties' reasonable expectations and without regard to the usually significant costs entailed for their contract parties to enforce those expectations in court.[36]

Businesses self-regulate in performing and negotiating their contracts also when they take into account persons affected by their contracts but not party to them (in this context, "third parties"). It is often the case that third parties are affected by contracts between two businesses (e.g., their employees and their local communities). Businesses self-regulate if, in performing their contracts, they give due consideration to possible harm to third parties (e.g., such as personal injury or property damage) and generally to the communities where they operate. Businesses self-regulate if, in negotiating their contracts, they anticipate possible harm to specific individuals or communities and agree ways to try to reduce the risk of harm and allocate responsibility for any actual harm.

Through industry associations

Industry initiatives are the third forum in which issues of self-regulation arise. Industry forums (such as industry associations) expand the potential scope for self-regulation because an individual company sometimes hesitates to take self-regulatory initiatives even where the benefit to third parties is clear. Individual companies sometimes hesitate because doing so can increase their costs or reduce their revenue, thereby putting them at a competitive disadvantage. By addressing legal and ethical concerns on an industry-wide basis, individual companies can overcome their competitive concerns about the increased cost and reduced revenue sometimes associated with self-regulatory measures.[37]

To the extent that competition within an industry is global, effective self-regulation also needs to be global. Accordingly, there is a proliferation of international confederations of national industry associations. The same competitive concerns for costs and revenues pushing individual companies to look to national industry associations for self-regulatory initiatives is pushing national industry associations to look to international confederations. National industry associations attempt to harmonize their self-regulatory efforts internationally through these confederations. In fact, the international confederations frequently take the lead with self-regulatory initiatives.[38]

4

Private Property Rights

INTRODUCTION

This chapter is intended as an introduction to private property, including the relationships amongst owners of private property and between owners and those agreeing to act on their behalf.

The legal framework for business around the world

The use and transfer of private property, i.e., assets a person "owns," provide the legal framework for practically all business activities around the world. As indicated in Chapter 3, most business activity consists of a person using some of his, her or its private property (i.e., fixed assets and raw materials) to deliver other private property intended for sale (i.e., final goods and services).

From a legal perspective, a corporation is a fictional person using and transferring its private property for the purpose of conducting business activity. As a result, a clear understanding of private property, including an understanding of the relationships arising from the use and transfer of assets owned by a corporation, is necessary in order to understand business activity around the world.[1]

The definition of private property rights

As you may recall from Chapter 3, "private property rights" are legal rights held by one or more persons in specific assets. For all types of assets, private property rights consist of the owner's exclusive right to possess, use and profit from those assets (the "use rights"). Private property rights in assets also include the right to transfer the "use rights" in those assets, either in whole or in part, to other persons. "Ownership" of certain assets consists of holding:

(a) all of the present and future use rights in those assets; and
(b) the right freely to transfer all of those use rights to others, together with the right freely to make further transfers.

Ownership is sometimes said to consist of "all right, title and interest" in and to certain assets. A person who holds all right, title and interest in an asset is said to be the "owner" of the asset.

While "use rights" are enforceable against others (i.e., non-owners) without their consent and so are not set forth in any contracts, transfers of private property rights are enforceable against owners only with their consent – as embodied in contracts between transferors and transferees. Accordingly, even though use rights are not enforceable against non-owners pursuant to contracts, holders of use rights must be able, upon demand, to demonstrate their status as owner of those use rights, usually by producing a document evidencing the creation or transfer of those use rights in their favour.

Transfers of private property rights

Transfers of private property rights are subject to the innumerable definitions, terms and conditions devised by owners and buyers concerning those transfers. For example, owners can transfer some, but not all, of their use rights in assets while retaining the remaining use rights for themselves; and owners can transfer all of their use rights in assets without transferring the right freely to make further transfers of those use rights.

The terms and conditions pursuant to which owners and buyers agree to transfer private property are, of course, set forth in contracts. An owner's use rights can be enforced against all other persons without their consent. Use rights exist pursuant to law, so contracts are not necessary to define them. Transfers of private property rights, on the other hand, can be enforced only between sellers and buyers (i.e., former owners and current owners) and only on the basis of their mutual consent. Accordingly, contracts are necessary for transfers of private property.

Limitations and obligations

Generally, owners can freely exercise their private property rights, both use rights and transfer rights, In other words, owners are allowed to use and transfer assets as they see fit – not as the government dictates. The owners' freedom in respect of their assets does not mean, however, that private property rights are not subject to limitations and burdens. Government regulation of business, for example, constitutes an important limitation on the exercise of private property rights by business. General obligations constitute an important burden in connection with businesses' exercise of private property rights.

TYPES OF ASSETS

Tangible assets, intangible assets and documents

Private property rights can exist in tangible assets, intangible assets and documents. Tangible assets are valuable objects. Tangible assets include land, buildings, equipment and materials. Intangible assets are valuable rights. Intangible assets include intellectual property rights and contractual undertakings. Documents are writings embodying the right to receive delivery of tangible assets or payments of money. Documents include warehouse receipts and negotiable instruments.

Land, fixtures and personal property

Within the system of private property rights, land is classified as "real property." In fact, other tangible assets are defined within the system of property rights by their relationship to land:

(a) assets attached to land, such as plants and buildings, are classified as "immovable property" or "fixtures"; while
(b) all other assets, i.e., those not attached to land, are classified as "movable property" or "personal property."

Animals and equipment are examples of personal property.

It is possible for the same asset to shift amongst classifications within the system of private property rights, always depending on its relationship to land. Minerals are usually considered to be part of the land – and therefore real property – before they are extracted. After minerals are extracted, they become personal property. Crops are considered to be fixtures until they are harvested, when they become personal property. Seeds separated from plants are personal property until they are planted and take root, when they become fixtures.

TANGIBLE ASSETS

Land

For ownership purposes, "land" is typically defined in terms of space, usually a horizontal plane at the earth's surface level (not necessarily sea level) with its boundaries determined by reference to certain fixed points – such as latitude and longitude. Land also includes all of the space located vertically directly above and below that horizontal plane: the space "from heaven to hell." Any minerals, water and immovable objects located within the three-dimensional space so defined are called "real property," the ownership interest in land.

Transfers of real property are always evidenced by a "deed," a document naming the owner and signed and delivered by the person from whom the owner obtained ownership. Often, the deed is also signed by the owner. There can be further formalities involved in evidencing ownership in real property. In some jurisdictions, for example, it is necessary to have the deed signed by a public official, such as a notary or notary public. The official involved certifies any or all of the following:

1   that the seller's and buyer's signatures are authentic;
2   that the seller and buyer have understood the terms of the transaction; and
3   that, sometimes subject to filing as a public document, the transaction has been completed – so that ownership has actually transferred in accordance with the terms of the deed.

A deed evidencing ownership of real property must also be filed as a "public record." In other words, the person receiving ownership must ensure that the deed is filed with a government office where it is available for inspection by the public. A transferee's ownership of real property is enforceable against the transferor on the basis of the deed evidencing the transfer. A transferee's ownership of real property is not enforceable against other persons until the deed is registered.

Fixtures

Fixtures are tangible personal property attached to land. Personal property, as defined immediately below under a separate heading, becomes a fixture as soon as it is attached to land. Personal property ceases to be a fixture as soon as it is no longer attached to land. As indicated in the preceding paragraph, fixtures are usually considered to be a part of the real property to which they are attached. Accordingly, ownership in fixtures is established by the deed establishing ownership in the land to which they are attached. When owners transfer real property rights, they are deemed to have transferred the property rights both in land and in the fixtures attached to that land.

While the concept of fixtures can be easily defined, applying the definition to specific assets can be difficult. The proper application of the definition is usually important because fixtures are often valuable assets. On occasion, it is difficult to determine whether the owner and buyer intend for a specific asset to be included in a land transfer as a fixture. While the law should – and usually does – consider the price paid for the purpose of identifying the

assets intended for transfer, the law also considers whether a particular asset is "attached to the land."

For example, in connection with the sale of "land" by one business to another, it is clear that any building on the land, including its plumbing, electrical wiring and systems for heating and cooling, are "fixtures." Accordingly, unless the transfer contract indicates a contrary agreement between owner and buyer, they are included in the real property transfer. It is also clear – unless the transfer contract indicates a contrary agreement between owner and buyer – that raw materials, final products, supplies and tools are not "fixtures" and so are not included in the land transfer.

It might not be clear, however, whether specific equipment and furniture are "fixtures" to be included in a real property transfer. Even if the value of specific equipment is significant, it may not be possible to infer an owner's and buyer's intention from the purchase price because the equipment's value is a relatively small portion of the entire price for the real property transfer. In such cases, the law will attempt to determine whether the equipment is "attached to the land," sometimes with disappointing results for either the owner or the buyer.

Personal property

Personal property consists of all tangible assets subject to ownership other than land and fixtures. Intangible assets, discussed below under a separate heading, are also often classified as personal property.

As a general rule, ownership in personal property is usually evidenced by simple possession. Accordingly, ownership in personal property is transferred simply by transferring possession of the personal property. For example, if you have a watch around your wrist, you are presumed to own it. If you physically deliver the watch to someone else and he or she puts it around his or her wrist, then he or she is presumed to own it.

Unlike real property ownership, it is usually not necessary – or even possible – for owners of personal property to sign, deliver, certify and file transfer documents in their favor in order to establish ownership of personal property. There are, however, many exceptions to this general rule.

First, evidencing ownership of certain types of tangible personal property can require transfer documents in the same manner as required for evidencing ownership of real property. Such tangible assets include vehicles like automobiles, aircraft, boats and ships.

Second, while not necessary, it is sometimes possible and, upon challenge to their ownership, sometimes useful for persons in possession of personal property to evidence their ownership of those tangible assets by producing transfer documents such as bills of sale or invoices coupled with proof of payment. Conversely, it is sometimes possible for persons with transfer documents evidencing their ownership of tangible assets to rebut the presumption that another person in possession of those assets owns them.

Third, "security interests" in personal property must be evidenced by transfer documents signed by the personal property's owner and filed as a public document. A "security interest" is the right in favor of a bank or other source of funding, in exchange for a loan:

(a) to take possession of a borrower's personal property – often the personal property purchased with the proceeds from the loan – in the event that the borrower defaults on repayment or other loan obligation; and

(b) to sell that personal property and apply the moneys received from the sale to the repayment of the loan.

Fourth, evidencing ownership in most intangible assets – frequently considered to be personal property – can require transfer documents in the same manner as required for evidencing ownership of real property.

"Intellectual property" and contract rights

As noted above, intangible assets are all assets other than tangible assets. Typically, they consist of valuable rights granted or awarded by governments. Types of assets for which governments grant property rights include original works of art ("copyrights"), names ("trademarks"), inventions ("patents") and information ("trade secrets"). Contract rights are also intangible assets.

"Intellectual property"

Property rights in intellectual assets, generally called "intellectual property," will be explained more fully in a separate chapter. Inventions provide an excellent example of one type of intangible asset which governments protect with intellectual property rights. Patents are property rights to inventions awarded by governments.

Patents consist of the right to commercialize an invention. For these purposes, "commercialization" includes the exclusive right to make, use or sell a patented product or the exclusive right to use a patented method or process. As with copyrights, patents can be clearly distinguished from the tangible assets to which they apply. Since pharmaceutical medicines are based upon synthetic chemicals, they are also based on inventions. Specific quantities of pharmaceutical medicines are tangible personal property. As with other personal property, "ownership" of some quantity of medicine (e.g., a few tablets) is presumptively evidenced and transferred by possession. However, a person does not own the patent to the medicine simply by virtue of his possession of a few tablets. In other words, a person does not acquire the right to make the medicine and sell it commercially simply because that person purchases a few tablets. In fact, only an inventor can own a patent. In this case, only the inventor of the medicine can own the exclusive right to make, use or sell the medicine. An inventor owns a patent by virtue of the fact that he or she makes the invention. No person can own the patent unless the inventor transfers the right to own the patent to that person, quite separate and apart from a transfer of the medicine. In summary, a patent is an asset quite separate and apart from the tangible medicine. Since the patent is not embodied in any tangible asset, it is an intangible asset.[2]

Contract rights

Contractual undertakings typically consist of a person's promise to make one or more future payments or to provide future goods or services or, conversely, the right to receive payments, goods or services. Like copyrights, contractual undertakings are intangible assets because they can be clearly distinguished from the form in which the undertaking is expressed – typically a written agreement. A person does not have any right to a contractual undertaking simply because that person holds a copy of the written agreement in which the contractual undertaking is expressed. The only person(s) entitled to receive a contractual undertaking are the person(s) specified in accordance with the terms of the written agreement, without regard to whether other persons hold a signed original or copy of the written agreement. In addition, the person(s) entitled to receive a contractual undertaking in accordance with the terms of a written agreement are entitled to receive it only once, even if they hold multiple signed originals or copies of the written agreement. In summary, a contractual undertaking is an intangible asset quite separate and apart from the written agreement in which it is set forth.

DOCUMENTS

Receipts, bills, instruments and certificates

Documents are writings embodying the right to receive delivery of tangible assets or payments of money. Documents include warehouse receipts, bills of lading, negotiable instruments and corporate share certificates.

Documents can be distinguished from other contractual undertakings set forth in writing because the right to receive payments, goods or services as evidenced by a document does not exist apart from the document itself. In order to receive the payments, goods or services in accordance with the terms of the document, the document must be presented along with demand for performance in accordance with its terms and, upon such performance, the document must be surrendered. Any person who holds the document properly – sometimes called a "holder in due course" – holds the "ownership" of the assets identified on the document.

Documents exist in two forms: bearer form and order form. In the "bearer form," a document is issued in favor of the "bearer," i.e., literally, the person who has physical possession of the document. In the absence of fraud or theft, a document in bearer form is held properly by any person who holds the document in his, her or its possession. In "order form," the document is issued in favor of a named individual. In the absence of fraud, documents in "order form" are held properly by any person who bears it with evidences of "negotiation" from the individual in whose favour it was issued. The term "negotiation" refers to transfer of the document in the manner required by law from the individual named in the document to the

bearer. Evidence of negotiation usually consists of "endorsement," i.e., the signature of the individual named in the document, together with that individual's indication of an intention to transfer the document to the bearer. In either bearer or order form, documents reflect the right to claim ownership rights in the assets identified in the document.

Warehouse receipts and bills of lading

For example, a warehouse receipt is issued by a public warehouse to persons who deposit goods (i.e., personal property) in the warehouse for safe storage. Similarly, a bill of lading is issued by a transport company (often called a "carrier") to persons who deposit goods (i.e., personal property) with the carrier for safe transportation.

The warehouse receipt or bill of lading is simultaneously:

(a) the warehouse's or carrier's acknowledgment to the owner that it – i.e., the warehouse or carrier – does not own certain goods in its possession; and

(b) the warehouse's or carrier's agreement to release possession of the goods, and thereby to grant title in the goods, to anyone who
  (i) properly holds the warehouse receipt or bill of lading,
  (ii) presents it to the warehouse or carrier demanding physical delivery of the goods identified in the document, and
  (iii) surrenders the document – or has it "cancelled" by the warehouse or carrier – upon receipt of those goods.

If the warehouse receipt or bill of lading is issued in the name of the "bearer" (i.e., quite simply, the person who physically holds the receipt or bill), then the warehouse or carrier will release the goods to anyone who presents the receipt or bill, demanding delivery and surrendering the document. If the warehouse receipt or bill of lading is issued in the name of the person who deposited the goods, then the warehouse or carrier will release the goods either:

(a) to that person upon presentation, demand and surrender of the receipt or bill; or

(b) to any other person who demands delivery of the goods and surrenders the receipt or bill after presenting the receipt or bill, together with evidence that the receipt has been rightfully transferred to the person holding it.

Bills of exchange

Bills of exchange are identical to warehouse receipts and bills of lading, except that the goods evidenced by receipts and bills of lading are replaced by money evidenced by the bills of exchange. In addition, the warehouse or carrier is replaced by a debtor, i.e., either:

(a) a borrower of an outstanding loan;
(b) a purchaser of goods for which payment remains due and owing; or
(c) a bank holding a deposit.

A bill of exchange issued by a borrower of an outstanding loan is called a "promissory note." Bills of exchange issued by a purchaser of goods for which payment remains due and owing is called a "trade acceptance."

Bills of exchange issued in respect of bank deposits are referred to as "checks." Checks are different from promissory notes and trade acceptances in that checks are not issued by banks in the way that notes and acceptances are issued by borrowers and trade debtors. Checks are issued by depositors, i.e., the persons owning money held by banks, and so do not constitute depositors' promises to deliver money to the holder of the check. Instead, checks constitute instructions from depositors to their banks to deliver money to the holder of the check.

Checks take this different form, i.e., an instruction from the depositor rather than a promise from the bank, because bank practices are different from practices of borrowers and trade debtors. It is customary for borrowers and trade debtors pursuant to promissory notes and trade acceptances to deliver at one time all of the money they owe – just as warehouses and carriers customarily deliver at one time all of the goods in their possession. This custom does not carry over, however, to bank practices in respect of money deposited with them. On the contrary, banks customarily deliver the money they owe to depositors in partial lots, on several occasions over a period of time. Checks reflect this different custom, which is in fact a service banks provide to depositors.

Negotiable instruments

Generally, in order to be generally acceptable in international trade, a bill of exchange (i.e., a promissory note, trade acceptance or check) must qualify as a "negotiable instrument." In order to qualify as a negotiable instrument, the bill of exchange must be;

(a) an unconditional promise from a borrower/trade debtor or an unconditional instruction from a depositor to a bank;
(b) to pay a definite sum of money;
(c) either to the bearer of the bill of exchange or to the person designated therein;
(d) on demand or at a definite time; and
(e) signed by the borrower, trade debtor or depositor.

In addition, in order to receive payment from the borrower, trade debtor or bank upon presentation, demand and surrender, the presenter must be either:

(a) the bearer of a "bearer instrument";
(b) the person designated in an "order instrument" as the person entitled to receive payment (the "named payee"); or
(c) a person designated in an endorsement of an order instrument, as signed by the instrument's named payee.

Corporate share certificates

Of course, corporations are separate legal entities. They are fictional persons with the ability to hold ownership and other private property rights in the same manner and to the same extent as individuals, i.e., natural persons.

At the same time, corporations are owned by their shareholders, again either natural persons or other legal entities. Of course, shareholders as a whole own all, right, title and interest in and to corporations, while corporations, in turn, own all of the assets – and owe all of the liabilities – used or accrued in the conduct of its business, all as reflected on a corporate balance sheet.

Ownership of corporations is usually divided into shares and often, but not always, evidenced by share certificates. In the absence of classes of shares, each share constitutes an equal undivided ownership interest in distributions made by the corporation to its shareholders, either in the form of:

(a) dividends in the normal course of business; or

(b) distributions in partial or total liquidation of the corporation.

Corporate ownership arrangements will be discussed more fully in the chapters on corporate law and securities law. Here, it is sufficient to state that a share certificate is similar to other documents in that they reflect an ownership interest in certain assets, in this case intangible assets, i.e., the right to receive distributions from a corporation.

TYPES OF ASSETS WHICH CANNOT BE PRIVATE PROPERTY

It sometimes is the case that private property rights in certain types of assets will not be recognized and enforced by governments because of prevailing community ethical norms. In this context, community ethical norms are sometimes referred to as "public policy reasons."

In all countries, people

First, since the end of World War I (and in some places earlier), people have not been subject to ownership as private property in most countries around the world. In other words slavery has been almost universally abolished around the world. Instead, each person is deemed to "own" his or her own labor and is free to sell that labor as a service.

In some countries, natural resources

Second, since the end of World War II (and in some places earlier), natural resources have not been subject to ownership as private property in some countries around the world. Instead, the people within a country are deemed to "own" the natural resources located there. These natural resources are typically oil or other minerals. In the absence of the community ethical norms within some countries, natural resources are scarce assets which could be and have been owned, i.e., possessed, used and transferred, as private real property. In those countries where natural resources are not subject to ownership as private property, governments exercise ownership rights on behalf of all people in part for the purpose of preventing the use of the valuable natural resources by any one person, i.e., businesses.

In most countries, bodies of water (with important exceptions)

Third, naturally occurring bodies of water (i.e., rivers, lakes, seas and oceans) are typically not subject to ownership as private property anywhere around the world – even in those places where water constitutes a scarce resource. Typically, however, governments do not exercise ownership rights on behalf of all of the people in part because preventing the use of water by any one person (e.g., a business), is typically not part of the public policy.

An important exception to the typical rule for bodies of water exists for naturally occurring and artificially created bodies of water which lie entirely within a single parcel of real property. Such bodies of water typically include lakes and do not include rivers, seas and oceans. In such circumstances, water standing in a lake is considered to be a part of the parcel(s) of land surrounding it and so is subject to ownership as private property.

In those places where water is a scarce resource, another important exception exists for water running in a river. In such places, river water is considered to be a part of the land touching it and so is subject to ownership as private property.

In all countries, air (with an important exception)

Fourth, air is typically not subject to ownership as private property anywhere in the world, in part because of community ethical norms but also because it is not a scarce resource. Obviously, governments do not exercise ownership rights on behalf of all of the people in part because preventing the use of air by any one person is not part of the public policy.

The absence of government ownership of air does not mean, however, that the use of air by single persons, i.e., businesses, does not raise public policy issues. When one person pollutes the air to be used by another person, then air becomes a scarce resource. In such circumstances, polluters can use air freely, but subject to an important quali-fication: Polluters must pay to use air, either through government permits or by installing pollution-reduction equipment. Of course, the same qualifi-cation exists in respect of water: users must pay to pollute water.

OWNERSHIP INTERESTS

Ownership is "all right, title and interest" in and to certain assets. As already noted, "ownership" consists of holding:

(a) all of the present and future use rights in those assets; and
(b) the right freely to transfer all of those use rights to others, together with the right freely to make fur-ther transfers (e.g., by sale, gift, testament or the laws of intestacy).

Assets are often owned by a single person but two or more persons can:

(a) simultaneously hold present and future ownership interests in the same asset; or
(b) concurrently hold present ownership interests in the same asset. Individuals' ownership interests in real property, as customarily defined under com-mon law, offer some of the best examples of future and concurrent ownership interests.

As you review the following examples of custom-ary forms of "ownership" interests under common law, please bear in mind that ownership interests can be defined, divided and transferred in many ways other than in the customary manners described below. The only real limitations in this area of law are the transferors' imagination and the transferees' inter-ests. Indeed, as you contemplate the following cus-tomary ownership arrangements (for which the details can vary significantly under the law of differ-ent jurisdictions and in accordance with the terms of specific contracts establishing those arrangements), you will probably conclude that it is best to under-stand completely the intricacies and implications of the ownership arrangements in which your business is involved, both by understanding local law and by clearly defining those ownership arrangements in transfer agreements.

INDIVIDUAL OWNERSHIP IN THE PRESENT

Freehold estates

Under common law, an ownership interest in land is called an "estate." There are three customary individ-ual "estates" in land:

1   a fee simple absolute;
2   a life estate; and
3   a fee simple defeasible.

Under each of these arrangements, the individual owner holds the right to possess and use the land and to profit from the land (again, the "use rights") – all as he or she sees fit, subject only to applicable govern-ment regulations and the law of general obligations.

Under the "fee simple absolute," the owner holds the use rights in the land theoretically forever and in practice during his or her entire lifetime. The holder of a fee simple absolute also has the right freely to transfer all of those present and future use rights in the land to others, together with the right freely to make such further transfers. The holder of a fee sim-ple absolute has the right to transfer his or her estate by sale, gift or testament and, in the absence of any such transfer, by the laws of intestacy.

Under the "life estate," the owner holds the use rights in the land during his or her life time, both in theory and in practice. Upon the death of the holder of life estate, the use rights in the land revert to the original transferor. For example, a sister might transfer land and a building to her brother for as long as he lives, with the land and building reverting to the sister as soon as the brother dies. In the event that the brother dies after the sister dies, then the land and building will revert to her heirs (e.g., husband and children) in accordance with the terms of her testament and the laws of intestacy. Like the holder of a fee simple absolute, the holder of the life estate has the right to transfer his or her estate by sale or gift, but the interest transferred will expire upon the transferor's death. Unlike the holder of a fee simple absolute, the holder of a life estate cannot transfer his or her interest by testament or the laws of intestacy. Holders of a life estate cannot do so for the obvious rea-son that their interests expire at the time of their death.

Under the "fee simple defeasible," the owner holds the use rights in the land for as long as certain condi-tions are fulfilled (e.g., "for as long as the land and building are used as a library"). As soon as the conditions are no longer fulfilled, the use rights in the land terminate and revert to the original transferor of the fee simple defeasible. For example, a person might transfer land and a building to a city for as long as they are used as a library, with the land and building reverting to the person as soon as the land and building are no longer used as a library. In the event that the city ceases to use the land and building as a library after the person dies, then the land and building will revert to the transferor's heirs in accordance with the terms of his or her testament and the laws of intestacy.

Unlike the holder of a fee simple absolute, the holder of the fee simple defeasible typically does not have the right to transfer the estate by sale, gift, testament or the laws of intestacy. While transfers of a fee simple defeasible are theoretically possible, restrictions on transfers tend to exist for the purpose of supporting the conditions imposed on the use of the land. In the example cited in the preceding paragraph, the person might provide that the city cannot transfer its fee simple defeasible as a way of ensuring the land and building are in fact used as a library.

Reversions, remainders, mortgages and security interests

As indicated by the previous discussion, under common law, it is possible for a person to hold a future ownership interest in land without holding a present interest. Such future interests in land are called "reversions," "remainders," the "possibility of reversion" and "mortgages." "Security interests" in personal property are similar to mortgages in real property.

REVERSIONS AND REMAINDERS

For example, as indicated above: upon the death of a life-estate holder (e.g., the original owner's brother), the use rights in the land subject to the life estate revert to the original owner (i.e., to the sister). Before that death, the original owner's (i.e., the sister's) future interest in the land subject to the life estate is called a "reversion."

It is also possible that the original owner (e.g., the sister) transferred the "reversion" to another person (e.g., her daughter) at the same time that she transferred the life estate to her brother. A reversionary interest held by anyone other than the original owner (e.g., the daughter) is called a "remainder."

The use rights in a fee simple defeasible of the land terminate and revert to the original owner as soon as the conditions imposed on the fee simple defeasible are no longer fulfilled. The original owner's future interest in the land subject to the fee simple defeasible is called a "possibility of reversion." If the future interest is held by someone other than the original owner, the future interest is called a "possibility of remainder."

MORTGAGES AND SECURITY INTERESTS

Finally, in most countries, purchasers of land often do not have sufficient money to purchase the land. In such circumstances, banks are willing to loan the necessary money to purchasers – subject, of course, to purchasers' promise to repay the loan amount with interest. Moreover, in order to facilitate enforcement of the borrower–purchaser's promise of repayment, the bank will take a "mortgage" in the land purchased by the borrower with the proceeds of the loan. A mortgage is simply a "contingent future ownership interest" in land. Mortgages give banks the right to claim "all right, title and interest" in land if borrowers default on their promises to repay loans used to purchase land. In the event of such a default, the banks claim a present ownership interest in the land covered by the mortgage, take possession of the land and sell it in total or partial satisfaction of the borrower's repayment obligation. Since mortgages are used to secure borrowers' personal undertakings, mortgages include the restriction that borrowers must fully repay their loans before (or, in any event, no later than) the borrowers sell their interest in lands subject to mortgages.

In many countries, similar arrangements exist for lenders financing the purchase of personal property. Such "contingent future ownership interest" in personal property in favor of lenders and exercisable upon borrowers' defaults are called "security interests."

CONCURRENT OWNERSHIP ARRANGEMENTS

Tenancy in common and joint tenancy

Two customary "concurrent estates" are:

(a) tenancy in common; and
(b) joint tenancy.

Under both a "tenancy in common" and a "joint tenancy" two or more individuals each hold an undivided interest in a single parcel of land. In other words, under both arrangements, each tenant is free to possess and use any and all of the land. Under both systems, each tenant can freely transfer his or her interest to another person without the other tenant's consent, even a transferee who is unrelated and unknown to the continuing tenant. In such circumstances, under both systems, either tenant is free to request a "partition" of the land held jointly or in common. In other words, the undivided ownership in the entire land is rearranged so that each person holds a specified portion of the partitioned land, i.e., the divided land, in fee simple absolute.

In a tenancy in common, each tenant's interest survives his or her death and each is free to transfer his or her tenancy by sale, will or inheritance. A joint tenancy differs from tenancy in common in that each joint tenant's ownership interest terminates at the time of his or her death. In effect, the remaining joint tenants have the right to receive the interest of the deceased tenant by reason of his or her death. This right in the surviving joint tenants is called a "right of survivorship." The entire joint tenancy terminates at the time of the death of the second-to-last surviving tenant. In accordance with the "right of survivorship," the last surviving tenant receives the interest as the last joint tenant and continues to hold the real property in fee simple absolute.

NON-OWNERSHIP INTERESTS

Possessory leaseholds

As explained above, "ownership" of assets consists of holding:

(a) all of the present and future right to possess, use and profit from those assets; and
(b) the right freely to transfer all of those rights to others, together with the right freely to make further transfers.

Under the heading of "ownership interests," I explain how more than one person can hold the entire bundle of use and transfer rights, either simultaneously (with concurrent rights) or sequentially (with future rights). For the purpose of explanation, I use the example of real property rights under common law.

It is also possible for persons to hold less than an entire ownership interest. Very generally, persons can hold such interests by receiving from the owner a transfer of no more than the right to possess, use and profit from assets for an agreed time. Such rights are called a "lease," "license," "easement" or "profit." Persons holding such limited rights are called, respectively, tenants, licensees, easement holders, or profit holders. In all such circumstances, the owner of an asset retains at all times:

(a) the rights of possession, usage and profit not transferred; and
(b) the right freely to transfer their ownership interests to persons other than the tenants, licensees and easement or profit holders. In addition,
(c) the transferred rights revert to the owner upon the expiration of the lease, license, easement or profit.

Again, I will use the example of estates in land under common law to illustrate these various non-ownership interests.

Tenants and landlords

The exclusive right to enter on to, take possession of, and use land and fixtures is called a "leasehold interest" or a "possessory interest." Lease holders are usually called "tenants." Owners of real property who grant leasehold interests to one or more tenants are called "landlords," at least in the context of the relationship with their tenants.

For the duration of leases, landlords no longer have the right freely to enter on to and take possession of the land subject to the lease. As soon as the lease enters into force, landlords have:

(a) no right to take possession of the land and fixtures subject to the lease; and
(b) only a limited right to enter on to the land, solely for the purposes reasonably necessary to exercise their rights as landlords.

In fact, landlords have the obligation to assure that no one disturbs their tenants' rights to peaceful enjoyment of their leaseholds. The tenants' right, as created by these restrictions and obligations on landlords, is called the right of "peaceful enjoyment."

In addition to the right of peaceful enjoyment, tenants also have the right to use, as they see fit, and to profit from the land and fixtures subject to their lease-hold interest. Tenants' use rights are, however, subject to many possible limitations. The property can be used only in a manner suitable and legal for the nature and location of the land and fixtures. In addition, while tenants are not typically liable for normal wear and tear in connection to their possession and use of land and fixtures, tenants are liable for repairing any damage or destruction they cause. Finally, as is generally true with all transfers of private property interests, tenants are subject to any terms and conditions contained in the transfer documents. Such terms and conditions typically include restrictions on their rights to use land and fixtures as they see fit.

Various durations

Leasehold interests are often called "tenancies" and are usually classified according to their duration. A "tenancy for years" is a leasehold with a duration of a specified period of time – not necessarily a year. "Tenancy for years" can have a duration specified in the lease agreement of a day, month, year or longer.

"Periodic tenancies" have no duration specified in the lease agreement. Periodic tenancies do, however, specify intervals for the payment of rent from tenant to landlord. Periodic tenancies continue indefinitely, until the tenant fails to pay rent at the specified interval or otherwise breaches a leasehold obligation. For example, a lease agreement without a specified duration and calling for monthly rent payments is a periodic tenancy from month to month. A lease agreement without a specified duration and calling for weekly rent payments is a periodic tenancy from week to week.

"Tenancies at will" are leasehold interests granted by landlords to tenants "for as long as both agree." Under this arrangement, both landlords and tenants have the right to terminate the leasehold at any time.

"Tenancy at sufferance" is not really a leasehold interest. A "tenancy at sufferance" continues only for as long as landlords allow tenants to possess and use land and fixtures after their leasehold interests have expired.

Transfers by landlords and tenants

Interesting issues are raised when landlords or tenants want to transfer their ownership or possessory interests in land and fixtures subject to a leasehold interest. Landlords typically can transfer their ownership interest in land and fixtures in spite of tenants' leasehold interests. The landlords' rights and obligation in respect of leaseholds are simply transferred along with all other rights and obligations associated with the ownership interest (or, using the terms of the common law of real property: right and obligations "appurtenant to" the ownership interest). In other words, landlords can transfer their ownership interests because their obligations in respect of the leasehold are not considered to be "personal obligations" – so that the tenant has no legitimate interest in the identity of the person performing them. Tenants typically cannot transfer their possessory interest in land and fixtures because their obligations under the lease agreement are considered to be "personal obligations" – so that the landlord has an interest in the identity of the person performing them. Of course, all of these transfer arrangements can be modified in the lease agreement between landlords and tenants – so that the leasehold terminates if landlords transfer their ownership interests or tenants have the right to transfer all or part of their possessory interests (pursuant to, respectively, an assignment or a sublease). In the absence of a prior agreement to the contrary, tenants' assignments and subleases do not release them from their leasehold obligations – so that tenants tend to act as guarantors for those to who they assign or sublease their leasehold interests.

Non-possessory licenses, easements and profits

Licenses, easements and profits are called "non-possessory" estates or interests because they do not give the holder the right to take possession of land. In other words, holders of non-possessory interests do not have a right of peaceful enjoyment. Licenses, easements and profits only give the holder the right to enter on to land only for specific purposes.

Licenses

The right to enter

A license is the right to enter on to land for a specific purpose, but without the right to remove anything from the land. For example, patrons have a license to enter a restaurant for the limited purpose of eating there or to enter a cinema for the limited purpose of viewing a film there. Patrons exceed the scope of their license if they engage in any activity other than eating or viewing, if they disrupt other patrons in their eating or viewing or if they remain in the restaurant or cinema longer than necessary to eat or view the film. Employees have no more than a license to enter on to the property possessed by their employers for the purpose of discharging their employment obligations. Employees exceed the scope of their license if they engage in any activity other than discharging their employment obligation, if they disrupt other employees in discharging their obligations or if they remain on their employers' premises longer than necessary to discharge their employment obligations.

Easements

The right to enter and maintain fixtures

An easement is the right to enter on to land, usually for the purpose of transversing it, i.e., traveling across it, again without the right to remove anything from the land. Easements usually include the easement holder's right to maintain such fixtures as are a necessary incident to exercising the easement rights. For example, an electrical utility has the right to maintain power transmission facilities on land over which it exercises the right to transmit electricity. Easements can be held as a right connected with the ownership or possession of adjacent land ("appurtenant easements") or without respect to the ownership or possession of adjacent land ("easements in gross"). Electrical utilities, for example, usually own easements "in gross." In other words, utility companies possess easements on land even though they do not own any adjacent land.

Profits

The right to enter, maintain fixtures and remove assets

A profit is the right to enter on to land and to take away some part of the land (such as minerals) or some produce from the land (such as crops or ani-

mals). As with easements, profits include the profit holder's right to maintain such fixtures as are a necessary incident to exercise the profit rights. For example, an oil company with the profit rights in oil under the surface of land owned by another person has the right to maintain a well and road necessary to extract and remove the oil from the land. As with easements, profits can exist as appurtenances to adjacent land or "in gross," without regard to whether the profit holder owns or possesses adjacent land. Of course, an oil company would tend to hold its oil profit rights "in gross."

Transfers of licenses, easements and profits

A license cannot be transferred because it is a right personal to the individual holding it (e.g., a patron or employee).

An easement or profit can continue to be imposed on land after the ownership interest in that land is transferred only if the purchaser is aware of the easement or profit before the transfer of ownership. Accordingly, it is usually possible, customary and important for holders of easements and profits on land owned by others to record those easements and profits as a public record in the land registry. Land can continue to benefit from an appurtenant easement or profit even after ownership in that land is transferred.

Some agency arrangements

As noted above, in particular under the heading of documents, it is often the case that owners transfer to other persons some, but not all, of their ownership rights in certain assets, i.e., the rights of possession, usage, profit and transfer. Of course, businesses do not transfer private property rights gratuitously. They transfer private property rights for specific purposes.

"Agent" is a term used to describe a person who, in pursuit of a business's specific purposes, accepts some – but not all – of that business's ownership rights in specific assets. "Principal" is the term used to describe businesses who, in pursuit of their specific purposes, transfer to agents some – but not all – of their ownership rights in specific assets. Within the scope of the agency arrangement, the agent is said to act "on behalf of" the principal. Depending on the terms of the agency arrangement, the agent may additionally have the right to act "in the name of" the principal.

In other words, appointments of agents create a relationship involving trust, the principals' trust of their agents. The "trust" involved in agency arrangements consists generally of the agents' obligations:

(a) to exercise the transferred property rights for the principal's specific purposes; and
(b) to respect the present and future private property rights not transferred to the agents.

The agent's trust obligations are a necessary incident to principals' property rights. Since property rights can be enforced against all persons without their consent, principals can enforce their right to trust their agents even if those specific rights are not set forth in the agreement creating the agency arrangement. (Owners can, however, effectively waive those rights in the transfer agreements creating the trust relationship.)

An agent's trust obligations generally take the form of:

(a) a duty of care;
(b) a duty of loyalty; and
(c) a duty to render accounts and reports.

Again, these obligations exist generally under the law – in addition to agents' contractual undertakings to follow principals' instructions and to render specifically designated personal services in furtherance of the principals' stated purposes.[3]

Typical agency arrangements involving transfer of some, but not all, ownership rights include: commercial representations, bailment agreements, corporations and trusts.

COMMERCIAL REPRESENTATION

Sales agents

Pursuant to "commercial representations," owners of final products available for sale – i.e., businesses – often give other persons, typically called "sales agents," the right to agree to transfer ownership in those products to unrelated third parties, i.e., to customers. The owners do not transfer to their sales agents any elements of ownership other than the right to agree to

transfer ownership in final products. Businesses do not transfer to sales agents the right to possess, use or profit from the final products.

The specific personal service rendered by sales agents, the reason businesses entrust certain private property rights to sales agents, is to agree to transfer ownership in their final products pursuant to the corporations' specific instructions and otherwise in a manner consistent with the agents' duties of care and loyalty.

BAILMENTS

Warehouses and carriers

Pursuant to "bailment arrangements," owners transfer possession of personal property to other persons without transferring to them any other elements of ownership, i.e., without transferring to them the rights of use, profit or transfer. Such transferees are called "bailees." Businesses often give bailees possession of personal property for the purpose of storage (i.e., warehouses) or transportation (i.e., carriers).

The specific personal service rendered by warehouses and carriers – the reason businesses entrust certain private property rights to them – is to agree, respectively, to store and to transport goods pursuant to the businesses' specific instructions and otherwise in a manner consistent with the warehouses' and carriers' duties of care and loyalty.

CORPORATIONS

Officers and directors

Of course, corporations give specific individuals, typically called "officers and directors," the right to possess, use and transfer corporate assets. Corporations do not, however, transfer to their officers and directors the right to profit from those assets. The profits derived from the possession, use and transfer of the corporate assets – all as decided by the officers and directors – belong to the corporation.

The specific personal service rendered by corporate officers and directors – the reason corporations entrust certain private property rights to them – is to make decisions concerning the exercise of possession, use and transfer of the corporations' assets pursuant to the corporations' specific instructions and otherwise in a manner consistent with officers' and directors' duties of care and loyalty.

BUSINESS TRUSTS

Trustees

While not currently common, in the past and even today in some places, some types of businesses were and still are conducted in the form of a trust. Business trusts are like corporations. Business trusts give one or more individuals, typically called "trustee(s)," the right to possess, use and transfer the trust's assets. Business trusts do not, however, transfer to their trustee(s) the right to profit from those assets. The profits derived from the possession, use and transfer of the trust's assets, all as decided by the trustee, belong to the trust.

As with corporate officers and directors, the specific personal service rendered by business trustees – the reason trusts entrust certain private property rights to them – is to make decisions concerning the exercise of possession, use and transfer of the trusts' assets in a manner consistent with officers' and directors' duties of care and loyalty. (Trusts typically do not issue any instructions to trustees.)

General Obligations (Tort Law)

INTRODUCTION

Contract rights can be enforced against other persons because of their consent. Property rights can be enforced against others without their consent. Of course, contract obligations complement contract rights. Similarly, "general obligations" complement property rights. General obligations are enforceable against individuals who exercise private property rights. Like private property rights, general obligations are enforceable without the consent of the individuals subject to them.

The law of general obligations is a term used in civil law jurisdictions to denote obligations arising out of the exercise of property rights. In common law countries, the law of general obligations is called "tort law." A "tort" is a breach of a general obligation. (The word "tort" is derived from French, meaning a "wrong.")

Just as the law of general obligations is separate and apart from contract law, so the law of general obligations exists separate and apart from government regulation of business. It is possible for businesses to breach their general obligations (a "tort") without violating any government regulation (frequently constituting a "crime"). Similarly, it is possible to commit a crime without committing a tort, but a violation of a government regulation is often taken as evidence, sometimes conclusive evidence, of a breach of a "duty of care," an essential element to any breach of the law of general obligations. If the same act or omission constitutes both a breach of general obligations and a violation of government regulations, then the business in question can be subject to sanctions both for the tort and the crime.

Plaintiffs' "burdens of proof"

Persons alleging torts are called "plaintiffs." Their allegations are called "complaints." Businesses alleged to have committed torts are called "defendants," with their responses to complaints called "answers" or "defenses." Plaintiffs usually have the burden of proving three elements of alleged torts (i.e., harm, duty of care and causation). Such a burden is called a "burden of proof."

In tort trials, plaintiffs must both:

(a) "allege," i.e., claim, that each element of a tort occurred; and
(b) offer "evidence," i.e., facts presented in a form required by law that each element of a tort has occurred.

In order to carry the burden of proof, each of the plaintiffs' allegations must be accepted as a fact in court "by a preponderance of the evidence," i.e., after balancing all of the evidence presented both by plaintiffs and defendants, "the allegation is more likely to be true than not to be true" – or, there is a 51 percent likelihood that alleged events actually occurred or alleged conditions actually existed. In other words, for a business to be legally liable to pay damages for a tort, a person harmed must allege that a business breached its duty, thereby causing harm to that person – and convince a judge or jury that it is "more likely than not" that the elements of tort in fact occurred.

Plaintiffs' "burden of proceeding"

Plaintiffs also have the "burden of proceeding." In fact, the burden of proceeding is the first burden plaintiffs must satisfy. In order to satisfy – or "carry" – the burden of proceeding, plaintiffs must convince courts that a reasonable person could conclude, on the basis of evidence presented by plaintiffs, that the defendants are liable for the alleged tort. The plaintiffs must carry their "burden of proceeding" before the defendants have any obligation to submit any evidence. If the plaintiffs carry their burden of proceeding, then defendants must present evidence showing that they are not liable for the alleged tort, with the judge or jury deciding the case by a "preponderance of the evidence," as explained below.

Defendants' "burdens of proof"

A court can, as it deems appropriate, allocate evidentiary burdens between plaintiffs and defendants. While it is invariably true that the plaintiffs must carry their burden of proceeding, it is sometimes the case that courts place the burden of proof on defendants rather than plaintiffs. For example, if defendants assert "affirmative defenses," i.e., facts tending to exonerate the defendants, then the defendants typically have the burden of proof for the affirmative defenses.

In addition, courts will sometimes shift to defendants the burden of proof concerning some elements of plaintiffs' allegations. In such cases, the defendant has the burden of proving, by a preponderance of the evidence, that one of the plaintiffs' allegations is not true, again by a preponderance of the evidence. Courts will shift the burden of proof if, for example, the defendants are in possession of significant relevant evidence while plaintiffs are not in possession of any relevant information.

In addition, courts will sometimes shift to defendants the burden of proof concerning some element of plaintiffs' allegations. In such cases, the defendant has the burden of proving, by a preponderance of the evidence, that one of the plaintiffs' allegations is not true, again by a preponderance of the evidence. Courts will shift the burden of proof if, for example,

the defendants are in possession of significant relevant evidence while plaintiffs are not in possession of any relevant information.

ELEMENTS OF A TORT

A tort is a breach of general obligations which causes harm. There are four elements to the commission of a tort:

1 a protected harm to plaintiffs or their property;
2 a sufficient causal link between the harm to plaintiffs and an act or omission by defendants';
3 defendants' breach of an applicable duty of care; and
4 the absence of an affirmative defense.

All four of these elements must be true for a business to be legally liable to pay damages for the harm.

HARM TO PERSONS OR THEIR PROPERTY

Generally, persons are free to engage in activities, including the use of their private property, on the condition that they do not cause bodily injury to other persons or physical damage to their property. In its simplest form, tort law provides compensation to individuals for bodily injury and physical damage to their tangible property. If a manufactured product contains a defect resulting in death when used as intended, then the product obviously causes "bodily injury." If a manufacturing process deposits toxins on neighboring land, then the process obviously causes "physical damage" to land.

At the same time, bodily injury and physical damage to tangible property encompass many, but not all, of the types of harm giving rise to possible compensation for torts under the law of general obligations. In a business context, protected harm can have a scope much broader than bodily injury or physical damage to tangible assets.

CAUSATION

As noted above, there are four elements to the commission of a tort:

1 a protected harm to plaintiffs or their property;
2 a sufficient causal link between the harm to plaintiffs and an act or omission by defendants;
3 defendants' breach of an applicable duty of care;
   and
4 the absence of an affirmative defense.

The second element of a tort is "a sufficient causal link between the harm to defendants and an act or omission by plaintiffs." The bottom line concerning this element of a claim under tort law is whether the plaintiffs' acts or omissions are sufficiently related to the defendants' harm that the plaintiffs should pay compensation and even punitive damages by virtue of plaintiffs' acts or omissions.

In reaching this conclusion, there are two general areas of consideration under tort law. The first element in analyzing causation is called "but for" causation. In this element of the analysis, the law asks whether there is, in fact, any causal link between the defendants' harm and a previous act or omission by plaintiffs. The second element in analyzing causation is called "proximate causation." For this element of the claim, the law asks whether, at the time that the plaintiffs acted, they foresaw – or should have foreseen – that their acts or omissions would cause the type of harm which actually occurred.

"But for" or actual causation

In order to satisfy the "but for," or actual, causation in a tort claim, plaintiffs must show "by a preponderance of the evidence" – i.e., a 51 percent likelihood – that plaintiffs' act(s) or omission(s) was one of the actual causes of defendants' harm.

The most important observation about "but for," or actual, causation is the following: it does not matter that plaintiffs could have been injured or their property damaged in another way. For example, if a business makes a chemical and the chemical causes injury to one of its customers, it does not matter that other businesses supply identical chemicals for the same use and that the customer could have been injured or would have been injured using the other chemical. In this regard, the legal analysis for determining causation under tort law differs from economic analysis for determining prices under market conditions.

It also does not matter that the aggregate overall economic benefits created by having the chemical

available on the market are outweighed by certain individuals' costs and losses arising out of injuries caused by having the chemical available. Legal analysis under tort law is made exclusively on the basis of the costs incurred and losses suffered separately by each individual, not on the basis of balancing overall benefits against overall disadvantages. In my example, the business supplying the chemical can be legally liable to pay compensation for specific individuals' injuries even though the aggregate benefit to "the economy" or "the society" is greater than the costs and losses arising out of all of those individuals' injuries.

Finally, "but for" or actual causation is a relatively broad concept. In order to satisfy this element of a tort claim, plaintiffs must show only that defendants' act(s) or omission(s) was "one of the actual causes" resulting in the injury or damage. It is not necessary for plaintiffs to show that, taken alone, the defendants' acts or omissions would have been sufficient to cause the injury. To satisfy this element of a tort claim, it is also not necessary for plaintiffs to show either that defendants' act(s) or omission(s) was an important cause or that it was the most important cause.

"Proximate" or foreseeable causation

In addition to showing "but for" or actual causation, plaintiffs must show "by a preponderance of the evidence" – i.e., a 51 percent likelihood – that the type of harm actually caused was foreseeable at the time of the defendants' act(s) or omission(s).

The most important observation about proximate causation is the following: it does not matter whether defendants in fact foresaw the specific injury or damage which occurred. It does not even matter whether the defendants in fact foresaw the type of injury or damage which actually occurred. It is only important that, in the opinion of the judge or jury, that the defendants could have foreseen the type of injury or damage which actually occurred.

As with determinations pursuant to the other elements of a tort claim, determinations of "proximate causation" necessarily imply a value judgment in addition to a factual determination. In determining that defendants could have foreseen certain types of harm, judges and juries are also making a judgment that the defendants should have foreseen those types of harm. Again in my example, in determining that a chemical supplier could have foreseen that using its chemical would cause certain types of injury, a judge or jury is also in effect making the judgment that the chemical supplier should have foreseen the type of injury which actually occurred.

The duty of care imposed on defendants is obviously important in determining whether this element of a tort claim is satisfied. In my example, a judge or jury could reasonably conclude that an average person could not have foreseen the type of injury caused by the use of a chemical but that the average chemical supplier could have foreseen the type of injury caused by the use of its chemical.

DUTY OF CARE

Once again, there are four elements to the commission of a tort:

1   a protected harm to plaintiffs or their property;
2   a sufficient causal link between the harm to plaintiffs harm and an act or omission by defendants;
3   defendants' breach of an applicable duty of care; and
4   the absence of an affirmative defense.

The third element, a duty of care, is a more-or-less objective standard against which a judge or jury measures defendants' conduct. General standards applied to all persons' conduct – not just businesses – are usually classified as:

1   intentional;
2   negligent; and
3   strict liability.

Intentional breaches

If the applicable duty of care is "intention," then defendants are not liable for injuries they cause if they are unaware of a foreseeable harm or fail to take precautions against a foreseen risk. To be liable under this standard, it is necessary that defendants "intend" – i.e., want to cause – a certain harm. In my example, in order to be liable for an intentional tort, it is not enough that the chemical supplier is unaware of a foreseeable risk of injury to customers or fails to take precautions against injuries to customers. It is neces-

sary that the chemical supplier actually wants to injure its customers.

As you can imagine from my example, intentional torts are relatively uncommon in business because most businesses do not want to cause bodily injury and property damage. Nonetheless, intentional injury or damage is required for some torts. In fact, some element of intentionality is required for business torts other than infringement. In other words, defamation, wrongful interference in contracts, fraud, conversion and misappropriation of trade secrets all require that defendants' act(s) or omission(s) evidence some element of intention.

In the case of each intentional tort, the specific scope of the required intention is an important issue. In general, to be liable for an "intentional tort," i.e., a tort for which the duty of care is intentional, it is not sufficient that defendants merely intend to take certain actions – after all, most business acts are taken intentionally. To be liable for an "intentional tort," it is necessary that businesses taking certain actions also intend to cause certain injuries or damage.

For example, in the case of conversion, is it not sufficient that defendants intend to exercise property rights in respect of certain assets. It is necessary that defendants intend to exercise property rights inconsistent with plaintiff-owners' rights. If a warehouse refuses to release goods to the owner who delivered them for storage upon the owner's presentation of a warehouse receipt, then the warehouse is liable for conversion. If a warehouse refuses to release goods to the owner who delivered them for storage because the owner cannot present and surrender a warehouse receipt, then the warehouse is not liable for conversion.

In the case of each intentional tort, the time at which defendants had the required intention is also an important issue. It is necessary that defendants have the required intention at the time of the act(s) or omission(s) causing the injury. In my example, the warehouse can arguably become liable for conversion even though the owners cannot present a warehouse receipt for their goods, as soon as the owners present irrefutable evidence of their identity, together with irrefutable evidence of the fact that the warehouse receipt has been destroyed. At that point in time, by continuing to refuse delivery, the warehouse is arguably exercising property rights inconsistent with the owners' rights.

Persons liable for intentional torts can also be guilty of crimes. Employees who steal funds from the companies where they work in the payroll department are guilty of the tort of conversion. At the same time, they are guilty of the crime of embezzlement. Persons guilty of murder, i.e., intentionally killing another person, are also liable for wrongful death, i.e., negligently causing another person's death. On the other hand, it is possible for defendants to be liable for wrongful death without being guilty of murder.

Infringement requires a special note. Infringement is a business tort but does not require intent. It is not necessary that an infringer to intentionally use another business's copyright, patent or trademark. A business can be liable for infringing other businesses' intellectual property without intending to do so. At the same time, various countries have enacted statutes imposing penalties in excess of compensatory damages, payable to businesses owning intellectual property rights, for intentional infringement of other businesses' intellectual property rights.

Negligent breaches

As explained above, causing harm to certain types of business interests does not constitute a business tort unless defendants intend to cause the harm. At the same time, many – probably most – torts do not involve business torts; instead, they involve bodily injury and property damage. Legal liability for bodily injury or property damage does not require that defendants intend to cause the injury or damage.

Liability for bodily injury or property damage requires only that defendants are "negligent" concerning the risk of harm. In order to be negligent, it is enough that either:

(a) defendants do not foresee risks of bodily injury or property damage which they should foresee; or
(b) defendants foresee those risks but fail to take adequate precautionary measures to avoid the bodily injury or property damage.

In either case, concluding whether businesses are liable for negligently causing personal injury or property damage, it is necessary to define an applicable standard for determining:

(a) whether the defendants should have foreseen the risk; or
(b) whether their precautionary measures were adequate.

In other words, it is necessary to define the applicable "duty of care" in order to conclude whether the defendants were negligent.

"Reasonable person" standard

The best known standard applied to claims of negligence under tort law is the standard of the average "reasonable person": the person with common sense but no special knowledge or experience in a specific field. Using this standard, plaintiffs claim that:

(a) an average person would have foreseen the risk of injury or damage which actually occurred; and
(b) that an average person could have and would have taken precautionary actions adequate to avoid the injury or damage.

Community standards

Community standards are similar to the standard of the average "reasonable person." Using this standard, plaintiffs claim that:

(a) an average person at the time and place where the defendants took their actions – or alternatively, where the plaintiffs suffered their harm – would have foreseen the risk of injury or damage which actually occurred; and
(b) an average person at such time and place could have and would have taken precautionary actions adequate to avoid the injury or damage.

While the community standard is obviously similar to the "reasonable person" standard, its relationship to the "reasonable person" standard is ambiguous. If the applicable community standard is higher than the standard of conduct expected of a reasonable person, then a judge or jury is more likely to conclude that defendants negligently caused bodily injury or property damage. Of course, if the community standard is lower, then a judge or jury is less likely to conclude that defendants are negligently caused bodily injury or property damage.

Regulatory standards

One of those standards is "regulatory standards," i.e., the standards established by statutes governing business conduct. If the same act or omission by a business causes injury or damage at the same time that it violates a statute governing its conduct, then it is often possible – but not always required by tort law – that a judge or jury will determine that the statute is the applicable standard for judging whether the business conduct was negligent. A judge or jury is particularly justified in making such a determination when the statute's express purpose is to prevent the type of injury or damage caused by the business conduct. In such cases, it is possible for businesses to be guilty both of violating criminal statutes (with penalties owing to the government) and of negligently causing injury or damage (with compensation owing to the persons harmed).

Professional and industry guidelines

"Professional and industry guidelines" are another standard often applied to determine whether businesses negligently cause bodily injury or property damage. These standards tend to be even higher than regulatory standards and, where they exist, are often found to be the applicable standard for determining businesses' duty of care.

These guidelines tend to be even higher than regulatory standards because, of course, it does not make sense for professional and industry associations to adopt guidelines embodying standards lower than applicable statutes and other government regulation. On the contrary, those associations adopt guidelines in part in an attempt to preempt government regulation.

For at least three reasons, these guidelines are often found to be the applicable standard for determining whether businesses negligently cause injury or damage. First, professional and industry guidelines typically cover a wider range of business conduct than government regulation. Second, guidelines expressly address business practices in specific industries, including appropriate sorts of precautionary measures. Third, many guidelines are specifically intended to avoid bodily injury and property damage.

Strict liability

In order to be strictly liable for causing bodily injury or property damage, it is enough that business conduct actually causes bodily injury or property damage. In other words, under the standard of strict liability, it is not necessary for plaintiffs to prove "proximate causation," "intention" or "negligence." Traditionally, in order to be strictly liable for injury or damage, businesses must have created a hazard, including – but not limited to – a product or service which is defectively designed or manufactured.

Generally, if a business is strictly liable for a hazard – including but not limited to a defective product or service – a judge or jury often determines that:

(a) the business could and should have foreseen all of the injuries and damages actually caused by the hazard (i.e., any injury or damage caused by the hazard is foreseeable and thus a "proximate cause"); and
(b) the business could and should adopt the measures necessary to prevent all such injuries and damage (i.e, the business is necessarily "negligent" in connection with any injury or damage caused by the hazard).

Preferences of defendants and plaintiffs

Business defendants most prefer to argue that the average "reasonable person" standard is the duty of care applicable to their conduct. They make this argument because – compared to the regulatory or industry standards – by applying the reasonable person standard it is less likely for a judge or jury to conclude that a business negligently breached its duty of care. An average person – even a reasonable one – probably would not foresee many risks of bodily injury and physical damage inherent in business and adopt adequate precautionary measures.

Plaintiffs most prefer to argue that the "strict liability" standard is the duty of care applicable to defendants' conduct. While plaintiffs cannot always argue successfully for strict liability, plaintiffs are often able to argue successfully that regulatory or industry standards are better suited than the reasonable person standard for determining whether businesses have been negligent, in part because the regulatory and industry standards often specifically address business risks giving rise to possible tort liability.

ABSENCE OF AFFIRMATIVE DEFENSES

If plaintiffs are able to carry their burden of proceeding and their burden of proof for the first three elements of a tort claim (i.e., harm, causation and duty of care), then the burden of proof shifts to defendants to establish an "affirmative defense," i.e., facts tending to exonerate defendants. Unlike plaintiffs, who must establish all elements of the tort claim in order to establish defendants' legal liability, defendants must establish only one affirmative defense in order to avoid all legal liability.

Generally, affirmative defenses tend to show that an intervening event contributed so substantially to causing the alleged harm that defendants should not be legally liable for the harm even though defendants might otherwise have violated their general obligations. Defendants' actions, i.e., the actions of the persons whose interests are harmed, are often the basis for asserting an affirmative defense. For example, if defendants can show by a preponderance of the evidence that plaintiffs "assumed the risk" – i.e., plaintiffs were aware of the risk causing their harm and accepted that risk – such facts are often accepted as exoneration for defendants' tort. Similarly, defendants are also often exonerated if they can show, in respect of the risk causing the harm, either that:

1   plaintiffs were "reckless" – i.e., plaintiffs were aware of the risk causing their harm and ignored that risk; or
2   plaintiffs were "negligent" – i.e., plaintiffs should have been aware of the risk causing the harm and should have avoided it.

The actions of persons other than defendants can also be a good defense, but such actions are not typically called affirmative defenses. Such actions are not the basis for affirmative defenses because one defendant is not necessarily exonerated from legal liability if he or she can show that another person – other than plaintiffs – contributed substantially to causing the alleged harm. Instead, both the defendant and the other person contributing substantially to the alleged harm are "jointly liable" for the tort. Generally, if two persons are jointly liable for causing the same harm, then each of them is individually liable for compensating plaintiffs for their harm in its entirety. This approach to joint liability is based on the general principle of tort law: a person should be compensated for

harm if that harm is caused by one or more other persons.

By showing that a person other than plaintiffs contributed substantially to causing the alleged harm, defendants can at most expect that other persons causing harm will share the obligation to compensate plaintiffs for their harm. In other words, a defendant can at most expect that the other persons will be "co-defendants."

CONSEQUENCES OF COMMITTING TORTS

In general, the consequence of committing a tort is – at a minimum – the payment of the monetary equivalent of the personal injury or property damage suffered by the person or persons experiencing the injury or damage. In addition, the person committing the tort can be required to pay punitive damages in an amount sufficient to discourage that person – and other persons – from committing such a tort in the future. If the actions or omissions constituting a tort also violate a government regulation, then – in addition to paying compensatory and punitive damages – the person committing the tort can be required to pay penalties to the government for violating the government regulation. Finally, if the tort is committed by a business and the tort violates community ethical norms (as is often the case), then the business can experience a loss of future revenue in the manner and to the extent outlined in Chapter 2.

Paying compensation

Compensatory damages are the payments made by defendants to plaintiffs for the harm actually suffered by plaintiffs pursuant to torts committed by defendants.

In connection with bodily injury or tangible property damages, actual damages can include:

1   costs incurred to repair or cure the harm suffered – both personal injury and property damages; plus
2   to the extent that the harm is irreparable or incurable, an estimate of the value of the losses associated with the personal injury or property damages.

Obviously, the costs incurred include medical expenses for personal injury and contractors' expenses for property damage, all of which can be determined with some accuracy. The value of irreparable losses usually cannot be determined with accuracy and so is based on an estimate by a judge and jury. The estimated amount can be considerable but must be reasonably related to the losses actually suffered.

In connection with business torts, i.e., injury to businesses or their intangible property, compensatory damages also include lost profits and other consequential damages. These consequential damages are related to the value of the business as a going concern. As with other types of losses, lost profits and other consequential damages are difficult to determine and so are based on estimates by judges and juries. The estimated amounts can be considerable but must be reasonably related to some objective standard – such as past profits.

Paying punitive damages

As illustrated by the Ford Pinto Case in Chapter 2, defendants can be required to pay punitive damages as a consequence of committing torts. Punitive damages can be imposed both:

(a) in addition to compensation for consequential damages, such as irreparable harm and lost profits, as discussed above; and
(b) in addition to penalties imposed for violations of government regulations, as discussed below.

Punitive damages are intended not only to compensate plaintiffs for past harm. Punitive damages are intended to influence defendants' future conduct. More precisely, punitive damages are intended to deter future tortious conduct by depriving defendants of any profit from past tortious conduct. In order to achieve this purpose, punitive damages should be even greater than the greater of:

1 the amount by which defendants' profits exceed their profit after taking into account the harm actually suffered by defendants; and
2 the costs defendants would have incurred to avoid the injury.

As a result, punitive damages tend to be significant.

Since punitive damages are supposed to deter future tortious conduct, punitive damages are some-

times limited to past torts which involve some intentional acts by defendants, for example:

(a) intentionally ignoring a known risk; or
(b) failing to take precautionary measures adequate to avoid a known risk.

In order to deter defendants' future intentionally tortious activity, defendants do not need to pay punitive damages to plaintiffs. It is enough that defendants are deprived of their profits from past tortious activity, e.g., by paying punitive damages to governments. In fact, government regulations imposing criminal penalties on business for tortious activity achieve the same effect as punitive damages awarded pursuant to tort claims. In order to achieve such effect, however, it is necessary for government agencies to take action pursuant to their regulations. The payment of punitive damages to plaintiffs provides an incentive for plaintiffs to assume the uncertainties involved in pursuing tort claims.

Paying government penalties

As previously noted, the same action can constitute a tort, leading to the payment of compensatory and punitive damages, and a violation of government regulations, leading to the payment of fines and other penalties.

Paying fines is usually not an alternative to compliance. Governments establish the possibilities of fines as an incentive for businesses to comply with their regulations. Accordingly, in addition to paying fines, compensatory damages and punitive damages, acts and omissions constituting both torts and violations of government regulations can entail belatedly incurring the cost of compliance.

Finally, acts and omissions constituting both torts and violations of government regulation can result in sanctions in addition to the payments of monetary fines. Governments also claim the right to suspend business operations until businesses comply with regulations or – at the very least – agree with government a plan for implementing compliance.

Losing future revenue

In addition to the payment of compensatory and punitive damages, committing a tort which offends community ethical norms can result in the loss of future income. Persons situated similarly to the harmed persons will take the tort into account in determining their future dealings with defendants, potentially disrupting commercial relationships. Such disruptions of commercial relationship can, of course, result in losses of future revenue.

SOME TORTS ALLEGED BY BUSINESSES

Business torts often alleged by business are described below. As a preliminary matter, it is useful to note that businesses are not protected from all harm, even harm intentionally afflicted upon them. Competition amongst companies, in particular, inevitably results in harm to some companies. In the absence of some improper action by competitors, however, a company's interests are not protected against harm caused by competitors.

At the same time, if one company improperly harms a competitor's business or intangible assets, then consumer choice also suffers. Accordingly, a business tort committed by a company against its competitor(s) can constitute "unfair competition," subjecting the company both to paying compensation for committing the tort and to paying penalties for violating competition law.

Defamation and libel

In a business context, personal injury includes harm to a company's reputation. Tortious harm to reputations is called "defamation." Making a verbal defamatory statement is called "slander." Making such a statement in writing is called "libel." In order to constitute defamation, a statement must be false and it must injure a company's or individual's business reputation, typically by subjecting the individual or company to contempt, ridicule or hatred, e.g., by indicating that the individual or company is incompetent or dishonest.

Wrongful interference with contractual relationships

In a business context, personal injury also includes harm to a person's relationships. Tortious harm to business relationships is sometimes called "wrongful interference with contractual relationships." In order to constitute wrongful interference, there must be a valid contract between two businesses and a third person – not a party to the contract – must induce one of the two parties to the contract to breach its contractual obligations.

Fraud

"Fraud" can also be a business tort. As already noted, contract law and tort law are separate and distinct. At the same time, it is possible to breach both contract obligations and general obligations in respect of a contract. If a party enters into a contract with the (secret) intention of breaching it, then the act of entering into the contract constitutes a fraud, a violation of general obligations. Such a violation of general obligations is called "fraud in the inducement."

Conversion

In a business context, property damage includes "conversion." Very generally, conversion consists of exercising ownership rights in certain assets inconsistent with the real owners' rights in the same assets. In a business context, conversion often arises in the context of transactions where owners entrust possession of property to another person, i.e., a trustee or agent such as a warehouse, carrier or employee. If the person entrusted with possession uses the property for a purpose inconsistent with the scope of the trust arrangement, then the person who exceeds the scope is liable for conversion. For example, if a warehouse or carrier sells goods entrusted to them for storage or delivery, then selling the goods constitutes conversion. If employees use their employers' raw materials for family purposes, then the employees are liable for conversion. Conversion is also a good example of the principle that the same acts can be both a tort and a crime. The actions constituting the tort of conversion also constitute the crime of embezzlement.

Infringement

Business torts also include "infringement" of intellectual property rights such as infringement of copyrights, trademarks and patents. Governments grant owners of copyrights, patents and trademark, as with owners of other forms of property, the right to exclude others from using their property. In the case of copyrights, trademarks and patents, governments grant creators, inventors and businesses the right to exclude others from using, respectively, works of art, inventions and fanciful names used to designate origin. If persons other than owners of copyrights, patents and trademarks use those intangible assets without the owners' consent, then the persons engaged in the unauthorized use are liable for "infringement" of the intellectual property rights. Infringement of intellectual property rights differs from conversion because "infringers" of intellectual property rights do not need to take possession of those intangible assets in the same way that "converters" need to take possession of tangible assets. Even though infringers do not deprive owners of the use of their copyrights, patents and trademarks, infringers deprive owners of some of the revenue from those intellectual property rights while possibly degrading their value.

Misappropriation of trade secrets

"Misappropriation of trade secrets" is another business tort. This business tort is very similar to infringement but given a different name because of the difference between the nature of trade secrets and other forms of intellectual property. The exclusivity accorded by copyright, patent and trademark is based in the first instance upon a grant by the government to creators of works of art, names or inventions (with "first use" establishing some rights to trademarks in common law countries). The exclusivity accorded by trade secrets is based in the first instance upon the actions taken by inventors to keep their inventions secret. Misappropriation of trade secrets is another good example of the principle that the same acts can be both a tort and a crime. Some misappropriations of trade secrets have become a federal crime in the United States under the Industrial Espionage Act.

Tort claims

In addition to the torts discussed above, businesses are often subject to tort claims. Common sorts of tort claims include: toxic tort, worker compensation and product liability are types of torts important to business.

Toxic torts

If a business's use of its property causes contamination resulting in personal injury or property damage, then the business is subject to paying compensation. Personal injury or property damage resulting from contamination is called "toxic torts." Since toxic torts cause injury to many people or their property, they are also often called "mass torts," qualifying for treatment as "class actions." Toxic torts, mass torts and class actions are discussed more fully in the chapter on "Environmental Law."

Here, it is sufficient to note that a business can be liable to pay compensation for a toxic tort without regard to whether it causes contamination intentionally, recklessly or negligently. In fact, as with the creation of other hazards, a business can be strictly liable for all personal injury or property damage caused by its contamination.

In addition, as with business torts, committing a toxic tort can also constitute a violation of government regulations, subjecting defendants to all of the potential consequences of violating government regulations – in this case: environmental regulations.

Worker compensation

Employees are often injured at work. Employees also often – at least arguably – contribute to their own injuries. The employment relationship does not – as a matter of law – detract from employees' ability to claim compensation for personal injuries for torts suffered at work. In many cases, however, the employers' ability to argue that employees contributed to their own injuries does – in fact – detract from employees' ability to claim compensation under tort law for such injuries.

In order to address this issue, many jurisdictions have adopted government regulations establishing arrangements for compensating employees injured at work without regard to whether they negligently contribute to their own injuries. In the United States, such regulations are called "workers compensation statutes." In return for the limitation of liability for negligent injury to employees, employers are required to provide guarantees of their ability to pay workers' compensation claims, often by carrying insurance called "workers compensation insurance."

By accepting payments under workers compensation statutes, injured employees waive the right under tort law to claim compensatory and punitive damages from their employers. At the same time, by accepting such payments, employees do not need to overcome the – more or less inevitable – affirmative defense that their negligence contributed to their injuries.

Product liability

If a business's use of its property creates a hazard causing personal injury or property damage, then the business can be strictly liable for compensatory and punitive damages. As we have already seen, this rule regarding hazards applies to environmental pollution. The same rule applies to making and selling hazardous products, i.e., products defective in design or manufacture. In other words, businesses can be strictly liable for all bodily injuries and property damage they cause by making or selling defective products. In addition, if businesses negligently make or sell defective products, then they can be liable for consequential damages such as lost profits.

Strict liability has long been available as a basis for product liability claims in Britain, the United States of America and in Britain's other former colonies. Product liability in the United States has attracted the most attention because in the United States there is no statutory limitation on the amount of punitive damages plaintiffs can recover pursuant to product liability claims. In other respects, the law in Britain and Commonwealth Countries is substantially similar to product liability law in the United States.

In 1985, the European Union adopted a directive requiring its member states to implement product liability regulations meeting certain minimum standards. Those minimum requirements are similar to the product liability law in Britain. In fact, the scope of the EU's minimum requirements appears to be broader than its British precedent because the EU does not require that a product's defect be "unreasonably dangerous" in order to impose strict liability on businesses for making or selling it.

The scope of defendants – usually businesses – involved in product liability cases is very broad. First, it is not necessary for businesses to make a product in order to share in liability for any harm caused by defects. Businesses selling products can share in the product liability of the products they sell. Second, manufacturers of ingredients and components can share the product liability for final products incorporating their ingredients or components.

The scope of plaintiffs – both individuals and businesses – involved in product liability cases is also very broad. The ability to make a product liability claim includes businesses' customers but is not limited to them. Any person using a product, even unintended users, can make product liability claims against businesses which made it, sold it or contributed ingredients or components.

TECHNICAL TRAINING PROGRAMS

As indicated in this chapter, negligence can be an important basis for legal liability under tort law. Negligence involves either or both of the following:

(a) employees' failure to be aware of risks of which they should be aware; and
(b) employees' failure to take adequate measures to avoid harm arising from risks of which they are aware.

In either case, a good technical training program is not only an important part of businesses' customer satisfaction efforts. A good technical training program is an important part of businesses' legal compliance programs.

6

Contract Rights and Obligations

INTRODUCTION

Property is a legal fiction facilitating business by granting important legal rights. Holders of "property" can enforce their legal rights against other persons without the consent of those other persons. (For example, I do not need a contract with you to keep you out of the house I own.) Contracts are another legal fiction facilitating business. Holders of "contracts" can enforce their rights against other persons only because of the prior consent obtained from those other persons. (For example, I can occupy your house if you agree to rent it to me.)

Contracts are ubiquitous in business. They create various consensual relationships (e.g., employee or customer). In order to understand contracts generally, we will look at contracts for the sale of goods and the customer relationships they create. We will look at contracts with customers as our example for contracts, instead of contracts creating other business relationships, in part because relationships with customers (especially other businesses) are governed to a great extent purely by concepts of contract law, in part because all businesses have customers and in part because, together with shareholders, customers are often considered to be the most important business constituency.

Commercial law applies only to the sale of goods – i.e., movable tangible assets – by merchants to merchants. At the same time, commercial law is an excellent example of all contract law because commercial law is nothing but a compilation of those contract terms which have proven to be most effective over the centuries for the sale of goods between mer-

chants. Those terms were developed by merchants for merchants to govern transactions spanning continents and the globe.

ESSENTIAL TERMS IN COMMERCIAL TRANSACTIONS

The essential elements on the international sale of goods are:

1 delivery of goods by the seller to the buyer; and
2 payment for the goods by the buyer to the seller.

In those cases where the deliveries of payment and of goods cannot be accomplished simultaneously and face-to-face, then it is usually necessary for sellers or buyers to promise to complete their deliveries after the other has completed their deliveries. Such promises to complete deliveries are called "covenants."

First, we will look at delivery and payment terms most prevalent in international trade. These terms are:

1 the International Commercial Terms ("INCO-TERMS"); and
2 the Uniform Customs and Practices for Documentary Credits ("UCP").

Both of these terms for commercial transactions were promulgated by the International Chamber of Commerce (the "ICC"). The ICC is an international non-governmental organization. Accordingly, the INCOTERMS and UCP are important examples of international self-regulation by business.

Delivery terms

Together with payment terms, delivery terms are the only truly essential elements of a contract for any sale of goods, including international sales of goods. At the same time, the term "delivery" of goods is a vague term. First, the term "delivery" can be construed to refer to the "transfer of physical possession of goods." Second, the term "delivery" can be construed to refer to the "transfer of title to goods."

In its INCOTERMS, the ICC has adopted a third approach: "transfer of the risk of loss and damage." The ICC does not focus on "physical possession" to define delivery in its INCOTERMS in part because goods are handled by warehouses and carriers, not sellers and buyers, in the course of international sales transactions. The ICC does not focus on "title" to define delivery in part because title to goods is determined in part by payment in full of the goods, an issue not addressed in the INCOTERMS.

The place of delivery

To define delivery terms, the ICC focuses first on the exact geographical location where transfer of risk of loss and damage passes from sellers to buyers. In general, under the INCOTERMS, sellers have the obligation to "place goods at the disposal of the buyer" or to "make goods available to the buyer," at a place specified in the sales contract, i.e., the point of delivery. The risk of loss and damage transfers at that point of delivery. Under the INCOTERMS, the point of delivery can be:

(a) the seller's place of business;
(b) the buyer's place of business; or
(c) any point between the seller and buyer where physical possession of the goods has just passed or is about to pass from one carrier to another carrier.

Arrangements and costs of carriage and insurance

Second, based on definition of the point of delivery, the INCOTERMS allow sellers and buyers to determine how "functions and costs" should be divided between themselves in connection with the transfer of

the goods and the risk of loss. Those main "functions" are arranging and paying for carriage and insurance. Other functions are arranging and paying for:

(a) documents of title and shipment;
(b) providing export and import licenses;
(c) packaging goods;
(d) quality, quantity and damage inspections; and
(e) notifying the other party of any arrangements made.

Sellers' and buyers' obligations in respect of these functions are typically divided in terms of the point of delivery, but they have some flexibility.

For example, sellers and buyers can agree that goods are "delivered," i.e., risk of loss and damage passes from sellers to buyers, when sellers place the goods on board a ship at a port specified in the sales contract, e.g., Baltimore USA. They can also agree that sellers have the obligation to arrange and pay for carriage and insurance to the point of delivery but not thereafter. Such a delivery term is called "FOB – Baltimore USA," meaning "Freight On Board – Baltimore USA." Alternatively, sellers and buyers can agree that, even though risk of loss and damages passes to buyers as soon as sellers make goods available to buyers on board a ship at Baltimore USA, sellers have the obligation:

(a) to arrange and pay for carriage from Baltimore to buyers' place of business; or
(b) to arrange and pay for both carriage and insurance from Baltimore to buyers' place of business. Such delivery terms are called, respectively, "C&F – Baltimore USA" or "CIF – Baltimore Maryland,' referring to sellers' obligations to arrange for cargo and freight or cargo, insurance and freight.

Care is required in designating delivery terms

The ICC does not, however, grant unlimited flexibility in its INCOTERMS. The ICC sets forth thirteen specific formulations for delivery terms, each of which relates to a specific delivery arrangement for shifting the risk of loss and obligations for arranging and paying carriage and insurance. Most of those formulations consist of three letters, such as "FOB" or "CIF." A complete set of the INCOTERM formulations is set forth in the notes at the end of this book, together with a brief definition of each.[1]

As with other provisions of commercial law, international buyers and sellers are free to derogate from the INCOTERMS by mutual agreement. For at least two reasons, sellers and buyers should, however, exercise caution in using delivery terms other than the INCOTERMS. First, warehouse people and carriers are involved in international sales transactions and are most familiar with INCOTERMS. Second, INCOTERMS are defined very clearly in great detail. In the absence of INCOTERMS, buyers and sellers must define their delivery arrangements equally clearly and in equal detail.

Finally, sellers and buyers should expressly designate the legal framework used to define their delivery terms. In addition to INCOTERMS, national laws also provide a complete legal framework for designating points of delivery and the legal consequences of delivery. Moreover, national laws tend to use the same three-letter designations for delivery terms as those used by the ICC, e.g., FOB and CIF – but give those designations different meanings. Accordingly, to avoid confusion, sellers and buyers should reference the appropriate legal framework for all delivery terms, e.g., "FOB – Baltimore USA (Maryland USA Uniform Commercial Code)" or "FOB – Baltimore USA (INCOTERMS, 2000)."

ESSENTIAL TERMS IN COMMERCIAL TRANSACTIONS

Payment terms

The timing of payment is important in all commercial transactions, including international sales transactions. Sellers do not want to relinquish physical possession or title to their goods before they receive payment from buyers. Buyers do not want to make payment before they receive physical delivery and title to the goods from sellers. In most commercial transactions, this conflict is resolved through simultaneous "closings" or "completions." At a closing or completion, sellers deliver their goods to buyers, together with title documents, at the same time that buyers deliver their payment to sellers.

In the event of a closing or completion, the payment arrangements involve the completion of all formalities for the delivery of cash or cash equivalents from buyers to sellers, just as sellers complete all formalities for the delivery of goods or services (or, if agreed in advance with the buyer, for the delivery of a promise to deliver goods or services in the future). Such a payment can take the form of currency, a check (sometimes a cashier's or certified check) or an electronic wire transfer of funds from the buyer's bank to the seller's bank. Typically, the closing or completion is not considered to be consummated (and none of the actions taken at the closing or completion have any legal effect) until all of the delivery formalities for payment are finished to the seller's reasonable satisfaction.

Other covenants

The delivery and payment terms set forth in commercial law are an excellent example of all delivery and payment terms for all contractual relationships.

This essential exchange is simplest to arrange and document when the exchange is a simultaneous, face-to-face exchange of money for goods, i.e., for movable tangible assets, also called personal property. In such cases, buyers personally deliver payment to sellers at the same time that sellers personally deliver to buyers physical possession of the goods, together with evidence of title. All complications in the essential exchange (i.e., buyers' delivery of payment for sellers' delivery of goods or services) are due to the fact that:

1 exchanges are not simultaneous;
2 exchanges are not face-to-face;
3 buyers do not deliver money;
4 sellers do not deliver goods, i.e., movable tangible assets; and/or
5 sellers do not intend to transfer title to buyers.

Addressing complications concerning the essential exchange between sellers and buyers requires additional contract provisions. These contract provisions are generally called "covenants." As mentioned previously, covenants are:

1 promises made by sellers to complete their deliveries after buyers have completed payment; or
2 promises made by buyers to complete payment after sellers have completed their deliveries. Sometimes both the sellers and buyers need to make covenants, for example: if

(a) buyers begin to arrange or make payments before sellers have completed their deliveries, at the same time that

(b) sellers begin to arrange or make deliveries before buyers have completed their payments.

In such cases, both sellers and buyers need to make covenants, i.e., promise to complete performance, as an inducement to the other to begin their performance.

In a situation where a seller and a buyer enter into contracts governing their entire transaction before they begin arranging and making deliveries and payments, the contracts will set out as "covenants" all of each party's promises of future performances, including the promises to make deliveries and payments. In such circumstances, the exchange giving rise to a contract between sellers and buyers is not an exchange of assets for payment but an exchange of promises: seller's promise to deliver assets for buyer's promise to deliver payment – and all performance obligations are "covenants," i.e., promises to render some performance in the future.

LETTERS OF CREDIT

Simultaneous closings or completions are not possible in international sales of goods because sellers and buyers are geographically remote from each other. To resolve the conflict concerning the timing of payment in international sales transactions, sellers agree to accept – before relinquishing possession and title to their goods – an irrevocable promise of payment from a clearly creditworthy source as a substitute for actual payment from buyers. The "clearly creditworthy source" acceptable to sellers is sellers' local bank. The irrevocable promise of payment is called a "letter of credit."

Just as the ICC has developed terms for the delivery of goods which are widely accepted in international trade, i.e., INCOTERMS, so the ICC has developed terms for issuing and confirming letters of credit in international sales transactions. Those terms are called Uniform Customs and Practices for Documentary Credits (the "UCP"). The UCP are widely used by banks in defining the exact procedures concerning payments under letters of credit. A summary of those procedures is set forth in the notes at the end of this book.[2]

The letter of credit from sellers' local bank is irrevocable but it certainly is not "unconditional." In order for sellers to receive payments from their local banks under letters of credit, sellers must deliver certain documents to their local banks. Local banks generally require two types of documents from sellers before making payment to sellers pursuant to letters of credit: title documents and shipment documents.

Title documents

For goods requiring registration of ownership with governmental authorities, title documents consist of the originals of those ownership registrations as issued by governments. For all other types of goods (including most goods sold in international trade), title documents consist of a "bill of sale" evidencing transfer of title from sellers to buyers. Bills of sale are simple one-page documents signed by sellers evidencing their intention to transfer title to certain assets to buyers.

Shipping documents

Shipping documents consist of certificates issued by warehouses and carriers – typically warehouse receipts and bills of lading – evidencing the fact that sellers have "entrusted" the goods to the warehouses or carriers, i.e., the warehouses or carriers accepted physical possession of certain goods from sellers without claiming title to those goods. The shipping documents must show that the warehouses and carriers have accepted possession of the goods under terms consistent with the sales contract between sellers and buyers. Typically, the shipping documents must show that the goods will be transported to the place of delivery and there made available to buyers.

If sellers have obligations in addition to physical delivery of goods, then sellers' local banks make their payments under letters of credit conditional upon sellers' delivery of certificates evidencing fulfillment of those obligations. For example, if sellers are obligated to:

(a) provide export and import licenses;

(b) arrange for quality, quantity and damage inspections of goods; and

(c) obtain cargo insurance, then their local banks will expect sellers to deliver, respectively:

  (i) such export and import licenses;
  (ii) certificates of such inspections; and
  (iii) certificates of insurance, all before making payment pursuant to their letters of credit.

Invoices

Finally, in order to make payments under their letters of credit, sellers' local banks insist that they receive a formal demand for payment. Such demand for payment includes presentation of an invoice issued by sellers to buyers. The invoice must be in accordance with the terms of the letter of credit concerning two important matters:

(a) the price to be paid; and
(b) the description of the goods purchased.

Issuing banks and confirming banks

Of course, sellers' local banks will not issue letters of credit for goods to be delivered to foreign buyers unless sellers' local banks have an irrevocable promise of payment from a clearly creditworthy source as a substitute for actual payment from those foreign buyers. The "clearly creditworthy source" acceptable to sellers' local bank is buyers' local bank. The irrevocable promise of payment from buyers' local bank to sellers' local bank is also called a "letter of credit." The actions taken by buyers' local banks are called "issuing letters of credit," while the actions of sellers' local banks are called "confirming letters of credit." Buyers' banks are often called "issuing banks." Sellers' banks are often called "confirming banks."

INCIDENTAL TERMS IN COMMERCIAL TRANSACTIONS

All contract terms other than deliveries, payments and covenants are incidental to the essential exchange of buyers' payments for sellers' assets. Other contract terms can be necessary or important, but they are not essential. They are not essential simply because sellers or buyers might not need to per-

form any obligations pursuant to them in addition to the obligations they perform pursuant to their delivery terms, payment terms and other covenants.

Such other contract terms tend to address two important issues:

1 assumptions made by sellers or buyers in entering into the contractual exchange; and
2 contingencies, i.e., events which might occur or conditions which might exist in the future but will not necessarily occur or exist.

Contract terms other than delivery, payment and covenants can be broadly categorized as:

1 conformity provisions or warranties;
2 remedies; and
3 "liability" provisions, i.e., provisions regulating liability under the law of general obligations (also called "tort law").

The ICC does not address these incidental contract terms in its INCOTERMS or UCP. Instead, the international community has addressed them under the United Nations' Convention on Contracts for the International Sale of Goods (the "CISG"), also known as the Vienna Convention of 1980. Accordingly, we will examine conformity provisions or warranties, sellers' remedies, buyers' remedies and liability provisions under the CISG.

Of course, the United Nations is an international governmental organization, so the CISG is an example of international governmental regulation. Please note also that the CISG, like other examples of international governmental regulation, can facilitate business as well as burdening them.

"CONFORMITY" OR "WARRANTY" PROVISIONS

"Conformity" provisions in the CISG and the statutes of civil law countries – or "warranties" under the law in common law countries – are simply assumptions buyers and sellers bring into their commercial transactions, e.g., that sellers hold title to the goods they deliver to buyers. ("Conformity" provisions – or warranties – are "incidental" contract provisions, at least in the way I have defined "incidental," because, if they are true, sellers or buyers do not need to perform any obligations pursuant to them in addition to the already-agreed delivery, payment and other covenants.)

By expressing those assumptions in the CISG (Articles 35 (1) and (2)), those assumptions are converted into enforceable promises for the sales transactions to which the CISG applies. Since the assumptions set forth in the CISG are enforceable even if they are not set forth in the sales contracts to which the CISG applies, such conformity provisions – as well as similar provisions under the statutes of civil law countries and the law of common law countries – are called "warranties implied in law" or "implied warranties."

It is interesting to note that all of the warranties described below apply to sellers' deliveries. In fact, most warranties are given by sellers because buyers in commercial transactions deliver money while sellers deliver real property, personal property or services. Money, by its nature, has an exact and obvious value. Real property, personal property and services, on the other hand, do not have an exact and obvious value. As a result, it is important for buyers to include in their contracts warranties confirming the assumptions they use in purchasing and valuing sellers' deliveries.

Implied warranties

Under the CISG, the implied conformity provisions – or implied warranties – include:

1 title;
2 merchantability;
3 fitness for a particular purpose;
4 samples or models; and
5 packaging.

All of the warranties or conformity provisions implied by the CISG are available to all sellers and buyers to which the CISG applies unless sellers or buyers expressly disclaim them in the contract. In addition, all of the warranties implied by the CISG are cumulative unless the contract specifically provides otherwise.

The conformity provisions – or warranties – implied by the CISG are a good list of warranties which, at a minimum, should be in all contracts, including both:

(a) contracts for the purchase of real property, intangible assets and services; and
(b) contracts for sales of goods to which the CISG does not apply.

Those warranties are described below.

"Title"

In all commercial transactions to which the CISG applies, sellers make an implied promise, stipulated by the CISG, that they own the goods they deliver to buyers. As explained elsewhere, "ownership" in certain assets entails:

1 the right freely to use those assets; and
2 the right freely to transfer physical possession of those assets together with title in them, i.e., the right freely to use and transfer those assets in the future.

"Title," then, is clearly an important assumption made by buyers.

This conformity provision – or the implied warranty of title – also applies under the law of most civil law and common law counties. In common law countries, it is called the "implied warranty of title."

"Merchantability"

In all commercial transactions to which the CISG applies, sellers make an implied promise, stipulated by the CISG, that the delivered goods are "fit for the purposes for which goods of the same description would ordinarily be used." Sellers do not need to know anything about buyers' intended uses or conditions for this warranty to apply.

This conformity provision – or implied warranty of merchantability – also applies under the law of most civil law and common law counties. In common law countries, this conformity provision is called the "implied warranty of merchantability."

"Fitness for a particular purpose"

In all commercial transactions to which the CISG applies, sellers make an implied promise, stipulated by the CISG, that the delivered goods are "fit for any particular purpose expressly or impliedly made known [by the buyers] to the sellers at the time of the conclusion of the contract."

In other words, sellers are not bound by this promise unless they know about buyers' intended uses and conditions of use. Moreover, under the CISG, this provision is not available to a buyer if "the buyer did not rely, or that it was unreasonable for [the buyer] to rely, on the seller's skill and judgment."

In order to ensure that their "particular purpose [is] made known to the sellers at the time of the conclusion of the contract," buyers usually state their purposes in their contracts with sellers. In addition, buyers also tend to state that they are relying on "seller's skill and judgment." In other words, buyers usually attempt to provide expressly for "fitness for a particular purpose" in their contracts if they intend to enforce such a conformity provision or warranty.

This conformity provision – or implied warranty of merchantability – also applies under the law of most civil law and common law counties. In common law countries, this conformity provision is called the "implied warranty of fitness for a particular purpose."

"Samples or models"

In all commercial transactions to which the CISG applies, sellers make an implied promise, stipulated by the CISG, that the delivered goods "possess the qualities of goods seller has held out to the buyer as a sample or model."

There is no implied warranty concerning samples or models in common law countries. Accordingly, if buyers in common law countries want to ensure that goods delivered conform to samples or models, they need to make an express warranty or covenant concerning samples or models.

"Packaging"

In all commercial transactions to which the CISG applies, sellers make an implied promise, stipulated by the CISG, that the delivered goods are "contained or packaged in the same manner usual for such goods or, where there is no such manner, any manner adequate to preserve and protect the goods."

There is no implied warranty concerning packaging in common law countries.

Accordingly, if buyers want to ensure proper packaging in a common law country, they need to make an express warranty or covenant concerning packaging.

Express warranties

In addition to the conformity provisions or warranties implied by law, sellers and buyers can expressly provide for additional conformity provisions or warranties in their contracts. In fact, it is customary for buyers to request warranties in addition to those implied by law. Two typical express warranties are set forth below: "specifications" and "no infringement."

It is important to note that many conformity provisions and warranties are implied by law only in commercial transactions, i.e., only in transactions for the purchase and sale of goods (movable tangible assets). In order to benefit from the conformity provisions and warranties in other sorts of transactions – such as the purchase of real estate, intangible assets or services – it might be necessary for the buyers expressly to state this important assumption in their contracts.

"Specifications"

In a commercial context – i.e., in sales transactions between merchants – buyers typically do not rely exclusively on the implied warranties of merchantability and fitness for a particular purpose. In addition, buyers typically include in their contracts reasonably detailed descriptions of the products they intend to purchase. Such conformity provisions or warranties are called "specifications."

In addition to detailed specifications, buyers also often stipulate that:

(a) materials they purchase should be free from contaminants; and
(b) manufactured goods should be free from defects in design, materials or workmanship.

Cautious buyers often include such express warranties in their contracts because detailed specifications do not necessarily insure freedom from contaminants and defects.

"No infringement"

With the increase in the importance of intellectual property rights – e.g., patents and trade secrets – it has become more common for buyers to include in their contracts express warranties that

1   sellers have not infringed any third party's intellectual property rights by making and selling the goods to buyers; and
2   buyers' use of the products will not infringe any intellectual property rights.

In the absence of such a provision, it would be possible that an owner of intellectual property rights could claim that a purchaser of, for example, capital equipment collaborated in the sellers' intentional infringement of patent rights. A seller's breach of a patent typically would not prevent a buyer from continuing to use an infringing product because patent holders' rights are usually exhausted upon sale of a product containing a patent. Nonetheless, a seller's patent infringement, even an unintentional one, could disrupt future supplies of goods, such as capital equipment, important to a buyer's continuing business operation.

Buyers' and sellers' remedies

The purpose of remedies under commercial and contract law is the same as damages under the law of general obligations: compensation. Under tort law the purpose of damages is to "put plaintiffs in the same position" as if the harm had not occurred. Under commercial and contract law, the purpose of remedies is to "put the plaintiff in the same position" as if the contract had been fully performed.

Under tort law, there is a possibility of additional damages above and beyond compensation, i.e., "punitive" damages, especially if defendants have the required intent (i.e., ignoring a known risk or failing to take any remedial measures). Under commercial and contract law, there is a possibility of additional damages above and beyond compensation, but only if defendants committed "fraud," i.e., only if defendants intended to breach the contract at the time that they signed the contract. Accordingly, in the absence of fraud, there is no legal penalty or punishment for breaching contractual obligations.

Since there is no penalty for breaching contracts, there is often insufficient incentive under the law for buyers and sellers to perform contracts which appear to have become disadvantageous after they are signed. Instead, continuing commercial relationships with contract parties or concern about commercial reputations (i.e., the possibility of future contractual relationships with the contracting parties or with other persons) provide the incentive for sellers and buyers to perform contracts which appear to have become disadvantageous. In the absence of commercial relationships and reputations, it may be rational and, in fact, is relatively common for buyers and sellers simply to refuse to perform such contracts. Given the costs, delays, uncertainties and emotions involved for plaintiffs to enforce their contracts in court, such refusals might not be surprising.

The best way to understand remedies under commercial contract law is to focus on the point in time at which sellers or buyers breach their contracts. By viewing remedies in this way, it becomes clear that the purpose of remedies is to compensate plaintiffs by putting them in the same position as if the contract had been fully performed.

Buyers' remedies

If sellers breach contracts before buyers pay the price and before sellers ship goods, then buyers have the right to cancel the contract. If sellers breach contracts after buyers pay the price but before sellers ship goods, then buyers have the right to cancel the contract and recover the price paid. If sellers breach contracts after they ship goods but before buyers accept them, i.e., by delivering non-conforming goods, then buyers have the right to refuse delivery and hold the non-conforming goods for sellers to retrieve. If sellers breach contracts after they ship goods and after buyers accept them, i.e., again by delivering non-conforming goods, then buyers have the right – within a limited period of time – to reject the goods and, again, to hold the non-conforming goods for sellers to retrieve.

Since these various buyers' remedies set forth above are available at different times during sellers' performance of the contract, they are necessarily mutually exclusive. There are, however, "cumulative" remedies, available to buyers at all times during sellers' performance of the contract. "Cover" is the cumulative remedy available to buyers. "Cover" is buyers' right:

1 to purchase substitute goods at market or other reasonable prices; and
2 to recover from sellers any additional amounts paid for the substitute goods above and beyond the price set for such goods in contracts between buyers and sellers.

In addition to cover, buyers also have the cumulative remedy of recovering "damages." The damages available under commercial and contract law differ only slightly from the damages available under tort law. Under tort law, damages focus on personal injury and property damage. Under commercial and contract law, damages focus on "direct, incidental and consequential" economic costs and losses suffered by buyers. The most notorious of these types of contractual damages are the "consequential damages." Consequential damages refer to revenues lost by buyers as a result of sellers' contractual breaches. "Direct and incidental damages" refers to costs incurred by buyers as a result of sellers' contractual breaches, e.g., the costs of holding the goods for sellers to retrieve.

Sellers' remedies

If buyers breach contracts before they pay the price and before sellers ship goods, then sellers can withhold shipment, resell the goods to another buyer (i.e., sellers' cover) and recover from buyers the amount by which the contract price exceeds the actual sales revenue. Alternatively, sellers can withhold shipment, hold the goods at buyers' disposal and recover the contract price for the goods. If buyers breach contracts before they pay the price and after sellers ship goods, sellers have all the same remedies, except that they will stop shipment in route rather than withhold shipment. (It is unusual for buyers to breach their contracts after they have paid the price, so remedies in such circumstances will not be considered here.)

Obviously, the sellers' remedies set forth above, including sellers' cover, are necessarily mutually exclusive. Like buyers, sellers also have the cumulative remedy of recovering "direct, incidental and consequential damages."

Tort liability

Unlike the previous terms for delivery, payment, warranties and remedies, there are no provisions in commercial law concerning liability under general obligations. Instead, sellers and buyers are liable to each other for their torts, i.e., breaches of the law of general obligations, without regard to their performance of their contracts.

Accordingly, sellers and buyers can have unlimited liability to each other for any personal injury or property damage caused by them to the other during their performance of their contract obligations, even if sellers and buyers fully perform all of their contract obligations – and so do not breach or incur any liability under their contract obligations. On the other hand, sellers and buyers can incur liability to each other under both contract law and the law of general obligations – including unlimited liability under the law of general obligations – if they cause personal injury or property damage to each other at the same time that they fail fully to perform, and so breach, their contract obligations.

Finally, sellers and buyers can incur unlimited liability to persons other than each other, i.e., to third parties, under the law of general obligations if they cause personal injury or property damage to those third parties in the course of performing their contracts. It does not matter at that sellers or buyers are performing obligations under the contract when they cause the personal injury or property damage. In the absence of an indemnification provision (as discussed below), each contract party is solely and exclusively liable for any personal injury or property damage he, she or it causes in performing his, her or its contract obligations.

CONTRACTUAL MODIFICATIONS IN COMMERCIAL TRANSACTIONS

As previously explained, commercial law is a compilation of commercial customs and conventions adopted by merchants for merchants over the centuries. With the advance of the nation-state, countries have simply incorporated into their national laws – more precisely into their commercial codes – the customs and conventions merchants applied amongst themselves when emperors, kings, counts and dukes ruled.

As such, most provisions of commercial law are not mandatory or, in French, *obligatoire*. Most provisions of commercial law are merely permissive or, in French, *facultative*. In other words, sellers and buyers can derogate from the terms of otherwise applicable commercial law, including the terms of the CISG, simply by introducing into their contracts provisions expressly modifying the terms of commercial law. In the absence of such express provisions, the terms of the applicable commercial law apply.

In fact, sellers and buyers often expressly derogate from the terms of commercial law by introducing contractual modifications, especially as regards: warranty disclaimers, exclusive remedies, limitations of liability and indemnifications. A model of standard terms and conditions for a commercial sales arrangement is set forth at the end of this book.[3]

Warranty disclaimers

As previously noted, most conformity provisions (warranties) burden sellers and benefit buyers. In addition, all conformity provisions (warranties) implied by law are cumulative. At the same time, under the CISG – and the commercial law of most countries – parties are free to derogate from warranties implied by law by express contractual provisions.

Consequently, sellers often introduce "disclaimers" of all conformity provisions or "disclaimers" of warranties implied by law. Having thus eliminated all implied warranties, sellers provide such "limited and exclusive express warranties" as are mutually acceptable to sellers and buyers. Such a disclaimer provision, together with a limited and express warranty, is set forth below. Under the law of some countries, disclaimers of warranties must appear prominently in a contract, e.g., through the use of capital letters.

Limited and Exclusive Express Warranties. Seller offers no conformity provision or warranty of any kind, express or implied, except that (1) seller owns the products, and (2) the products conform to seller's standard specifications. The warranties set forth herein are made only to buyer and are not transferable by buyer to its customers or any other party.
DISCLAIMER OF ALL IMPLIED CONFORMITY PROVISIONS AND ALL IMPLIED WARRANTIES. SELLER MAKES NO OTHER COMMITMENT, REPRESENTATION OR WARRANTY OF ANY KIND, EXPRESS OR IMPLIED, AS TO MER-

CHANTABILITY, FITNESS FOR A PARTICULAR PURPOSE, OR ANY OTHER MATTER WITH RESPECT TO THE PRODUCTS, INCLUDING WITHOUT LIMITATION PATENT INFRINGEMENT AND THE ABSENCE OF CONTAMINANTS AND DEFECTS.

Exclusive remedies

Under the commercial law of most countries, including the CISG, all remedies provided by law are fully available – either as alternatives or cumulatively – to sellers and buyers for breaches of warranties and other contractual obligations owed to them. At the same time, the parties are free to derogate from warranties implied by law by express contractual provisions.

Consequently, sellers and buyers often introduce "exclusions" of remedies provided by law. Having thus eliminated all remedies, they provide such "limited remedies" as are mutually acceptable to sellers and buyers. An example of such an "exclusive and limited remedy" provision is set forth below, in this case: an exclusive and limited remedy for a breach of a warranty. Under the law of some countries, exclusions of remedies must appear prominently in a contract, e.g., through the use of capital letters.

EXCLUSIVE AND LIMITED REMEDY. In the event that buyer notifies seller of a failure of a product to conform with the limited and exclusive express warranty set forth in this contract within ten (10) calendar days after buyer's receipt of the product, then seller shall, at seller's sole option, either replace the non-conforming product or refund the purchase price thereof. Any transportation charges incurred by buyer in returning of the products shall not be reimbursed unless authorized in advance by seller. SUCH REPLACEMENT OR REFUND SHALL BE BUYER'S SOLE AND EXCLUSIVE REMEDY FOR BREACH OF THE LIMITED AND EXCLUSIVE EXPRESS WARRANTY SET FORTH IN THIS CONTRACT.

Limitations of liability

Under the law of general obligations (tort law) of most countries, sellers and buyers can have unlimited liability to each other for any personal injury or property damage they cause to each other during the performance of their contract obligations, even if sellers and buyers fully perform all of their contract obligations – and so do not breach or incur any liability under their contract obligations.

Subject to one important qualification, this unlimited liability for torts (breaches of the law of general obligations) is not addressed or affected by commercial law. Using "limitation of liability" provisions set forth in their contracts, sellers and buyers can, and often do, contractually agree to limit – or even eliminate – their liability to each other under the law of general obligations. Such "limitations of liability" in effect constitute waivers by the contract parties who otherwise would have the right to recover compensation for personal injury or property damage caused by the other contract parties. The important qualification is that it is not possible to limit liability for intentional torts. Contractually agreed limitations of liability are restricted to damages caused by negligence.

An example of such a "limitation of liability" provision is set forth below, in this case: seller limits its total liability to buyer – arising out of negligence or otherwise – to the price paid by buyer to seller under the contract. Under the law of some countries, limitations of liability must appear prominently in a contract, e.g., through the use of capital letters.

LIMITATION OF SELLER'S LIABILITY. SELLER'S TOTAL LIABILITY FOR ANY and all direct, indirect, incidental, special, consequential, exemplary or punitive costs, losses or damages claimed, incurred, suffered by buyer and arising out of any cause whatsoever (WHETHER SUCH CAUSE BE BASED ON CONTRACT, WARRANTY, STRICT LIABILITY, TORT – INCLUDING NEGLIGENCE – OR OTHERWISE) SHALL IN NO EVENT EXCEED THE PURCHASE PRICE OF THE PRODUCTS. SELLER SHALL NOT UNDER ANY CIRCUMSTANCES BE LIABLE TO BUYER FOR ANY "BUYER INDEMNIFIED DAMAGES," AS SUCH TERM IS DEFINED IN THIS CONTRACT. This limitation of liability shall survive the failure of the sole and exclusive remedy provided in this contract. The limitations of Seller's liability in this paragraph are without prejudice to any other limitation or restriction available to Seller under contract, statute, other law or equity.

Indemnification provisions

Finally, as noted above, sellers and buyers can incur unlimited liability to persons other than each other, i.e., to third parties, under the law of general obligations if they cause personal injury or property damage to those third parties in the course of performing their contracts.

Unlike sellers' and buyers' liability to each other under the law of general obligations, sellers and buyers cannot contractually agree to limit or eliminate their liability to third parties for torts committed in the course of performing their contracts. Using "indemnification" provisions set forth in their contracts, sellers and buyers can, however, agree to allocate the third-party liability either of them incurs in performing their contract obligations. For example, sellers can agree to indemnify buyers for any third-party liability buyers incur in buyers' performance of their contract obligations.

Such indemnification provisions usually allocate two potential costs:

1 the costs of paying any third-party liability claim, either by settlement or final judgment; and
2 the costs of defending against any third-party liability claim. Such indemnification provisions also usually address at least the following three issues:
   (a) notification to the indemnifying party of any third-party liability claim against the indemnified party;
   (b) control of any settlement or defense by the indemnifying party; and
   (c) cooperation by the indemnified party with the settlement and defense efforts by the indemnifying party.

Buyer Indemnifies Seller. Buyer shall indemnify seller from and against any and all direct, indirect, incidental, special, consequential, exemplary or punitive costs, losses or damages claimed, incurred, suffered by any and all persons other than buyer and arising out of any cause whatsoever whether such cause be based on contract, warranty, strict liability, tort – including negligence – or otherwise (collectively "Damages"), including any claims made against or paid by seller or buyer to any other person on the basis of any such Damages, either by way of settlement or judgment, including without limitation the costs of settling and defending claims for Damages (collectively the "Buyer Indemnified Damages"). Seller shall promptly notify buyer of any Buyer Indemnified Damages promptly upon Seller's obtaining any knowledge or receipt thereof. Buyer shall control the settlement or defense of any Buyer Indemnified Damages. Seller shall cooperate with buyer in Buyer's efforts to settle and defend any Buyer Indemnified Damages.

SELF-REGULATION

In closing, most importantly, I would like to remind you that contracts are businesses' second opportunity for self-regulation. (The first opportunity arises as each business decides how to use its property.) In order to take full advantage of this opportunity, sellers need to be honest and buyers need to be diligent.

CONSUMER PROTECTION

In closing, I would also like to remind you that this chapter has focused on contract law in a commercial setting. The same laws apply generally in a consumer setting. There are however additional government regulations intended to protect consumers. Those additional government regulations are addressed in Chapter 8.

PART THREE

Government Regulation

7

Relationships with Competitors

Competition law

INTRODUCTION

As explained in Chapter 3, in order to protect buyers from harm, in the first instance, most governments attempt to give buyers real choices whenever possible. With real choice, buyers can protect themselves from future harm without more intrusive government regulation. In order to give buyers real choices, most governments rely on competition amongst sellers in the market place. By enforcing competition, governments effectively elevate buyers' economic interest in real choice to the status of a legal right instrumental in protecting their general and contract rights. At the same time, governments effectively make competition law the most fundamental form of business regulation.[1]

As we will see throughout this chapter, there are two fundamental rules for competition law. First, businesses should not enter into agreements in restraint of trade, including any form of cooperation with competitors. Second, if a business does not have effective competition, then it must treat its customers fairly. Of course, there are vague terms in each of these brief statements and important exceptions to each rule. In addition, some elements of competition law are, as we will see, rather complex. Still, one or both of these simple rules covers most violations of competition regulations. Such actions include price fixing, bid rigging and customer allocation.

Finally, before looking at the substance of competition law, let's consider the following question: why is competition regulated by governments and not exclusively self-regulated by competitors themselves? The answer: consumers generally benefit individually

from competition but many individual businesses do not benefit from competition.[2] Generally, established businesses prefer to cooperate with their large competitors against smaller competitors, and all existing competitors prefer to join together against any potential competition.[3]

A BIT OF HISTORY: 1776 WAS AN EVENTFUL YEAR

In 1776, Anne Robert Jacques Turgot, Baron de Laune (Baron Turgot) was the Controller General of Finances for Louis XVI of France. In that year, Baron Turgot attempted to introduce two measures, both of which met with strong opposition from powerful vested interests in French towns and the French countryside. First, he attempted to abolish the trade guilds ("*chambres de commerce*"), because he considered their monopolies on training, goods and services to be restrictive to economic wealth. Second, he attempted to eliminate the "*corvée*," the labor owed by commoners to the state and used by landed nobility to force peasants to work their land. In effect, he was attempting to create more competitive markets for goods and for rural labor. Both of Turgot's laws were enacted by decree but neither was successfully implemented.

In matters of political economy, Baron Turgot was a follower of François Quesnay (1694–1774), the court physician to Louis XV and founder of the "Physiocratic" school of political economy.[4] Another of Quesnay's followers was Vincent de Gournay (1712–1759). Gournay identified two principles important for a "natural order" in economic affairs: "*Laissez-Faire*" and "*Laissez-Passer.*" With the term "*laissez-faire*" Gournay admonished the king to let agricultural landowners (at that time, by far the largest part of the economy) "do as they please" (*laissez faire*) regarding the use of their land. Second, with the term "*laizzez-passer*," Gournay admonished the king to let agricultural produce "pass freely" (*laissez-passer*) within France, i.e., without the imposition of internal tariffs. Of course, by admonishing the king to allow individuals freely to exercise their property rights, including the sale of products on open markets, Gournay, Turgot and other physiocrats were arguing in favor of competition.

In Scotland in 1776, Adam Smith published his most famous work, *An Inquiry into the Nature and Cause of the Wealth of Nations* ("Wealth of Nations") considered to be one of the classic works in favor of competition. Adam Smith had met Turgot in Paris in 1766 and, while in France, had studied the physiocratic school of economics.[5] Adam Smith was greatly influenced by the concepts of "*Laissez-Faire*" and "*Laissez-Passer.*" In fact, he retained both concepts in *Wealth of Nations*, using the term, "invisible hand," to amplify on the concept of *laissez-passer*. Adam Smith used "invisible hand" to explain how the material wealth of a nation can be increased by maintaining free markets ("*laissez-passer*"). Of course, in free markets, each person – seller and buyer – intends to pursue his or her own self interest. At the same time, as if directed by an "invisible hand" (in particular, without government intervention in individual market transactions), market participants unintentionally increase the material wealth of their nations. Of course, Adam Smith's arguments in favor of markets also favor competition.

Finally in 1776, the United States of America declared its independence from England. In other words, the USA was created at a time when the importance of free markets was already recognized. Moreover, the free market concepts of *laissez-faire* and *laissez-passer* did not encounter in the USA the resistance encountered by Baron Turgot in France (i.e., from trade guilds and landed aristocracy). In the USA, in the absence of a native aristocracy, the "natural order" – i.e., free markets – predominated, just as the physiocrats had explained. Accordingly, it should not be surprising that the USA took the lead as the first nation to enact legislation protecting free markets by adopting the Sherman Act in 1890.

RESTRAINTS ON TRADE

The United States and the European Union are the two leading jurisdictions regulating competition. The various states of the United States and, more importantly, the various member states of the European Union have their own competition law which applies to conduct within those states or member states.

The fundamental United States law (1890)

The United States law against agreements in restraint of trade is articulated in Section 1 of the Sherman Act (1890):[6]

> Every contract, combination in the form of a trust or otherwise, or conspiracy in restraint of trade or commerce among the several states, or foreign nations, is hereby declared to be illegal.
> (Section 1 of the Sherman Act (1890) (hereinafter, the "Sherman Act"))

A "contract … in restraint of trade or commerce" is any agreement which restricts or distorts the free negotiation of buyers with individual businesses in the purchase of goods and services. In other words, each business not only has the right to use its private property as it sees fit (as explained in Chapters 2 and 3). Pursuant to competition law, each business has the obligation to use its private property as it alone sees fit, without the benefit of agreements with competing businesses. Of course, the purpose of avoiding any restriction or distortion in free markets is, as explained earlier, to permit buyers to protect their legal rights and promote their other material interests while, at the same time, increasing the national wealth.

The fundamental European Union law (1957)

Following World War II, six countries in Europe formed the EEC, or "European Economic Communities" (France, Germany, Italy, The Netherlands, Belgium and Luxembourg). Based on the perceived success of the United States economy, and in reaction to the threat of communism from the former Soviet Union, the EEC adopted competition law as one of its fundamental legal principles. The fundamental importance attributed to competition law is indicated by the fact that:

1 EEC's competition law was incorporated into the constitutive treaty (The Treaty of Rome) in 1957; and
2 competition law and customs law were the only two areas of law for which the EEC claimed directive legislative and executive powers over the members states.[7]

Although the EEC has been transformed into the European Union (the "EU") with twenty-five member states, the original treaty provisions still apply and directly control the competition matters to which they apply:

[A]ll agreements between undertakings, decisions by associations of undertakings and concerted practices … [are prohibited if they] have as their object or effect the prevention, restriction or distortion of competition within the common market.
(Article 81(1) of The Treaty Establishing the European Community (consolidated text) O.J. 325 of 24.12.2002 (hereinafter, the "Treaty") (originally Article 85 (1) of the Treaty of Rome))

The "rule of reason"

Under the express terms of the fundamental US and EU statutes cited above, literally all agreements in restraint of trade are illegal. In other words, the legality of a restraint on trade is not determined by the facts and circumstances surrounding the agreement containing the restraint. Under the express terms cited above, a restraint on trade is illegal even if consumers obtain advantages from the restraint and even if those advantages outweigh the disadvantages to consumers.

In the early 1900s, the US courts and US Congress soon realized that it was necessary to determine whether consumers obtained any advantages from the restraint and, if so, to consider whether to permit the restraint of trade in those cases where the advantages to consumers arising out of the restraint were greater than the disadvantages to consumers.

In other words, a "rule of reason" was necessary. Pursuant to the rule of reason, all agreements in restraint of trade are prohibited (as provided in the Sherman Act) unless the advantages to consumers arising out of the restraint are greater than the disadvantages to consumers. If the advantages to consumers are greater than the disadvantages, then the agreement is legal even though it contains a restraint of trade.

The process of articulating such a rule in the USA has lasted for decades and continues even today. The European Union has benefited from the US experience to articulate a set of circumstances in which an agreement in restraint of trade would be permissible:

An agreement [in restraint of competition] is exempt from competition law if:

1 the agreement contributes to improving the production or distribution of goods, or promoting technical or economic progress, [and]
2 the agreement allows consumers a fair share of the resulting benefit, and
3 the agreement does not impose … restrictions which are not indispensable … , or afford … the possibility of eliminating competition.
(Article 81 (3) of the Treaty (originally Article 85 (3) of the Treaty of Rome))

In other words, if the advantages to consumers outweigh the necessary disadvantages, then an agreement in restraint of trade is permissible. The same rough calculus applies under both competition law in the United States of America and under competition law in the European Union.

Per se illegality

After giving due consideration to the "rule of reason," the authorities in the United States and Europe have determined that the advantages to consumers arising out of some agreements never outweigh the necessary disadvantages. All such agreements are "*per se*" illegal, i.e., prohibited without giving further consideration to any benefits obtained by consumers.

As with the "rule of reason," the United States developed its understanding that certain agreements were always illegal through a long series of executive actions, court cases and congressional enactments. Drawing in part on the United States' experience, the

Treaty provides a clear list of restraints on competition which are always impermissible:

(a) directly or indirectly fixing purchase or selling prices or any other trading conditions;
(b) limiting or controlling production, markets, technical development, or investment;
(c) sharing markets or sources of supply;
(d) applying dissimilar conditions to equivalent transactions;[8]
(e) making the conclusion of contracts subject to … supplementary obligations which … have no connection with … such contracts.[9]
(Article 81 (1) of the Treaty (originally Article 85 (1) of the Treaty of Rome))

The USA and EU classify as "*per se*" illegal virtually all of the same types of agreements in restraint of trade. In fact, all countries adopting competition laws have classified the same restraints of trade "*per se*" illegal. Accordingly, the practices above listed as illegal "*per se*" in the European Union (i.e., always impermissible under EU competition law) are also always impermissible in the United States and most other countries with competition laws. In other words, for all practical purposes, agreements amongst competitors to fix prices, rig bids, limit production or allocate customers are always illegal around the world.

HORIZONTAL RESTRAINTS ON TRADE

Competition law prohibits "agreements in restraint of trade." As explained in the next section, agreements with consumers, distributors and suppliers can constitute restraints of trade, i.e., vertical restraints. The common understanding of the term "restraints of trade" applies, however, to contracts between and among competitors within the scope of their competition, i.e., horizontal restraints.

Competing sellers violate the law when they substitute cooperation for competition in their dealings with buyers.[10] By substituting cooperation for competition, sellers eliminate real choice for buyers and discourage new sellers from entering markets. In this way, cooperation amongst sellers undermines both the national wealth and buyers' ability to promote their own interests, including the protection of their general and contract rights.

In fact, most forms of cooperation between and among competitors are *per se* violations of competition law, i.e., experience shows that most forms of competitor cooperation never benefit consumers and so are always illegal. In fact, most of the forms of cooperation listed as *per se* illegal under the Treaty are forms of cooperation amongst competitors. Such illegal cooperation includes agreements to fix prices, to rig bids, to limit production and to allocate customers. In each of these cases, cooperation by competitors eliminates buyers' choice without yielding any advantages for buyers.

Joint ventures with competitors

Experience shows that the advantages to consumers from some forms of horizontal restraints, i.e., some forms of cooperation by competitors, can outweigh the necessary disadvantages to buyers and therefore are permissible under a rule of reason – provided that they avoid unnecessary disadvantages to consumers.

Joint ventures are an excellent example of such cooperation between competitors. There are basically three forms of joint ventures: research, production and marketing.[11] Considering each of these forms under the rule of reason tends to yield slightly different results.

Using the factors outlined by the EU under the rule of reason, it appears that marketing joint ventures are least likely to "allow[s] consumers a fair share of the … benefit" resulting from the joint venture, i.e., consumers are least likely to gain significant advantages from marketing joint ventures. Marketing joint ventures can improve systems for the "distribution of goods," but they seem unlikely to share the benefits with consumers because marketing joint ventures tend to eliminate at least one choice for consumers in markets where each joint venturer is already independently active.[12]

Production joint ventures also offer potential benefits to consumers. They offer potential benefits by reducing the cost of producing an existing product. Rather than having each producer bear the costs and risks associated with independent production, joint producers can share facilities, thereby sharing fixed costs and risks. Production joint ventures are particularly advantageous where they can be used to avoid the construction of additional plant and equipment. At the same time, each of the production joint venturers is likely to share with consumers the benefits derived from reduced production costs because each of them competes independently with the other to sell the jointly-produced goods.

Finally, research joint ventures offer potential benefits to consumers. As with production joint ventures, they offer potential benefits through a reduction in cost, i.e., the costs and risks of researching and developing a new product. Research joint ventures are easiest to justify where the costs of researching and developing a new, potentially useful product would be prohibitive in the absence of the joint venture. As with production joint ventures, each of the research joint venturers is likely to share with consumers the benefits derived from reduced research costs because each of them competes independently with the other to produce and sell the jointly developed goods.

An important limitation on the formation of joint ventures by actual or potential competitors is the scope of cooperation. The scope of cooperation between (and among) the competitor(s) should be limited to the activities necessary to obtain the benefits for consumers. In other words, the joint venture should not "impose ... restrictions which are not indispensable" to the joint venture's purpose of researching a new product, making or marketing an existing product. For example, it may not be necessary for a production joint venture to obtain all of its raw materials from the joint venturers.[13]

VERTICAL RESTRAINTS ON TRADE

Unless a business is a monopoly (as discussed below), it is generally free to unilaterally choose the customers to whom it will sell its products. However, once a business has chosen to deal with a particular customer, the antitrust laws generally require a business to respect that customer's freedom to conduct its commercial policy as it sees fit. For example, a business may not control its customers' purchase of products from competitors or the price at which customers resell products. At the same time, experience has shown that the advantages to consumers from such controls sometimes outweigh their disadvantages. Accordingly, pursuant to the "rule of reason," vertical restraints – i.e., restrictions on consumers, distributors and suppliers – are sometimes permissible under competition law.

Restraints on consumers

For example, consumers often enter into long-term purchase arrangements with manufacturers, whereby the consumers agree to buy all – or a substantial portion – of their requirements for a specific product exclusively from a single manufacturer. Such long-term purchasing arrangements benefit consumers because they enable consumers to negotiate relatively fixed prices for future raw materials or services, thereby avoiding the risk of fluctuations in spot markets and enabling consumers to plan their businesses with more certainty. At the same time, having long-term sales arrangements allows selling manufacturers to plan their production with more certainty, enabling them to offer not only relatively stable prices but also relatively low prices.

Exclusive purchasing

At the same time, exclusive purchasing arrangements raise issues under competition law. They raise issues because the manufacturer's competitors are foreclosed (i.e., precluded or prevented) from making sales to the manufacturer's customers for the duration of the exclusive purchasing arrangement. Such foreclosure is a disadvantage, certainly to the manufacturer's competitors and even possibly to the manufacturer's customer. For example, the exclusive purchasing arrangements can be disadvantageous to the customer if the duration of the exclusive purchasing arrangement is longer than necessary in order for the customer to obtain the benefits in terms of relatively inexpensive supplies. Nonetheless, in the absence of an abuse of monopoly power by the selling manufacturer, such exclusive purchasing agreements are generally held to be permissible under competition law.[14]

Tying and full-line forcing

In addition to exclusive purchasing obligations, manufacturers sometimes attempt "tying" and "full-line forcing." "Tying" is a commercial practice whereby a manufacturer requires a consumer to purchase a second, unwanted product in order to obtain the product the consumer wants to purchase and use. "Full-line forcing" is a commercial practice whereby a manufacturer requires a consumer to purchase a full range of products in order to obtain the single (or few) product(s) the consumer wants to purchase and use. Unlike exclusive purchasing arrangements, there are typically no advantages to consumers in "tying" or "full-line forcing." At the same time, both practices constitute a restraint on trade by foreclosing competitors from making sales of the "tied" product or "forced" product lines. Accordingly, "tying" or "full-line forcing" are generally considered to be illegal *per se*.

Restraints on distributors

Long-term exclusive purchasing agreements tend to be ruled permissible under competition law because courts are not eager to review in hindsight determinations made by consumers at the time they enter into contracts. Courts are more active in reviewing vertical restraints under competition law when the purchaser is not the consumer but a distributor, i.e., a business buying goods from a manufacturer for the purpose of resale to business or individual consumers. Courts are more willing to intervene in distributorship arrangements in part because the consumer is not a party to the vertical restraints agreed between manufacturers and their distributors. The restrictions on long-term exclusive distributorship arrangements (nothing other than a special form of long-term purchasing agreement) are dictated by concerns for the ultimate consumer, the distributors' direct or indirect customer.

Exclusive purchasing

Manufacturers often enter into exclusive purchasing arrangements with their distributors. Under these arrangements, manufacturers prohibit their distributors from purchasing goods for resale from any competing manufacturers. These and similar restrictions are evaluated under the "rule of reason." They are permissible if the advantages to consumers – in this case, the distributors' customers – outweigh the disadvantages to those consumers.

"Interbrand competition" and "intrabrand competition" are important considerations in determining whether restrictions on distributors are permissible under the rule of reason. "Interbrand competition" refers to the availability to consumers at a single location of substitute goods from different manufacturers (e.g., the choice between Renault and Opel automobiles in Arnheim, The Netherlands). "Intrabrand competition" refers to the competing channels through which consumers in a single location can purchase a single manufacturer's goods (e.g., such as the availability of Renault automobiles at more than one dealer in Arnheim, The Netherlands).

Imposing exclusivity on distributors tends to reduce interbrand competition. Exclusive distributorships tend to reduce interbrand competition by foreclosing a distributor from dealing in competing goods, i.e., making a distributor unavailable as an outlet for more than one competing product. On the other hand, exclusive distributorships tend to increase interbrand competition by forcing each distributor to focus its marketing efforts on selling goods from a sole manufacturer. To the extent that consumers benefit from the exclusive distributorships more than they are disadvantaged (i.e., to the extent that interbrand competition is increased more than it is decreased), then exclusivity imposed by a manufacturer on its distributors is considered permissible under the rule of reason.

Territorial restrictions

In addition to exclusivity, manufacturers impose other restrictions on their distributors. Such other restrictions include limitations on the territories where distributors may conduct marketing activities, such as constructing warehouses, showrooms and sales offices.[15] Imposing territorial limitations on exclusive distributors tends to reduce intrabrand competition by making it more difficult for consumers to obtain products from more than one channel, i.e., from any distributor other than the distributor assigned to the territory where they are located. On the other hand, territorial limitations on distributors tend to increase interbrand competition by encouraging each distributor to focus its marketing efforts on selling products within its assigned territory while giving each distributor some assurances that it will not be subject to intrabrand competition from within its territory. To the extent that consumers benefit from the territorial limitations more than they are disadvantaged (i.e., roughly: to the extent that interbrand competition is increased more than intrabrand competition is decreased), then territorial limitations imposed by a manufacturer on its distributors' marketing activities are considered permissible under the rule of reason.

Resale price maintenance

In addition to exclusive purchasing and territorial restrictions, manufacturers also impose restrictions on the prices distributors may charge for the products they purchase for resale from the manufacturer. Such restrictions can be either minimum permissible prices or maximum permissible prices. It is generally agreed that maintaining minimum resale prices (i.e., a minimum price below which distributors are not permitted to resell a product) is illegal *per se*. Minimum resale price maintenance is illegal *per se* because it is generally agreed that the advantages to consumers never outweigh the disadvantages. Maintaining maximum resale prices, however, has recently become permissible in many cases because recently competition law authorities have recognized that setting maximum prices frequently increases interbrand competition without restricting intrabrand competition.[16]

Full-line forcing

Finally, in addition to restrictions, manufacturers impose obligations on their distributors. Such obligations can include the duty to purchase and carry minimum inventories, duties to maintain warehouses, a sales organization, after-sales service within the assigned territory and "full-line forcing".

The difference between permissible restraints on consumers and permissible restraints on distributors is most clearly illustrated by the differing position of "full-line forcing." While it is generally illegal for a manufacturer to force a consumer to purchase a full-line of the manufacturer's goods, it is generally legal for a manufacturer to force a distributor to purchase a full-line of the manufacturer's goods.

The reason for the different status of "full-line forcing" in the two circumstances is as follows: there is no benefit to the consumer (i.e., the manufacturer's direct customer) if it is forced to purchase a product which it does not want to use. There is a potential benefit to the consumer (i.e., the distributor's direct or indirect customer) if the distributor is forced to purchase and offer for resale goods the distributor does not want to offer for resale.

VERTICAL RESTRAINTS ON SUPPLIERS

Of course, all of the restraints on consumers and distributors, as outlined immediately above, are restraints imposed by suppliers of goods and services. At the same time, restraints imposed by consumers and distributors on suppliers are also subject to review under competition law.

Consumers' primary restriction on dealings with suppliers is to select suppliers and to establish terms and conditions for purchases without discussion or agreement with that supplier's others customers and potential customers.[17]Multilateral agreements not to deal with certain suppliers are called "group boycotts" and are similarly illegal *per se*.

More importantly, reciprocity agreements are *per se* illegal under competition law. Reciprocity agreements are conditions imposed by buyers on the purchase of goods or services. Pursuant to reciprocity agreements, buyers agree to make purchases only on the condition that the supplier purchases certain goods or services from the buyer.[18] Such reciprocity agreements are illegal *per se* because they make free market sales by the buyer's competitors to its suppliers subject to conditions other than price, quality and the terms of sales, i.e., conditions which the buyer's competitors cannot necessarily meet.[19]

OTHER POSSIBLE RESTRAINTS ON TRADE

Both US and EU competition laws outlaw forms of informal cooperation. The Sherman Act outlaws "conspiracy," while Article 85 of the Treaty prohibits "concerted practices" which have as their object or effect the prevention, restriction or distortion of competition.

Industry association activities, exchanges of commercial information, and other concerted activity between or among competitors can be a violation of the competition law even in the absence of a formal contract. In particular, simply discussing prices, general terms and conditions of sale, and profit margins can constitute violations of competition law. Accordingly, you should never discuss any of those topics with competitors.[20]

Verbal agreements

The US and EU competition authorities interpret very broadly the phrases "conspiracy" and "concerted practices." Certainly, impermissible agreements need not be embodied in a formal written agreement. Agreements can be established verbally and inferred from circumstances, such as a meeting followed by parallel actions.

For example, in the EU, it is not necessary for more than one party to accept restrictions. On the contrary, it is enough if two parties' agreement concerning cooperation benefits another business, not a party to the agreement. Therefore, if one distributor promises to a supplier not to sell in a second distributor's territory, then there is an "agreement" even though the second party is not a party to the agreement.

Concerted practices

It is important to understand that a violation of competition law, in either the EU or USA, does not even depend on the existence of an express written or oral agreement.[21] The existence of an unlawful agreement may be inferred from circumstantial evidence; i.e., from a combination of words and subsequent actions (e.g., a group of competitors attends a meeting at which representatives complain about low industry prices, after which meeting the companies represented at the meeting raise their prices).

In fact, when competitors speak or meet, they are presumed to be involved in sharing information or other impermissible activity.[22] Accordingly, if a business speaks or meets with one or more competitors, then the business has the burden of proof to establish that the conversation or meeting was limited to permissible topics and activities. In other words, you will have the burden of proving that there was *no* exchanging of impermissible information or other impermissible activity.

Since unlawful agreements, conspiracies and concerted practices can be inferred from circum-

stantial evidence, such as meetings and conversations with competitors followed by parallel price movements. Meetings and conversations with competitors should be avoided. If meetings and conversations cannot be avoided, then exchanges of information should be as limited as possible. In addition, the meetings or conversations should be carefully supervised and documented in reasonable detail.

Trade associations

As explained in Chapter 3, participation in industry and professional associations ("trade associations") is an important form of self-regulation. At the same time, trade association activities risk violating competition law if not properly supervised and documented. In general, trade associations are not permitted to serve as forums to discuss, to coordinate or to facilitate members' discussion or coordination of commercial terms (such as prices and product offerings).

Generally, trade associations are allowed to develop and promulgate codes of conduct and good practice guidelines, including standards-setting, statistical analysis, and benchmarking. For example, trade associations provide a lawful service by collecting and releasing aggregate information about an industry's past production and past pricing. In this regard, it may be legal for a trade association statistical program to include aggregated reports on members' past prices, production volume, operating costs, credit experience, labor statistics and inventories. A statistical reporting program is illegal, however, where it is used to promote or coerce concerted action on prices, production or other future commercial conduct.

Some trade associations also develop uniform performance standards or specifications that the members' products should meet. Such programs are legitimate where they have as their goals improving safety, upgrading or maintaining product quality, improving the substitutability of products or enhancing customers' ability to compare goods or the prices and other terms on which the goods are offered for sale. A standard-setting program is illegal, however, if it is used to fix prices, control production, boycott particular suppliers or exclude competitors.

MONOPOLIES

A monopoly is a business with a "dominant position" or "monopoly power" in the market in which it is active.[23] Having a dominant position or monopoly power does not mean the absence of competitors. Instead, it means that a business is in a position:

1 to have an "appreciable influence on the conditions" under which the relevant market will develop; and
2 to act largely in disregard of its competition.[24] Generally, having a dominant position or monopoly power requires a 40 percent or more share in the relevant market.[25]

Becoming or being a monopoly, in and of itself, is not a violation of competition law. In other words, obtaining or possessing a dominant position or monopoly power does not, in the absence of other actions, violate competition law in the EU or USA. A violation of competition law will be found only if the dominant position or monopoly power is created, maintained or extended[26] by means other than competition. For the purpose of this analysis, competition is the attempt to influence customer decisions through the quality of goods and services, prices and other terms of sale. Creating, maintaining or extending a dominant position or monopoly power is referred to as "monopolization" in the USA. The same actions are referred to as an "abuse of a dominant position" in the EU.[27]

"Natural monopolies" are markets in which consumers obtain unique benefits from having all goods or services supplied by a single company. As we will see later, networks (such as communications and transportation) are usually natural monopolies

A dominant position in a natural monopoly or any other market can be obtained by competing fairly with other suppliers or by undermining competition. Success in becoming the dominant supplier in a natural monopoly or in any other market does not violate competition law, provided that the dominant position is obtained by fair competition. It is a violation of competition law, however, to use methods other than fair competition to attempt to create a dominant position in a natural market or in any other market, without regard to whether the attempt is successful.

In natural monopolies, competition inevitably tends to eliminate all but one (or a few) of the competitors. Once established in a dominant position in a natural monopoly, businesses are not subject to effective competition, in part because of the benefits consumers necessarily obtain from having a single supplier and in part because of the difficulties necessarily encountered by potential competitors in establishing themselves in the natural market. Instead of being subject to regulation under competition law, dominant suppliers in a natural monopoly are exempted from competition law and subject to their own intrusive forms of government regulation specifically intended to address potential abuses on an industry-by-industry basis.

In markets other than natural monopolies, competition does not inevitably eliminate all competitors. In other markets, it is possible for effective competition to continue indefinitely. Nonetheless, like in natural markets, it is possible for one supplier to obtain a dominant position. Unlike natural monopolies, however, dominant suppliers in other markets can still be subject to effective competition even after they establish a dominant position. Dominant suppliers in markets other than natural monopolies are subject to continuing competition, at least potentially:

1 in part because consumers do not necessarily obtain benefits from having a single supplier; and
2 in part because potential competitors do not necessarily encounter significant difficulties.

There are basically three regulatory regimes for abuses of a dominant position:

1 prohibition of "monopolization," i.e., actions creating, maintaining or extending dominant positions by means other than competition;
2 prior notification of acquisitions tending to create, maintain or extend dominant positions; and
3 regulation of dominant suppliers in natural monopolies.

PROHIBITION OF MONOPOLIZATION

Businesses are tempted to use the same actions to undermine actual or potential competition both to create and maintain dominant positions in natural monopolies and in other markets. The USA, the EU and, increasingly, other governments around the world have enacted government regulation prohibiting such actions.

The fundamental US law (1890)

The US statute has been in place since 1890:

> Every person who shall monopolize, or attempt to monopolize, or combine or conspire with any other person or persons, to monopolize any part of the trade or commerce among the several States, or with foreign countries, shall be deemed guilty of a misdemeanor.
> (Section 2 of the Sherman Act)

Section 2 of the Sherman Act prohibits monopolization, attempts to monopolize, and conspiracies to monopolize. The offenses of monopolization and attempted monopolization may be committed by one company acting alone. Conspiracies to monopolize require complicity by two or more parties. The offense of attempted monopolization requires both intent to achieve monopoly power and the taking of some step toward achieving that end.

The fundamental EU law (1957)

As with "restraints of trade," the EU regulation of abuses of dominant positions is considered to be fundamental to the proper working of the common market in Europe. Accordingly, it also appears in the Treaty since 1957:

> Any abuse by one or more undertakings of a dominant position within the common market or in a substantial part of it shall be prohibited as incompatible with the common market in so far as it may affect trade between Member States.[28]
> (Article 82 of the Treaty (originally Article 86 of the Treaty of Rome))

Article 82 of the Treaty is substantially similar to Section 2 of the Sherman Act. Article 82 of the Treaty refers to "abuse of a dominant position" rather than monopolization. Both Article 82 of the Treaty and Section 2 of the Sherman Act make clear the offenses may be committed by one company acting alone or by complicity between two or more companies. Article 82 does not, however, deal with attempts to abuse a dominant position. It would appear, therefore, that there must be an actual effect on commerce within the EU in order to violate Article 82.

It is most important to note that any action by a company in a dominant position can constitute an abuse of a dominant position. For example, the practice of *building "patent fences"* is an abuse of dominant positions. Patent fences are a thicket of patents filed by one competitor to surround the core patents of another competitor. Each patent in the fence covers a different conceivable improvement in the competitor's core patent. With development of improvements on its core patent foreclosed, the "fenced-in" competitor has an incentive to license his core patent to the "fencing" competitor in exchange for access to the improvements. While building patent fences may be legal for competitors without a dominant position, patent fencing definitely subjects a dominant supplier to a claim of "abuse."

Specific abuses: "Refusals to deal"

Another practice perfectly legal for most companies but constituting an abuse of a dominant position is a "*refusal to deal.*" Suppliers are sometimes willing to forgo business because they prefer their leisure – or for any other reason. Refusals to deal are perfectly legal for suppliers not in a dominant position. After all, if suppliers in competitive markets refuse to deal with certain customers, then those customers can simply turn to alternative suppliers. Suppliers in a dominant position are not in the same position. In the absence of their goods or services, customers would have no alternatives and would be harmed. Accordingly, suppliers in a dominant position cannot refuse to deal with any customers.[29]

Abuses involving pricing

A common abuse of a dominant position is "*monopoly pricing.*" Monopoly pricing consists of charging all customers the same high price, i.e., a price in excess of the prices which would prevail in competitive markets. In fact, monopolists tend to limit production and compromise on quality in ways which would not be sustainable in competitive markets.[30]

Monopoly pricing is clearly an abuse of a dominant position. Other abuses are less clear. One such abuse is called "*predatory pricing*." Predatory pricing consists of pricing goods or services to some or all customers on the basis of marginal costs (and even below marginal prices), as opposed to a price above average costs.[31] The purpose of predatory pricing is eliminating competitors in the short run, thereby reducing competition. Predatory pricing causes antitrust concerns because it raises the possibility that, once weaker competitors have been eliminated, the dominant supplier will increase its prices to monopolistic levels. A single episode of predatory pricing cannot only eliminate actual competition. It can also discourage future competition as potential suppliers fear that the dominant supplier will again use predatory pricing.

Another form of abuse makes clear that dominant positions are not limited to markets with only one supplier. This form of abuse is "*price signaling*." Price signaling is a practice whereby a dominant supplier takes the lead in publicly announcing increases or decreases in its prices (or other changes in terms and conditions, including product offerings), with other suppliers in the same market making the same changes relatively promptly and in a relatively uniform manner. Such prompt and uniform responses by potentially competitive suppliers suggest that the market in which they operate is no longer subject to competitive forces. As you can imagine, such parallel action becomes more likely as there are fewer suppliers in a given market.[32]

PRE-ACQUISITION NOTIFICATION REQUIREMENTS

As noted earlier, it is permissible to create and maintain a dominant position through competition with alternative suppliers. It is not permissible to create or maintain a dominant position through any other means, such as refusals to deal, monopoly pricing, predatory pricing, tying and full-line forcing.

Acquiring competitors is another impermissible means for obtaining a dominant position. Mergers and acquisitions are subject to a "rule of reason." Business combinations can result in significant benefits for consumers, through resulting "synergies" – both in terms of reduced costs and in terms of improved quality in goods and services. In certain circumstances, acquisitions can clearly enhance competition.

On the other hand, acquisitions can significantly reduce the amount of competition, without the promise of any benefit to consumers. At the same time, acquisitions are virtually impossible to "unwind." In other words, it is virtually impossible for competition regulators to enforce an effective remedy if they prohibit an acquisition after it has been completed. As a result, in order to apply a "rule of reason" to acquisitions, the rule of reason must be applied before the acquisition is complete.

To this end, governments have adopted "pre-acquisition notification requirements" for mergers and acquisitions. Pursuant to these regulations, if the governments intend to oppose a notified acquisition, then they are required to do so before the acquisition is completed. To give the governments a reasonable opportunity to review notified acquisitions, pre-acquisition notification requirements typically require parties to an acquisition (i.e., the buyer and seller) to respect a specified "waiting period" before the acquisition is completed. The waiting periods tend to run from thirty to ninety days, in order to avoid unreasonable delays in completing acquisitions.

The Hart-Scott-Rodino Act in the USA

The United States was the first country to adopt a pre-merger notification requirement: The Hart-Scott-Rodino Antitrust Improvement Act of 1976 ("the Hart-Scott-Rodino Act"). It obligates an acquisition to be notified if the value of the acquired business exceeds $200 million. An acquisition must be notified also if:

1 the value of the acquired company exceeds $50 million; and
2 one of the parties to the acquisition (i.e., buyer or seller) has annual revenues or assets of over $100 million and the other party has annual revenues or assets of over $10 million.

Pursuant to the Hart-Scott-Rodino Act, the buyer and seller must separately submit various descriptive and quantitative information concerning themselves, the acquired business and the markets in which each of them operates. The US government (Federal Trade Commission) has thirty days after receiving the notifications from both buyer and seller in order to oppose the acquisition – or to request that the parties agree to conditions making the acquisition acceptable to the government. The US government also has the ability to request additional information at any time during the thirty day "waiting period" and to take the additional time reasonably necessary to consider that information.

It seems that the most important factor in approving an acquisition under the Hart-Scott-Rodino Act is the extent to which the acquisition will result in a concentration of market power in the relevant market. Of course, acquisitions of competitors will always result in the elimination of one supplier in the relevant market. The important question under the Hart-Scott-Rodino Act is the extent to which the buyer and seller have enhanced their market power.

In order to answer this question, the US government applies the Herfindahl-Hirschman Index ("HHI"). HHI attempts to quantify the monopolizing effect of an acquisition. The HHI is the sum of the squares of the percentage market shares of all of the suppliers in the relevant market. For the purpose of determining an acquisition's effect on competition, the HHI is calculated before the acquisition and after giving effect to the acquisition. For example, if there are four competing suppliers before an acquisition with, respectively, market shares of 30 percent, 30 percent, 20 percent and 20 percent, then the HHI before the acquisition equals 2,600 ($30^2 + 30^2 + 20^2 + 20^2 = 2,600$). If the third competitor acquires the fourth, then the HHI after the acquisition is 3,400 ($30^2 + 30^2 + 40^2 = 3,400$), an increase of 800 points in the HHI.

In order to interpret these results, it is necessary to consult a chart setting forth schematically the US government's attitudes towards increases in market concentrations pursuant to acquisitions. Such a chart is set forth as the last page of this chapter as Annex A. As you can see, the US government considers a market with a HHI index of 2,600 to be "highly concentrated." As a result, it is "likely" that the US government will "refuse" the acquisition because it increases the concentration in the relevant market by more than 100 HHI points.

Acquisitions in a market with more suppliers do not tend to raise issues pursuant to the HHI system. Assuming, for example, that there are ten suppliers in a relevant market and that each supplier holds a 10 percent market share, then the HHI index before the acquisition is 1,000 ($10^2 + 10^2 + 10^2 + 10^2 + 10^2 + 10^2 + 10^2$

$+ 10^2 + 10^2 + 10^2$). If one competitor acquires another, then the HII increases to 1,200 ($10^2 + 10^2 + 10^2 + 10^2 + 10^2 + 10^2 + 10^2 + 10^2 + 20^2$), an increase of 200. It would appear that the US government will "challenge" the merger, asking for explanations of its intention and effect, as well as – possibly – negotiating conditions for the government's acquiescence to the acquisition.

Prior notification of large acquisitions in the EU

In 1989, the European Union adopted its own prior notification requirement for large acquisitions. The EU's notification requirement has a very high threshold, leaving prior notification and review of all other acquisitions (even reasonably large ones) to review in each of the member states in which the buyer, seller or acquired businesses have assets or sales.[33]

Under the EU's regulation, prior notification is required if the acquisition involves assets or sales in any two or more member states. In order to require prior notification, three conditions must be met:

1   the combined worldwide sales revenue of the buying and selling groups of companies must be more than 5 billion Euros;
2   the combined EU-wide sales revenue of either the buying or selling group is more than 250 million; and
3   the buying group of companies and the selling group of companies each realizes at least one-third of its sales revenue in two different EU member states.

There is also an alternative formula if the buying and selling groups have sales revenues from more than two EU member states.[34]

REGULATION OF NATURAL MONOPOLIES

"Natural monopolies" are markets in which consumers benefit from having all goods or services supplied by a single company – and there is no way for consumers to obtain those benefits by having more than one supplier. There are no laws against becoming or remaining a dominant supplier in a natural monopoly. In fact, dominant suppliers in natural monopolies are beneficial to consumers.

In natural monopolies, competition inevitably tends to eliminate all but one (or a few) of the competitors. Once established in a dominant position in a natural monopoly, businesses are not subject to effective competition, in part because of the benefits consumers necessarily obtain from having a single supplier and in part because of the difficulties necessarily encountered by potential competitors in establishing themselves in the natural market. In the absence of effective competition, dominant suppliers in a natural monopoly are subject to intrusive government regulation.

Networks of all sorts

Networks of all sorts are the best example of a natural monopoly. Examples of such networks are telephones, railroads, shipping, trucking, airlines and utilities such as water, electricity and gas.[35] Each of these industries – or important parts of each of these industries – is essentially a network. Moreover, all of these networks – as with all networks generally – derive their value, at least in part, from the fact that they are monopolies. Finally, each of these monopolies is valuable, at least In part, because of the high start-up costs, which constitute a barrier to entry.[36]

The high cost of real choice in natural monopolies

As discussed in Chapter 3, natural monopolies do not afford consumers real choices, but providing choice in naturally monopolistic markets implies creating a second network. At the same time, creating a separate network often diminishes the advantages to consumers from the natural monopolies. In addition, creating a second network often entails high costs, greatly exceeding the benefit obtainable through consumer choice.[37]

The low value of information without real choice

Without real choices for consumers, information is also not a useful tool to enable consumers to protect their legal rights and to promote their other interests. Accordingly, again as explained in Chapter 3, govern-

ments have recourse to various sorts of more intrusive regulation of natural monopolies. In the case of natural monopolies, intrusive government regulation often takes the forms of controls over commercial policies. In general, it is common for governments to regulate the availability and prices of goods and services provided by natural monopolies. Examples include obligations on railroads and airlines to provide comprehensive services throughout a region (even to and from locations which are not profitable) and price schedules for railroads and airlines negotiated or reviewed with government authorities. Utilities such as water, gas and electricity, if they are not owned by government authorities, are usually subject to similar regulatory obligations and procedures regarding availability and pricing of goods and services.

Again, dominant firms in markets other than natural monopolies are not subject to this third basic form of monopolies regulation, i.e., industry-specific regulation of pricing, availability and other commercial policies. Dominant firms in markets other than natural monopolies are subject to "prohibitions on monopolization" (referred to as "abuses of dominant positions" in the EU), the second basic form of monopolies regulation. Microsoft is generally believed to have a monopoly in operating systems and to have obtained the monopoly by competitive means.[38] Some consider Boeing to be an example of a monopoly obtained primarily through competition.

THE EFFECTS DOCTRINE

Of course, business conduct outside of a country or group of countries (such as the USA or the EU) can affect trade within that country or group of countries. Accordingly, in order to be effective, the competition law of each place (e.g., the USA or EU) needs to reach business conduct outside its borders if that conduct has an appreciable effect on competitive conditions within its borders.

The "effects doctrine" is the legal principle whereby each country or group of countries asserts jurisdiction over business conduct outside of its borders. Under the "effects doctrine," a business is subject to the competition laws of a country or group of countries in which that business has assets or makes sales. The only important question is whether the amount of assets in the country or group of countries seeking to apply the "effects doctrine" – or, more frequently, the amount of sales into that place – is sufficient for the business's conduct abroad to have an appreciable effect there.

The "effects doctrine" rule is justified because the consumers within each country or group of countries are the persons intended to benefit from competition law.

ANNEX A

Herfindahl-Hirschman Index

HHI	Government characterization	Government challenge
Under 1000	"Unconcentrated"	Unlikely
1000–1800	"Moderately concentrated"	Likely to be challenged if the deal increases HHI over 100 points
Over 1800	"Highly concentrated"	Likely to be challenged if the deal increases HHI 50 to 100 points
		Likely to be refused if the deal increases HHI over 100 points

8

Relationships with Consumers

Consumer protection

INTRODUCTION

There are important differences between commercial transactions (i.e., merchant-to-merchant sales of goods and services) and consumer transactions (i.e., merchant-to-consumer sale of goods and services), especially consumer transactions in mass markets.

First of all, commercial transactions tend to be negotiated, while consumer transactions are not subject to negotiation. Second, in commercial transactions, both seller and buyer are experts. In consumer transactions, only the seller is an expert. Third, in commercial transactions, a small abuse by a seller in commercial transaction tends to lead to relatively small abuses for buyers, both individually and in the aggregate, primarily because the number of transactions is relatively limited. In consumer transactions, a small abuse by a seller leads to small abuses for individual buyers but significant abuses of all buyers in the aggregate, in part because the number of transactions is relatively great. Fourth, buyers in commercial markets tend to be better informed about sellers' practices (because the communities of buyers are relatively small). Buyers in mass consumer markets tend to be less informed about sellers' practices (because the community of buyers is relatively large).[1]

At the same time, at the beginning of the 1900s, consumer transactions were regulated primarily by contract and commercial law, the laws developed and applicable to commercial transactions. Government regulation has been developed to address the differences between commercial transactions and consumer transactions. In other words, government regulations have been developed to the extent that contract and commercial law have been inadequate to prevent harm to consumers' economic and other personal interests, including their rights to freedom from personal injury and property damage. In addition, government agencies have been created to enforce these laws and even to facilitate communication and coordination amongst consumers.

All three levels of government regulation as identified in Chapter 3 – competition, disclosure obligations and quality controls – play a role in consumer protection. At the same time, disclosure obligations play the predominant role. I have chosen to present relationships with consumers as the second relationship important to senior management – relationships with competitors was the first important relationship – because consumer relations are an important example of the second level of government regulation: disclosure obligations. In consumer markets, real choice – as protected by competition law – has sometimes been insufficient to prevent certain types of harm to buyers. Real choice coupled with disclosure obligations – in other words "the right to know" – often has proven to be sufficient to enable consumers to protect themselves from personal harm, including physical injury and economic loss.

"THE RIGHT TO KNOW"

Before outlining consumer relationships, I would like to discuss briefly the context for the "right to know." I want to discuss the right to know because it provides the justification for disclosure obligations, an important aspect of consumer protection regulations, as well as government regulation of other important business relationships.

The corporate context

The decision-making process commonly used in corporations does not involve all affected parties in the decision-making process. Affected parties (even shareholders) are not usually consulted or given information as an integral part of corporate routines. Instead, affected parties' interests are identified and evaluated entirely by corporate decision-makers.

For example, in the Ford Pinto Case, discussed in Chapter 1, Ford did not inform Pinto purchasers about its decision to manufacture the Pinto without redesigning the gas tank. (In fact, as mentioned in Chapter 1, it probably would not be commercially feasible for Ford to make such a disclosure.)[2]

The moral context

"The right to know" is generally accepted to be an individual right implicit in freedom of choice, including the freedom of contract: If one person lies to another person in connection with a choice to be made by that other person, then the person telling the lie effectively denies that other person his freedom of choice. In other words, manipulating another person's decisions by telling lies violates that other person's individual rights. The same reasoning can be applied to keeping secrets.[3]

Accordingly, moral philosophers generally argue that individuals with all relevant information are morally responsible for their decisions. Moreover, philosophers generally argue that those who misrepresent relevant information to decision-makers (or withhold that information from them) are morally accountable for the decisions to the extent that the misrepresentation (or concealment) alters the decision.[4]

Viewed entirely from this perspective, in the Ford Pinto Case, moral philosophers would argue that the individuals who purchased and operated the Pinto with an undisclosed, potentially lethal defect in the gas tank would *not* be morally responsible for injuries caused by the defect. Instead, they would argue that Ford Motor Company (or, at least the individual manager(s) responsible for Ford's decision) is morally responsible for those injuries.

The economic context

Access to all relevant information is a fundamental assumption in establishing that market transactions are economically efficient.[5] Conversely, those who withhold relevant information are impeding the markets' work in efficiently allocating scare resources and maximizing economic returns. Consistent with this reasoning, market economists would tend to argue that Ford undermined market mechanisms by failing to disclose or eliminate the design defect in the Pinto gas tank. The risk of personal injury resulting from the defective gas tank was, in effect, a hidden cost which prevented Pinto purchasers from making rational decisions.[6]

Even though complete information is necessary for efficient markets, it is not necessarily true that complete information is freely available as an integral part of market activities.[7] On the contrary, information available to some market players is frequently not available to others, or information is available at different costs. Moreover, the availability and cost of information can vary from market to market. Consumer markets are arguably markets where information about sellers (e.g., the quality of different sellers' products and services and the honesty in their business practices) is not readily available to buyers as an integral part of their market activities.

It is important to note that the "right to know" tends to favor buyers more than it favors sellers in consumer transactions. Consumers and businesses are in very different positions regarding the possession of relevant information and the need to discover it. In addition to information provided by individual sellers in market transactions (such as price), consumers often need information possessed by sellers in order to make sound decisions concerning the goods and services they purchase. Businesses do not need such information because the value of money – the property the consumers typically propose to exchange for businesses' goods and services – is apparent and unambiguous.

The contract and commercial context

Under general principles of contract and commercial law applicable in most countries, sellers of goods and services are legally liable for any misrepresentations they make to buyers. This general rule of contract and commercial law is applicable to and protects purchasers of goods and services, including both merchants and consumers. This general rule of contract and commercial law is also consistent with the moral and economic justifications for the "right to know."

Under general concepts of contract and commercial law, however, sellers are not legally liable for any secrets they keep from buyers.[8] Sellers are not generally liable for their secrets in spite of the moral and economic arguments in favor of such a rule of law. In other words, under general principles of contract and commercial law, businesses are responsible for lies but not for secrets; and no purchasers – neither merchants nor consumers – have a "right to know." If buyers consider certain information to be material for their decisions, then they must request that information. If the buyers do not receive the information, then their only recourse is to decline to purchase the goods or services.

Under these principles, Ford would not be liable to all Pinto purchasers simply because Ford did not disclose the defect to them. Ford is legally liable only to those purchasers (and others) who suffered personal injury or property damage as a result of the undisclosed defect.[9]

Consumer context

Governments often go beyond the established principles of contract and commercial law by giving consumers a "right to know," i.e., by requiring businesses to disclose all relevant information to consumers. Under these government regulations, businesses are responsible for both lies and secrets. In other words, consumers have a "right to know" even if they do not ask for all material information. Such regulatory disclosure obligations are considered justified in part because consumers do not have opportunities to negotiate for relevant information from businesses. In such circumstances, too frequently consumers do not receive the information necessary for them to make choices which effectively protect their legal rights and promote their other interests.

Governments rely on the "right to know" (i.e., governments impose disclosure obligations) partly because governments prefer *not* to interfere in corporate decision-making. Governments prefer to rely on the "right to know" also because the "right to know"

as a regulatory mechanism is very flexible: it enables individual consumers to determine the value they assign to specific risks and rights and to protect their individual rights and other interests as they see fit. In addition, governments prefer to rely on the "right to know" because it is a relatively inexpensive, unobtrusive, non-invasive form of government regulation.

FAIR DEALING – IN GENERAL

"Fair dealing" is a central concept in respect of consumer relationships. It is broad enough to incorporate both:

1 competition law;[10] and
2 disclosure obligations imposed pursuant to the right to know.

As we will see, "fair dealing" also addresses:

3 contract issues in consumer transactions.

Where fair dealing does not protect consumers from personal injury and property damage, legislatures have little alternative but to adopt:

4 more intrusive legislation protecting consumer health and safety.

We considered issues of competition law in the last chapter. The other aspects of "fair dealing" and "consumer protection" are discussed below.

The fundamental US law (1914)

Section 5 of the FTC Act (1914) creates a government agency, "The Federal Trade Commission" (or "FTC"), charged with preventing unfair and deceptive practices affecting commerce – in particular such practices detrimental to consumers.

The [US Federal Trade] Commission is hereby empowered and directed to prevent persons, partnerships, or corporations … from using … unfair or deceptive acts or practices in or affecting commerce.

(Federal Trade Commission Act, Section 5 (15 USC Section 45(a)), enacted in 1914, as amended by Wheeler-Lee Amendment in 1938)[11]

The FTC is broadly charged to prevent unfair and deceptive practices likely to prompt consumers to act to their own detriment. In fact, most of these practices have concerned misleading advertising and unfair consumer contracts. The broad powers granted to the agency are an important element of the regulatory scheme. As you can see, the express terms of the statute provide nothing more than very broad goals and purposes. The statute defers to and relies upon the FTC to adopt specific rules and to take appropriate action to enforce those rules. As discussed in Chapter 3, the broad powers granted to the FTC are similar to the broad powers granted to other government agencies pursuant to other forms of government regulation. While the scope of government regulation tends to be set in statutes, the specific content of the regulations and the responsibility for enforcing them rests with the government agencies.

The fundamental EU law (1999)

As we saw in Chapter 7, competition law is a fundamental legal principle in the European Union and accordingly is incorporated into the Treaty Establishing the European Community (the "Treaty"). Similarly, consumer protection is incorporated into the Treaty. Unlike competition law, however, consumer protection was *not* recognized as a fundamental community principle at the Union's inception in 1957. The provision concerning consumer protection was incorporated into the Treaty effective 1 May 1999:

> In order to promote the interests of consumers and to ensure a high level of consumer protection, the Community shall contribute to protecting the health, safety and economic interests of consumers, as well as to promoting their right to information, education and to organize themselves in order to safeguard their interests.
> (Treaty Establishing the European Community. Title XIV Consumer Protection, Article 153 (1))[12]
> (Text added by the Treaty of Amsterdam, effective 1 May 1999)

The European Union established its Health and Consumer Protection Directorate General in 1995 (on the basis of a previous Treaty provision). As with the FTC in the USA, the EU's Health and Consumer Protection Directorate General has broad powers, commensurate to those of the FTC in the United States. For example, the Commission Directorate has the power, pursuant to the Treaty, to fund consumer protection groups within the European Union – and the Directorate regularly does so.[13] The Directorate's power will only increase as the Union shifts from a diplomatic institution, representing separate nations, to a democratic institution, representing the peoples of those various nations.

FAIR DEALING – DISCLOSURE OBLIGATIONS

Disclosure obligations in dealings with consumers are, of course, governmental attempts, in the absence of negotiation between businesses and individual consumers, to give consumers information adequate to protect their general legal rights and to promote their other interests. The disclosure obligations prevent businesses both from telling lies to consumers and from keeping secrets from consumers.

The attempts to prevent lies take the form of government regulation of deceptive practices, including misleading advertisements. In Europe, until very recently comparative advertising was considered a form of advertisement fraught with potential for deception and accordingly was largely prohibited or strictly regulated. In the USA, on the contrary, regulators have encouraged comparative advertising.

The attempts to prevent secrets take the form of labeling requirements for goods and services. Disclosure requirements in respect of consumer financial services, such as mortgage lending and franchising, take a form more extensive than labels on containers. Still, disclosure requirements in respect of consumer financial services have the same goal as product labeling: preventing businesses from keeping secrets.

Deceptive practices

As explained above, sellers in commercial transactions are not allowed to lie but generally are allowed to keep secrets. With specific exceptions, merchants are left to negotiate for the information they consider necessary in connection with their purchases. If merchants do not receive such information, their remedy is simply to find an alternative supplier or forgo the purchase.

In modern mass consumer markets, consumers do not have the opportunity to negotiate for information. In the absence of an opportunity to negotiate, governments have imposed disclosure obligations on businesses supplying goods and services to consumers. In fact, eliminating "deceptive practices" has been an essential element of government regulation of consumer relations since the inception of such regulation.

As noted above, the FTC is charged to prevent deceptive practices. As identified by the FTC, such deceptive practices include:

1 false oral or written representations about a product or service;
2 misleading price claims;
3 sales of hazardous or systematically defective products or services without adequate disclosures;
4 use of "bait and switch" schemes; and
5 failure to perform promised services and systematic failure to meet warranty obligations.[14]

As you can see, all of these practices involve some form of deception. The use of "bait and switch techniques" is a good illustration of the deceptive practices regulated by the FTC. In a "bait and switch scheme," businesses advertise (or "bait") a certain product or service at a low price. Enticed by the advertisement of a low price, consumers travel to the business location for the purpose of buying the product or service. When consumers arrive at the business location, they discover that the business no longer has any of the advertised product or service available for sale. A "bait and switch scheme" is a good example of deceptive practices because:

1 it shows how the deception is used together with transaction costs to induce consumers to make purchases (e.g., the time and cost of traveling to and from a business location); and
2 a relatively small transaction cost for consumers can result in large gains for businesses.

As with the FTC in the United States, the Directorate General of Consumer Affairs is charged generally with "fair dealing."[15] There is a wide divergence among European countries in their approaches to dealing with the issues of fair dealing between businesses and consumers.[16] As a result, there is currently considerable debate in the European Union as to the scope of future regulation in this area.[17] At the same time, there is a consensus within the Union that "misleading and deceptive practices" are at the core of fair dealing with consumers.[18]

Misleading advertising

Misleading advertising is prohibited within the EU. Comparative advertising is permitted but subject to regulation.[19] Misleading advertising can be defined as any advertising which in any way, including its presentation, deceives or is likely to deceive persons and which, by reason of its deceptive nature, is likely to affect economic behavior or which, for those reasons, "injures or is likely to injure a [consumer]."[20]

Misleading advertising is also prohibited in the USA. In dealing with misleading advertising, the FTC focuses on whether advertisers and advertising agencies have a "reasonable basis" to substantiate claims made in advertisements.[21] Although the terms of reference are quite different between the EU and the USA, both specifically attempt to prevent misleading advertising.

Comparative advertising

Comparative advertising is any form of advertising which, explicitly or implicitly, identifies a competitor or goods or services offered by a competitor. On 16 September 1998, the European Council adopted the Directive on Comparative Advertising, effective May 2000, requiring harmonization of the national legislation on comparative advertising. Prior to the adoption of the Directive, most European countries effectively prohibited or severely restricted comparative advertising on the grounds that it constitutes unfair competition. Accordingly, the adoption of the Directive on Comparative Advertising constitutes a significant liberalization of European laws and eliminates a substantial barrier to trade within Europe. Still, several restrictions apply to the use of comparative advertising in Europe, including the requirement that it "objectively compares" features which are "material, relevant and verifiable."[22]

In the United States, the situation on comparative advertising has been quite different. While most

European countries have traditionally taken a restrictive stance against comparative advertising (subject, as explained above, to recent relaxation pursuant to an EU Directive), the United States regulators have a long-standing policy in favor of comparative advertising:

> [FTC] policy in the area of comparative advertising encourages the naming of, or reference to competitors, but requires clarity, and, if necessary, disclosure to avoid deception of the consumer. ... Comparative advertising, when truthful and non-deceptive, is a source of important information to consumers and assists them in making rational purchase decisions. Comparative advertising encourages product improvement and innovation, and can lead to lower prices in the marketplace.
>
> (13 August 1979 FTC Statement of Policy regarding Comparative Advertising)

In other words, the FTC encourages comparative advertising provided that it is truthful and substantiated to the same extent as any other advertising. In fact, the FTC carefully scrutinizes any industry or professional associations' guidelines which intentionally or effectively attempt to limit comparative advertising.[23]

Labeling and no secrets

In the United States and in Europe, foods, drugs, medicines, cosmetics and other products and services must have labeling or packaging that discloses information (such as ingredients, shelf-life, hazards, and instructions for transportation, storage, use, care and disposal). The purpose of all of these labeling requirements is to require businesses to supply consumers with the information necessary to prevent personal injury and property damage and otherwise to obtain the promised value of goods and services.

The various labeling requirements are typically administered by various government agencies, each one responsible for the goods or services from a particular industry. As a result, it would be impossible and, ultimately, not useful to list all such labeling requirements. At the same time, these various requirements clearly play an important role in terms of consumer protection.

Viewed from the perspective of the "right to know," these innumerable labeling requirements are the best example of the principle that, in consumer relationships, businesses cannot keep secrets. In other words, the various labeling regulations require businesses to disclose information government regulators believe is relevant to consumers purchasing and using the labeled products and services.

Trade associations (industry and professional) are excellent sources for beginning to learn about the labeling requirements applicable to various goods and services.

Franchises and financial services

Franchises and other financial services have also given rise to government regulations intended to ensure – like the labeling requirements just discussed – that there are "no secrets" in consumer transactions.[24]

Experience shows that consumers often do not understand the essential elements of franchising, mortgage lending and other financial services. Too frequently, individuals have entered into such arrangements on terms which, in retrospect, were not well understood and became unbearably burdensome.

In response, consumer protection regulation has required that the essential terms of the mortgage lending, franchising and other consumer financial services be disclosed simply, completely and accurately. In mortgage transactions, for example, the total amount borrowed, the total amount to be repaid and the effective interest rate must be disclosed simply and clearly. In franchise arrangements, the franchisees' many continuing obligations to the franchisor must be stated simply and clearly: These obligations can include:

1 trademark licenses;
2 continuing full-line purchase obligations; and
3 compliance with franchisor standards for maintenance of facilities and the many different aspects of business operations.

The disclosure requirements in respect of consumer financial services (such as mortgage lending and financial services) are very similar to disclosure obligations in respect of securities laws. Indeed, as we will see in a later chapter, securities regulation probably has more in common with consumer protection regulation than with corporate law.

FAIR DEALING – REASONABLE CONTRACTS

Enabling consumers to protect themselves also involves a further level of regulation, beyond disclosure obligations. Even if a business did not tell any lies or keep any secrets in connection with a consumer transaction, it often occurs that the transaction was not understood and agreed by the consumer. Consumer protection regulation will intervene, pursuant to the principle of "fair dealing," to enable consumers to avoid unreasonably burdensome contract provisions.

Government regulators reason that, if consumer contracts contain unreasonably burdensome provisions, then the consumers either:

1 did not understand the provisions; or
2 did not effectively agree to them.

In either case, consumers can avoid the unreasonable contract terms and, in some cases, even the entire contract. At the same time, the business can be subject to sanctions under consumer protection regulations including fines and suspension of operations.

At the European Union, the applicable directive – quoted below – asserts that consumer contracts can be "unfair" because they are not really negotiated.[25] In other words, there is in fact no agreement on the many or most contract terms in a consumer transaction.

A contractual term which has not been individually negotiated shall be regarded as unfair if, contrary to the requirement of good faith, it causes a significant imbalance in the parties' rights and obligations arising under the contract, to detriment of the consumer. … Where any seller or supplier claims that a standard term has been individually negotiated, the burden of proof in this respect shall be incumbent upon him. A term shall always be regarded as not individually negotiated where it has been drafted in advance and the consumer has therefore not been able to influence the substance of the term, particularly in the context of a pre-formulated standard contract.

(Article 3 (1) and (2) of Council Directive 93/13/EEC of 5 April 1993 on unfair terms in consumer contracts)

The principle that contracts with consumers are not negotiated and therefore contain "unfair" provisions is primarily applicable to incidental elements of the contract – those elements in addition to price and product quality which may not have captured a consumer's attention in the sales transaction.[26] For example, the potentially unfair contract provisions identified by the Commission of the European Union include:

1 limitations on the business's potential liability;
2 limitations on the consumer's remedies; and
3 penalties imposed on consumers for failure to perform their obligations under the contract.[27] For

The USA has its own concept of "unfair" contract terms. As in the EU, the concept of "unfair" contracts applies where sales terms are not actually negotiated (i.e., understood and agreed by the consumer). In the absence of an agreement in fact, the FTC will intervene to assist consumers in avoiding unduly burdensome contract provisions.[28]

[For the FTC] to justify a finding of unfairness the injury must satisfy three tests: [(1) The injury to consumers] must be substantial; [(2) the injury] must not be outweighed by any countervailing benefits to consumers or competition that the practice produces; and [(3)] it must be an injury that consumers themselves could not reasonably have avoided.

(17 December 1980 FTC Policy Statement on Unfairness)

Under FTC policy, in most cases a substantial injury involves some sort of monetary harm, as when sellers coerce consumers into purchasing unwanted goods or services or when consumers buy defective goods or services on credit but are unable to assert against the creditor claims or defenses arising from the transaction. The FTC also attempts to determine whether the consumer was subject to overt coercion, as by allowing a repairman to dismantle a home appliance for "inspection" and then having him or her refuse to reassemble it until a service contract is signed. Another example of such an abuse is exploiting particularly susceptible classes of purchasers, e.g., by promoting fraudulent "cures" to seriously ill cancer patients. Unwarranted health and safety risks may also support a finding of unfairness.[29]

QUALITY STANDARDS – CONSUMER HEALTH AND SAFETY

The previous material shows how government regulation attempts to provide consumer protection by buttressing consumers' economic rights: If consumers are offered accurate and complete information and reasonable contract terms (especially in respect of the many terms incidental to their purchases of goods and services), then, even in the absence of negotiation, consumers are often enabled to protect themselves over a broad range of issues through the real choices provided by competitive markets.

If the government concludes, on the basis of experience, that regulations enhancing consumers' economic rights are not effective in allowing consumers to protect their general legal rights and to promote their other interests, then governments can and do impose other obligations on businesses dealing with consumers.

These further governmental regulations generally take the form of quality standards such as:

1 minimum educational requirements and professional licensing for suppliers;
2 standards for business procedures and practices of all sorts;
3 specifications for goods and services; or
4 any combination of the foregoing quality standards, all prescribed in a relatively detailed fashion.

Governments attempt to enforce these various quality standards by licensing, by inspections, by reviews and by approvals of final products, all on a relatively regular basis. For example, governments have imposed such quality standards on industries such as utilities, pharmaceuticals, food, building construction and the professions (e.g., architects, accountants, doctors and lawyers). Such regulatory schemes tend to be the least flexible and the most expensive, obtrusive and invasive form of regulation.

Governments typically impose the more intrusive quality standards in those instances where consumers' health and safety are at risk. Medicines are a good example. While the governmental regulation for dispensing medicines varies from country to country, there is a general consensus that some medicines can be purchased directly by consumers in stores simply with the proper labeling (i.e., complete disclosures of relevant information concerning the medicine from the consumer's perspective). Other medicines can be dispensed only with a doctor's authorization and only by a pharmacist. Dispensing by a pharmacist with a doctor's authorization is justified in part because labeling would be considered inadequate to secure the benefit of such medicines for consumers while protecting them from potential harm.

As with labeling requirements, the many government regulations imposing quality standards are too numerous to list usefully. Trade associations are again a good place to begin to understand the many governmental quality controls applicable to various goods and services.

A REMINDER ABOUT TORTS

If businesses make accurate and complete disclosures to consumers, as required under government regulation; if businesses enter into consumer contracts containing only reasonable terms; and if businesses comply with any and all applicable quality standards, then they can be exonerated from "legal liability" for personal injury or property damage suffered by the consumers using or exposed to their products. In other words, consumers can be deemed to have "assumed the risk" for their own conduct by virtue of a business's accurate and complete disclosures.

At the same time, businesses are not necessarily exonerated from liability to consumers under the law of general obligations (i.e., potential tort liability) by complying with all applicable consumer protection regulations. In other words, consumers are not necessarily deemed to have "assumed the risk."[30] As explained in Chapter 5, the law of general obligations (i.e., torts) giving rise to judicial remedies is an area of law separate and apart from government regulation. While compliance with government regulations can be a factor in determining legal liability under the law of general obligations, compliance with government regulations is not the sole and decisive factor.

The relationship between government regulations and general obligations will be discussed more closely in my chapter on general obligations.

ANNEX

EU COUNCIL DIRECTIVE 93/13/EEC

Terms referred to in Article 3(3)

"Unfair terms in consumer contracts"

(a) excluding or limiting the legal liability of a seller or supplier in the event of the death of a consumer or personal injury to the latter resulting from an act or omission of that seller or supplier;

(b) inappropriately excluding or limiting the legal rights of the consumer *vis-à-vis* the seller or supplier or another party in the event of total or partial non-performance or inadequate performance by the seller or supplier of any of the contractual obligations, including the option of offsetting a debt owed to the seller or supplier against any claim which the consumer may have against him;

(c) making an agreement binding on the consumer whereas provision of services by the seller or supplier is subject to a condition whose realization depends on his own will alone;

(d) permitting the seller or supplier to retain sums paid by the consumer where the latter decides not to conclude or perform the contract, without providing for the consumer to receive compensation of an equivalent amount from the seller or supplier where the latter is the party canceling the contract;

(e) requiring any consumer who fails to fulfill his obligation to pay a disproportionately high sum in compensation;

(f) authorizing the seller or supplier to dissolve the contract on a discretionary basis where the same facility is not granted to the consumer, or permitting the seller or supplier to retain the sums paid for services not yet supplied by him where it is the seller or supplier himself who dissolves the contract;

(g) enabling the seller or supplier to terminate a contract of indeterminate duration without reasonable notice except where there are serious grounds for doing so;

(h) automatically extending a contract of fixed duration where the consumer does not indicate otherwise, when the deadline fixed for the consumer to express this desire not to extend the contract is unreasonably early;

(i) irrevocably binding the consumer to terms with which he had no real opportunity of becoming acquainted before the conclusion of the contract;

(j) enabling the seller or supplier to alter the terms of the contract unilaterally without a valid reason which is specified in the contract;

(k) enabling the seller or supplier to alter unilaterally without a valid reason any characteristics of the product or service to be provided;

(l) providing for the price of goods to be determined at the time of delivery or allowing a seller of goods or supplier of services to increase their price without in both cases giving the consumer the corresponding right to cancel the contract if the final price is too high in relation to the price agreed when the contract was concluded;

(m) giving the seller or supplier the right to determine whether the goods or services supplied are in conformity with the contract, or giving him the exclusive right to interpret any term of the contract;

(n) limiting the seller's or supplier's obligation to respect commitments undertaken by his agents or making his commitments subject to compliance with a particular formality;

(o) obliging the consumer to fulfill all his obligations where the seller or supplier does not perform his;

(p) giving the seller or supplier the possibility of transferring his rights and obligations under the contract, where this may serve to reduce the guarantees for the consumer, without the latter's agreement;

(q) excluding or hindering the consumer's right to take legal action or exercise any other legal remedy, particularly by requiring the consumer to take disputes exclusively to arbitration not covered by legal provisions, unduly restricting the evidence available to him or imposing on him a burden of proof which, according to the applicable law, should lie with another party to the contract.

2. Scope of subparagraphs (g), (j) and (l):

(a) Subparagraph (g) is without hindrance to terms by which a supplier of financial services reserves the right to terminate unilaterally a contract of indeterminate duration without notice where there is a valid reason, provided that the supplier is required to inform the other contracting party or parties thereof immediately.

(b) Subparagraph (j) is without hindrance to terms under which a supplier of financial services reserves the right to alter the rate of interest payable by the consumer or due to the latter, or the amount of other charges for financial services without notice where there is a valid reason, provided that the supplier is required to inform the other contracting party or parties thereof at the earliest opportunity and that the latter are free to dissolve the contract immediately.

Subparagraph (j) is also without hindrance to terms under which a seller or supplier reserves the right to alter unilaterally the conditions of a contract of indeterminate duration, provided that he is required to inform the consumer with reasonable notice and that the consumer is free to dissolve the contract.

(c) Subparagraphs (g), (j) and (l) do not apply to: – transactions in transferable securities, financial instruments and other products or services where the price is linked to fluctuations in a stock exchange quotation or index or a financial market rate that the seller or supplier does not control; – contracts for the purchase or sale of foreign currency, traveler's cheques or international money orders denominated in foreign currency;

(d) Subparagraph (l) is without hindrance to price-indexation clauses, where lawful, provided that the method by which prices vary is explicitly described.

9

Relationships with Local Communities

Environmental law

INTRODUCTION

Chapter 7 introduced you to competition law, obviously an important topic in a business's relationship with its competitors. Chapter 8 introduced you to disclosure and other fair dealing obligations, an important topic in a business's relationship with consumers.

This chapter introduces you to environmental law – both toxic tort and environmental regulation – an important topic in a business's relationship with the communities where it operates. Environmental law is also a good example of the third (and last) level of government regulation: intrusive intervention of all sorts in business operations to prevent personal injury and property damage. (The first two types of government regulation are competition law and disclosure obligations.)

Pollution

An unintended consequence of industrialization

Economic development usually entails changes in the environment. For example, even building a house or road changes the place where the house or road is built. With the industrial revolution came steam engines, internal combustion and electricity. They provided the power to develop the economy more quickly and the power to change the environment more drastically.

The industrial revolution began in England in the 1830s and spread first to Europe and the United States, becoming well established in those places before World War I. By the beginning of the twentieth century, businesses located in countries around the North Atlantic had learned to extract tremendous material wealth from the earth's natural resources but were unaware of the unintended consequences of those economic activities. They gave little consideration, for example, to the impact of building the railroad on coal and iron ore supplies or on the contamination of air, water and public lands. In the United States, farmers and foresters gave little consideration to the impact of clearing land on forest depletion and on soil erosion by wind and water.

After World War II, businesses gave little consideration to the impact on the environment (air, water and soil) of pesticides, herbicides, fertilizers, heavy metals and the waste produced from the manufacture of plastics and other synthetic chemicals. Environmental degradation increased with the spread of a consumer-oriented economy in more and more developed and developing countries.

By the end of the twentieth century, the industrial revolution had expanded to every continent on earth, accompanied by a spread in consumer society and, especially in developing and underdeveloped countries, by a population explosion. The general public, governments and businesses became increasingly aware of the unintended environmental consequences of the resulting increase in economic activities. In fact, many of those consequences were proving to be negative, imposing significant costs on personal health and the quality of life.

Some possible solutions

During the 1970s, the public, governments and businesses began asking: How do we handle the unintended, negative effects to the environment from the rapid increases in population, consumption and economic activity? For individuals whose personal health or property was damaged, the answer – at least in part – seemed to lie in tort law, i.e., in recovering monetary compensation for specific businesses' breaches of their general obligations to those individuals. The resulting class actions and punitive damages have resulted – and continue to result – in compensation to large numbers of individuals at a significant cost to business. Still, compensating specific individuals – or groups of individuals – for harm already suffered seemed to be an inadequate response to the risk of personal injury to large portions of the general population and of damage to their property, as well as damage to natural resources such as air and rivers.

Preventing the creation and spread of environmental contamination seemed to provide a better solution than solely paying compensation for harm resulting from pollution. The nature of the resulting government regulation has varied – generally according to whether a technology causing pollution is implemented on an economically significant scale before or after the risk of harm from the pollution is discovered. Preventive measures can be devised if the potential risks are discovered before the technology is implemented on a large scale. Remediation – along with preventive measures – is necessary if the negative impact is discovered after commercialization.

Most recently, environmental concerns have reached a new dimension, raising questions about the sustainability of many industries and, more generally, about the sustainability of a consumer-oriented economy.

Some definitions

Throughout this chapter, the terms "contamination" and "pollution" have the same meaning and so are interchangeable. In each case, I am referring to "environmental contamination" or "environmental pollution." The meaning of all of these terms includes altering the air, water or soil by introducing a toxic substance in such a way as to cause personal injury to animals or humans who ingest or are exposed to the air, water or soil.

"Ingestion" occurs when animals or humans introduce pollution into their bodies, typically by breathing or eating. Animals and humans can ingest pollution intentionally by eating contaminated plants or meat or unintentionally by consuming other contaminated substances (e.g., children ingesting contaminated soil when they put toys in their mouths). The manner in which humans ingest pollution is often called the "critical path." Once humans ingest pollution, the problems raised become public health issues as well as environmental issues.

Of course, contaminating or polluting air, water and soil can reduce the value of those physical assets for users and owners. The value of physical assets can be derived either from their use or from their transfer.[1] Through migration, pollution can spread to other air, water and soil, thereby reducing their value as well. "Migration" occurs when the action of gravity, wind or water carries pollution from originally contaminated air, water or soil to other air, water or soil.

JUDICIAL REMEDIES

Compensation for contamination

As we learned in Chapter 3, if people's uses of their property cause personal injury or property damage to another person, then they must pay compensation for the injury or damage. The people exercising their property rights must pay compensation because they have violated their general obligations. In other words, they have committed a tort.

The law of general obligations (tort law) applies, of course, to environmental contamination caused by businesses. If a business's use of property (i.e., to manufacture a product or provide a service) causes contamination and the contamination results in personal injury or property damage to others, then the business must pay compensation for the personal injury or property damage.[2]

Potential strict liability

It is important to note that businesses causing environmental pollution can be legally liable for the resulting personal injury and property damage even if those businesses do not intend to cause the pollution, injury or damage.[3] Businesses can certainly be legally liable for pollution if they could have known, and in fact knew, that their operations would cause pollution, injury or damage. (The business can be legally liable because it breached a general obligation with its "reckless" attitude toward the risk of pollution.) Businesses can also be legally liable if they could have known, but in fact did not know, about the risk of pollution, injury or damage. (The business can be legally liable because it breached a general obligation with its "negligent" attitude toward the risk of pollution.) In fact, businesses can be legally liable even if they could not have known, and therefore certainly did not know, that their operations would cause pollution, injury or damage. Legal liability in such circumstances is referred to as "strict liability."

Toxic torts, mass torts and class actions

Personal injury and property damage resulting from air, water and soil pollution are referred to as "toxic torts."

Toxic torts are often referred to as "mass torts" because a single source of environmental contamination often causes "mass" injury and damage, i.e., injury and damage to many persons and their property. In the United States, mass torts are often handled as "class actions" in court systems. A class action is a lawsuit in which many plaintiffs, referred to as a "class," bring a single case against one (or a few) defendant(s). Plaintiffs typically prefer class actions because class actions facilitate legal claims. Class actions are favored by courts because they expedite trials. For the same reasons, class actions are disfavored by defendants.

Punitive damages

As illustrated by the case of the Ford Pinto in Chapter 2, a business operation can be very profitable even if the business pays full compensation for all of the injuries or damages resulting from the operation. In such circumstances, plaintiffs often request and courts award punitive damages, i.e., an additional monetary award in an amount sufficient to discourage the harmful practice. In the United States, plaintiffs in mass tort cases usually request – and courts often award – significant punitive damages because,

in the absence of significant punitive damages, business operations which contaminate the environment are often very profitable even if businesses pay full compensation for all of the injuries or damages actually resulting from the environmental contamination. Thus, significant punitive damages are necessary to deter businesses.

An inadequate solution to pollution?

Even with the ability to bring class actions and to recover punitive damages, potential plaintiffs consider judicial remedies to be a burdensome response to environmental pollution. For example, the burden of proving all or most of the elements of their claims (i.e., pollution, illness, damage and causation) falls on the plaintiffs. Even if plaintiffs are eventually able to prove their cases, trials are typically very long, very expensive and very emotional for the alleged victims of pollution.

Potential plaintiffs also often consider judicial remedies to be an unreliable response to environmental pollution. First, it is sometimes difficult to identify pollution. Sometimes, pollution is identifiable only after several years of gradual accumulation. Second, it is frequently difficult to detect illnesses and property damage, especially the sorts of illness and damage caused by pollution. Such illnesses and property damage frequently manifest themselves only after years of exposure. Third, it is often difficult to prove that an illness or property damage resulted from exposure to specifically identified pollution. Fourth, the payment of damages awarded by a court is usually delayed as defendants appeal legal issues to a higher court. As a result, even though the damages awarded can be significant, their payment to the plaintiffs is often delayed for considerable periods of time.

Finally, potential plaintiffs and many others agree that judicial remedies are an inadequate response to environmental pollution. Judicial remedies are inadequate because monetary damages, even punitive damages, are insufficient to compensate for the death of a family member or the loss of good health. In addition, in the absence of government regulation, the payment of compensation for past harm to certain individuals does not entail either:

(a) an obligation to eliminate the cause of the harm (i.e., the obligation to remediate the pollution); or

(b) an obligation to pay for future harm to those same individuals or for past harm to other individuals, even if the harm results from the same existing or continuing pollution.

Moreover, judicial remedies are not available for the deleterious effects of environmental pollution other than personal injury and property damage. The air, rivers, oceans and most lakes are not anyone's personal property. Accordingly, judicial remedies for breaches of general obligations are not available for contamination of those natural resources. In other words, in the absence of government regulation, individuals and businesses are free to contaminate the air, rivers, oceans and most lakes with impunity unless and until that contamination causes injury (i.e., an illness) to other persons or damage to their personal property.

GOVERNMENT REGULATION

In general

As we learned in Chapter 3, competition and disclosure obligations are the two forms of government regulation favored both by government and by business. In a competitive environment, businesses are influenced to use their assets to provide the greatest benefit to consumers, thereby realizing the greatest financial return on their assets.[4] At the same time, by virtue of disclosure obligations, consumers are able to make the purchases which best protect their general and contract rights and promote their other interests.[5]

Competition and information are inadequate

Competition and information are not usually considered to be effective to prevent environmental pollution because individual businesses have not usually been willing to increase their operating costs above those of competing suppliers for the purpose of preserving clean air, water and soil. Individual consumers, for their part, have also been unwilling to assume the cost of avoiding the environmental pollution incidental to the supply of goods and services they purchase. Consumers have been unwilling to do so in part because the consumers of specific goods and services are not usually the individuals who bear

the burden of environmental pollution incidental to the supply of those goods and services. Instead, the environmental burden is borne by the communities where businesses operate or, through the migration of water and air pollution, more remote communities who use air and water after it has been used by businesses to supply goods.

More intrusive regulations are required

Since competition and information have not been adequate to prevent environmental contamination, governments have resorted to more intrusive forms of regulation. As discussed below, these more intrusive forms of regulation have taken many different forms. Some of the regulations apply to "remediation," i.e., cleaning up pollution after it occurs. Other regulations apply to preventing pollution before it occurs.

The polluter pays

Whether government regulation focuses on remediating or preventing pollution, the general scheme for environmental regulation is that the polluter pays for pollution. If the pollution has already occurred, then the polluter pays for the remediation, i.e., for cleaning up the pollution. The polluter pays for remediation either:

(a) by paying the cost of the clean up;
(b) by paying a fine; or
(c) very often, paying both costs and a fine.

In addition, the polluter can be subject to judicial remedies requiring monetary compensation for personal injury and property damage resulting from pollution.

If the pollution has not yet occurred but is the inevitable consequence of an industrial or agricultural operation, then the polluter pays for preventing the pollution. The potential polluter pays by designing, integrating and installing the proper equipment and procedures to prevent releases of potentially polluting materials above regulatory tolerances. If the potential polluter fails to install the necessary equipment and procedures voluntarily, then the polluter will be subject to fines for the pollution above regulatory tolerances while retaining the obligation to install the necessary procedures and equipment.

In addition, polluters will be responsible for remediation under separate regulations and, as with remediation, subject to judicial remedies requiring monetary compensation for personal injury and property damage caused by their pollution.

Remediating pollution

As noted in the introduction to this chapter: since the 1970s, the public, governments and businesses began asking: How do we handle the unintended, negative effects to the environment from the rapid increases in population, consumption and economic activity?

The answer depends on several factors, including the following: Is the potential for pollution known at the time a technology is commercialized? If we become aware of the possible environmental pollution before the technology is commercialized, then commercialization can include preventive measures. If we become aware of a technology's potential for pollution only after a technology is commercialized, then – in addition to measures designed to prevent future pollution – the environmental issues will typically include remediation of past pollution.

Remediation

Technical methods

Remediation involves cleaning up accumulated contamination. Since soil contamination is usually more "persistent" than water or air contamination – i.e., soil is the environmental element where pollution lingers and accumulates most easily – most remediation deals with cleaning up soil contamination. Pollution sometimes accumulates in standing bodies of water, requiring remediation, but air and water pollution are addressed primarily with preventive measures, as discussed below.

Viewed from a technical perspective, soil is most often remediated through removal and incineration. All three common soil remediation measures typically involve digging up the contaminated soil. With "removal" remediation techniques, the soil is taken to a remote location, where it is isolated so as to prevent all further harm through migration to air, water or soil or through ingestion by animals or humans. Incineration typically involves exposing contami-

nated soil to a high temperature. Through incineration, the contaminants are boiled (or evaporated) out of the soil and captured for safe disposal – usually through the use of cooling towers and tanks. Incineration sometimes also alters the chemical formulation of contaminants, rendering them harmless.[6]

The "green field" standard

An important issue regarding remediation is "regulatory tolerances," i.e., the level of residual contamination acceptable to environmental regulators – government officials – after soil or water has been remediated. Some national and local environmental regulators take the position that polluted soil must be remediated to its initial, pristine state, i.e., as if the pollution had never occurred. This position is referred to as a "green field" standard. Needless to say, the green field standard is very expensive. In fact, the green field standard is so expensive that it often inhibits the sale and continuing use of land which has been used only once in a polluting operation, either industrial or agricultural. The green field standard often impedes the sale and continuing use of such land because a buyer is not willing to purchase land subject to such an expensive regulatory burden. Similarly, the seller is not willing to incur the high costs of complying with green field standards because the seller will not be able to recover the high compliance costs from buyers.

The "brown field" standard

As a result of the green field standard, land used only once for a polluting industrial or agricultural purpose often lies idle, while ever increasing amounts of new land, previously unused and therefore unpolluted, are applied to polluting uses. In response to the perceived waste from the single use of polluted facilities, regulators have developed a "brown field" standard for soil remediation. Generally, under the "brown field" standard, land must be remediated only to the standard required by a new buyer for its continued use. Frequently, such a standard requires no remediation. Under the brown field standard, the regulatory focus shifts to preventing humans and animals from ingesting existing pollution and to preventing migration of existing pollution to neighboring areas.[7]

Who is supposed to know about existing contamination?

Another important issue regarding remediation is the obligation of an owner or user of real property to know about – i.e., to test for – existing environmental pollution and, if so, to remediate the known contamination.

Under current regulatory standards owners and occupiers sometimes have an obligation to disclose and remediate existing contamination, of which they are aware.[8] At the same time, owners and occupiers of real property generally do not have an obligation to know about – i.e., to test for – existing environmental pollution. Notwithstanding these rules, real estate buyers generally insist on having the seller-owner conduct such tests as a condition precedent to their purchase of real estate.[9]

Who is supposed to pay for remediation?

Another important issue regarding remediation is the identification of the businesses or individuals required to pay for remediation of past pollution. Of course, if a certain polluting facility has been owned and operated by a single business or individual during its entire operation, then that individual is responsible for remediating the pollution. It is sometimes the case, however, that one business or individual owns the real estate where a polluting facility is located while another business or individual operates the facility itself. It is even more common that a single polluting facility has been owned and operated by a series of businesses or individuals. In these cases, regulators are uncertain about the identity of the persons actually causing contamination and therefore arguably responsible for remediation. Regulatory regimes often resolve the uncertainty by imposing joint responsibility on the current owner, the current operator and on each of the past owners and operators. Each of them is required to pay for the entire remediation, with those who actual pay for the remediation demanding contribution from the others in a lawsuit.[10]

Is it an adequate solution to pollution?

Remediating past pollution has significant technical disadvantages to preventing future pollution. First, remediation techniques differ dramatically from pre-vention techniques and are often less effective. ("An ounce of prevention equals a pound of cure.") Second, continuing water and air pollution usually manifest themselves after a significant delay in time, in some form of soil pollution or public health problem – usually over a relatively broad geographic area and sometimes at a considerable distance from the polluting facilities.

Remediation also has economic disadvantages to prevention. First, in addition to being technically more difficult, remediation is frequently more expensive. Second, only regulations which prevent pollution before it occurs enable businesses to shift the cost for pollution to consumers, by increasing prices for goods and services to cover the cost of the preventive measures. Third, recovering the costs of remediation from a polluting business poses difficulties, in part because businesses typically do not have sinking funds for possible remediation. As a result, revenues from polluting operations have usually been applied to other uses before remediation is required.[11]

Preventing pollution

Based on the foregoing discussion, it appears that dealing with environmental issues through prevention is technically easier and less expensive than dealing with such issues through remediation. In any event, remediation of past pollution does not obviate the need for prevention of future pollution, but prevention of future pollution can eliminate the need for remediation. As a result, potential pollution identified before commercialization of a technology is typically addressed, within the limits of technical feasibility, through preventive measures. Pollution concerns identified after such commercialization are addressed with a combination of remediaton (for past pollution) and prevention (for future pollution).

Prevention

Technical methods

Unlike remediation, which focuses primarily on soil contamination, preventive measures involve keeping continuing contamination from entering all three environmental elements, i.e., air, water and soil.

Since the polluting material (e.g., a toxic substance) is usually waste incidental to an industrial or agricultural operation, from a technical perspective, preventive measures typically involve:

(a) design of a planned operation to reduce polluting inputs and outputs;
(b) intervention in an existing operation to reduce polluting inputs and outputs;
(c) capture and containment for planned or existing operations; or
(d) separate efforts to recover the polluting material.

Of course, these techniques are not all mutually exclusive. Some can be applied to a single planned or existing operation.

As regards design of a planned operation, the raw materials and process materials used in a product or process can be changed or modified – eliminating the toxins or toxin-producing substances and procedures – before a technology is commercialized. A redesign of products and processes can be the least expensive sort of preventive measure because it can be introduced before investment in plant and equipment. Intervening in an existing operation is similar to designing a planned operation to avoid pollution, but intervening in an existing operation involves both:

(a) the cost and effort of redesigning products and processes; and
(b) the expense of investments to modify or replace existing plant and equipment.

Capture and containment do not entail modification of an industrial or agricultural operation to eliminate or reduce polluting wastes. Instead, they involve extensions of planned or existing operations. Accordingly, both involve investments in additional plant and equipment. The sort of additional investment depends largely on the waste's toxicity and on its physical state: gas, liquid or solid. In each case, after capture, the waste is:

(a) reused;
(b) collected and safely disposed; or
(c) treated to render it harmless before it is expelled into the environment within regulatory tolerances.

Finally, to the extent that the first three steps are not selected or effective at: (a) eliminating or (b)

reducing and containing polluting materials, measures intended to prevent environmental pollution include separate efforts to recover polluting material for proper disposal. This step applies in particular in those instances when the potentially polluting substance is not a waste product but the final product – or other by-product – from an industrial or agricultural operation. In such cases, the business making and selling the potentially polluting final product or by-product assumes responsibility for the product's transportation, storage, use and disposal by customers (and by the customers' customers), even after legal title has passed from the producing business.

Regulatory tolerances

As with remediation (green field or brown field), tolerances are an important issue for government regulations intended to prevent environmental pollution. There are various approaches to establishing the tolerances within which pollution is acceptable under government regulation.[12]

First, there is the approach of "set outcomes." With this approach, government regulators establish a maximum quantity of various pollution materials which can be emitted into the environment within a certain area and accordingly from certain operations within that area. The quantities tend to be established as a rate (e.g., absolute amounts per day, week or month). The tolerances take the form of permits (i.e., licenses to pollute up to a set maximum) issued by environmental regulators and enforced, for example, through monitors installed at industrial facilities. Sometimes, the licenses are transferable. In such cases, a market for licenses develops as businesses operating well within the limits of their licenses sell unused tolerances to businesses wishing to operate beyond the limits of their licenses.

Second, there is the approach of "continuous improvement." Continuous improvement is, in effect, a variation of set outcomes. With the approach of continuous improvement, environmental regulators both prescribe a set outcome for current tolerances and set a higher standard (i.e., a stricter tolerance) for a specific time in the future. As a first step in a continuous improvement regime, environmental regulators can set an outcome (stricter than current industry practice or available technology) for a specific deadline in the future.

THREE

Third, there is the approach of "best available technology" or "BAT." With this approach, government environmental regulators prescribe the specific preventive technology they consider to be the best (e.g., bags or scrubbers to capture particulate pollution from the exhaust of power plants). Using a variation of BAT, regulators require that businesses must achieve the results of a specific BAT, but do not require that businesses use the specified BAT. In other words, businesses have complete flexibility as to how to achieve those "BAT results." Such a variation of the BAT approach is an incentive to business to develop less expensive or more efficient techniques of preventing environmental pollution.

International coordination

Remediation regulations, by their nature, do not often raise the issue of international coordination. Since remediation usually applies to existing soil pollution, each nation has its own concerns which can be adequately addressed by its own national regulation. The only exception to this general observation is the remediation of bodies of water which form the boundaries between nations, i.e., rivers, lakes and seas; and rivers which flow from one nation into another nation. As regards these boundary waters, nations often attempt to coordinate environmental regulation.

Preventive regulations, on the contrary, often raise the issue of international coordination because, frequently, one nation cannot effectively control continuing air or water pollution without coordination and cooperation from neighboring nations or, indeed, from nations around the world. Examples of such pollution include acid rain, ozone depletion and global warming. The most important form of international coordination is harmonization of standards.[13] Such harmonization deals with two issues: the types of pollution subject to regulation and the acceptable regulatory tolerances.

The harmonization of international standards for preventing environmental pollution usually takes the form of international treaties. In these treaties (e.g., The Montreal Protocol or The Kyoto Treaty), nations typically recognize a common risk from an existing form of air or water pollution (e.g., ozone depletion from chlorofluorocarbons or global warming from carbon dioxide), acknowledge that they cannot effec-

tively manage the risk without international cooperation, and agree on a standard, including regulatory tolerances. The standards and tolerances set usually exceed (i.e., are more restrictive) than the standards and tolerances currently in place in most nations.

Permissive and precautionary approaches

It is often said that environmental regulations are either "permissive" or "precautionary" and that, in any case, they should be "science based." Unfortunately issues invariably arise about the permissive and precautionary approaches and about the scientific basis needed for specific environmental regulations.[14]

"Prove it's harmful" or "prove it's safe"?

Environmental regulators inevitably face an important policy issue: Should the government use a permissive approach in adopting its preventive environmental regulations or should the government adopt a precautionary approach? With the "permissive approach," the government takes the position that potentially polluting materials (i.e., waste products, by-products or final products) are safe until proven to be harmful. For example, with a permissive approach, bio-engineered crops are considered to be safe for the environment until proven harmful. With the "precautionary approach," the government takes the approach that potentially polluting materials are harmful until proven to be safe. For example, with a precautionary approach, bio-engineered crops are considered to be harmful for the environment until proven safe.

Allocating the burden of proof

Implicit in this policy decision is the allocation of a burden of proof. Under the permissive approach, it is incumbent on environmental interests (or, for example, the government on their behalf) to prove that a potentially polluting material is harmful. Under the precautionary approach, it is incumbent on producers (or, for example, the government on their behalf) to prove that the potentially polluting material is safe. For example, with a permissive approach, environmentalists, independent research facilities or the government must prove that bio-engineered crops are harmful to the environment in order to prohibit commercialization. With a precautionary approach, producers, independent research facilities or the government must prove that bio-engineered crops are safe for the environment before they can be commercialized.

Establishing a required level of confidence

Establishing a presumption and thereby allocating the burden of proof is a not sufficient basis to formulate preventive environmental regulations. Environmental regulations – under both the permissive and precautionary approach – claim to be "science based." Accordingly, an important issue related to both is the general nature of scientific conclusions. What does it mean, for example, to say that a product is "proven to be safe"? For many scientists, it is impossible to state that any scientific hypothesis is definitely "proven to be true"; it is only possible to state that a scientific hypothesis has – or has not – been "proven to be false." In other words, it is impossible to state with certainty that any potentially polluting material, such as a bio-engineered crop, is definitively proven to be safe.[15]

Since absolute certainty is not possible, the regulators must also establish the level of confidence with which scientific conclusions must be drawn. For example, with a permissive approach, in order to prohibit commercialization, do environmentalists need to show that bio-engineered crops are harmful to the environment by a preponderance of the evidence, by clear and convincing evidence or beyond any reasonable doubt? Finally, should it be enough for environmentalists to show some evidence of harm? Similarly, with a precautionary approach, before producers can commercialize bio-engineered crops, do they need to show that bio-engineered crops are safe for the environment by a preponderance of the evidence, by clear and convincing evidence or beyond any reasonable doubt? Finally, should it be enough for businesses to show that there is some evidence of safety?

Combining the two

To the extent that permissive and precautionary approaches relate to burdens of proof regarding the environmental safety or harm of a potentially polluting material, the two can be combined.

It would be possible, for example, to require that producers offer some evidence (as established by regulators) that materials are environmentally safe. If producers cannot satisfy their burden of proof for a specific material, then they cannot commercialize the material. If producers satisfy their burden of proof, then the material can be commercialized unless other evidence – presented, for example, by environmental groups or by the government itself – provides some evidence that the product is harmful to the environment. In fact, this is the system applied, for example, to synthetic chemicals.[16]

Moreover, permissive and precautionary can incorporate a "risk-based" analysis of potential environmental contamination, including a study of critical paths leading to injury to humans. In fact, most materials tend to raise only certain types of environmental risks and only in a certain context and to a certain extent. After collecting all of the evidence tending to show that a potentially polluting material is safe or harmful government regulators can take a relatively balanced, risk-based approach to preventive environmental regulation.[17]

Presumptions can vary by type of material and over time

Of course, governments can adopt different regulatory approaches (precautionary or permissive) for different types of materials. Important factors are the perceived benefits to be derived from making a product commercially available and the perceived risks from releasing the products into the environment.[18] In addition, appropriate regulatory attitudes can evolve over time, for example: from permissive to precautionary or precautionary to permissive.[19]

Avoiding the greater risk

Obviously, a government taking a precautionary approach will be more actively engaged in preventing potential environmental pollution and, potentially, in restricting economic progress. A government taking a permissive approach will be less actively engaged in preventing potential pollution and, potentially, in allowing environmental releases to cause personal injury and property damage. For any product at any time, one way to adopt a reasonable policy might be to avoid the greater risk, i.e., unnecessary restrictions on economic progress (by adopting a precautionary approach), or avoidable personal injury or property damage (by adopting a permissive approach).[20]

BUSINESS SELF-REGULATION

As outlined in this chapter, environmental law is often the subject of government regulation, but it can also be the subject of business self-regulation. Business prefers self-regulation on environmental issues for the same reasons business prefers self-regulation in other areas: because business usually considers self-regulation to be more effective and less intrusive than government regulation. Self-regulation on environmental matters is conducted at various levels: individual companies, industry associations, and independent testing institutions. Of course, the standards for all of these forms of environmental self-regulations must exceed the requirements of the most stringent applicable government regulations.

By individual companies

First, individual companies sometimes engage in self-regulation on environmental issues because they find it easiest from a technical point of view to establish the same global operational standards throughout their organization, even for environmental matters. Companies adopting this form of self-regulation tend to do so for two reasons. First, maintaining a single operating standard, including for environmental matters, offers some cost savings. With the same global operational standards, a company can save costs by interchanging the same designs, equipment and personnel between the company's various locations. Second, maintaining the same global operating standards offers benefits in terms of consistent product quality. In an era of global customers and global sourcing, it is important for a company to offer the same quality in its products from its various locations. Some companies have found that it is not possible to maintain a consistently high product quality among different locations without the same operating standards, including for environmental matters.

By industry associations

Second, individual industries often engage in environmental self-regulation both nationally and internationally. Environmental self-regulation at the industry level, typically through the industry association, affords individual companies all of the benefits of self-regulation at the company level. In addition, industry-wide programs offer at least two advantages over individual programs.

First, individual companies avoid the potential cost disadvantages of instituting their own environmental self-regulation. Adopting industry policies also costs less for the individual companies than formulating their own polcies, but of course does not obviate the need to implement those policies at the company level. Second, industry associations can advertise and otherwise promote their environmental regulations to important corporate constituencies more effectively and less expensively than individual companies can do so. Such advertising and promotion can be important because environmental matters are a major concern for governments and general publics.

Governments allow business self-regulation on environmental matters at the industry level, both nationally and internationally, because governmental competition regulators do not consider environmental matters to be commercial issues giving rise to competition within an industry.

By independent testing agencies

Finally, independent third party testing agencies, in particular the International Standards Organization ("ISO") in Switzerland, have become involved in "non-governmental" regulation on environmental matters. "Self-regulation" is not the correct term to describe ISO's involvement in environmental matters because they adopt and monitor environmental standards for other industries, not for themselves. In fact, the ISO's independence gives credibility to its standards and certifications. The ISO's standing in this arena, as well as the importance of environmental self-regulation, is illustrated by the fact that many companies undertake to obtain ISO environmental certification in response to customer requests.

WTO NEGOTIATIONS

The increased global awareness of environmental issues is evidenced by recent attempts to include environmental issues among the trade issues incorporated into the GATT.

From the perspective of countries with relatively strict environmental standards on production, their WTO obligations to maintain open markets occasionally threaten the effectiveness of their environmental regulation, at least as regards the importation of products from abroad processed or made in violation of the importing country's stricter standards (e.g., Mexico's successful WTO challenge to the USA's ban on tuna caught in nets which snare dolphins).

Countries with relatively strict environmental standards also see imports from countries with more relaxed environmental standards as a threat to an equitable global trading system. In their view, the free importation of those products without an offsetting "environmental tariff" unfairly favors imports at the same time that it undermines the effectiveness of their tougher environmental regulations.

SUSTAINABILITY

As mentioned at the beginning of this chapter, environmental pollution is a broader issue than the scope presented in this chapter. For example, this chapter does not discuss depletion of natural resources. Depletion is very important for industries based on non-renewable or slowly renewable natural resources (for example: metals, petroleum, forestry and fishing).

Sustainability is another broad issue important for business but not squarely addressed in this chapter. Sustainability is based on the observation that, as production, consumption and populations increase ever more rapidly on a global basis, there are more people on earth – with each one of them using more of the earth's natural resources. Sustainability has at least three aspects.

First, the environmental costs incidental to current high-consumption life-styles are becoming less negligible as the worldwide rates of consumption increase. As environmental costs associated with current life-styles become more significant, those life-styles become less sustainable. For example, it might be sustainable for most adults in North America and Europe to travel primarily in individual automobiles with internal combustion engines. Those experts and interests focusing on sustainability are concerned, however, that it might not be sustainable – from a purely environmental perspective – for those adults, together with most of the other adults around the world, to do so. Those experts and others argue that, if the freedom and efficiency of individual travel is to become generally available to all adults around the world, everyone's equipment and method for achieving that goal might need to change.

Second, experts and interests focusing on sustainability are concerned that entire industries – such as the automobile industry – are not viable in their present forms. Unless those industries are fundamentally transformed (e.g., by creating vehicles using less non-renewable energy), the benefits they initially afforded might not remain generally available.

Third, as more and more of the earth's resources are accessible to our global system of production and consumption, resources for which no economic value has been established are eliminated in favor of those resources with proven economic value. For example, cultivated rice varieties decrease as farmers throughout Asia abandon locally traditional varieties in favor or varieties with larger yields. Experts and interests focusing on sustainability are concerned that eliminating diversity can foreclose future technological progress and economic development. Eliminating diversity, they argue, can even undermine the viability for current systems of production and consumption. For example, as diversity in cultivated food crops decreases, more and more of the world's food supply could well be vulnerable to the same diseases.

THREE

10

Relationships with Employees

Employment and labor law

UNITED STATES

INTRODUCTION

This section deals primarily with employment and labor law issues affecting employees in private companies. Although many of the laws discussed here also affect employees in the public sector, other bodies of law beyond the scope of this section – such as the Constitution, civil service systems and public-sector labor relations statutes – play an even more important role in the work lives of government workers.

Individual employment

Employment-at-will doctrine

The relationship of employer and employee exists when, pursuant to an express or implied agreement of parties, one person, the employee, undertakes to perform services or to do work under the direction and control of another, the employer, for compensation.

In most instances of individual employment contracts the employment contract does not state any time or duration. It is an employment-at-will contract. In contrast, the employment contract may state that it shall last for a specified period of time. An employer cannot terminate a contract for a definite period of time at an earlier date without justification as contemplated by the parties to that agreement. Under classic at-will rule, both the employer and employee

are free to terminate the relationship with or without cause.

This rule, which gives an employer the right to terminate an employee for any reason –good cause, no cause, or bad cause – has been uniformly recognized throughout the country. However, judicial and, in some instances, legislative intervention has had an impact on its application. There are four exceptions under which a wrongful discharge suit can be supported:

1 public policy violation (whistleblowing cases);
2 abusive discharge;
3 express or implied guarantee of continued employment; and
4 good faith and fair dealing in employment contracts.

It is important to mention that employees are protected against discrimination practices. In addition, employers cannot retaliate against an employee for exercising his or her rights.

Non-competition agreements

Employers commonly seek to restrict employees who have access to trade secrets or other confidential information from competing against them subsequent to leaving the employers' business. They do so by having their employees sign non-competition agreements, sometimes called *covenants not to compete*, as part of their employment contracts. These covenants will be enforced where:

1   the restraint is reasonably necessary to protect the employer's business;

2   it is not unreasonably restrictive on the employee; and

3   it is not antagonistic to the general public.

Employer liability for torts of employees

The legal concept of imposing liability on an employer for the wrongs of its employees is known as *vicarious liability*. It imposes liability, however, only when an employee is acting within the course of employment. The concept is justified on the grounds that the business should pay for the harm caused in the undertaking of the business, that the employer will be more careful in the selection of employees if made responsible for their actions, and that the employer is in a position to obtain liability insurance to protect against claims of third persons.

It is important to mention that if the work is done by an independent contractor, the employer is generally not liable for harm caused by the contractor to third persons or their property. An exception exists, however, when the work undertaken by the contractor is inherently dangerous.

PERSONAL RIGHTS IN THE EMPLOYMENT CONTEXT

The Privacy Act of 1974

This Act provides federal employees limited protection from the dissemination of personal records without the prior written consent of the employee. Eleven exceptions exist including use by officers or employees of the agency that maintains the records who have a need for the records in the performance of their agency duties and court orders for the records. The Privacy Act also bars disclosure of information about federal employees unless it would be required under the Freedom of Information Act.

Private sector employees are not subject to the same restrictions imposed on public sector employees by the federal constitution. Private employers, then, are generally less restricted in conducing searches in some States based on the State constitution, statutes, or the common law.

The Fair Credit Reporting Act of 1971

In many organizations, the employment process includes a credit check on the applicant. The purpose of such checks is to obtain information about the individual's "character, general reputation," and various other personal characteristics. Typically, companies can obtain this information by using two different approaches. The first is through a credit reporting agency, similar to the type that is used when you apply for a loan. In this instance, the employer is required to notify the individual that a credit report is being obtained. However, if an applicant is rejected based on information in the report, the individual must be provided a copy of the credit report, as well as a means for how to appeal the accuracy of the findings. The second type of credit report is obtained through a third-party investigation. Under this arrangement, not only is one's credit checked, but people known to the applicant are interviewed regarding the applicant's lifestyle, spending habits, and character. For an organization to use this type of approach, the applicant must be informed of the process in writing, and as with the credit report, must be notified of the report's details if the information is used to negatively affect an employment decision.

The Drug-Free Workplace Act of 1988

Under this Act, government agencies, federal contractors, and those receiving federal funds ($25,000 or more) are required to actively pursue a drug-free environment. In addition, the Act requires employees of companies regulated by the Department of Transportation (DOT) and the Nuclear Regulatory Commission who hold certain jobs to be subjected to drug tests. For all organizations covered under this Act, other stipulations are included.

The Employee Polygraph Protection Act of 1988 (EPPA)

This Act makes it unlawful for private employers to use pre-employment lie detector (polygraph) tests while screening applicants for employment or to take any disciplinary action or deny employment or promotion to any individual who refuses to take a polygraph test. However, federal, state and local government employers are exempt from any restrictions on the use of polygraph tests, and the federal government may also test private consultants under contract to the Defense Department, CIA, FBI, the National Security Agency or the Department of Energy. The law also permits private security firms and drug companies to administer polygraph tests to job applicants and employees.

Under the law a limited exemption exists that allows employers to request an employee to submit to a polygraph test if:

1 the test is administrated in connection with an ongoing investigation involving economic loss or injury to an employer's business, such as theft or embezzlement;
2 the employee had access to the property in question;
3 the employer has "reasonable suspicion" of the employee; and
4 the employer gives a written statement to the employee of the basis for its reasonable suspicion.

LABOR UNIONS AND COLLECTIVE BARGAINING

The American labor relations system differs from its European counterparts in a number of ways. First, the system is based on an adversarial model. In most cases, unions obtain bargaining rights in contested elections administered by a federal agency. In such elections, management has a right to, and often does, speak out in opposition to the union. Companies may not have a role in initiating or supporting "labor organizations," a term that is broadly defined to include any mechanism by which employees deal with their employer on terms and conditions of employment. The labor laws are based on a fundamental division of interest between labor and management: unions can seek bargaining authority on behalf of non-managerial and non-supervisory workers, but managers and supervisors are deemed representatives of the firm who have no right to form unions or insist on collective bargaining. The scope of bargaining also reflects this division between spheres of influence: the parties must bargain over wages, hours and working conditions, but decisions involving the disposition of assets and the strategic position of the firm, including plant closings, are deemed to be part of management's realm of unilateral action; management must bargain over the effects of such decisions but not the decisions themselves.

Second, collective bargaining is highly decentralized. Unions acquire bargaining authority on a plant-by-plant basis, often among a subgroup of workers in the plant. Unlike the German, French and Swedish systems, regional bargaining between labor federations and multi-employer organizations in the United States is exceptional; multi-employer bargaining units are formed only by consent and in many industries they have unraveled.

Finally, unions are predominantly multi-employer organizations representing employees of competing firms. Unlike Japan's enterprise unions, employee associations representing only the employees of a particular firm are rare in the United States, and tend over time to affiliate with national labor organizations that are members of the central labor federation, the American Federation of Labor-Congress of Industrial Organizations (AFL-CIO). Enterprise-based works councils – found in most continental European countries – are non-existent in the United States. American unions typically negotiate agreements with single companies, often applicable only to a particular facility; while making every effort to ensure that such agreements conform to the national "pattern" for that industry.

The regulatory framework

It is probably most useful to understand labor law, i.e., the relationship between unions and employer interests (i.e., management, individual companies and entire industries) by reviewing the applicable regulations chronologically. The following description of regulation in the United States offers a historical overview of labor relations in the United States.

The Railway Labor Act of 1926

This Act provided the initial impetus for widespread collective bargaining in the United States. Although the Act covers only the transportation industry, it was important because workers in these industries were guaranteed the right to organize, bargain collectively

with employers, and establish dispute-settlement procedures in the event that an agreement was not reached
at the bargaining table. This dispute-settlement procedure allows congressional and presidential interces-
sion in the event of an impasse.

The Federal Anti-Injunction Act of 1932

Commonly referred to as Norris-La Guardia Act, this
Act was the first law to protect the rights of unions
and workers to engage in union activity. The Act for-
bids federal courts to issue injunctions (orders prohibiting certain activities) against specifically
described union activities and outlaws yellow-dog
contracts (in which employees agree that continued
employment depends on abstention from union
membership or activities).

Section 7 ensures the Act may not be used as a
cover for violent and destructive actions. An injunction may be issued if:

1 substantial or irreparable injury to property will
  occur;
2 greater injury will be inflicted on the party
  requesting the injunction than the injunction
  would cause on the adversary;
3 no adequate legal remedy exists; and
4 authorities are either unable or unwilling to give
  protection.

The National Labor Relations Act of 1935

Commonly referred to as the Wagner Act, this Act
is the basic "bill of rights" for unions. This law guarantees workers the right to organize and join
unions, to bargain collectively, and to act in concert
to pursue their objectives. In terms of labor relations,
the Wagner Act specifically requires employers to
bargain in good faith over mandatory bargaining
issues – wages, hours and terms and conditions of
employment.

This Act established the National Labor Relations
Board (NLRB), whose main responsibilities include
determining appropriate bargaining units, conducting
elections to determine union representation, and preventing or correcting employer actions that can lead
to unfair labor practice charges. The NLRB, however,
has only remedial and no punitive powers.

The Labor Management Relations Act of 1947

Commonly referred as the Taft-Hartley Act, its major
purpose was to amend the Wagner Act by addressing
employers' concerns in terms of specifying unfair
union labor practices. In addition, this Act declared
illegal one type of union security arrangement: the
closed shop. Under this arrangement, an individual
would join the union, be trained by the union, and
sent to work for an employer by the union.

This Act included provisions that forbade secondary boycotts, and gave the president of the United
States the power to issue an 80-day cooling-off
period when labor–management disputes affect
national security. A secondary boycott occurs when a
union strikes against Employer A (a primary and legal
strike), and then strikes and pickets against Employer
B (an employer against which the union has no complaint) because of the relationship that exists between
Employers A and B, such as Employer B handling
goods made by Employer A.

Taft-Hartley also set forth procedures for workers to
decertify, or vote out, their union representatives. Also,
this Act created the Federal Mediation and Conciliation
Service (FMCS) as an independent agency separate
from the Department of Labor. The FMCS's mission is
to send a trained representative to assist in negotiations.
Both employer and union have the responsibility to
notify the FMCS when other attempts to settle the dispute have failed or contract expiration is pending. An
FMCS mediator is not empowered to force parties to
reach an agreement, but he or she can use persuasion
and other means of diplomacy to help them reach their
own resolution of differences.

The Labor Management Reporting and Disclosure Act of 1959

It is also known as the Landrum-Griffin Act. This Act
was passed to address the public outcry over misuse
of union funds and corruption in the labor movement. This Act, like Taft-Hartley, was an amendment
to the Wagner Act.

The thrust of the Landrum-Griffin Act is to monitor internal union activity by making officials and
those affiliated with unions (e.g., union members,
trustees, etc.) accountable for union funds, elections,
and other business and representational matters.
Restrictions are also placed on trusteeships imposed

by national or international unions, and conduct during a union election is regulated.

Much of this Act is part of an ongoing effort to prevent corrupt practices and to keep organized crime from gaining control of the labor movement. The mechanisms used to achieve this goal are requirements for annual filing, by unions as organizations and by individuals employed by unions, of reports regarding administrative matters to the Department of Labor – reports such as their constitutions and bylaws, administrative policies, elected officials and finances.

This Act also included a provision that allowed all members of a union to vote irrespective of their race, sex, national origin and so forth. Landrum-Griffin also required that all who voted on union matters would do so in a secret ballot, especially when the vote concerned the election of union officers.

Executive Orders 10988 and 11491

Both of these executive orders deal specifically with labor legislation in the federal sector. In 1962, the Executive Order 10988 permitted for the first time federal government employees the right to join unions. The order required agency heads to bargain in good faith, defined unfair labor practices, and specified the code of conduct to which labor organizations in the public sector must adhere. Strikes, however, were prohibited.

In 1969, Executive Order 11491 made federal labor relations more like those in the private sector and standardized procedures among federal agencies. This order gave the assistant secretary of labor the authority to determine appropriate bargaining units, oversee recognition procedures, rule on unfair labor practices, and enforce standards of conduct on labor relations. It also established the Federal Labor Relations Council (FLRC) to supervise the implementation of Executive Order 11491 provisions, handle appeals from decisions of the assistant secretary of labor, and rule on questionable issues.

Both of these executive orders served a vital purpose in promoting federal-sector unionization. However, if a subsequent administration ever decided not to permit federal-sector unionization, a president would have had only to revoke a prior executive order. To eliminate this possibility, and to remove federal-sector labor relations from direct control of a president, Congress passed the Civil Service Reform Act.

Racketeering Influenced and Corrupt Organization Act of 1970 (RICO)

Its primary emphasis with respect to labor unions is to eliminate any influence exerted on unions by members of organized crime. That is, it is a violation of RICO if "payments or loans are made to employee representatives, labor organizations, or officers and employees of labor organizations," where such action occurs in the form of "bribery, kickbacks, or extortion."

The Civil Service Reform Act of 1978

Title VII of the Civil Service Reform Act established the Federal Labor Relations Authority (FLRA) as an independent agency within the executive branch to carry out the major functions previously performed by the FLRC. The FLRA was given the authority to decide, subject to external review by courts and administrative bodies, union election and unfair labor practice disputes, and appeals from arbitration awards, and to provide leadership in establishing policies and guidance. An additional feature of this Act is a broad-scope grievance procedure that can be limited only by the negotiators. Under Executive Order 11491, binding arbitration had been optional. While the Civil Service Reform Act of 1978 contains many provisions similar to those of the Wagner Act, two important differences exist. First, in the private sector, the scope of bargaining includes wages and benefits, and mandatory subjects of bargaining. In the federal sector, wages and benefits are not negotiable – they are set by Congress. Additionally, the Reform Act prohibits negotiations over union security arrangements.

LABOR UNIONS AND COLLECTIVE BARGAINING

Union recognition and representation process

Employees are unionized after an extensive and sometimes lengthy process called the organizing campaign. Efforts to organize a group of employees may begin by employee representatives requesting a union to visit the employees' organization and solicit members; the union itself might initiate the membership drive.

The union must secure signed authorization cards from at least 30 percent of the employees it wishes to represent. Employees who sign the cards indicate that they wish the particular union to be their representative in negotiating with the employer.

It is important to mention that parties, union and employer, should not engage in unfair labor practices, which provide grounds for setting aside the election.

To become the certified bargaining unit, the union must be accepted by a majority of those eligible voting workers. Acceptance in this case is determined by a secret-ballot election. This election held by the NLRB, called a representation certification, can occur only once in a 12-month period.

Collective bargaining

Under the NLRA, once the union has been certified, the parties are under a duty to meet and confer at reasonable times and engage in "good faith" bargaining. There is no legal obligation to make concessions or reach agreements.

The duty to bargain is limited to "wages, hours and other terms and conditions of employment." These are considered "mandatory" subjects over which the parties must bargain (and provide information to substantiate bargaining positions) and are free to press their disagreements to the point of "impasse." Bargaining is not required over subjects like plant closings, advertising budgets, and capital investments that are considered to lie within the realm of "entrepreneurial control"; subjects that affect the union's relationship with its members such as strike and contract ratification votes; or subjects that alter the established framework of negotiations, such as proposals to bargain with coalitions of unions or to submit disagreements over the content of labor contracts to arbitration. These are considered "permissive" subjects over which the parties have no duty to bargain and may not be a basis for deadlock over mandatory subjects.

If the parties have reached an "impasse" over mandatory subjects, the NLRA permits resort to self-help after notice is given to the Federal Mediation and Conciliation Service (FMCS) and a 60-day "cooling off" period has expired. The employer may lock-out its employees and/or unilaterally implement its final offer to the union. The union may exercise its right to strike, which is legally protected. Although the employer may not discharge striking workers, it can,

in the interest of maintaining operations, hire permanent replacements even without a showing that it could not maintain operations by other means. Even if permanent replacements have been hired, strikers remain "employees" and have preferential rights to job openings as they occur, once the strikers have offered unconditionally to return to work. If the strike is in protest over the employer's unfair labor practices, the employer may not hire permanent replacements and returning strikers will displace replacement workers. Also, if the employer resorts to a lock-out, locked-out employees may not be permanently replaced.

Collective redundancies

Unlike the situation in Europe, there are no "redundancy" laws in the United States. Employees covered by collective bargaining contracts typically are protected by a seniority principle that requires lay-offs to occur in reverse order of length of service; very few labor agreements prohibit lay-offs outright. In 1988, the Congress passed the Worker Adjustment and Retraining Notification Act of 1988 (WARN).

This is also called the Plant Closing Bill. It places specific requirements on employers considering significant changes in staffing levels. Under WARN, an organization employing 100 or more individuals must notify workers sixty days in advance if it is going to close its facility or layoff fifty or more individuals. Should a company fail to provide this advance notice, it is subject to a penalty not to exceed "one day's pay and benefits to each employee for each day's notice that should have been given."

However, the law does recognize that under certain circumstances, advance notice may be impossible. Assume, for example, a company is having financial difficulties and is seeking to raise money to keep the organization afloat. If these efforts fail and creditors foreclose on the company, no advance notice is required.

TRANSFERS OF UNDERTAKINGS

The successor's obligation to bargain is based on the language of Sections 8(a)(5) and 9(a) of the National Labor Relations Act – an employer must bargain with the "representatives designated or selected for the purposes of collectively bargaining by the majority of the employees in a unit appropriate for such purposes."

In determining whether a new employer must recognize and bargain with a union that has represented the predecessor's employees, the NLRB looks to the totality of the circumstances to determine whether there have been changes that have significantly altered the employees' working conditions, expectations, and needs for representation.

Factors considered by the Board in determining whether a new employer is obligated to recognize a union are the following:

Continuity of the workforce: A majority of the employees must have worked for the predecessor employer for the union to succeed. If the new owner purposefully avoids hiring union members to escape designation, the majority requirement is waived, and the employer will ordinarily be subject to a bargaining order.

Continuity of operations: The Board looks to the continuity of the functions performed by the employees, the continuation of the business at the same location with the same or similar equipment, and the continuity of customers.

Continuity of the appropriateness of the unit: The bargaining unit of the new employer must continue to be appropriate for a successorship finding.

Hiatus: A hiatus between the cessation of production of the old employer and the commencement of the new employer's operations will be considered by the Board. However, it does not preclude a successorship finding where the hiatus period is viewed as the normal concomitant of a new management and a new approach to a failing business.

Employer defenses: The new employer may avoid the successorship obligations to recognize and bargain with a union where the continuity and hiatus factors do not support a finding of successorship. The new employer may also avoid these obligations if it has not committed unfair labor practices and demonstrates a bona fide doubt as to the union's lack of majority support.

"Alter ego" employers: A successor employer must be distinguished from an "alter ego" employer. An entity is an alter ego of another discontinued entity where it is "merely a disguised continuance of the old employer." In alter ego cases the Board determines whether there is a continuation of ownership and control of the new enterprise by the former

owner, stating it will find alter ego status "where the two enterprises have substantially identical management, business purpose, operations, equipment, customers, and supervision, as well as ownership." The alter ego employer is bound by the terms of the predecessor's agreement.

WAGES AND WORKING TIME

Fair Labor Standards Act of 1938 (FLSA)

This Act contained several provisions that affected organizations and their compensation systems. These included issues surrounding minimum wages, overtime pay, record-keeping and child labor restrictions. Nearly all organizations, except the smallest businesses, are covered by the FLSA. The Act also identified two primary categories of employees –*exempt* and *nonexempt*.

Exempt employees would include, for instance, employees in professional and managerial jobs. Under the Act, jobs categorized as exempt are not required to meet FLSA standards, especially in the area of overtime pay.

Nonexempt employees receive certain protections under the FLSA. Specifically, employees in these jobs are eligible for premium pay – typically time-and-a-half – when they work more than 40 hours in a week. Moreover, these jobs must be paid at least the minimum wage.

Both federal and state governments have also enacted laws requiring employers who contract with the government to pay what are called *prevailing wage rates*. In the federal sector, the secretary of labor is required to review industry rates in the specific locality to set a prevailing rate which becomes the minimum under the contract prescribed under the Walsh-Healy Act. Under this Act, government contractors must also pay time-and-a-half for all work in excess of eight hours a day or forty hours a week.

SOCIAL SECURITY

Social security and medicare taxes

The Social Security Act of 1935 created the social security insurance, which provides benefits such as a source of income for American retirees, disabled workers, and for surviving dependants of workers who have died. Social Security also provides some health insurance coverage through the federal government-sponsored Medicare program (created by the Medicare Act of 1965).

Social Security insurance is financed by contributions made by the employee and matched by the employer, computed as a percentage of the employee's earnings. Additionally, 2.9 percent is assessed for Medicare on all earned income. Similar to Social Security, both the employer and employee split this assessment, paying 1.45 percent each in payroll taxes.

To be eligible for Social Security, employees must be employed for a minimum of forty quarters, or ten years of work. During this work period, employees must have also earned a minimum amount of money each quarter, and for the entire year. Social Security benefits vary, based on the previous year's inflation, one's additional earnings, and the age of the recipient.

Federal unemployment taxes

Unemployment compensation laws provide benefits to employees who meet the following conditions: they are without a job, have worked a minimum number of weeks, submit an application for unemployment compensation to their State Employment Agency, register for available work, and are willing and able to accept any suitable employment offered them through their State Unemployment Compensation Commission. The premise behind unemployment compensation is to provide an income to individuals who have lost a job through no fault of their own (e.g., layoffs, plant closing). Being fired from a job, however, may result in a loss of unemployment compensation rights.

The funds for paying unemployment compensation are derived from a combined federal and state tax imposed on the taxable wage base of the employees'. At the federal level the unemployment tax (based on the Federal Unemployment Tax Act of 1935 – FUTA) is 6.2 percent on the first $7,000 of earnings of employees. State unemployment compensation tax is often a function of a company's unemployment experience; that is, the more an organization lays off employees, the higher its rate.

It is important to mention that major groups that are excluded include self-employed workers, employees who work for organizations employing fewer than four individuals, household domestics, farm employees and state and local government employees.

LEAVE

The Family and Medical Leave Act of 1993 (FMLA)

This Act requires covered employers to provide up to twelve weeks of unpaid, job-protected leave to "eligible" employees for certain family and medical reasons. Employees are eligible if they have worked for a covered employer for at least one year, and for 1,250 hours over the previous twelve months, and if there are at least fifty employees within 75 miles. Unpaid leave must be granted for any of the following reasons:

1 to care for the employee's child after birth, or placement for adoption or foster care;
2 to care for the employee's spouse, son or daughter, or parent, who has a serious health condition; or
3 for a serious health condition that makes the employee unable to perform the employee's job.

At the employee's or employer's option, certain kinds of paid leave may be substituted for unpaid leave. The employee may be required to provide advance leave notice and medical certification.

Taking of leave may be denied if requirements are not met. The employee ordinarily must provide thirty days' advance notice when the leave is foreseeable. An employer may require medical certification to support a request for leave because of a serious health condition, and may require second or third opinions (at the employer's expense) and a fitness for duty report to return to work. For the duration of FMLA leave, the employer must maintain the employee's health coverage under any "group health plan." Upon return from FMLA leave, most employees must be restored to their original or equivalent positions with equivalent pay, benefits, and other employment terms. The use of FMLA leave cannot result in the loss of any employment benefit that accrued prior to the start of an employee's leave.

Military leave

The Uniformed Services Employment and Re-employment Rights Act of 1994 (USERRA) clarifies and strengthens the Veterans' Reemployment Rights (VRR) Statute.

USERRA is intended to minimize the disadvantages to an individual that occur when that person needs to be absent from his or her civilian employment to serve in their country's uniformed services. Specifically, USERRA expands the cumulative length of time that an individual may be absent from work for uniformed services duty and retain reemployment rights.

USERRA potentially covers every individual in the country who serves in or has served in the uniformed services and applies to all employers in the public and private sectors, including Federal employers. The law seeks to ensure that those who serve their country can retain their civilian employment and benefit, and can seek employment free from discrimination because of their service. USERRA provides enhanced protection for disabled veterans, requiring employers to make reasonable efforts to accommodate the disability.

ANTIDISCRIMINATION STATUTORY FRAMEWORK

The Civil Rights Act of 1866

Section 1981 of Title 42 of the US Code, referred to as the Civil Rights Act of 1866, coupled with the Fourteenth Amendment to the Constitution (1868), prohibited discrimination on the basis of race, sex, and national origin. Although these earlier actions have been overshadowed by the 1964 Act, they have gained prominence in years past as being the laws that white male workers could use to support claims of reverse discrimination.

The Equal Pay Act of 1963

This Act mandates that organizations compensate men and women doing the same job in the organization with the same rate of pay. This Act was designed to lessen the pay gap between male and female pay rates. The Equal Pay Act requires employers to eliminate pay differences for the same job. That is, salaries should be established on the basis of skill, responsibility, effort, and working conditions.

Title VII of the Civil Rights Act of 1964

This Title prohibits discrimination in hiring, compensation, and terms, conditions, or privileges of employ-

ment based on race, religion, color, sex or national origin. Title VII also prohibits retaliation against an individual who files a charge of discrimination, participates in an investigation, or opposes any unlawful practice. Most organizations, both public and private, are bound by the law. The law, however, specifies compliance based on the number of employees in the organization. Essentially, as originally passed in 1964, any organization with twenty-five or more (amended to fifteen or more in 1972) employees is covered. This minimum number of employees serves as a means of protecting, or removing from the law, small, family-owned business.

Section 703 of this Act defines what employment activities are unlawful. This same section, however, also exempts several key practices from the scope of Title VII enforcement. The most important are:

1 The *bona fide occupational qualification (BFOQ)* exception: Section 703(e) stipulates that it shall not be unlawful employment practice for an employer to hire employees on the basis of the religion, sex, or national origin in those certain instances where religion, sex or national origin is a BFOQ reasonably necessary to the normal operation of a particular enterprise. The so-called BFOQ clause is construed narrowly by the courts, and the burden of proving the business necessity for any such restrictive occupational qualifications is on the employer.

2 The *testing and educational requirement* exception: Section 703(h) of the Act authorizes the use of "any professionally developed ability test [that is not] designed, intended, or used to discriminate." The EEOC has issued *Uniform Guidelines of Employee Selection Procedures* to assist employers in their compliance with EEOC laws. The *Uniform Guidelines* establish a "four-fifths" rule of thumb for determining when an adverse impact exists in employee selection. If the selection rate for a protected class of employees is less than four-fifths of the selection rate for the rest of the workforce or the qualified applicant pool, the test or requirement has an adverse impact. Although some courts use the four-fifths rule as a guideline, it has not been universally adopted.

3 The *seniority system* exception: Section 703(h) provides that differences in employment conditions that result from a bona fide seniority system are sanctioned as long as the differences do not stem

from an intention to discriminate. The term *seniority system* is generally understood to mean a set of rules that ensures that workers with longer years of continuous service for an employer will have a priority claim to a job over others with fewer years of service.

The Age Discrimination in Employment Act of 1967 (ADEA)

This Act prohibited the widespread practice of requiring workers to retire at the age of 65. It gave protected-group status to individuals between the ages of 40 and 65. Since 1967, this Act has been amended twice – once in 1978, which raised the mandatory retirement age to 70, and again in 1986, where the upper age limit was removed altogether. As a result, anyone over age 39 is covered by the ADEA. Organizations with twenty or more employees, state and local governments, employment agencies, and labor organizations are covered by the ADEA.

The Equal Employment Opportunity Act of 1972 (EEOA)

This Act was designed to provide a series of amendments to Title VII. Probably the greatest consequence of the EEOA was the granting of enforcement powers to the Equal Employment Opportunity Commission (EEOC). The EEOC was granted authority to effectively prohibit all forms of employment discrimination based on race, religion, color, sex or national origin. The EEOC was given the power to file civil suits (individuals may also file a suit themselves if the EEOC declines to sue) against organizations if it was unable to secure an acceptable resolution of discrimination charges within 120 days. In addition, the EEOA also expanded Title VII coverage to include employees of state and local governments, employees of educational institutions, and employers or labor organizations.

Title VII, as it exists today, stipulates that organizations must do more than just discontinue discriminatory practices. Enterprises are expected to actively recruit and give preference to minority group members in employment decisions. This action is commonly referred to as *affirmative action*.

Affirmative action

Affirmative action means that an organization must take certain steps to show that it is not discriminating. For example, the organization must conduct an analysis of the demographics of its current work force. Similarly, the organization must analyze the composition of the community from which it recruits. If the work force resembles the community for all job classifications, then the organization may be demonstrating that its affirmative action program is working. If, however, there are differences, affirmative action also implies that the organization will establish goals and timetables for correcting the imbalance, and have specific plans for how to go about recruiting and retaining protected group members. It is important to mention two consequences of discrimination, such as *adverse impact* and *adverse treatment*.

Adverse impact can be described as any employment consequence that is discriminatory toward employees who are members of a protected group. Protected status categories include race, color, religion, national origin, citizenship status, sex, age 40 and above, pregnancy-related medical conditions, disability and Vietnam-era veteran military status.

Adverse treatment occurs when a member of a protected group receives less favorable outcomes in an employment decision than a non-protected group member.

Executive Orders 11246, 11375 and 11478

Executive Order 11246 prohibited discrimination on the basis of race, religion, color, or national origin by federal agencies as well as by contractors and subcontractors who worked under federal contracts. This was followed by Executive Order 11375, which added sex-based discrimination to the above criteria. In 1969, President Richard Nixon issued Executive Order 11478 to supersede part of Executive Order 11246. It stated that employment practices in the federal government must be based on merit and must prohibit discrimination based on race, color, religion, sex, national origin, political affiliation, marital status or physical disability.

These Orders cover all organizations that have contracts of $10,000 or more with the federal government. Additionally, those organizations with fifty or more employees and/or $50,000 in federal grants must have a written active affirmative action program.

The Rehabilitation Act of 1973

The right of "handicapped persons" to enjoy equal employment opportunities was established on the federal level with the enactment of the Rehabilitation Act of 1973.

Although not designed specifically as an employment discrimination measure but rather as a comprehensive plan to meet many of the needs of the handicapped, the Rehabilitation Act does contain three sections that provide guarantees against discrimination in employment. These sections are:

1 Section 501 of the Act applies to the federal government itself;
2 Section 503 applies to federal contractors; and
3 Section 504 applies to the recipients of federal funds.

Title I of the Americans with Disabilities Act of 1990 (ADA) extends employment protection for disabled persons beyond the federal level to state and local governmental agencies and to all private employers with fifteen or more employees. The ADA refers to *qualified individuals with disabilities* as opposed to the term *handicapped persons* used in the Rehabilitation Act.

The Pregnancy Discrimination Act of 1978 (PDA)

This Act (and supplemented by various state laws) prohibits discrimination based on pregnancy. Under the law, companies may not terminate a female employee for being pregnant, refuse to make a positive employment decision based on one's pregnancy, or deny insurance coverage to the individual. The law also requires organizations to offer the employee a reasonable period of time off from work. Although no specific time frames are given, the pregnancy leave is typically six to ten weeks. At the end of this leave, the worker is entitled to return to work. If the exact job she left is unavailable, a similar one must be provided.

The Americans with Disabilities Act of 1990 (ADA)

This Act prohibits employers from discriminating "against a qualified individual with a disability because of the disability of such individual." A qualified individual with a disability is one "who, with or without reasonable accommodation, can perform the essential functions of the employment position." Therefore, to establish a viable claim under the ADA, a plaintiff must prove by a preponderance of the evidence that:

1 he or she has a disability;
2 he or she is qualified for the position; and
3 an employer discriminated against him or her because of a disability.

Disability under the ADA is a term of art. Section 3(2) of the Act defines it as:

1 a physical or mental impairment that substantially limits one or more of the major life activities of such individual;
2 a record of such an impairment; or
3 being regarded as having such an impairment.

Section 101(9) of the ADA defines an employer's obligation to make "reasonable accommodations" for individuals with disabilities to include

1 making existing facilities accessible to and usable by individuals with disabilities; and
2 restructuring jobs, providing modified work schedules, and acquiring or modifying equipment or devices.

An employer is not obligated under the ADA to make accommodations that would be an "undue hardship" on the employer. The Act excludes from its coverage employees or applicants who are "currently engaging in the illegal use of drugs." The exclusion does not include an individual who has been successfully rehabilitated from such use or is participating in or has completed supervised drug rehabilitation and is no longer engaging in the illegal use of drugs.

The Civil Rights Act of 1991

This Act prohibits discrimination on the basis of race and prohibits racial harassment on the job; returns the burden of proof that discrimination did not occur back to the employer; reinforces the illegality of employers who make hiring, firing, or promoting decisions on the basis of race, ethnicity, sex, or religion; and permits women and religious minorities to seek punitive damages in intentional discriminatory claims. Additionally, this Act also included the Glass Ceiling Act – establishing the Glass Ceiling Commission, whose purpose is to study a variety of management practices in organizations.

OCCUPATIONAL SAFETY AND HEALTH

The Occupational Safety and Health Act of 1970 (the "OSHA") established comprehensive and specific health standards, authorized inspections to ensure the standards are met, empowered the OSHA to police organizations' compliance, and required employers to keep records of illness and injuries, and to calculate accident ratios. The Act applies to almost every US business engaged in interstate commerce. Those organizations not meeting the interstate commerce criteria are generally covered by state occupational safety and health laws.

Typically, OSHA enforces the standards based on a five-item priority listing. These are, in descending priority: imminent danger; serious accidents that have occurred within the past 48 hours; a current employee complaint; inspections of target industries with a high injury ratio; and random inspections.

To fulfill part of the requirements established under the OSHA, employers in industries where a high percentage of accidents and injuries occur must maintain safety and health records. Organizations that are exempt from record-keeping requirements – like universities and retail establishments – still must comply with the law itself; their only exception is the reduction of time spent on maintaining safety records. Employers are required to keep these safety records for five years.

Any work-related illness must be reported. Injuries, on the other hand, are reported only when they require medical treatment (besides first aid), or involve loss of consciousness, restriction of work or motion, or transfer to another job.

An OSHA inspector has the right to levy a fine against an organization for noncompliance. Fines are not for safety violations only. If a company fails to keep its OSHA records properly, it can be subject to stiff penalties.

Under this Act, if an employee death occurs, executives in the company can be criminally liable.

WORKERS' COMPENSATION

The rationale for workers' compensation is to protect employees' salaries and to attribute the cost for occupational accidents and rehabilitation to the employing organization.

Workers' compensation benefits are based on fixed schedules of minimum and maximum payments. When comprehensive disability payments are required, the amount of compensation is computed by considering the employee's current earnings, future earnings, and financial responsibilities. The entire cost of workers' compensation is borne by the organization. Its rates are set based on the actual history of company accidents, the type of industry and business operation, and the likelihood of accidents occurring. The organization, then, protects itself by covering its risks through insurance. Some states provide an insurance system, voluntary or required, for the handling of workers' compensation. Some organizations may also cover their workers' compensation risks by purchasing insurance from private insurance companies. Finally, some states allow employers to be self-insurers. Self-insuring – while usually limited to large organizations – requires the employer to maintain a fund from which benefits can be paid.

Most workers' compensation laws stipulate that the injured employee will be compensated by either a monetary allocation or the payment of medical expenses, or a combination of both. Almost all workers' compensation insurance programs, whether publicly or privately controlled, provide incentives for employers to maintain good safety records

HEALTH INSURANCE

As a general matter, the United States does not mandate provision of employee benefits. Other than modest social security payments for retirees and disabled workers (funded by a payroll tax) and the minimum wage, maximum hour, and overtime protections provided by the FLSA and state laws, benefits are a matter of contracts. Most private employers, whether unionized or not, do provide a fairly extensive array of benefits, the most important of which are health insurance and retirement programs. Tax law favors employer provision of such benefits by allowing employers to deduct their cost and employees to receive them on a tax-free or tax-deferred basis.

The purpose of health insurance is to minimize employees' out-of-pocket expenses for medical care. Any type of health insurance offered to employees generally contains provisions for coverage that can be extended beyond the employee. Specifically, the employee, the employee's spouse, and their children may be covered. The specific types of coverage offered to employees will vary based on the organization's health insurance policy. Generally, three types appear more frequently than others: traditional health-care coverage, Health Maintenance Organizations (HMOs), and Preferred Provider Organizations (PPOs).

The Health Maintenance Act of 1973

This Act created Health Maintenance Organizations (HMOs). It also required employers who extended traditional health insurance to their employees to also offer alternative health-care coverage options. HMOs seek efficiencies by keeping health-care costs down; one means of achieving that goal is by providing preventive care.

COBRA notifications

This Act established the continuation of employee benefits for a period up to three years after the employee leaves the company. When employees resign or are laid off through no fault of their own, they're eligible for a continuation of their health insurance benefits for a period of eighteen months, although under certain conditions, the time may be extended to twenty-nine months. The cost of this coverage is paid by the employee. The employer may also charge the employee a small administrative fee for this service. However, COBRA requires employers to offer this benefit through the company's current group health insurance plan.

RETIREMENT ARRANGEMENTS

Employees cannot rely on the government as the sole source of retirement income. Instead, Social Security payments must be just one component of a properly designed retirement system. The other components are retirement monies and savings amassed over the years. Regardless of the retirement vehicles used, it is important to recognize that retirement plans are highly regulated by the Employee Retirement Income Security Act of 1974 (ERISA).

ERISA

The Employee Retirement Income Security Act of 1974 (ERISA) was passed to deal with one of the largest problems of the day imposed by private pension plans – employees were not getting their benefits. That was due chiefly to the design of the pension plans, which almost always required a minimum tenure with the organization before the individual had a guaranteed right to pension benefits, regardless of whether or not they remained with the company. These permanent benefits – or the guarantee to a pension when one retires or leaves the organization – are called vesting rights. In years past, employees had to have extensive tenures in an organization before they were entitled to their retirement benefits.

ERISA requires employers who decide to provide a pension or profit sharing plan to design their retirement program under specific rules. Typically, each plan must convey to employees any information that is relevant to their retirement. Currently, vesting rights in organizations typically come after six years of service, and pension programs must be available to all employees over age 21. Employees with fewer than six years of service may receive a pro-rated portion of their retirement benefit. ERISA enables pension rights to be portable.

ERISA also created guidelines for the termination of a pension program. Should an employer voluntarily terminate a pension program, the Pension Benefit Guaranty Corporation (PBGC) must be notified. Similarly, the Act permits the PBGC, under certain conditions (such as inadequate pension funding), to lay claim on corporate assets – up to 30 percent of net worth to pay benefits that had been promised to employees. Additionally, when a pension plan is terminated, the PBGC requires the employer to notify workers and retirees of any financial institution that will be handling future retirement programs for the organization.

Another key aspect of ERISA is its requirement for a company to include what is commonly called a Summary Plan Description (SPD). Summary Plan Descriptions are designed to serve as a vehicle to inform employees about the benefits offered in the company in terms the "average" employee can understand.

This means that employers are required to inform employees on the details of their retirement plans, including such items as eligibility requirements, and employee rights under ERISA.

The Retirement Equity Act of 1984

This Act decreased plan participation from age 25 to 21. It also requires plan participants to receive spouse approval before a participant is able to waive survivor benefits.

401(k) plans

Among the different retirement programs, 401(k)s are one of the most popular. Under the Tax Equity and Fiscal Responsible Act (TEFRA), capital accumulation programs, more commonly known as 401(k) or thrift-savings plans, were established. A 401(k) program is named after the IRS tax code section that created it. These programs permit workers to set aside a certain amount of their income on a tax-deferred basis through their employer. In many cases, what differentiated the employer-sponsored 401(k) from an IRA was the amount permitted to be set aside, and the realization that many companies contributed an amount to the 401(k) on the employee's behalf. Because of this matching feature, many companies call their 401(k) a matching-contribution plan, meaning that both the employer and the employee are jointly working to create a retirement program.

FOREIGN WORKERS

The status of foreign workers in the United States is addressed under federal legislation related to immigration laws, employer discrimination and visas.

Employment-related immigration laws

The Immigration Reform and Control Act (IRCA) of 1986 addressed problems associated with illegal immigration to the United States through a broad amnesty program and the initiation of both criminal and civil sanctions against employers who employ undocumented aliens.

The Immigration Act of 1990 reformed legal immigration to the United States. This Act provides for 140,000 visas annually for employer-sponsored immigrants.

Section 101 of the IRCA makes it illegal to hire, recruit, or refer for a fee unauthorized aliens. The law also makes it illegal for an employer to employ an alien in the United States knowing that the alien is (or has become) an unauthorized alien with respect to employment.

The law requires employers to verify that each new employee hired after 6 November 1986 is authorized to work in the United States. The Immigration and Naturalization Service (INS) has designated Form 1–9, Immigration Eligibility Verification Form, as the official verification form to comply with the IRCA. Documents that both identify and support an individual's eligibility to work are a US passport, a certificate of US citizenship, a certificate of naturalization, an unexpired foreign passport with attached visa authorizing US employment, or an Alien Registration Card with photograph. Where the individual does not have one of the above documents, the individual may provide a document evidencing his or her identity and another document evidencing the right to employment. Thus, a state-issued driver's license is sufficient to provide identity and a Social Security card or official birth certificate issued by a municipal authority is sufficient to prove employment eligibility. 1–9s must be kept for three years after the date of hire.

In an action against the employer under the IRCA, the government must establish that the employer had "actual knowledge" that the employee was unauthorized to work in the United States. This standard is one of the highest standards of proof under law.

Employer discrimination

Under Section 102 of the IRCA and Title VII of the Civil Rights Act, it is an unfair practice to discriminate against a person in employment situations on the basis of national origin. Additionally, Section 102 of the IRCA makes it an unfair immigration-related practice to discriminate against an individual in hiring, discharging, recruiting or referring for a fee because of an individual's national origin or, in the case of a citizen or intending citizen, because of that individual's citizenship status.

The Immigration Act of 1990 strengthened the antidiscrimination provisions of the IRCA by prohibiting employers from demanding too much documentation. Section 535(a) of the 1990 Act provides that employers' requests for more or different documents than required under the IRCA or refusal to honor documents that on their face reasonably appear to be genuine shall be treated as an unfair immigration-related employment practice.

Types of visas

Nonimmigrant B-1 business visas are issued by a US consular office abroad after it has been shown that the visitor:

1 has an unabandoned foreign residence;
2 intends to enter the United States for a limited period of time; and
3 will engage solely in legitimate business activities for which the visitor will not be paid in the United States.

Certain investors qualify for E-2 business visas. Principal foreign investors responsible for development and direction of an enterprise in the United States are granted such a visa. An E-2 visa is very desirable because it is issued for extended periods of time, usually four to five years, and may be renewed indefinitely so long as the alien maintains her or his role with respect to the investment. An E-2 visa will not be issued to an applicant who has invested "a relatively small amount of capital in a marginal enterprise solely for the purpose of earning a living."

L-1 visas allow qualifying multinational businesses to make intracompany transfers of foreign persons to the United States when the individuals are employed in management or have "specialized knowledge." L-l visas are good for up to seven years for executives and managers. "Specialized knowledge" personnel may stay for five years.

H-1 classification visas allow aliens of "distinguished merit and ability" to enter and work in the United States on a temporary basis. These persons include architects, engineers, lawyers, physicians and teachers. The American Competitive and Workforce Investment Act of 1998 increased the number of temporary, foreign, high-tech, "highly-skilled" workers that US companies may employ from 65,000 in FY 1998 to 107,500 in FY 2001. These workers are classified as H-1B visa employees. The hiring employer must attest that it will not layoff an American employee ninety days before or after the filing of a petition to employ a foreign worker regarding any position to be filled by the foreign worker. H-1B professionals must be paid the higher of the actual or prevailing wage for each position in order to eliminate economic incentives to use this foreign workers' program.

Temporary agricultural workers are admissible to the United States under the H-2A category of the 1990 Act. An H-2B nonagricultural worker is an alien who is coming temporarily to the United States to perform temporary services or labor, is not displacing US workers capable of performing such services or labor, and whose employment is not adversely affecting the wages and working conditions of a US worker. The 1990 Act places an annual limit on the number of H-2B visas at 66,000.

The 1990 Act created new categories of visas. The R visa facilitates the temporary entry of religious workers into the United States. The Q visa allows private businesses to bring individuals into the country for cultural events. The O and P visas apply to professional entertainers and athletes.

EUROPE

INTRODUCTION

This section will not seek to analyze employment and labor standards in each European country. For the present purpose this section will discuss the Union as a whole and the experience of its larger members. The experience of some of the smaller member countries will be touched on where useful.

EVOLUTION OF THE EUROPEAN UNION

The formation of the European Economic Community (now part of the European Union) under the Rome Treaty of 1957 brought a new influence into labor markets. The Treaty itself had little to say about labor except for the following comments:

1 to call for equal pay for men and women workers;
2 to require freedom of movement of labor throughout the Community; and
3 to require establishment of a European Social Fund, from which help could be provided, for instance, to workers displaced, or threatened with displacement.

By the 1970s, the European Union (then called the European Common Market) was seeking to extend its influence in continental Europe with "directives" concerning procedures for collective dismissals: conditions to apply to workers when their enterprise is taken over by a new owner. Significantly, the directives protected workers' right to payments due to them when an enterprise closes. ("Directives" are binding resolutions addressed by the European Council to the Member States – i.e., countries who are members of the European Union – and obligating the Member States to adopt national regulations reasonably intended to achieve the results specified in the directives.)

As part of its efforts to expedite the formation of a single European market, in the mid-1980s, the Commission set about extending its efforts in labor regulation. It reasoned that if the Union wanted workers to support the single market, it should be seen to serve their interests as well as those of entrepreneurs. In 1989 it put forward a Social Charter, which formed the basis for a legislative program, which it then pursued. It stepped up dialogue with the European trade unions and employers' organizations that, according to the Maastricht Treaty of 1991, were given the right to put forward agreements that the Union could accept as a basis for legislation by the Union. Legislation passed in pursuit of the Charter has included the following:

1 directives requiring the setting up of European works councils in multinational enterprises operating in more than one member country;
2 a framework for working time (including a minimum of four weeks' paid vacation);
3 parental leave; and
4 the working conditions of part-time workers.

The European Court of Justice – the judicial arm of the Union – has also made some influential judgments concerning workers' conditions, notably a ruling against discrimination in occupational pension

rights. In 1997 the Commission decided to put forward a proposal requiring countries to make it obligatory for employers to give their workers rights to information and consultation. The Amsterdam Treaty, signed in June 1997, again signified support for the Union's role in social policy, in establishing an employment chapter and incorporating the Maastricht Social Chapter in the main European Treaty.

INDIVIDUAL EMPLOYMENT

The European Union differentiates two types of contracts, the "fixed-duration contracts of employment" and "temporary employment":

1 *fixed-duration contracts of employment:* concluded directly between the employer and the worker, where the end of the contract is established by objective conditions such as: reaching a specific date, completing a specific task or the occurrence of a specific event;
2 *temporary employment:* relationships between a temporary employment business which is the employer and the worker, where the latter is assigned to work for and under the control of an undertaking and/or establishment making use of his services.

(Articles 1(1) and 1(2) of Directive No. 91/383 of 25 June 1991)

These definitions are rather broad. In certain legal systems fixed-duration contracts relate exclusively to contracts which specify their duration, and thus are distinguished from seasonal contracts or contracts for a specific task to be performed.

Also the definition of temporary work may differ from what is prevalent in some Member States as certain definitions relate only to certain types of work, e.g., of a limited temporary nature and the like.

Termination

European workers tend to have considerably more job security than American workers do. Most have the possibility of appealing a dismissal to some form of labor court. The burden of proof may lie with the employer, and the dismissal may have to be socially justifiable. In the Netherlands the employer is required to ask the Regional Labor Office for permission to terminate a worker's employment. In the case of collective dismissals for economic reasons, invariably the law stops short of vetoing the employer's decision, but it usually requires advance notice and discussion with workers' representatives, aimed at mitigating the effects on workers. In Germany, if the works council is not satisfied with the help offered by the employer, it can refer the matter to an arbitration panel, whose decision is binding. Except that misconduct normally justifies dismissal without notice, there is usually a scale of minimum notice to be given, often based on years of service.

Notice

In Europe, many countries mandate fairly long advance notice periods, particularly for skilled workers. In addition, in most countries, advance notice periods increase with seniority. In Belgium, for instance, the mandatory advance notice for skilled workers with ten years of seniority is nine months, while for workers with twenty years of seniority it is fifteen months. In Sweden, all workers with ten years of seniority are entitled to an advance notice period of five months; whereas for a worker with twenty years of seniority, the mandatory advance notice period is six months.

Unemployment and severance

Unemployment pay and assistance are clearly important. Apart from the generally held view in Europe that unemployment requires workers to receive long-term financial support and help by public services to find a new job, there is considered to be a risk of social disturbance if the unemployed are not helped. There is a wide variety of unemployment insurance and benefits schemes in European countries, providing a similarly wide variety of levels of support; some of the benefits are paid on an earnings-related basis and others on a flat-rate basis.

For many dismissals compensation must be paid. In Spain, the most generous case, basic compensation is twenty days' pay per year of service up to twelve months' pay, or if the dismissal is unfair, forty-five days per year up to forty-two months' pay. For some workers a new rate was established in 1997, of thirty-three days per year, up to a maximum of twenty-four months' payment.

Dispute resolution

Under the Directive 91/553 EEC of 14 October 1991, the employees who consider themselves wronged by failure to comply with the obligations arising from this directive have the right to pursue their claims by judicial process after possible recourse to other competent authorities.

Member States may, however, provide that access to the means of redress is subject to the notification of the employer by the employee and the failure by the employer to reply within fifteen days of notification. The formality of poor notification may in no case be required in the cases of expatriates, nor for workers with a temporary contract of employment relationship, for employees not covered by a collective agreement or by collective agreements relating to the employment relationship (Article 8(2)).

COLLECTIVE BARGAINING

In Europe, unions have often evolved out of a class struggle, resulting in labor as a political party. Recently, unions have begun dropping their "class struggle" rhetoric and slogans to pursue a "partnership" with management. For example, in the United States, "collective bargaining" implies negotiations between a labor union and management. In Sweden and Germany, it refers to negotiation between the employers' organization and a trade union for the entire industry.

American firms have been more inclined to keep labor relations centrally located at corporate headquarters. Many European countries, by contrast, have small home markets with comparatively larger international operations; thus, they are more inclined to adapt to host-country standards and have the labor relations function decentralized.

Union recognition

Whatever the size of an undertaking in France, the exercise of trade union rights is recognized. The law of 1982 abolished the minimum threshold of fifty employees for the creation of a trade union branch. Such a branch can now exist in any undertaking whatever the number of employees. On the other hand, this threshold of fifty will still apply if such a branch is to be entitled to designate a shop steward.

The ability to establish a trade union branch is confined to representative trade unions. Organizations are deemed representative at national level whatever their actual representation in the undertaking. Any trade union which is not affiliated to one of these organizations can create a trade union branch if it can prove that it is representative. Whether a branch is representative depends on a certain number of criteria which include the number of members, the payment of subscriptions, the length of time for which it has been established, and its independence.

Representation process

In France there are two major categories of representatives of the workforce: *workers' representatives* and *works councils.*

Workers' representatives exist once the undertaking (or its branch) has at least eleven employees. The essential role of the workers' representative is to present to the employer all individual or collective complaints concerning wages, and the application of the Employment Code and other laws and regulations, as well as collective labor agreements which apply to the undertaking. Moreover, for undertakings having between eleven and fifty employees, they also perform the function which in undertakings having more than fifty employees is reserved for the works council.

The *works council* has three principal functions:

1 *Professional:* It is consulted on a whole range of problems (hours and times of work, rest, holidays, absence, conditions of work, health and safety, employment of staff, professional training).
2 *Economic and financial:* The head of the undertaking must keep it regularly and punctually informed on certain points.
3 *Social:* It manages all the social and cultural activities of the enterprise.

French law also provides for the existence of branch councils and group councils. The importance of these two organs should be borne in mind. Indeed, once the numerical threshold is reached, they

become compulsory and any failure to these institutions constitutes a criminal offense.

Agreements at the national level

Collective bargaining agreements in countries such as Spain, France and Greece, which are negotiated by a minority, are extended to almost all employees.

In France, the law of 13 November 1982 established the principle of the right of employees to negotiation within the undertaking, and fixed the general conditions under which it was to take place. This legislation applies to the whole of the private sector and must be put into practice between, on the one hand, the employer, and on the other hand the trade union organizations which are representative in the undertaking. Thus, the negotiation can only be carried out, whether it is a one-off negotiation or even a compulsory annual negotiation, in undertakings in which there is at least one shop steward designated by a representative organization.

Bearing in mind that in undertakings having less than fifty employees, a workers' representative can be given this role of shop steward, the applications of provisions relating to negotiation will thus be limited in practice to undertakings in which there are at least eleven employees.

If no trade union organization is represented in the undertaking, it will not be possible for any collective agreements to be entered into. In the absence of trade union representation in the undertaking, the employer will be able to enter into arrangements with representatives of the staff but these will not have the legal status of a collective agreement or negotiation.

Agreements at the European level

A collective agreement is an agreement between one or more employers or employers' association(s) and one or more trade unions, including other *bona fide* representatives of employees, concerning the terms and conditions of employment and the rights and the obligations of the contracting parties.

Agreements at European level can be:

1 European company agreement;
2 European industry agreement;

3 European multi-industry-wide agreement; and
4 European multi-regional agreement (Blanpain, 2002, p. 510).

Third-party resolution of disputes

In Germany, the methods of exerting pressure by the opposing sides in industrial relations disputes are strikes and lockouts, and the detailed provisions governing these are established by judge-made law. Often industrial disputes are conciliated by neutral mediation by public figures such as, for instance, former ministers. Political strikes or sympathy strikes are unlawful and the trade unions and employees are obliged to compensate for the resulting loss. Collective bargaining is frequently accompanied by warning strikes.

WORKER PARTICIPATION

The German and Dutch models of worker participation are significant in and of themselves. At the same time, they have been influential in shaping worker participation in other European countries and at the level of the European Union.

The German model

In the German (two-tier) system, elected employees or trade-unionists are members of the supervisory organ of the company. They constitute one-third of the members in companies which employ from 500 to 2,000. If one-third is more than three, trade unionists can have a seat on the board. In companies that employ 2,000 employees or more, a system of quasi-parity prevails in the supervisory organ. There are namely as many members representing the shareholders as there are members representing the employees. The chairperson of the supervisory organ, however, is always a representative of the shareholders and has a casting vote in the case of deadlock. It should be mentioned that this latter German model provides for a specific place in the supervisory organ of a representative of the (higher) middle-management, namely of the so-called *leitende Angestellten*. This representative is chosen out of a list of two, nominated by the *leitende Angestellten,* by all the white-collar workers, *leitende Angestellten* included.

The Dutch model

The Dutch (two-tier) model starts from the reasoning that there is no room in the supervisory organ either for employees or for trade-union representatives. In order to avoid unnecessary confrontation and to guarantee a smooth decision-making process a system of co-option has been set up.

Under this model, whenever a vacancy on the board comes up, the remaining members of the board will co-opt candidates from a list of candidates, nominated separately by shareholders, management and the works council, which is composed of employees only in the Netherlands. Out of these nominees, the remaining members of the board will choose a new member. That new member can neither be an employee nor a trade-unionist, as indicated, but should be an independent and socially accepted person. If one of the groups (shareholders, management or works council) is of the opinion that the co-opted nominee does not qualify, it can pronounce a veto against him or her in which situation the case can be brought before the *Enterprise Chamber* (Court) of Amsterdam, which will decide whether to sustain or not sustain the veto. It is self-evident that trade unions have lists of social commissionaires candidates, which they provide to the works council, and that there is a *de facto* consultation among the groups involved in order to arrive at a consensus.

Employee participation through a body representing company employees

This model means that a workers' council is established at the level of the enterprise which has the right, in relation to the company's management organ, to regular information and consultation on the administration, situation, progress and prospects of the company, its competitive position, credit situation and investment plans. It also has the same rights to information as those conferred on the members of the supervisory organ or the non-executive members of the administrative organ. The workers' representatives need furthermore to be consulted in cases in which the supervisory organ needs to grant authorization (closure, transfer, etc.). If the opinion of the employees' representatives is not followed by management, the reasons for this decision must be communicated.

Participation through collectively agreed systems

In this model, employee participation is regulated in accordance with collective agreements concluded between the company and organizations representing its employees. These collective agreements will provide for comparable right to information and consultation as in the other models.

COLLECTIVE REDUNDANCIES

In the event of a "collective redundancy" as defined below, the employer shall give prior written notice to the public authorities and workers' representatives. The employer shall, moreover, consult with the workers' representatives prior to finalizing the plans for the collective redundancy.

A "collective redundancy" is a dismissal effected by an employer for one or more reasons not related to the individual workers concerned and affecting several employees as follows. The number of dismissals is: either,

1 over a period of ninety days: at least twenty, whatever the number of workers normally employed in the establishments in question; or
2 over a period of 30 days:
   (a) at least ten in establishments normally employing more than twenty and less than 100 workers;
   (b) at least 10 percent of the number of workers in establishments normally employing at least 100 but less than 300 workers;
   (c) at least thirty in establishments normally employing 300 workers or more.
      (Directive 98/59 EC of 20 July 1998 Council Directive on the approximation of the laws of the Member States relating to collective redundancies)

Although the directive primarily deals with collective dismissal of workers it holds that "for the purpose of calculating the number of redundancies ... termination of an employment contract which applies to the individual workers concerned shall be assimilated to redundancies, provided that there are at least five redundancies" (Article 1(b) of Directive 98/59 EC of 20 July 1998).

The Directive in principle also applies to collective redundancies where the establishment's activities are terminated as a result of a judicial decision.

TRANSFERS OF UNDERTAKINGS

The employees who are employed on the date of transfer are automatically transferred to the new employer with all their acquired rights, whether they or the new employer want it or not. Therefore, the terms of the contract work or of the working relationship may not be altered with regard to the salary, in particular its day of payment and composition, notwithstanding that the total amount is unchanged (The Council Directive 77/187/EEC of 14 February 1977 on the Approximation of the Laws of the Member States relating to the Safeguarding of Employees' Rights in the event of Transfers of Undertakings, Businesses or Parts of Businesses).

The transferee shall, following the transfer, continue to observe the terms and conditions agreed in any collective agreement on the same terms applicable to the transferor under that agreement, until the date of termination or expiry of the collective agreement or the entry into force or application of another collective agreement. The directive does not oblige the transferee to continue to observe the terms and conditions agreed in any collective agreement in respect of workers who are not employed by the undertaking at the time of the transfer. Member States may limit the period of observing such terms and conditions, with the proviso that it shall not be less than one year (Article 3(3) of Directive 77/187/EEC of 14 February 1977).

The transferee undertakings are not precluded, however, from altering the working relationship with the new head of the undertaking in so far as the national law allows such an alteration independently of a transfer of the undertaking.

WAGES

Several European countries have a national minimum wage – Belgium, France, the Netherlands, Spain and the UK – shortly to be joined by Ireland – though not Germany, Italy or Sweden. Collective bargaining plays a much greater part in setting minimum wage rates. The OECD has found that collective bargaining coverage in twelve European countries ranged from 47 percent in the UK to 98 percent in Austria, with five of the countries having coverage of 90 percent or more. Incidentally, several continental European countries have arrangements of "extension," whereby the authorities can extend the provisions of a collective agreement to employers and employees who are not affiliated with the respective bargaining parties.

WORKING TIME

Since unemployment started to be a serious post-war European problem in the late 1970s, several European governments and virtually all the trade unions have seen reduction of working time as a key measure for reducing unemployment. Thus, comparing annual hours actually worked per person in employment in 1996, the OECD found figures of 1,578 (Germany); 1,645 (France); 1,738 (UK); and 1,810 (Spain), compared with 1,951 in the US. What is more common is to agree on introducing more flexibility into the arrangement of shorter hours, so that, for instance, enterprises could vary their workweek throughout the year, according to need. Some German industries have done this for more than a decade now.

Daily rest

Every worker is entitled to a minimum daily rest period of eleven consecutive hours per twenty-four-hour period (Article 3 of Council of Directive 93/104/EC concerning certain aspects of the organization of working time).

Break

Where the working day is longer than six hours, every worker is entitled to a rest break, the details of which, including duration and the terms on which it is granted, shall be laid down in collective agreement or agreements between the two sides of industry or, failing that, by national legislation (Article 4 of Council of Directive 93/104/EC).

Weekly rest period

Per each seven-day period, every worker is entitled to a minimum uninterrupted rest period of twenty-four hours plus the eleven hours' daily rest referred to in Article 3. If objective, technical or work organization conditions so justify, a minimum rest period of twenty-four hours may be applied (Article 5 of Council of Directive 93/104/EC).

Maximum weekly working time

The period of weekly working time is limited by means of laws, regulations or administrative provisions or by collective agreements or agreements between the two sides of industry. The average working time for each seven-day period, including overtime, does not exceed forty-eight hours (Article 6 of Council of Directive 93/104/EC).

Night work and shift work

Normal hours of work for night workers do not exceed an average of eight hours in any twenty-four-hour period. Night workers whose work involves special hazards or heavy physical or mental strain do not work more than eight hours in any period of twenty-four hours during which they perform night work.

Work involving special hazards or heavy physical or mental strain shall be defined by national legislation and/or practice or by collective agreements concluded between the two sides of industry, taking account of specific effects and hazards of night work (Article 8 of Council of Directive 93/104/EC).

LEAVE

Regulations apply to annual leave, maternity leave and parental leave.

Annual leave

Every worker is entitled to paid annual leave of at least four weeks in accordance with the conditions for entitlement to, and granting of, such leave laid down by national legislation and/or practice. The minimum period of paid annual leave may not be replaced by an allowance in lieu, except where the employment relationship is terminated (Article 7 of Council of Directive 93/104/EC).

THREE

Maternity leave

The European Union requires Member States to implement measures to encourage improvements in the safety and health at work of pregnant workers and workers who have recently given birth or who are breast feeding. The protective measures required by the Directive include:

1 temporarily adjusting working conditions;
2 worker leave including the payment of an adequate allowance;
3 providing an alternative to night work;
4 a continuous period of maternity leave of at least 14 weeks; and
5 the prohibition of dismissal of the workers from the beginning of pregnancy to the end of the maternity leave (Directive No. 92/85 of 19 October 1992 on Council Directive on the protection of pregnant women at work).

Parental leave

The agreement grants men and women workers an individual right to parental leave on the grounds of the birth or adoption of a child, to enable them to take care of that child, for at least three months, until a given age up to 8 years to be defined by Member States and/or management and labor. The right to parental leave is, in principle, granted on a non-transferable basis (Clauses 2(1) and 2(2) of Council Directive 96/34/EC of 3 June 1996).

Employees in Norway have been given much superior family leave. Fathers are granted four weeks of paid leave upon the birth of a child. Mothers, on the other hand, receive either fifty-two weeks of leave paid at 80% of their salary or forty-two weeks off at 100% of their salary.

EQUAL TREATMENT

The European Union has adopted a general framework for combating discrimination on the grounds of religion or belief, disability, age or sexual orientation as regards employment and occupation. The ultimate aim of the applicable directive is to establish the principle of equal treatment in the context of employment (Council Directive 2000/78/EC of 27 November 2000).

Definitions

The principle of "equal treatment" covers direct discrimination, indirect discrimination and harassment.

There is direct discrimination where one person is treated less favorably than another is, has been or would be treated in a comparable situation. There is indirect discrimination where an apparently neutral provision, criterion or practice would put persons having a particular religion or belief, a particular disability, a particular age, or a particular sexual orientation at an unjustified disadvantage compared with other persons.

Harassment is a form of discrimination when unwanted conduct takes place with the purpose or effect of violating the dignity of a person and of creating an intimidating, hostile, degrading, humiliating or offensive environment.

Positive action

With a view ensuring full equality in practice, the principle of equal treatment shall not prevent any Member State from maintaining or adopting specific measures to take positive actions to overcome barriers to equal treatment.

For example, employers must take appropriate positive measures, where needed in a particular case, to enable a person with a disability to have access to, participate in, or advance in employment, or to undergo training, unless such measures would impose a disproportionate burden on the employer.

OCCUPATIONAL SAFETY AND HEALTH

Employers have the duty to ensure the safety and the health of workers in every aspect related to the work (Council Directive No. 89/391 of 12 June 1989).

The employer must take the necessary measures, including the prevention of occupational risks and the provision of information and training (Article 6(1)). The employer of course carries the full financial burden: measures related to safety, hygiene and health at work may in no circumstances involve the workers in the financial cost (Articles 6(1) and 6(5) of Council Directive No. 89/391 of 12 June 1989).

The health and safety obligations apply to all sectors of activity, both public and private (industrial, agriculture, commercial, administrative, service, edu-cational, cultural, leisure, etc.), with the exception of certain specific activities in the civil protection serv-ices, such as the armed forces and the police.

PENSIONS

Fixed retirement ages are largely a function of the introduction of State pensions. Before that, most workers were likely to work as long as they were phys-ically able to do so, or as long as their employer allowed them to work. The most common age to receive a State pension is 65, though in Denmark it is 67 and in France 60. In Italy it was, until recently, 60 for men and 55 for women, but these ages are being increased gradually to 65 for men and 60/65 for women. Retirement ages are much more flexible than they used to be. Several countries have facili-tated early retirement schemes. Those schemes usually provide a higher pension than would be actu-arially justifiable, if a worker wanted to retire and the employer engaged a replacement from the unemployment register. However, such arrangements have lost favor among governments on account of their expense.

Public pension arrangements differ widely between countries, concerning the following factors:

1 the amounts paid;
2 how they are financed and administered;
3 whether they provide flat-rate amounts or are earnings-related;
4 who qualifies to receive them; and
5 how much flexibility they provide.

BENEFITS

The European Commission has calculated, based on the average industrial wage, that the benefits payable to a single person who is entitled to full basic pension on the basis of contributions paid, is around 75 per-cent of average net earnings. In the UK, Ireland and the Netherlands, however, the proportion is less than 50 percent.

Apart from state schemes, of which there may well be more than one in a particular country, there are also a considerable variety of occupational schemes and some personal pension arrangements, sometimes favored by tax concessions.

FREE MOVEMENT OF WORKERS

Free movement of workers entails the right to work in another Member State under the same conditions as national workers; it includes *the right to move freely* within the territory of Member States for this purpose and *the right to stay* in a Member State (Article 39(3)(b) of The Treaty Establishing the European Community (consolidated text) O.J. 325 of 24.12.2002).

The *right to move freely* as well as the right to entry and residence is linked to "an offer of employment actually made." There must be in the person of the worker a concrete offer of employment as a precon-dition for the right to move and residence. However, the Court is of the opinion that free movement for workers also entails the right to look for work when one wishes to pursue an effective and genuine activ-ity. From its side, the Council made on the occasion of the adoption of the directive in 1968 a declaration stating that a national of a Member State has the right to look for work on the territory of another Member State during a period of three months, and this right becomes defunct if the national concerned becomes dependent on the social assistance of the host Member State.

The *right to stay* in a Member State is contingent upon employment. The member of another State may be required to leave the territory of that State (subject to appeal) if he or she has not found employ-ment there after six months, unless the person con-cerned provides evidence that he is continuing to seek employment and he has genuine chances of being engaged.

Relationships with Taxing Authorities

International corporate income taxation

INTRODUCTION

Government relationships are clearly very important to business. Governments have the authority to regulate all business conduct for various purposes, for example: to protect the interests of individuals affected by business decisions (e.g., competitors, consumers and local communities)

In addition, governments have their own interests. In particular, governments need to generate revenue for themselves, both to provide public goods and services (such as transportation facilities and national defense) and to achieve public policy goals (such as income redistribution). Of course, government generates revenues by levying taxes, including various taxes on businesses. Since taxes can significantly reduce the returns available to business, taxes are an important issue in many business decisions.

Governments obtain revenues by imposing a wide variety of taxes, e.g., income taxes, value-added taxes, import duties, use taxes, property taxes and social security contributions. In this chapter, I will focus only on income taxes. I will focus on income taxes, first, because income taxes are imposed on businesses by most governments around the world. Second, the amount of income taxes can be significant, with marginal rates frequently rising to as much as one-third of business net income in many countries. Third, as opposed to some other types of taxes (such as import duties and value added taxes), income taxes appear as a separate line item on financial reports to shareholders. Fourth, international corporate income tax often poses significant difficulties

and challenges for international business transactions and multinational operations.

Most importantly, I will focus on income taxes because businesses – including multinational corporate groups – have opportunities to significantly reduce or defer income taxes, although rarely to avoid income taxes altogether, by anticipating them in their business decisions.

Preliminary observations

First, as with the other chapters in this text, this chapter will do no more than provide a general outline – in this case: an outline of the general principles used by many governments around the world to impose income tax on corporations. It will enable you to raise issues with appropriate experts and integrate their advice into your business decisions.[1]

Second, in addition to providing a brief outline of the most general principles for international corporate income taxation, I can do little more than provide a few brief illustrations of how the most important principles operate. Accordingly, examples are hypothetical in nature, are based on important simplifying assumptions and are given solely for the purpose of illustration only. Actual outcomes in actual tax cases depend on specific tax regulations beyond the scope of this chapter.[2]

Third, international corporate taxation provides a complete analytical framework, with sometimes seemingly compelling conclusions, for structuring international business transactions and multinational corporate group organizations. Please bear in mind that the structure of specific operations and organizations depends on many factors, including commercial, technical, human resources, regulatory and geographic considerations (e.g., the history of a corporation's foreign acquisitions).

In general

All international corporate income is subject to two different tax regimes. The first regime is the tax claimed by nations themselves. The second is the network of bilateral tax treaties which resolve conflicting claims amongst those nations, i.e., gives priority to one nation's income tax claim over another nation's claim.

INCOME TAXES CLAIMED BY NATIONS

There are three generally recognized bases for nations to claim the right to tax income realized by corporations: nationality, residency and source. The same nation can assert different bases for the purpose of taxing various income streams. In other words, in practice these various bases are not mutually exclusive.

The nationality principle

Under the nationality principle, a country claims the right to tax the income realized by all of its "nationals," without regard to the places where they reside or derive their income. Under the nationality principle, for example, the United States claims the right to tax US citizens residing in England on all of their worldwide income. Nationality for corporations and other legal entities is determined by the country in which they are incorporated or formed. For example, a company incorporated in the State of Delaware is a national of the United States.

The residency principle

Under the residency principle, a country claims the right to tax all of the income of its "residents" without regard to the residents' nationality or the source of their income. Under the residency principle, for example, the United States claims the right to tax

subjects of the United Kingdom on all of their worldwide income if they are registered in the USA as "resident aliens." In common law countries (the United Kingdom, its current dependencies and former colonies, including the United States), residency for corporations and other legal entities is determined by the place where their "central management and control" is exercised. In civil law countries, residency for corporations and other legal entities exists both in the place where they are incorporated and in the place where they maintain central management.[3] In other words, under civil law principles, a corporation is always resident in the country where it is a national.

The source principle

Finally, under the "source" principle, a country claims the right to tax all income realized by any individual or corporation from sources within its borders, without regard to that individual's or corporation's nationality or residency. Under the "source" principle, for example, the United States claims the right to tax United Kingdom subjects on all of their income derived from sources within the United States even if those UK subjects do not reside in the USA.

Nations often claim the right to tax the following types of income at their source:

1 income or gains derived from leasing, licensing or selling property located within the country;
2 income derived from a trade or profession conducted individually or, by a foreign corporation, through an unincorporated entity within the country; and
3 income derived from employment within the country.[4]

BILATERAL INCOME TAX TREATIES

The second regime is the network of bilateral income tax treaties maintained by each of the commercially active nations around the world (and by many of the other nations). By far the most important model for bilateral tax treaties is the OECD Model Convention with Respect to Taxes on Income and on Capital (the "OECD Model Convention"), which was last revised on 28 January 2003.[5]

Elimination of double taxation

Given the three different bases upon which nations assert the right to impose income taxes, it is not uncommon that the same income would be subject to income tax in more than one country. For example, income derived from the export sale could be fully subject to income tax in both the country of export and the country of import, each under the national taxing regime. In such a case, the exporting nation would claim income tax on the basis of the exporter's residency and the importing nation would claim tax as the source of the income.

At the same time, allowing more than one country to claim income taxes unabated on the same income, i.e., "double taxation," is considered to be unfair to the corporation subject to the double taxation. Double taxation is also considered to be a barrier to foreign trade and foreign investment (because they could give rise to income taxes in two different countries based on the differing principles, often residency and source).

As a result, bilateral tax treaties are intended to eliminate double taxation by resolving conflicting national claims for the imposition of income taxes. The bilateral treaties generally resolve these claims by establishing priorities amongst claims based on nationality, residency and source.

Priority given to the residency principle

Under the OECD Model Convention, the nation which imposes its taxes on the basis of the residency principle generally has priority over the nations which impose their income tax on the basis of nationality or source.[6]

Most importantly, a nation which taxes business profits on the basis of the residency principle has priority over the nations which impose their income tax on the basis of the source principle. For example, a company making export sales is subject to income taxation only in its country of residency, not in the country where its customers are located.[7]

This result is practical in part because business profits are not based on gross revenue. Business profits (the basis for most corporate income taxes) are based on a calculation of revenues less expenses. It would be relatively difficult for a nation claiming the right to tax business profits at their source (e.g., importing

nation) to calculate those profits because such a calculation would require an allocation of a portion of the exporting company's expenses to the income for which the importing country claims taxes. The resident nation (e.g., the exporting nation) can calculate business profits much more easily because the exporting nation does not need to allocate the exporting company's expenses between income derived from exports and income derived from domestic sales.

Taxing business profits (e.g., income from export sales) under the residency principle as opposed to taxing them the source principle is practical for another reason. It is difficult for the nation where the income is sourced (e.g., the importing nation) to enforce rules requiring non-resident corporations (e.g., importers) to file income tax returns and to provide other relevant information. Similarly, it would be difficult for nations relying solely on the "source" principle (e.g., importing nations) to collect income taxes due from non-resident corporations. The resident nation (e.g., the exporting nation) does not have such difficulties because the resident corporation (e.g., the exporter) is undoubtedly already subject to income tax reporting and payment requirements there. In addition, all of the tax rules of resident nations are easier to enforce because at least some of their resident corporations' assets and management are located there.

Two important exceptions to the priority for residency

Having established "residency" as the priority basis for a nation's right to impose corporate income tax on international business transactions, the OECD Model Convention also recognizes two important exceptions to this priority rule.

The first important exception is "permanent establishments." This exception allows nations to tax the business profits of non-resident corporations if they maintain a significant presence within their borders. Either:

(a) a place of business, such as an office with sales employees; or

(b) a contracting agent can constitute such a presence.[8]

The second important exception is "withholding taxes." The OECD Model Convention recognizes the right for a nation to "withhold" taxes at the source for certain types of income. The OECD Model Convention recognizes this right in particular for interest, royalties and dividends, in part because these types of income do not pose practical problems in terms of calculation, reporting and collection.

PERMANENT ESTABLISHMENTS

The exception for business profits

Having established that taxes can be imposed on business profits only by nations where a corporation is resident (i.e., where management exercises effective control), the OECD Model Convention also recognizes that a corporation "resident" in one nation can have such a significant presence in a second nation as to warrant the second nation's taxation on income attributable to that presence. Since each corporation can have its "residency" in only one nation under the OECD Model Convention, the corporation's taxable presence in the second nation is given another name: a "permanent establishment."

It is important to recognize that the concept of "permanent establishment" is a limitation on a nation's claim to tax a non-resident corporation's presence within its borders. Many nations claim income taxes on "trades or businesses conducted" within their borders by non-resident corporations.[9] Under the laws of such nations, a "trade or business" may require a minimal presence or activity within those nations' borders. A nation could conceivably claim, for example, that any importation of products into the nation constitutes the conduct of a trade or business there, requiring the payment of taxes on business profits. In this context, the permanent exception establishes that a nation can tax a non-resident corporation's trade or business within its borders (e.g., business profits from import sales) only if such trade or business constitutes a "permanent establishment."

Never subsidiary corporations

The first important observation about permanent establishments is that they are never corporations. If a corporation resident in one country establishes a second, wholly-owned corporation (i.e., a subsidiary)

in a second country, then the subsidiary corporation is not a permanent establishment for the non-resident corporation. Instead, the subsidiary corporation constitutes a new taxpayer "resident" in the second country under the OECD Model Convention – not a taxable presence of the first, non-resident corporation. The non-resident corporation, moreover, does not become a permanent establishment in the second nation simply by virtue of the fact that it owns a subsidiary in the second nation.

An unincorporated place of business

In other words, a permanent establishment is always a non-resident corporation's unincorporated presence in a second nation. An unincorporated presence constitutes a permanent establishment, subjecting the non-resident corporation to income taxes, if the unincorporated presence is "a fixed place of business through which the business of an enterprise [i.e., the non-resident corporation] is wholly or partly carried on" within that nation.[10] For example, a non-resident corporation has a permanent establishment within a nation if it maintains a one-employee office there for the purpose of soliciting purchase orders within the nation.

One important exception exists: As explained below, a fixed place of business is not a permanent establishment if its activities are exclusively "of a preparatory or auxiliary character." In other words, nations cannot tax a trade or business conducted by a non-resident corporation within their borders, even if the non-resident corporation's presence there otherwise would constitute a "permanent establishment," if the activities effectively connected with that presence are exclusively "preparatory or auxiliary" in nature.

A contracting agent

In addition, a non-resident corporation has a permanent establishment within a nation if it maintains an agent there who "has, and habitually exercises, [within the nation] an authority to conclude contracts in the name of the enterprise."[11]

There are two important exceptions to this rule. First, the agent is not a "permanent establishment" if the agent with contracting authority is an independent "broker, general commission agent or any other agent of an independent status, provided that such persons are acting in the ordinary course of their business."[12] Second, as explained below, the agent's contracting authority is limited to activities of a "preparatory or auxiliary character."[13] If either of these exceptions applies, agents are not permanent establishments – and so cannot provide the basis for a nation to tax non-resident corporations – even though the agents have contracting authority for the non-resident corporation.

Preparatory or auxiliary activities

Finally, as noted briefly above, fixed places of business and contracting agents can never be permanent establishments if their activities are limited to functions which are exclusively "preparatory or auxiliary in character," i.e., preparatory or auxiliary for generating income. "Preparatory or auxiliary" activities include maintaining warehouses, inventories, consignment inventories, showrooms and offices simply for the purpose of collecting information.[14]

Of course, maintaining a place of business or contracting agent for the purpose of purchasing goods and services can never constitute a permanent establishment because purchasing goods does not result in the generation of income. Purchasing goods is necessarily a preparatory or auxiliary activity to the conduct of any business.

Attribution rules

Subjecting non-resident corporations to income tax in the nations where their permanent establishments are located creates difficulties for calculating the income subject to taxation.

As previously noted, business profits (the basis for most corporate income taxes) are based on a calculation of revenues less expenses. At the same time, calculating the revenues and expenses "attributable" to a permanent establishment is not always evident. For example, agents might not be directly involved in any specific revenue-generating transaction for their affiliated non-resident corporations. In the face of such uncertainties, the OECD Model Convention provides in effect that a permanent establishment's profit should be calculated as if it were an unrelated incorporated entity:

[Each nation shall attribute to each] permanent establishment the profits which it might be expected to make if it were a distinct and separate enterprise engaged in the same or similar activities under the same or similar conditions and dealing wholly independently with the enterprise of which it is a permanent establishment.
(OECD Model Convention, Article 7(2))[15]

With such limited guidance, some nations have adopted the practice of taxing permanent establishments on the basis of an apportionment of the non-resident corporation's total profits. The OECD endorses this approach provided that it is not contrary to the provisions of the Model Convention.[16]

WITHHOLDING TAXES

The exception for interest, royalties and dividends

"Withholding taxes" are the other important exception to the rule giving priority to nations imposing tax on the basis of residency. The exception for certain "withholding taxes" in effect gives priority to nations imposing tax under the source principle for certain sorts of income.

Under a system of "withholding taxes," nations require their resident banks and other entities making certain types of payments abroad to non-resident corporations (e.g., German banks paying interest abroad to USA corporations) to surrender directly to their taxing authorities (i.e., to "withhold" from the non-resident payee corporation) the amount of taxes due by the non-resident corporation on the basis of its right to receive that payment. For example, Germany can require its resident banks:

(a) to withhold from US corporations the amount of the taxes due by the US corporations on the interest they receive from German banks; and
(b) to pay that amount to the German taxing authorities.

As with "permanent establishments," the treatment of "withholding taxes" in the OECD Model Convention operates both to allow (as an exception to the priority given to the residency principle under the Convention) and to limit (as a restriction on each nation's sovereign right to tax all income at its source) the income taxes nations can claim at the source on interest, royalties and dividends payable to non-resident corporations.[17]

Assessed on the basis of "gross revenue"

Withholding taxes are not imposed on the amount of "net income," i.e., the amount by which revenues exceed expenses. They are imposed on the amount of revenues without any reduction for expenses, i.e., on the basis of "gross revenues" of interest, royalties and dividends. Imposing taxes on the gross amount of certain types of income rather than the net amount avoids one of the practical difficulties raised by the possibility of imposing taxes at their source: calculating the amount by which taxable revenues exceed deductible expenses.[18]

Requires no collection from non-resident corporations

Withholding taxes are imposed only on types of income (e.g., interest, royalties and dividends) which do not pose the practical difficulty of collecting taxes from non-resident corporations. This practical difficulty is surmounted by collecting withholding taxes at their source – from the banks and other entities making payments to the non-resident corporations. In other words, the entities making payments abroad have an obligation to the nations where they are resident to "withhold" the taxes due by non-resident corporations on the basis of the payments the resident entities are making. In effect, each nation's right to collect taxes on certain types of income under the "source" principle is implemented by recognizing their right to impose a withholding obligation under the "residency" principle.

Requires no filings by non-resident corporations

By requiring resident entities making payments abroad (e.g., banks making interest payments to non-resident corporations) to withhold taxes at the source, nations also avoid the practical difficulties presented by requiring non-resident corporations to file income tax returns. The paying entities surrender directly to

the taxing authorities of their resident nations the amounts they have withheld "in the name of" the non-resident corporations receiving payments. In other words, pursuant to systems of withholding taxes, non-resident corporations do not receive the entire pre-tax amount of the interest, royalties or dividends due to them. Instead, they receive the post-tax amount due to them, i.e., the income due to them less the amount of taxes collected at the source. In this context, non-resident corporations do not file tax returns to establish the amount of taxes due; non-resident corporations file returns only for the purpose of obtaining refunds.

Subject to important limitations

Like other forms of income taxes, withholding taxes on interest, royalties and dividends are imposed on a percentage basis (e.g., 25 percent or 30 percent of the gross amount of the interest, royalties or dividends). Unlike other forms of income taxes, withholding taxes are usually not imposed on a progressive basis, i.e., with higher rates applied to higher gross amounts.

More importantly, withholding taxes are often subject to limitations negotiated in income tax treaties. For example, the OECD Model Convention itself provides that withholding taxes on dividends arising from non-resident corporate investments in subsidiaries shall not exceed 5 percent of the gross amount of the dividends. The withholding rate provided for dividends arising from other (i.e., portfolio) investments shall not exceed 15 percent of the gross amount of those dividends.[19] The maximum withholding rate is 10 percent for interest income.[20] The OECD Model Convention does not provide a maximum withholding rate for royalties.[21]

Withholding tax rates are often subject to important limitations because the nations imposing them often wish to promote foreign investment generally and in particular the domestic industries giving rise to the types of income subject to the withholding (i.e., banking, technology and holding company operations). Such nations can agree to reduced withholding rates for interest, royalties and dividends paid to non-resident corporations in part because they can do so without sacrificing:

(a) either their tax basis from other types of income; or
(b) their tax rates from resident tax payers (even taxes on residents' interest, royalties and dividends).[22]

MECHANISMS FOR AVOIDING DOUBLE TAXATION

As explained above, nations can tax income – either net income or gross income – on the basis of:

(a) a corporation's place of incorporation ("nationality");
(b) the location of effective management control ("residency"); or
(c) the place from which the income originates ("source").

These various bases for taxing authority give rise to conflicting claims among nations. The conflicting claims are resolved by giving priority to a corporation's residency, with limited exceptions permitting nations to impose:

(a) a tax on a non-resident corporation's business profits attributable to a trade or business conducted within their borders – but only if that trade or business constitutes a reasonably substantial presence ("permanent establishment"); or
(b) "withholding taxes," taxes collected at the source – but only for specific types of income payable to non-resident corporations, especially interest royalties and dividends.

Within this global regime for taxing international corporate income, there is no special mechanism necessary to establish residency as the priority basis for taxing corporations. The OECD Model Convention simply states that each nation shall have the right to tax the worldwide income of its resident corporations without regard to their nationality or the source of their income.[23]

Having established a comprehensive priority in favor of the residency principle, special mechanisms are necessary so that nations with priority authority to impose income taxes on the basis of residency defer to other nations' proper authority to impose income taxes on permanent establishments and to collect withholding taxes.

As outlined below, those special mechanisms take the form of exemptions and credits. It is important to note that a nation can grant exemptions and credits to its resident corporations on the basis of their foreign-sourced business profits even if a treaty does not obligate the nation to do so. The United States, for example, currently maintains a system of exemptions to provide tax relief for exports by its resident corporations.[24]

In fact, some nations (for example, in Europe) go beyond exemptions and credits, unilaterally surrendering their right to tax resident corporations on all forms of extra-territorial income. They limit their taxing jurisdiction to the "territorial" principle in part for historical reasons without regard to the extra-territorial rights recognized internationally.[25]

Exemptions

The first mechanism for avoiding double income taxation is the "exemption." Pursuant to an exemption, the nation where a corporation is resident defers to taxes imposed by another nation by subtracting from the income otherwise taxable in the resident nation the income subject to tax in the other nation. For example, pursuant to the "exemption" mechanism, Canada would allow Canadian corporations to deduct from their worldwide income – otherwise taxable in Canada – the amount of business profits subject to taxation in Chile or in any other country.[26]

The exemption mechanism is preferred by corporations because it can sometimes result in a corporation paying the lower of two applicable national tax rates. The corporation will pay the lower of two rates when the rate imposed on business profits or other income by the nation where it is not resident is less than the tax rate imposed by the nation where it is resident. For example, if Chile used a 12 percent tax rate to impose taxes of $120,000 on $1,000,000 of business profits earned in Chile by a Canadian corporation, and if Canada used the "exemption" mechanism to avoid double taxation, then the Canadian corporation would pay a total of only $120,000 (all of it going to Chilean taxing authorities) even though the 30 percent Canadian corporate tax rate would have resulted in a tax liability of $300,000 on the $1,000,000 of income earned in Chile.[27] The Canadian corporation would pay only $120,000 because it would not be subject to taxation in Canada on the $1,000,000 of business profits taxed in Chile. That $1,000,000 is exempted from tax in Canada because it was taxed in Chile.

Credits

The second mechanism for avoiding double income taxation is the "credit." Pursuant to a credit, the nation where a corporation is resident defers to taxes imposed by another nation by subtracting from the income tax otherwise due in the resident nation the amount of income tax paid to the other nation. For example, pursuant to the "credit" mechanism, Canada would allow a Canadian corporation to deduct from its Canadian income taxes – otherwise due and owing in Canada on its entire worldwide income – the amount of taxes paid by the Canadian corporation in Chile on its business profits realized there.

The credit mechanism is not preferred by corporations because it always results in a corporation paying the higher of two applicable national tax rates. For example, if Chile used its 12 percent tax rate to impose taxes of $120,000 on $1,000,000 of business profits of a Canadian corporation, and if Canada used the "credit" mechanism to avoid double taxation in respect of its 30 percent tax rate on business profits, then the Canadian corporation would pay:

(a) $120,000 to Chilean taxing authorities; plus
(b) another $180,000 to the Canadian taxing authorities.

The Canadian corporation would pay $180,000 in Canada because it would still be subject to Canada's 30 percent tax rate on the $1,000,000 of business profits taxed in Chile. In other words, that income is not exempted. Rather than receiving an exemption, the Canadian corporation would receive a "credit" for the taxes it paid in Chile. Pursuant to the credit, the Canadian corporation could subtract from the taxes due and owing in Canada on the income from Chile (i.e., $300,000 in Canadian taxes on the $1,000,000 income from Chile) the $120,000 in income taxes already paid to Chile in respect of the same income. As a result, the Canadian corporation effectively pays the higher of the two applicable taxes ($300,000), $120,000 in Chile and $180,000 in Canada.[28]

TAX EVASION AND TAX AVOIDANCE

Clearly, one of the focuses in international corporate taxation is the elimination of double taxation. Priority for "residency" nations, exceptions for permanent establishments, exceptions for withholding taxes, exemptions and credit arrangements are all intended to avoid the situation where the same corporate income is taxed in more than one nation.

It is also quite possible, within the global network of national regimes for taxing corporate income, that significant corporate income can escape taxation altogether, be taxed at relatively low rates or be taxed only years after it is earned. Reducing, deferring and entirely escaping corporate income taxation is not necessarily illegal. In other words, such results can be achieved not only as a result of tax evasion (which is illegal) but also as a result of tax avoidance (which is legal).

"Tax evasion" consists of activities subjecting taxpayers to possible criminal sanctions if known to taxing authorities. Examples of tax evasion are:

1 failing to file a required tax return;
2 filing a return based upon or containing intentional omissions or falsifications;
3 characterizing elements of ordinary earned income as reimbursement of expenses; and
4 characterizing earned income (e.g., business profits) as unearned income subject to a lower tax rate (e.g., interest, royalties or dividends).

Most taxpayers would agree that such activities necessarily constitute tax evasion – at least when the activities are undertaken knowingly.

"Tax avoidance" consists of activities which do not necessarily subject the taxpayer to criminal sanctions even if national taxing authorities are aware of them. Examples of tax avoidance are transfer pricing abuses and thin subsidiary capitalization arrangements.[29]

"Transfer pricing" occurs when one company sells goods or provides services to a related buyer, i.e., a buyer controlling the seller, controlled by the seller or under common control with the seller. Such transfer prices are quite common in domestic and international trade because related companies often provide raw materials, intermediate products and even final products to each other.

"Subsidiary capitalizations" occur when one company, the parent corporation, makes a contribution to the shareholder's equity of one of its subsidiaries. Subsidiary capitalizations are also quite common in domestic and international commerce because parent companies often fund the operations of their corporate groups by making contributions to their capital.

Transfer pricing arrangements and subsidiary capitalizations are, of course, legitimate and even necessary commercial transactions for multinational corporate groups. Neither one necessarily constitutes tax evasion or even tax avoidance. Transfer pricing abuses and thin subsidiary capitalizations can, however, constitute tax avoidance if they have the effect of preventing national taxing authorities from collecting income taxes properly due to them. In fact, transfer pricing abuses and thin capitalization can constitute tax evasion if they are undertaken with the intent of preventing national taxing authorities from collecting income taxes properly due to them.

Transfer pricing

In the normal course of business between unrelated parties, sellers demand that buyers pay the market price for their goods and services. In the absence of a clear market price, the price is determined on the basis of "arm's-length" negotiation between the seller and buyer.

Of course, each seller periodically calculates and pays its taxes on the basis of its profits, i.e., the prices paid by its buyers less the seller's costs. If a buyer resells the same goods as part of a trade or business, then that buyer's profit is its resale price less its costs (including the amount paid to the seller). Between unrelated sellers and buyers, the seller would not accept that its buyer pays an amount less than the market price because the lower price would decrease the seller's profits, with the seller receiving no benefit from the resulting equivalent increase in the buyer's profit.

However, if the seller and buyer are related parties (e.g., the seller is the buyer's corporate parent), then the seller can – without affecting the overall economic return for the corporate group – accept that its subsidiary-buyer pays a price less than the goods' market price (or less than some other "arm's-length" price).

In fact, if seller and buyer are related parties in two nations with different tax rates, then seller and buyer can improve the group's overall post-tax economics by adjusting the sales price on the basis of their relative tax burdens. For example, if the tax rate for a parent-seller's profits is less than the tax rate for its subsidiary-buyer's profits, then the seller and buyer can reduce their overall tax burden by having the buyer pay more than arm's-length value for the seller's goods. Conversely, if the tax rate applicable to the subsidiary-buyer's profits is less than the tax rate applicable to the parent-seller's profits, then the seller and buyer can reduce their overall tax burden by having the buyer pay less than arm's-length value for the seller's goods.[30]

In both cases, the related seller and buyer – located in different nations – have reduced their combined overall tax burden by shifting profits away from the nation with the higher tax rate. Such a practice is an abuse of "transfer pricing," recognized as unacceptable tax avoidance (or even tax evasion, if undertaken with the specific intention of defrauding competent taxing authorities) under the laws of most nations and under the OECD Model Convention.[31]

Most major commercial nations have their own national rules, both procedural and substantive, for contesting transfer prices between related companies in different nations and for establishing an arm's-length price for the purpose of assessing income taxes. Many times different nations' transfer pricing rules will lead them to reach different conclusions about the arm's-length price for the purpose of establishing the taxable profits of their resident corporations.

If, on the basis of differing assessments of arm's-length prices, the same business profits are taxed by two different national taxing authorities, then the taxing authorities are required to eliminate the double taxation, if necessary by meeting for a "competent authority proceeding."[32] These proceedings can result in intermittent meetings of taxing authorities and corporations for months or even years.

Thin capitalization

A parent corporation can fund its foreign subsidiaries in different ways. One fundamental choice for the parent is whether to provide funding as a loan or as a contribution to capital. At the same time, in a subsidiary's resident nation, there is typically a significant difference between the income tax treatment of interest (payments made to the parent on the basis of loans) and dividends (payments made to the parent on the basis of contributions to capital).

Foreign subsidiaries can deduct interest payments made to corporate parents from the business profits taxable in their resident nations. At the same time, foreign corporations typically cannot deduct dividend payments made to corporate parents. For this reason, both parents and their foreign subsidiaries generally prefer to make and receive funding in the form of loans rather than contributions to capital. As a result, there is often a risk that a foreign corporate subsidiary will be subject to "thin capitalization."

Thin capitalization exists where a subsidiary reflects an unreasonably large portion of funding from its parent as a loan rather than shareholders' equity. In theory, funding should be characterized as a loan, giving rise to deductible interest payments, only to the extent that there is a reasonable expectation that the subsidiary will be able to repay the principal amount of the funding on an arm's-length amortization schedule. Any funding provided by the parent to its foreign subsidiary in excess of such amounts should be characterized as a contribution to capital, giving rise to dividends – for which no deduction is typically allowed.

In practice, each nation has its own rules which can be used to recharacterize as dividends any excessive interest paid to parent corporations, thereby denying subsidiaries deductions for the excessive interest payments.[33]

Thankfully, issues of thin capitalization do not usually raise competent authority issues because interest and dividends received by parent corporations tend to be taxed in the same manner and at the same rate in the nations where the parents are resident. Accordingly, the sole issue is whether the foreign subsidiary claiming deductions for interest payments owes additional tax to the nations where it is resident.

Tax havens

A "tax haven" is a nation with a generally low corporate income tax rate, usually coupled with secrecy regulations (e.g., bank secrecy laws) making it difficult to trace funds transferred or accumulated there.[34] In addition, most tax havens historically have been small countries, not members of the OECD and not cooperating with taxing authorities of other nations in the manner proposed in the OECD Model Convention: competent authority proceedings, exchanges of information and assistance in the collection of taxes.[35]

Loans give rise to interest income. Technology gives rise to royalties. Shareholdings give rise to dividends. In other words, all of these forms of passive income (i.e., interest, royalties and dividends) are generated by intangible assets. At the same time, intangible assets are easy to relocate, even to move from one nation to another.[36] Such intangible assets can also be acquired and held from practically any location.

Accordingly, some corporations form subsidiaries in tax havens for the purpose of:

(a) transferring loans, technology or shareholdings to those subsidiaries; and
(b) transferring money to those subsidiaries for the purpose of acquiring such intangible assets.

In either case, the corporations often intend to accumulate the passive income from those intangible assets in the tax havens without paying taxes on them in their resident nations unless and until the income is repatriated to the resident nation.

If corporations (or other taxpayers) transfer intangible assets or money from their resident nations to tax havens without declaring those assets or money, as appropriate, as income in their resident nations and without paying any required tax on them there, then the corporations (or other taxpayers) have certainly committed an act of tax evasion in their resident nations. If corporations (or other taxpayers) transfer intangible assets or money from their resident nations to tax havens after properly declaring those assets or money as income in their resident nations and paying any required tax on them, then the corporations or other taxpayers have not committed an act of tax evasion in their resident nations.

To the extent that the corporations use tax havens as places to realize and accumulate income beyond the reach of the nations where they are resident, then resident nations sometimes take the view that their resident corporations are engaged in unacceptable tax avoidance. Accordingly, nations sometimes attempt to impose tax on at least some of the income their resident corporations realize and accumulate in tax havens through bank accounts, branches, subsidiaries, trust funds and other vehicles located there.

As of November 2000, twenty major nations (including France, Germany, Hungary, Japan and the USA) have adopted legislation imposing income taxes on foreign corporations whose shareholders are comprised predominantly of resident or national corporations or individuals ("controlled foreign corporations" or "CFCs") in those instances where the CFCs are:

(a) located in tax havens; and
(b) are accumulating either significant amounts of passive income or significant amounts of income from sources within the nations where their shareholders are resident.[37]

These CFC tax-avoidance rules are generally applicable to income from:

(a) loans, technology and shareholdings (i.e., interest, royalties, dividends and capital gains);
(b) transactions with companies related to the CFC's shareholders;
(c) sales made into the nation where the CFC's shareholders are residents or nationals;
(d) risks insured in the nation where the CFC shareholders are located; or
(e) international financial transactions such as factoring.

In addition to unilateral anti-tax-haven legislation of some "resident nations," the OECD has become involved in direct negotiations with practically all of the tax havens around the world in an attempt to put an end to the tax practices the OECD perceives as being harmful. In fact, since 1998, the OECD has obtained the undertaking of all but six of the world's "tax havens" to work for the elimination of harmful tax practices by 31 December 2005. In the meantime, each of the cooperative "tax havens" has agreed not to enhance existing harmful tax regimes and not to introduce new ones.[38]

Tax competition

"Tax competition" can lead to international corporate tax avoidance in the same way that tax havens lead to tax avoidance. Tax competition refers to tax incentives offered by nations which are not considered to be "tax havens" because, among other things, they maintain a relatively high level of corporate income tax on their own resident corporations and individuals.[39]

These nations are considered to be engaged in "tax competition," however, because they offer special income tax incentives intended to attract specific types of business operations from abroad.[40] Generally, these nations offer tax advantages for particular business operations identified as economically or socially desirable by the nation offering the advantage. In effect, nations involved in tax competition create special purpose tax havens for specific types of business operations (e.g., "Belgium is a tax haven for headquarters operations").

On 27 April 1998, the OECD issued a report on "Tax Havens and Harmful Tax Regimes, An Emerging Global Issue." It followed two years of study related to the growing practice among larger nations to adopt tax incentives similar to those available in tax havens but targeted at attracting specific business investments and activities from other nations. At the 1996 Lyon Summit, the G7 nations endorsed the OECD efforts with the following observation:

> Globalization is creating new challenges in the field of tax policy. Tax schemes aimed at attracting financial and other geographically mobile activities can create harmful tax competition between States, carrying the risk of distorting trade and investment and [leading] to the erosion of national tax bases.
> (1996 Communiqué Issued by the Heads of the G7 States) (as quoted in the OECD 1998 Report, page 7)

In 2000, the OECD identified forty-seven different tax regimes in twenty-one different countries as "potentially harmful preferential tax regimes."[41] The OECD recognized nine business operations considered to be desirable and so providing the basis for potentially harmful preferential tax regimes: insurance, financing and leasing, fund management, banking, headquarters operations, warehousing and distribution centers, service centers and shipping.[42]

The tax advantages available by virtue of tax competition vary dramatically from regime to regime. They can include: income tax holidays, capital allowances, carry forwards of tax allowances, import incentives (e.g., waivers of duties for equipment, spare parts and materials), export incentives (e.g., subsidies, waivers of export fees and waivers of import duties on intermediate goods), tax exemptions for expatriate employees and the deferment of corporate registration fees and duties.[43]

Many of the current complexities in international corporate income taxation deal with taking advantage of the various forms of available tax competition.

PART FOUR

Corporate Governance

12

Relationships with Shareholders

Corporate law

INTRODUCTION

Corporate law – at least in the USA – is often discussed but rarely understood, in part because corporate law is not federal law with no agency actively enforcing it. Securities law is better understood, in part because it is a federal law actively enforced by a government agency. The provisions of corporate law can be divided into two large topics.

First, corporate law contains provisions concerning each corporation's arrangements for proposing, making and implementing decisions. Within the scope of these provisions, corporate law is similar to the constitutional provisions of national governments and so can be referred to as corporate law's "constitutional provisions." Generally and with limited exceptions, corporate officers propose, make and implement corporate decisions.

Second, corporate law contains provisions concerning officers' and directors' personal liability for actions taken in their corporation's name and for its account. These provisions of corporate law are taken largely from rules of agency law. Generally, corporate directors and officers can be personally liable for failing to act diligently and in their corporation's best interests.

A BIT OF HISTORY[1]

Corporations have a long history, dating back at least to the time of the Roman Empire. Important themes throughout corporate history have included the purposes for which governments have allowed corporate formations (e.g., charitable, municipal and business), shareholders' involvement in corporate control and managers' personal liability to their corporations, to governments and to persons dealing with their corporations.

Roman corporations

Corporations have been controversial arrangements at least since the times of Ancient Rome. When asked for approval to establish an association of 150 firemen in Nicomedia, which had just been devastated by a fire, the Roman Emperor Trajan denied his approval with the following explanation: "Corporations, whatever they are called, are sure to become political associations." Nonetheless, Justinian's Corpus Juris records that charitable organizations such as hospitals, asylums and orphanages, as well as religious cults, churches and burial clubs, were accorded the status of corporations.

Medieval church corporations

Corporations were carried into the European Middle Ages as a part of church law, which gave them the status of "fictitious persons" for the purpose, in perpetuity, of owning church assets and conducting church activities. Such activities included operating churches, schools, universities, hospitals and poor houses. Corporations were also used to create other organizations if their purposes and duration were intended to extend beyond the life of any individual and his or her heirs. Such organizations included municipal corporations, i.e., cities and towns.

Guilds of tradesmen and of merchants

During both the Roman Empire and the European Middle Ages, groups of merchants and craftsmen were allowed to organize as corporations for the purpose of promoting and regulating their trades, including fixing prices. The "guilds" were established and maintained under imperial or royal charter and granted monopolies, i.e., exclusive right to engage in certain activities. Craft guilds manufactured and sold goods locally. Merchant guilds purchased goods abroad and sold them locally.

Italian Renaissance *commenda*

During the Renaissance, some individuals and families in the Italian city states of Genoa, Venice and Florence accumulated fortunes in trade with the Near East and the Far East – but at great risk. Others went bankrupt in the effort. The Italian Renaissance accountants developed double entry bookkeeping to enable those individuals and families to account for the expenses and revenues of individual expeditions. Italian Renaissance lawyers developed the legal facility of the "*commenda*," a legal entity similar to a limited partnership, to enable those same individuals and families to share the expenses and revenues from individual expeditions. Using the *commenda*, Italian Renaissance traders solicited funds from investors, i.e., other individuals and families, to finance expeditions. The potential liability of those investors was limited to the amounts they contributed to expeditions. The promoters, i.e., those individuals who actively managed expeditions, retained unlimited personal liability for any residual expenses.

Dutch and English joint stock companies

In Holland and England, joint stock companies were used to organize foreign trading enterprises, i.e., enterprises for buying goods overseas and returning them for resale in local and other markets. Unlike *commenda*, which typically required an accounting and distributions to members at the end of each expedition, joint stock companies had a continuing existence, with profits from one expedition reinvested in the next. Unlike the promoters of *commenda*, the directors of the joint stock had no liability to third parties for the business conducted by the company, but directors of joint stock companies – like promoters of *commenda* – continued to be potentially liable to members. Joint stock companies differed in other ways from *commenda*. Most importantly:

> [C]ommenda ... had to be reorganized on the death of the principals. Joint stock companies created a permanent fund from shares in the stock of the company ... managed by a select body (board of directors) drawn from the members (shareholders). When members died, their shares could be sold to new members. The crucial [advantage] of the joint stock company [over the *commenda*] was perpetuity [and transferability of shares].
>
> (Braithwaite and Drahos (2000), page 147)

Such joint stock companies included the East India Company in Holland and, later, its counterpart in England. Joint stock companies were also used to organize colonial enterprises, i.e., enterprises for making goods overseas and returning them for resale in local markets. Such companies included the Massachusetts Bay Company, the Virginia Company and the British South Africa Company.

Joint stock companies differed from *commenda* in other important ways. *Commenda* were organized amongst small groups of largely wealthy investors who presumably knew the business, each other and the promoter. The interests in commenda were not transferable, so their value depended entirely on the returns from individual trading expeditions – with promoters required to make distribution to members at the end of each expedition. Joint stock companies were organized amongst large groups of investors, many of whom were not wealthy or sophisticated. Investors in joint stock companies did not necessarily know the business, other investors or the promoter – with promoters relieved of the obligation to make distributions to members at the end of each expedition. Since shares were transferable, there were two ways in which to capture value: the returns from the trading and colonial enterprises and the sale of shares to other individuals. Indeed, stock markets arose in London,

Amsterdam and Paris for the purpose of trading shares in joint stock companies.

The South Sea Bubble Act

Some of the weaknesses inherent in the joint stock company became apparent in connection with the South Sea Company. The South Sea Company was formed for the purpose of engaging in slave trade with the "South Sea," a rather vaguely defined area. The business opportunity, if any, existed in connection with the prospective opening of the former Spanish colonies in America. The business opportunity owed its credibility in part to the then recent success of the East India Companies, both Dutch and English, in opening the Far East to European trade. The general enthusiasm for this opportunity among the general population is evidenced by the fact that, in 1711, England's national debt was repaid with shares in the South Sea Company. When the market for shares in the South Sea Company collapsed in 1720, the English parliament adopted the South Sea Bubble Act prohibiting the formation of new joint stock companies.

Business trusts

In the wake of the South Sea Bubble Act, English promoters took to organizing business enterprises as trusts. Creating trusts was a common way to form businesses from about 1720 until around 1900, when they were slowly replaced by modern corporations.

Trusts are surprisingly similar in structure to corporations. "Grantors" contribute assets to a trust in much the same way that shareholders contribute assets to a corporation. "Beneficiaries" in trusts receive the income from trust assets in much the same way that shareholders receive dividends from corporations. In fact, when grantors designate themselves as beneficiaries of the trusts to which they contribute assets, their status is very similar to the status of a shareholder in a corporation. The "trust" entities themselves are legal entities, i.e., fictitious persons, just like corporations. Trusts hold and exercise ownership rights in their "corpus" – i.e., the assets contributed to the trust by its grantors and the income derived from those assets – in exactly the same manner as corporations hold and exercise own-

ership rights in corporate assets. Finally, groups of "trustees" are appointed by grantors to administer trusts in the same manner that shareholders appoint directors to administer corporations.

The Industrial Revolution and modern corporations

The Industrial Revolution gained momentum with the application of steam power to railroads, shipping, mining, lumber and other heavy industries such as the manufacture of machine tools. Business trusts proved to be inadequate to provide the larger and larger pools of capital required to finance heavy industry. In response, national governments in Europe and the United States enacted modern corporation statutes in the second half of the 1800s. These statutes allowed individuals to form corporations for the conduct of all legal business. Although specific government approval was still necessary to the conduct of certain businesses, e.g., franchises for operating banks, railroads and utilities, generally there was no government approval required to conduct business in the corporate form. The statutes enacted before World War I are the statutes which continue to govern corporate conduct today. The general business corporation of the State of Delaware, the most influential of all corporate laws in the United States, dates from the early 1900s.

DEFINING MODERN CORPORATIONS

As explained below, the modern corporation tends to have the following characteristics: pooling of assets; corporate powers; owned by shareholders; ownership divided into shares; separation of shareholder and corporate ownership; and separation of shareholder and corporate control – all which help to set the stage for the role of corporate officers.

Pooling assets

A business corporation is a fictitious person, a legal entity – a business facility created by law. Subject to governmental authorization (either specifically in a government charter or generally in a statute), a business corporation is commonly formed and owned by its "shareholders," i.e., a group of individuals who pool their capital for the purpose of conducting business.

Corporate powers

Today, in most countries, corporations are empowered to conduct any business permitted by law, including the ownership of other corporations, but with some exceptions for businesses subject to special regulation (such as banking, insurance and hospitals). In such countries, individuals usually have the right to form corporations freely, as an expression of their private property rights and freedom of association. In other countries, corporations are still empowered to conduct only those businesses approved in advance by government, as evidenced by a corporate charter.

Owned by shareholders

Corporations in all countries tend to have the following characteristics: First, each of the shareholders is required to contribute some form of capital – money or assets – to the corporation, not just a promise of future personal services. In exchange, shareholders as a whole own all right, title and interest in and to corporations while corporations, in turn, own all of the assets used in the conduct of its business and owe all of the liabilities incurred in the conduct of the business, all as reflected on a corporate balance sheet.

Ownership divided into shares

Ownership of corporations is usually divided into "shares" and shares are often, but not always, evidenced by share certificates. In the absence of classes of shares (i.e., shares with preferential rights), each share constitutes an equal undivided right to participate in distributions made by the corporation to its shareholders, either in the form of:

(a) dividends in the normal course of business; or
(b) distributions in partial or total liquidation of the corporation.

In the absence of classes of shares (i.e., shares with preferential rights), each share has an equal vote in all decisions made by the shareholders in respect of the

corporation. Finally, in the absence of an agreement between or among shareholders, shares are freely transferable and the corporation survives the transfer of shares, whether the transfer is by sale, testament or the laws of intestacy.

Separation of shareholder and corporate ownership

There is a clear separation of shareholders' ownership of shares and the corporation's ownership of assets. Shareholders can directly exercise their ownership rights in shares, either personally or by delegation to others, but shareholders cannot personally exercise private property rights in corporate assets. Instead, corporations also have the ability to own assets and exercise private property rights in the same manner and to the same extent as individuals, i.e., natural persons.

Each shareholder's liability for the corporation's obligations is limited to the amount of capital contributed to the corporation. This principle is called "shareholders' limited liability" and is, needless to say, an incentive to conducting business in corporate form. Partnerships are also formed by individual investors pooling their assets to form a single enterprise. As partners, however, the investors cannot limit their personal liability for the costs and losses occasioned by the partnership's business.

Separation of shareholder and corporate control

In general partnerships, each partner can act in the partnership's name and, therefore, for the accounts of all other partners. In limited partnerships, one of the partners is designated by the other partners to act in the partnership's name and, therefore, for their accounts. Partners who cannot act in the partnership's name are called "limited partners." Their liability is limited to the amounts contributed to the partnership. Partners authorized to act in the partnership's name are called "general partners." General partners have unlimited personal liability – both to third parties and to the limited partners – for the actions they take in the partnership's name.

Unlike partnerships, corporations can exercise their private property rights only by delegation to one or more individuals. In other words, unlike partners, shareholders in corporations cannot act:

1 in the name and for the account of their corporations; or
2 in the name and for the account of other shareholders.

Instead, all of the authority to act in the corporation's name and on its behalf is delegated to a single individual. In civil law countries, such person is often called the corporation's "legal representative." In common law countries, such person is often called the corporation's "president" or "chief executive officer."

The legal representative or president typically delegates some of his or her power – in a manner allowed or required by the corporation's constitutional documents – to one or more subordinate individuals, authorized to act in the corporation's name in specific matters. The person or persons entrusted with the power to exercise the private property rights in corporate assets are called "corporate officers."

It is possible for shareholders to serve as legal representatives, presidents or other corporate officers. However, if shareholders serve as corporate officers, then they do so in the name and for the account of the corporation – not in their own names or for their own accounts.

The role of corporate officers

Very generally, all corporations have the goal of effective and efficient operation while complying with all applicable laws. Again very generally, legal representatives have the authority and, in exchange for their compensation, the obligation to propose, make and implement decisions in pursuit of that goal.

Within the scope of their authority, legal representatives have no liability to third parties, i.e., persons other than corporations they serve, under the law of general obligations or contracts for acts taken in the name and for the account of the corporations. Such is the risk for third parties in doing business with a corporation's legal representative. On the other hand, legal representatives and other corporate officers can be liable to their corporations under corporate law for their actions in the name and for the account of their corporations. Such is the risk of agreeing to serve as a corporation's legal representative.

BEFORE DECISIONS ARE MADE

Corporate constitutions

There is tremendous flexibility in structuring the corporate decision-making process. This flexibility is evidenced by the fact that the Commonwealth of Massachusetts and the Commonwealth of Virginia, now part of the USA, were originally corporations established under a charter of the King of England. Under their charters, settlers established their own decision-making processes, which included a "balance of powers" and served as models for the Constitution of the United States of America.

In modern business corporations, decisions are proposed, made and implemented largely by legal representatives (e.g., CEOs or presidents) and, pursuant to delegation from them, by other corporate officers.

The role of shareholders is limited to the election of directors and auditors – often nominated by legal representatives or other directors – while the role of directors is limited to selecting the legal representative and reviewing the corporation's accounts annually or, sometimes, more frequently. The only additional role for shareholders and directors is making decisions – again often proposed by legal representatives – on important matters outside of the corporation's ordinary course of business.

In any event, all corporate decisions – both in the ordinary course of business and extraordinary decisions – are implemented by legal representatives and other officers.

Shareholders and directors

With limited exceptions, shareholders' only role in the corporate constitution is the election of directors and independent auditors. Again with limited exceptions, the directors' only decisions are:

1 the election of the corporation's "legal representative," i.e., the person with all authority to act in the company's name and for its account; and
2 the approval of annual accounts prepared by the company's legal representative and presented to

the directors after the annual accounts have been reviewed by the company's independent auditors.

Shareholders and typically directors have no authority to take actions in the name and for the account of business corporations: only a corporation's legal representative and officers to whom he has delegated authority can act in the corporation's name and for its account.

In addition to the decisions listed above, pursuant to express provisions in corporate law or company constitutions, specific corporate decisions can be proposed and made by shareholders or directors. For example, shareholders or directors typically make decisions concerning the payment of dividends, changes in the corporation's business, mergers, acquisitions, divestments and the liquidation or partial liquidation of the corporation.

Legal representatives and other corporate officers

In the end, with the limited exceptions described above, in most countries all corporate decisions are proposed, made and implemented solely and exclusively by corporate officers. In fact, in the first instance, only one corporate officer, i.e., the corporation's legal representative, is authorized to propose, make and implement corporate decisions. However, legal representatives can delegate – and often are required to delegate – to other corporate officers the authority to propose, make and implement certain decisions.

Even in those instances where directors or shareholders make decisions, officers often have the ability to make the initial proposals and to organize the decision-making process. For example, even though shareholders typically elect directors and independent auditors, legal representatives usually retain the power to nominate directors and auditors for election – often selecting the sole nominee – and to organize the election process.

In those instances where directors and auditors are not nominated by the legal representative, directors and auditors tend to be nominated by the board of directors, or by a committee of the board formed for the purpose of making such nominations. Shareholders participate in the nomination of directors and auditors only in "closely held" corporations,

i.e., corporations with a limited number of shareholders – and no public market for readily selling shares.

AFTER DECISIONS ARE MADE

Officers' personal liability to corporations

As evidenced by the foregoing discussion, much of modern corporate law is dedicated to issues surrounding corporate constitutions, i.e., procedures for proposing, making and implementing corporate decisions. Officers' personal liability to their corporations is another important topic under corporate law.

Agents of the corporation

From a legal perspective, corporate officers are, in some ways, similar to bailees, such as warehousemen and common carriers. Like bailees, managers take possession of corporate assets – not title to them – and only as a necessary incident to performing their personal services.

Corporate officers agree to decide and act diligently and in the corporation's best interest when they take possession of corporate assets. In fact, corporate officers agree to decide and act diligently and in the corporation's best interests without regard to whether they have an obligation, before making decisions and taking actions, to consult with corporate shareholders or directors.

Obligations of trust

To the extent that corporate officers can decide and act without consultation, their relationship to their corporations is based on trust.[2] Since corporate officers make and implement practically all decisions in the ordinary course of a corporation's business without consulting shareholders or directors, the trust placed in corporate officers is practically complete.

Corporate officers, for their part, necessarily agree to respect the broad trust placed in them by their corporations when they accept their positions as officers. Corporate officers agree to respect their corporations' trust because corporate officers agree to decide and act without consulting with corporate shareholders or directors. In fact, trust is essential to the role of a corporate officer because, with very limited exceptions, neither shareholders nor directors want to be involved in making or implementing corporate decision. With very limited exceptions, shareholders do not even want to know about corporate officers' individual decisions before they are made. In fact, shareholders do not want to know about their officers' individual decisions after those decisions are made. Instead, shareholders want to know only about the aggregate results of all decisions after they are implemented – not the individual decisions or the results obtained from individual decisions – and they want to know those aggregate results only on a periodic basis – typically once each three-month, six-month or one-year period.

Reporting does not discharge trust obligations

Corporate officers are required to report periodically on the results of all operations. Reporting to shareholders is not, however, a substitute for respecting shareholders' trust in every decision officers make and implement. On the contrary, reporting to shareholders is a specific requirement for corporate officers, in addition to officers' obligations making and implementing decisions. All three obligations – making decisions, implementing decisions and reporting periodically on the aggregate results of all operations – are subject to the officers' overriding duties of care and loyalty.

Fiduciary duties

As already noted, all corporations have as their goal effective and efficient operation while complying with all applicable laws. In this context, legal representatives have the obligation to propose, make and implement decisions in pursuit of that goal. In discharging their obligations, corporate officers are subject to two specific "fiduciary duties," i.e., standards of conduct in respect of the businesses entrusted to them: the "duty of care" and the "duty of loyalty."

Duty of care

By accepting compensation from corporations, legal representatives and all other corporate officers necessarily agree that all of their actions in the name and for the account of their corporations will comply with the "duty of care," i.e., the officers will pursue their corporations' goals as prudently as if they owned the corporations.

The officers' duty of care has three elements. First, the officers must be acting "within the scope of their authority." This element of the duty of care relates to the corporation's by-laws, corporate resolutions and specific managerial instructions. If officers are not acting within the scope of these charter documents and authorizations, then the officers have breached their duty of care.

Second, the officers must not be acting "negligently." This element of the duty of care relates to the diligence exercised by officers in collecting facts relevant to their decisions. In collecting facts, corporate officers breach their duty of care if they do not use the diligence of an ordinarily prudent business person in similar circumstances. This element of the duty of care focuses on the facts available and known to officers at the time they make their decisions.

Third, the officers must be acting "in good faith." This element of the duty of care relates to the diligence exercised by officers in reaching conclusions based on the facts known to them at the time they make their decisions. In reaching conclusions, corporate officers breach their duty of care if they do not exercise the judgment of an ordinarily prudent business person in similar circumstances. This element of the duty of care focuses upon the manner in which officers' decisions are made.

Pursuant to the duty of care, corporate officers are not obligated to maximize shareholders' short-term return on investment. Under the duty of care, corporate officers are allowed to consider interests other than shareholder interests and to consider time frames other than the short-term. In order to comply with the duty of care, it is sufficient that officers' decisions are not inconsistent with shareholders' long-term interests.

The application of the duty of care to officers' decisions is subject to the "business judgment rule." In other words, courts apply the duty of care on the basis of the facts reasonably available to corporate officers, not on all actual facts. Moreover, courts apply the duty of care on the basis of results corporate officers can reasonably expect to achieve, not on the basis of results actually obtained. The business judgment rule does not apply to judicial application of the duty of loyalty.

Duty of loyalty

By accepting compensation from their corporations, all corporate officers also agree that all of their actions on behalf of their corporations will comply with the "duty of loyalty," i.e., the officers will avoid conflicts-of-interest between their corporations' interests and their own interests.

There are three elements to corporate officers' duty of loyalty. First, corporate officers agree to make decisions in their corporation's best interest without regard to their own best interests.

Second, corporate officers agree not to acquire interests in conflict with their corporation's best interests. To this element above the duty of loyalty corporate officers are prohibited from maintaining or entering into competitive undertakings and from appropriating corporate opportunities for themselves.

Third, in the event that officers' interests inevitably conflict with the best interests of their corporations, officers agree to disclose the conflict of interest to disinterested directors and to defer to them in making corporate decisions. Deciding officers' compensation is inevitably a conflict of interest.

Delegations of authority

Legal representatives and other corporate officers are not personally liable for acts and omissions of officers, employees or agents to whom they have delegated authority so long as the delegating officers have complied with their duties of care and loyalty in making the delegations.

Delegating officers can be personally liable for acts of subordinate officers in at least four circumstances. First, delegating officers can be personally liable if the delegation of authority is not permitted by corporate law or a corporation's charter documents. Second, delegating officers can be personally liable if they've violated their duties of care or loyalty in selecting the officers to whom the authority is delegated. Third, delegating officers can be personally liable if they fail to establish and maintain systems reasonably intended to prevent and punish violations of the duties of care and loyalty by subordinate officers, employees and agents. Fourth, delegating officers can be personally liable if they are in fact aware of and fail to prevent or mitigate violations of the duties of care and loyalty by their subordinate officers, employees and agents.

Specific contractual undertakings

In addition to the fiduciary duties of care and loyalty, corporate officers sometimes agree to additional specific undertakings in their contracts with their corporate employers. Contractual obligations can relate to a host of matters, such as secrecy requirements, performance standards and post-termination non-compete obligations. Additional contractual obligations are often related to compensation matters.

"Shareholder derivative actions"

Generally, there are no government agencies to enforce officers' personal liability to their corporations. The enforcement of such personal liability depends on legal actions by corporations against their officers. Needless to say, such action can present significant difficulties.

First, corporations take such legal actions, if at all, only after corporate officers are terminated. At the same time, corporate officers typically negotiate waivers from further personal liability in the context of their termination agreements.

Second, in the first instance such legal actions need to be authorized by the corporation's board of directors. At the same time, boards of directors often hesitate in bringing legal actions against corporate officers in part because of the moral issues such actions raise for continuing corporate officers.

Third, in the absence of legal action by boards of directors, shareholders are authorized to bring legal actions against corporate officers for their personal liability to their corporations. At the same time, allowing individual or small numbers of shareholders to bring legal actions against corporate officers can lead to confusion and wasting corporate assets. Such law suits are called "shareholder derivative actions."

In response to this third difficulty, shareholders who want to sue their corporate officers must follow procedures established under most corporate laws. Typically, shareholders are not allowed to sue in their own names; they are required to sue in the corporation's name. In addition, shareholders holding a relatively small percentage of outstanding shares are not allowed to sue; their lawsuits are subject to annulment by the corporation's independent directors; and they risk having to pay all expenses if they do not prevail in their claims against the corporate officers.

Officers' personal liability to others

As discussed below, in addition to potential liability to the corporations they serve, corporate directors and officers can also be subject to liability to governments for violations of government regulations and to creditors and creditors' groups if corporate directors' officers continue to serve as trustees to the bankrupt estate of their former corporations. In certain circumstances, corporation indemnifications and officers' and directors' liability insurance can be helpful as regards these various forms of potential liability.

Violations of government regulations

As noted in the chapters on government regulation, corporations can be subject to administrative penalties, criminal fines and civil liability for violating government regulations. Most government regulations subject violators to such sanctions because such sanctions are consistent with the purpose of most government regulation: preventing bodily injury, property damage or economic loss. Government regulations which impose potential sanctions on corporations include environmental law, tax law, trade law, consumer protection, worker health and safety and employment law.

Sanctions, including imprisonment, can also be imposed personally on corporate officers if they knowingly violate government regulations. In fact, the possibility of imposing sanctions on corporate officers is often considered to be an important deterrent for violations of government regulations. Possible sanctions against corporate officers are often considered important because, of course, corporate officers make and implement most corporate decisions. The business judgment rule is not available to protect corporate officers from sanctions for violations of government regulations.

Bankruptcy

Typically, corporate officers owe no fiduciary obligations to corporate creditors. Corporate creditors' rights are established solely and exclusively by their loan agreements with their corporate debtors.

The situation changes, however, as soon as corporate creditors file for the involuntary bankruptcy of their corporate debtors. In such circumstances, corporate officers are under fiduciary obligations to corporate creditors as beneficiaries of the estate of the bankrupt corporation.

In fact, corporate officers have fiduciary obligations to corporate creditors as soon as their corporations are not able to pay their debts in the ordinary course of business – in other words: as soon as corporate insolvency is apparently inevitable.

Corporate indemnifications

Corporations have the power to indemnify their directors, officers and employees for decisions made and implemented on behalf of the corporation. In the USA, corporations are empowered to do so if, in good faith, the officers believed that their actions were:

1 legal; and
2 not contrary to their corporations' best interest.

Corporations typically provide in their charter documents and employment agreements for the possibility of such indemnification. Corporations cannot, however, commit to indemnification in specific instances until they determine that indemnification is within their corporate powers. There are typically two potential elements to corporate indemnification of directors, officers and employees: paying the costs of defending third-party claims and paying the costs of judgment or settlement.

In the USA, corporate indemnification can be available even for the expenses incurred by corporate directors, officers and employees in defending law suits by the corporation itself or for defending shareholder derivative actions. Indemnification is not available for judgments imposed against corporate officers pursuant to such law suits or settlements paid by corporate officers to settle them.

Officers' and directors' liability insurance

In addition to indemnification by their corporations, insurance companies offer "directors and officers insurance" – sometimes called "D & O insurance." This insurance has some advantages over corporate indemnifications.

First, D & O insurance is available even if the corporation is bankrupt. Second, D & O insurance can cover risks of loss beyond the scope of corporate indemnifications permitted by law. Policies can cover "judgments, settlements and costs incurred by corporate directors and officers arising out of claims made by the corporation and third parties for alleged or actual errors, omission, statements, misleading statements and breaches of duty." The actual availability depends upon market conditions. Third, the coverage under D & O insurance is based upon the contractual terms of the insurance policy – drafted before the occurrence giving rise to the claim – not on the basis of resolutions of corporate directors – adopted after the occurrence giving rise to the claim.

D & O insurance is available both to corporate directors and officers and to the corporations paying indemnifications on behalf of directors and officers for insured losses. D & O insurance is typically a "claims made" policy, so that premiums must have been paid for the period of time during which the claim is made – not at the time of the occurrence giving rise to the claim. Insurers have no obligation to defend claims made and specific exclusions of coverage tend to apply to: actions taken outside of scope of an individual's duties as officer or director, deliberate criminal acts and breaches of the duty of loyalty. D & O insurance also typically expressly excludes risks covered by the corporation's general liability insurance: such as – as available – bodily injury, property damage, defamation and pollution.

REFERENCES

Braithwaite, J. and Drahos, P. (2000) *Global Business Regulation*, Cambridge: Cambridge University Press.

13

Relationships with Share Traders

Securities regulation

INTRODUCTION

Securities regulation and corporate law are usually considered to be closely related and indeed they are related in some ways. At the same time, securities regulation differs in important ways from corporate law.

First, corporate law promotes the legal institution of corporations. Securities regulation promotes securities exchanges, another institution which could not exist without legal support.

Second, corporate law is intended primarily for the benefit of shareholders, i.e., corporate investors for the periods of time that they hold their shares. Pursuant to corporate law, corporate officers report to corporate directors as shareholders' representatives. Securities regulation is intended primarily for the benefit of share traders, i.e., corporate investors at the moment that they sell or buy their shares. Pursuant to securities regulations, corporate officers report directly to the entire public, including all current shareholders as potential share sellers and all other persons as potential share buyers.

Third, corporate law is based on trust, i.e., corporate officers agree to act diligently in their corporations' best interests even though the vast majority of their decisions are not disclosed to directors and shareholders. Securities law, on the other hand, is based on disclosures. As in other types of market transactions, buyers of corporate securities rely primarily on disclosures from sellers – not their trust of sellers – to determine an agreeable purchase price. The most important element of trust in securities transactions is the trust placed, incidentally, both by sellers and by buyers in corporate officers to make adequate disclosures concerning their corporations' businesses – again: trust placed in corporate officers.

CORPORATE LAW IN GENERAL

Officers' responsibilities include reporting to directors

Corporate officers are agents for their corporations. As with all agency arrangements, corporate officers' responsibilities generally include:

1. the duty to render personal service within the agreed scope of the agency; and
2. the duty to render reports.

For corporate officers, the scope of agreed personal services is very broad: managing a corporate business, i.e., making and implementing all decisions in the corporation's ordinary course of business.

Under corporate law, one of the duties of all corporate officers is to report periodically to their boards of directors. In this regard, directors are acting in a supervisory capacity as the shareholders' representatives. The officers' periodic reports to directors include the following topics:

1. the results from ongoing businesses;
2. business plans; and
3. the few important matters to be decided by directors or shareholders (such as compensation, acquisitions and divestments).

The corporation's legal representative (usually, the CEO or president), the corporation's chief financial officer (i.e., the "CFO") and other invited officers typically report at each directors' meeting on all three of the matters enumerated above. Directors' meetings can be held as frequently as once each month and at the very least once each year. Directors' meetings are typically held on a quarterly or semi-annual basis.

Reports on results from ongoing businesses and business plans include – but are not limited to – reports on the corporation's financial condition and performance pursuant to generally accepted accounting principles. Reports to directors are not typically limited to generally accepted accounting principles:

(a) in part because the directors' supervisory duty requires them to examine past operations from perspectives other than cost accounting; and
(b) in part because important matters typically decided by boards, such as compensation, often require the preparation and review of pro-forma projections and other analyses.

Managing and reporting are separate responsibilities

The duties of care and loyalty apply to both of the officers' responsibilities: personal service, i.e., managing their corporations' businesses, and reporting on the results of those services. It is possible for corporate officers to breach their duties of care and loyalty regarding management without breaching their duties regarding reporting; it is possible for corporate officers to breach their duties regarding reporting without breaching their responsibilities regarding management; and it is possible for them to breach both separately.

Here is an example: Let's assume that a CEO embezzles $100 million from a privately-held corporation (i.e., a corporation that is not subject to securities laws). Let's also assume that the CEO discloses the embezzlement to the board of directors. Our embezzling CEO might have complied with reporting requirements under corporate law. Nonetheless, the CEO has certainly breached his duty of loyalty under corporate law in respect of personal services. (His actions are also, of course, a crime subjecting the CEO to restitution and imprisonment.)

Unlike our corrupt CEO, corporate embezzlers typically conceal their disloyal acts. Concealment violates reporting requirements under corporate law. Accordingly, corporate officers who breach their duty of loyalty in respect of personal services also typically breach their reporting responsibilities. By keeping secret their breach in respect of personal services, corporate officers also violate their reporting responsibility.

Reporting to directors is not a substitute for complying with the duty of loyalty concerning management. On the contrary, corporate officers are required to comply with their duties of loyalty and care under corporate law both in respect of management and in respect of reporting.

Securities reporting is different from corporate reporting

One of the duties for corporate officers of publicly traded companies is to report periodically to shareholders under securities law. Unless specifically stated in securities regulations, however, officers' reports under securities regulations are not a substitute for complying with officers' reporting duties under corporate law. On the contrary, officers are required to fulfill their reporting requirements under securities regulations in addition to fulfilling their reporting requirements under corporate law.

The reporting under securities regulations is not only separate from – and in addition to – reporting requirements under corporate law, it is fundamentally different from corporate reporting. Securities exchanges are not based on trust. Securities exchanges are based on disclosures. Purchasers of shares on securities exchanges do not trust share sellers in the same way that shareholders trust corporate officers. Pursuant to securities regulations, those purchasers look to share sellers for adequate disclosures before the purchasers make their purchase decisions. Pursuant to corporate law, shareholders look to corporate officers for adequate disclosures after the corporate officers make their management decisions.

The difference between reporting under securities regulations and reporting under corporate law is clear when you consider the following: Public corporations probably could not function well with complete disclosures to directors and shareholders before corporate decisions are made. Public securities markets could function perfectly well with complete disclosures to share sellers and buyers before they make their decisions – although such extensive disclosures certainly are not mandated by securities law.

Securities regulations are like consumer protection statutes

In the absence of "consumer protection" statutes, sellers of goods and services are allowed to keep secrets – even important secrets – about their products and services. Similarly, in the absence of securities regulations, sellers of corporate shares are allowed to keep secrets – even important secrets – about their shares and the corporations underlying those shares.

Securities regulation is, in fact, intended as a type of consumer protection for buyers of shares in corporations. This principle is evidenced by the following famous question and answer during the public debates concerning adoption of the US securities regulations in 1933:

US CONGRESSMAN:
"You think, then, that when a corporation … offers stock to the public …. the public has no right to know what [the corporation's] earning power is or [to] subject [the corporation] to any inspections …?"

CEO OF AMERICAN SUGAR REFINING COMPANY:
"Yes, that is my theory. Let the buyer beware … that is the way men are educated and cultivated."
(1933 Congressional testimony)

Securities regulations give buyers of company shares the "right to know" about their purchases just as consumer protection statutes give buyers of goods and services the right to know about their purchases. If the information supplied by sellers to buyers is complete in all material respects, then the market price for all items (goods, services and shares) is presumed to be fair.

Unlike other forms of consumer protection – which focus exclusively on the buyers' "right to know" – securities regulation is intended to benefit both buyers and sellers of shares in publicly-traded corporations. Because of the separation of ownership and control in publicly-traded corporations, shareholders – i.e., potential share sellers – have no immediate information about corporate affairs. As a result, securities disclosures provide information to share sellers as well as share buyers concerning the value of shares purchased and sold on securities exchanges. In other words, disclosures under securities regulations are made on behalf of share sellers but for the benefit of both share sellers and share buyers.

Of course, for publicly-traded corporations – the corporations subject to registration requirements under securities regulations – it is necessary to make disclosures to the general public, i.e., to all potential share sellers and buyers. While it is conceivable the corporations could communicate to their current shareholders through means other than public disclosures, the only way to communicate with all potential buyers of publicly-traded corporate securities is to make disclosures to the general public. Accordingly, disclosures under securities regulations are made to the general public.

Finally, since shareholders have no immediate information about corporate affairs, shareholders have no responsibility to make disclosures under securities regulations. Instead, the disclosures are made by corporations on behalf of their shareholders. Corporations, in turn, can act only through their corporate officers. Accordingly, disclosures under securities regulations are signed in three names: in the corporation's name, in the name of the corporation's chief executive officer, and in the name of the corporation's chief financial officer. Of course, the CEO and CFO sign for themselves. The CEO typically signs in the corporation's name.

Practical limitations on securities disclosures

There are at least three important practical limitations on corporate officers' ability to make securities disclosures.

Let's assume for the moment that corporate officers would, given their own preferences, prefer to disclose all corporate information to all shareholders at all times. In fact, let's assume that the corporate officers adopt a policy that any shareholder can at any time:

1 personally interview any management; and
2 visit the corporation to review its books and records.

Given these assumptions, I believe that we can quickly identify some practical limitations to the "open door" policy that the shareholders as a group would want to impose on management for the shareholders' own benefit.

First, as regards future business plans and prospects, I believe that the shareholders would not want corporate officers to disclose to individual shareholders or to all shareholders as a group any information prejudicing business opportunities. Disclosing such information could easily adversely affect corporate performance by reducing revenue. The "business opportunity" exception to the open door policy reasonably applies only to plans for future activity – not disclosures concerning past performance.

Second, as regards past performance, I believe that shareholders as a group would also want to limit disclosures because of the disruptions, administrative burdens and other costs involved in the completely "open door" policy. Continuous availability of all corporate information, even concerning past performance, would affect corporate results because of the high costs of providing that information. In other words, as a group, the shareholders would rather have the earnings from operations than immaterial information about those operations.

Third, I believe that the shareholders as a group would want to limit management's "open door" policy by preventing disclosures of material information to some, but not all, shareholders. Such "selective" disclosures would create an unfair advantage for certain shareholders for the period of time that they possess the additional material information. In other words, the shareholders would prefer that any disclosure to any shareholder be made simultaneously to all shareholders.

US SECURITIES REGULATION

Publicly issuing and trading corporate securities

Public disclosures pursuant to US regulation of corporate securities (typically, shares in the company's equity) can be divided into two general categories:

1   disclosures by corporations and their initial investors concerning securities they are issuing, i.e., selling, securities to the general public – usually called an "initial public offering"; and

2   disclosures by corporations concerning their publicly-traded shares, i.e., shares resold and purchased on public exchanges.

These two fundamental aspects of public disclosures pursuant to US securities regulation are set forth in two separate statutes:

1   the Securities Act of 1933 (the "1933 Act"), generally governing the issuance of securities by corporations; and
2   the Securities Exchange Act of 1934 (the "1934 Act"), generally governing the trading of corporate securities on public exchanges.

These two aspects of public disclosures pursuant to securities regulation are obviously closely related. When corporations and their initial investors issue equity securities to the public, the buyers of those securities expect to be able to offer those securities for resale publicly, i.e., on a securities exchange. In fact, most persons who buy equity shares in publicly-traded corporations do so with the intention, sooner or later, of reselling them. Pursuant to the 1933 Act, corporations register their securities so that they and their initial shareholders, usually a small group of founders and investors, can sell shares to the public. Pursuant to the 1934 Act, corporations maintain the registration of their securities so that the shares sold "to the public" can be resold "by the public" at any time on one of the securities exchanges maintained in the United States.

Securities and Exchange Commission

In keeping with the arrangements of many other regulatory schemes in the United States and around the world, the statutes governing the issuance and trading of corporate securities in the United States (the 1933 Act and the 1934 Act) are very broad. They do little more than state their purpose and create a regulatory agency to adopt and enforce regulations fulfilling that purpose. In the case of the US securities regulation, the agency's name is the "Securities and Exchange Commission." The SEC is authorized to adopt and enforce regulation for the following purposes:

To provide full and fair disclosure of the character of the securities sold in interstate commerce and through the mails, and to prevent fraud in the sale thereof.

(Preamble to the 1933 Act)

Whenever pursuant to this title the Commission is engaged in rulemaking and is required to consider or determine whether an action is necessary or appropriate in the public interest, the Commission shall also consider, in addition to the protection of investors, whether the action will promote efficiency, competition, and capital formation.

(Section 2(b) of the 1933 Act)

Filings with the SEC precede public disclosures

All public disclosures made pursuant to the US securities regulation – other than press releases – must first be filed with the SEC as a preliminary or tentative disclosure. The SEC is given an opportunity to review and comment on the filings but the SEC's failure to make objections or take exceptions with filings does not mean that the disclosures are approved by the SEC. Compliance with the filing requirements does not constitute approval of the securities offered for issuance or trading. In fact, the SEC requires that all prospectuses contain the following disclaimer:

Neither the Securities and Exchange Commission nor any state securities commission has approved or disapproved of these securities or determined if this prospectus is truthful or complete. Any representation to the contrary is a criminal offense.

(See, e.g., 17 CFR 229.501. Item 501(b) (7))

Accounting standards

Reports on financial performance and condition to directors under corporate law can use various accounting methods, e.g., pro forma, because of the specific issues addressed by directors and their face-to-face discussion of them. Public disclosures on financial performance and condition under securities regulations need to be limited to a single set of accounting standards in order to avoid confusion.

Accordingly, an important issue immediately confronting the SEC in 1933 was a determination of the accounting standards to be used for the purpose of making "full and fair disclosure of the character of the securities sold in interstate commerce." The 1933 Act authorized the SEC to adopt an approach based largely on self-regulation of public accounting, i.e., preparing financial statements for the purpose of reporting to the public on the financial performance and condition of publicly-traded corporations:

In carrying out its authority ..., the Commission may recognize, as "generally accepted" for purposes of the securities laws, any accounting principles established by a standard setting body that organized as a private entity.

(Section 19(b) of the 1933 Act and Section 13(b) of the 1934 Act)

In fact, since the SEC's inception, the SEC has relied on the US accounting profession to establish financial accounting and reporting standards for publicly-traded companies. Since 1974, the accounting profession's standards-setting body in the US has been called the Financial Accounting Standards Board (the "FASB"). Prior to 1974, the FASB was a part of the American Institute of Certified Public Accountants, the professional association for the US public accountants. The FASB was first called the "Committee on Accounting Procedure" (1936–59) and then the "Accounting Principles Board" (1959–73). Under the Sarbanes-Oxley Act, the FASB can continue as the standards-setting body in the USA, but its expenses must be funded by all issuers of corporate securities publicly traded in the United States. In addition, the FASB, is charged with dealing with emerging issues, as in the past, and with addressing issues of international convergence.

PERIODIC DISCLOSURE REQUIREMENTS

In the first instance, securities regulation in the United States depends on a system of periodic public disclosures. The basic public disclosures for corporate securities traded on exchanges in the United States are the annual and quarterly reports to shareholders. The annual report is intended as a "state-of-the-company" report, providing financial data, results of continuing operations, market segment information, new product plans, subsidiary activities and research and development activities on future programs. The quarterly report provided regular updates of the annual report at three-month intervals. Between annual and quarterly reports, current reports and/or press releases are required whenever there is a material change in a corporation's business.

The SEC's entire disclosure system begins when corporate securities are first offered for sale to the public, i.e., the initial public offering. Disclosures in addition to those required in annual reports to shareholders are required in connection with the initial public offerings. Those additional disclosures, together with the information required for an annual report to shareholders, are set forth in a "prospectus." The SEC calls corporations "issuers" of securities or "registrants" of publicly-traded securities.

In addition to the initial prospectus and other periodic reporting requirements, disclosures for publicly-traded shares include "proxy statements." Proxy materials differ from other public disclosures in that they are intended solely and exclusively for shareholders as opposed to share traders. Proxy statements contain disclosures needed by shareholders in those few instances when shareholder approval is required to take a corporate action – most commonly, the annual election of corporate directors.

The "prospectus" for an "initial public offering"

If a corporation – called the "issuer" for these purposes – offers to sell securities specifically to a small group of investors, then those investors are typically experienced and wealthy individuals. As experienced investors, they can make their own determinations concerning the information necessary to evaluate securities offered for sale. As wealthy investors, they can afford to make serious mistakes. Finally, as a small group, those investors are able to negotiate for the information, price and other terms and conditions – if any – pursuant to which they are interested in purchasing securities based on the available information, or lack of available information.

If a corporation offers to sell securities generally to members of the public, then the situation is different. The investors might not be experienced and wealthy individuals and, as a large group, they cannot negotiate information, price and other terms and conditions in connection with the sale of the securi-ties. As with consumers of manufactured goods and services, the public investors in corporate securities are offered a sale on a "take it or leave it" basis. As with the consumers of manufactured goods, the US government has determined – based on experience – that public investors in corporate securities need to have a statutory "right to know."

The right to know for investors purchasing corporate securities upon issuance is set forth in the 1933 Act. Pursuant to the 1933 Act, issuers of securities must deliver a "prospectus" to investors in the United States before those securities are issued to US investors. A "prospectus" is a document setting forth all of the information which, in the opinion of the SEC, an investor would reasonably want to know before purchasing a corporate security. The prospectus contains all of the information required in an annual report to shareholders, as discussed below. Generally, this information includes a description of the company's business and assets, with accompanying financial statements.

In addition to the information required in each annual report to shareholders, a prospectus includes the general terms of the offering, the plan for distributing the issued shares to the public (often called "underwriting" the shares), risk factors for a particular issuance (such as lack of an operating history, profitable operations or a market for securities to be issued), use of proceeds, such as debt repayment or construction of new facilities, and if any of the securities to be issued are offered for the account of a founder, officer or other private investor in the issuer, the name of such private investor, the number of such shares in the issuance and other relevant information.[1]

Annual report to shareholders

The statutory "right to know" for investors trading corporate securities on US exchanges is set forth in the 1934 Act. Pursuant to the 1934 Act, issuers of securities must issue annual, quarterly and current reports to shareholders, along with proxy solicitation materials in connection with all shareholder votes.

The Form 10-K is the annual report that most registrants file with the Commission. It is intended to provide an overview of the registrant's business. The Form 10-K must be filed within 90 days after the end of the registrant's fiscal year. The Form 10-K includes the "annual report to shareholders" and is the principal document used by most registrants to disclose corporate information publicly.

In addition to:

1 an opening letter from the corporation's chief executive officer, the annual report includes
2 a narrative description and general development of business by segments;
3 management's discussion and analysis of financial condition and results of operations;
4 a description of property and material legal proceedings;
5 financial information about segments and geographic areas, including acquisitions, divestments and changes in accounting methods, and changes in and disagreements with accountants.

The annual report also contains information concerning:

6 corporate "insiders," director and executive compensation plans, including equity compensation plans and employment, resignation and retirement agreements;
7 security ownership of officers, directors and 5 percent beneficial owners; and
8 certain relationships and related transactions with any of the foregoing persons.

Concerning the corporations' capital structure, the annual report discloses:

9 the number of shareholders;
10 amounts of dividends; and
11 recent sales of unregistered securities.

Most recently, pursuant to the Sarbanes-Oxley Act of 2002 (the "Sarbanes-Oxley Act"), the annual report contains:

12 report from the audit committee report of the corporation's board of directors;
13 the corporation's code of ethics; and
14 its internal controls and procedures.

A more extensive listing and description of the required contents for an annual report to shareholders is set forth as an annex in the notes to this chapter.[2]

Quarterly public disclosures

The Form 10-Q is a report filed quarterly by most reporting companies. It includes unaudited financial statements and provides a continuing view of the company's financial position during the year. The report must be filed for each of the first three fiscal quarters of the company's fiscal year and is due within 45 days of the close of the quarter.

Current reports and press releases

The Form 8-K is the "current report" that is used to report the occurrence of any material events or corporate changes which are of importance to investors or security holders and previously have not been reported by the registrant. This form is used as a filing to the SEC, sometimes in connection with and sometimes instead of the issuance of a press release.

In particular, the following events should be reported: a change in control of the registrant, an acquisition or disposition of operating assets, bankruptcy or receivership, changes in the registrant's certifying accountants and resignations of directors, changes in fiscal year and amendments to the registrant's code of ethics or any waiver of a provision of the code of ethics.

"Proxy statements"

Corporate law governs the circumstances under which shareholders are required to vote their approval of a corporate decision before the corporation acts upon that decision. Such decisions include the election of directors and, typically, mergers, consolidations, acquisitions and similar matters.

In the event that a shareholder vote is required to approve an action, the corporation itself, corporate directors or officers, one or more shareholders or another person usually makes a proposal to shareholders in the form of a draft resolution. For example, in the USA a corporation's chief executive officer commonly proposes a single candidate for each position as corporate director.

In connection with the proposed resolution (e.g., the election of a proposed candidate as corporate director), the person proposing the resolution both:

1   solicits the shareholders' votes by explaining the proposed resolution; and
2   requests that the shareholder sign and return a "proxy card."

A "proxy card" is a written declaration, signed by a shareholder, authorizing another person (called a "proxy") to represent the shareholder at a shareholders' meeting. The proxy card sometimes also contains an instruction for the proxy to vote for or against a specifically proposed resolution.

Under state corporate law, there is no clear method for soliciting shareholders' proxy cards, i.e., no clearly prescribed form and procedures for "proxy solicitation materials," also called "proxy statements." If a company's shares are publicly traded, however, the SEC has clearly prescribed a form and procedure for proxy solicitation materials. The SEC's form is intended to provide shareholders with the information necessary to enable them to vote in an informed manner on matters intended to be acted upon at shareholders' meetings. For example, proxy statements prescribed by the SEC in connection with the election of directors contain detailed information about officers' and directors' compensation and other information relevant to the election.

Since shareholders typically elect corporate directors at the shareholders' annual meeting, shareholders receive both an annual report to shareholders and a proxy statement in connection with the annual shareholders' meeting. Accordingly, proxy statements are usually considered to be part of the system of periodic public disclosures mandated for publicly-traded corporations in the United States. Most of the proxy statements in connection with annual shareholders' meetings contain information relevant to electing directors, such as current executives' and directors' compensation. Proxy statements for other purposes, such as shareholder approval of a merger, contain completely different information.

MISSTATEMENTS AND OMISSIONS

As described above, the SEC has established an integrated system of periodic disclosures:

1   beginning with the prospectus;
2   continuing with the annual, quarterly and current public disclosures; and

3   including forms and procedures for proxy solicitation materials.

The specific disclosures mandated in the periodic reporting are, in the SEC's opinion, reasonably intended to assure the "full and fair disclosure of the character of the securities sold in interstate commerce and through the mail." In other words, for general purposes, the SEC considers the expressly mandated disclosures, if reasonably accurate, to be reasonably complete for the purpose of evaluating investments in publicly issued and traded corporate securities.

For example, it would be a violation of securities regulations if an annual report did not contain a report from the corporation's audit committee, or a prospectus did not contain a plan of distribution or a statement concerning the use of proceeds. Similarly, it would be a violation of securities law if a corporation failed to disclose any of the events required to be disclosed in a current report, such as a resignation of a director or a change in auditors.

At the same time, the SEC realizes that it has necessarily granted registrants broad discretion in the formulation in their disclosures and that, in specific circumstances, the mandated disclosures may not be adequate for their intended purpose. Accordingly, the SEC expressly provides that registrants must provide such other information as is necessary to make the mandated statements "full and fair." The best known formulation of this rule is Rule 10b-5 of the 1934 Act:

> It shall be unlawful, in connection with the purchase or sale of any security, for any person, directly or indirectly ... to make any untrue statement of a material fact or to omit to state a material fact.
>
> (Rule 10b-5 of the 1934 Act)

In other words, in order to achieve the effect of full and fair disclosure, the SEC focuses on avoiding misstatements and omissions. In the first instance, as stated above, the SEC requires that corporations avoid "material" misstatements and omissions. As explained later in this chapter, the SEC also focuses separately on "intentional" misstatements and omissions.

If a company's external auditors detect a material or intentional misstatement or omission and it is not corrected in the normal course of the audit, then the external auditors are obligated to call it to senior management's attention (i.e., the CEO or CFO). If senior management does not correct the consequential misstatement of omission, then the auditor is required to call it to the directors' attention (typically through the board's audit committee) and thereafter to disclose the misstatement or omission to the SEC. The auditor is also required to qualify its audit report concerning any uncorrected misstatement or omission and is authorized to resign as the company's external auditors.

If a material or intentional misstatement or omission in any periodic report is not detected and corrected pursuant to audit procedures, then the person making the statement or omission is potentially liable to persons who bought or sold securities in reliance on those misstatements or omissions.

In addition, any misstatements and omissions must be corrected if they are material, intentional or correction is required according to generally accepted accounting principles.

Avoid all material misstatements and omissions

Clearly, making a material misstatement or omission in a periodic public disclosure required by US securities regulations is illegal.

Making determinations as to the "materiality" of a misstatement or omission has been less clear. Here are two definitions of "material fact" formulated by the SEC:

A material fact is any fact to which there is a substantial likelihood that a reasonable investor would attach importance in determining whether to buy or sell the securities registered.
(Definition of "Material," Rule 12b-2 – Definitions, the 1934 Act)

A "material fact" is any fact necessary [to state] in order to make the statements made not misleading in the light of the circumstances under which they were made.
(Rule 10b-5(b) under the 1934 Act)

In general, the test for the "materiality" of a misstatement or omission is taken to be as follows: "Would the inaccurate or incomplete statement mislead reasonable persons in their decisions to buy and sell shares?" The matters listed under SEC regulation of current reports on Form 8-K are clearly material, but that list is not complete. For example, the death of a chief executive officer would be a material fact. Failing to disclose the death would be a material omission. Other material omissions would include: failure to disclose the tapping of a large deposit of crude oil, winning a patent case affecting one-half of the company's annual revenue, and the imposition of a government fine totaling one-quarter of a company's annual revenue pursuant to the settlement of a price-fixing investigation.

Recently, the SEC substantially clarified the concept of materiality in financial disclosures. In the first instance, the statement or omission in a financial statement is material if it results in a misstatement of 5 percent or more in any line item in the consolidated balance sheet. All financial statements are considered both individually and together to determine compliance with the 5 percent rule. However, if the company can be more accurate than allowed by the 5 percent rule, then the company is required to make more accurate financial disclosures.

Avoid all intentional misstatements and omissions

Even if a misstatement or omission is not material according to the standards set forth above, the misstatement or omission is a violation of US securities regulation if it is intentional. In general, making any intentional misstatement or omission in a periodic public disclosure required by US securities regulations is illegal.

For example, even if a misstatement does not breach the 5 percent guideline set forth above, the misstatement is a violation of US securities regulations if it intentionally masks a change in earnings or other financial trends, hides a failure to meet analysts' expectations, changes a loss into income or is related to a segment the registrant has described as significant to its business.

A misstatement of less than 5 percent in any line item in a consolidated balance sheet is illegal, for example, if the misstatement is intended to evidence compliance with a regulatory requirement, demonstrate compliance with loan covenants or other contractual requirements, increase management's compensation or conceal an unlawful transaction.

SOME RECENT ABUSES

In 1998, the SEC identified a series of "accounting gimmicks" used by management to meet Wall Street earnings expectations on a quarterly basis. Those gimmicks included "big bath" charges, "cookie jar" reserves and "revenue acceleration."

In 2000, the SEC also addressed the issues of "selective disclosures," disclosures made by registrants to securities analysts but not to the general public.

"Big bath" charges

Companies engage in restructurings in response to competition and innovation. Just as often, the companies incur restructuring charges, which are supposed to reflect the cost of restructuring and the profile of the company's productive assets going forward.

Some companies intentionally overstate their restructuring charges. Such overstated charges are called "big bath" charges. They do so for two reasons. First, securities analysts are rather "forgiving" of one-time charges which include the promise of greater returns in the future. Second, overstating accrued restructuring charges gives management a cushion with which to restate earnings in future "down" quarters.

"Cookie jar" reserves

Companies are allowed to create liabilities on their balance sheets for such items as estimated sales returns, loan losses and warranty costs.

Some companies have intentionally overstated these estimates. Such overstated reserves are called "cookie jar" reserves. In good quarters, the estimates for sales returns and other reserves are exaggerated, allowing companies to avoid declaring revenues in excess of analysts' expectations. In bad quarters, the exaggerated estimates for sales returns and other reserves are reversed, allowing the company to "smooth out" its income from quarter to quarter, thereby meeting analysts' expectations.

One company took a large one-time loss to earnings to reimburse franchisees for equipment. That equipment, however, had not even been purchased by the franchisees. At the same time, the company announced that its earnings would increase by an impressive 15 percent in the next year.

Accelerating revenue

Under GAAP, revenue is recognized when all of the operations required to receive the revenue have been performed.

Some companies have intentionally accelerated revenue recognition to meet a short fall in quarterly earnings. For example, some companies recognize revenue before they have performed all of the operations required to receive the revenue – or while the customer still has the option to terminate, void or delay a purchase.

Selective disclosures

In recent years, corporate management has sometimes made "selective disclosures," i.e., disclosures of material non-public information to certain persons (in general, to securities analysts and to other securities market professionals in private or conference calls) without making a disclosure of the same information to the general public. Under new SEC regulations, corporate management must disclose the same information to the general public (e.g., with a press release). Intentional selective disclosures must be repeated simultaneously to the general public. Unintentional selective disclosures must be repeated promptly to the general public.

REGULATING POTENTIALLY FRAUDULENT PRACTICES

As stated earlier in this chapter, the SEC is charged "[t]o provide full and fair disclosure of the character of the securities sold in interstate commerce and through the mails, and to prevent fraud in the sale thereof … . By establishing a system of periodic disclosures, including rules for material and intentional misstatements and omission, the SEC has addressed the issues of "full and fair disclosure."

The SEC has adopted many regulations to avoid fraud and other manipulative practices concerning the issuance and trading of corporate securities. Some of those regulations are of special concern to corporate officers: insider trading, short swing trading and restricted stock.

Insider trading is clearly a fraudulent practice and so is prohibited. Short swing trading and restricted stock involve the potential for abuse and so are regulated.

Insider trading

Insider trading liability arises in connection with a trader's "use" or "knowing possession" of material non-public information. A person trades "on the basis of" material non-public information (and so violates the law) when the person purchases or sells securities while aware of the information.

"Short swing profits"

Corporate officers and directors must return to the company by which they are employed all of the profits which they receive from the purchase or sale of securities issued by that company within six months of any other purchase or sale of those same securities. In order to implement this regulation, corporate officers and directors are required to file publicly with the SEC their transactions involving shares in the corporations for which they serve as officers or directors. See Section 16(a) and (b) of the 1934 Act.

"Control stock" and "restricted stock"

The 1933 Act requires registration for the public issuance of shares. The 1934 Act regulates the trading of publicly issued shares on US securities exchanges, among other measures, by requiring their registration. Registrations for the purpose of trading on US securities exchanges apply to specific issuances of shares and therefore to specific shares (not entire classes of shares). Subject to certain conditions, certain individuals holding unregistered shares for a class of publicly-traded securities can sell their shares on US securities exchanges.

One clear set of conditions is set forth in Rule 144 on "Restricted and Control Securities." A person holding unregistered "restricted securities" or "control securities" can sell them on a US securities exchange without a prior registration statement of those shares, if:

1   the person selling the shares has held them for at least one year;

2   adequate current information is available about the issuer under the 1934 Act;

3   the person sells no more than 1 percent of all outstanding shares in any three-month period;

4   the shares are sold through routine trading transactions, with normal commissions paid to brokers; and

5   the person who sells the shares files a notice with the SEC for sales of more than 500 shares or for sales with a dollar value in excess of $10,000.

Any shares held by an "affiliate" are considered to be "control shares." An affiliate includes corporate directors, corporate officers and any other persons with the power to direct the management and policies of the issuer, whether by contract or otherwise. Any person who buys "control shares" from an "affiliate" acquires the shares as "restricted securities" unless the sale from the affiliate qualifies for an exemption under Rule 144.

SECURITIES EXCHANGES IN THE UNITED STATES

This chapter contains several references to securities exchanges. Securities exchanges are private associations, not government agencies. Securities exchanges in the USA – as well as other participants in US securities transactions, such as brokers, dealers and mutual funds – are regulated by US securities laws, primarily in the 1934 Act and regulations adopted pursuant to the 1934 Act. In SEC parlance, securities exchanges are called "self-regulatory organizations" (or "SROs"). The various governmental regulations applicable to securities exchanges are not immediately important to corporate executives.

It is important to corporate executives that, in the first instance, securities exchanges regulate themselves. In other words, securities exchanges such as the New York Stock Exchange (the "NYSE") and the NASDAQ adopt their own governing regulations – in much the same way that corporations adopt their own charter documents. In fact, securities exchanges such as the NYSE and NASDAQ are required to create rules that "allow for disciplining members for improper conduct and for establishing measures to ensure market integrity and investor protection."

Securities exchanges' self-regulation is immediately important to executives of companies listed, i.e., publicly traded, on those exchanges because those self-regulations extend to those companies in the form of "listing requirements." As discussed in more detail in Chapter 15 on "board supervision," NYSE listing requirements increasingly address issues related to corporate governance.

SECURITIES REGULATION IN EUROPE

For several reasons, this chapter is based on US law: US securities regulation is of longer standing than equivalent European laws, US securities regulation is more developed than European laws, the US securities regulation commission is fairly well respected, the USA has the largest markets in corporate equity securities, and the USA has a single set of securities regulations while national laws in Europe still govern the public issuance and trading of corporate securities.

Moreover, the US securities regulations have had a strong influence on evolving EU regulations.

At the same time, securities regulation is developing rapidly in Europe and around the world, with it exercising strong influence in the USA in some areas as the adoption and convergence of international accounting rules via the International Accounting Standards Committee ("IASC").

In addition, all securities commissions, including the US commission, see the need for cooperation in enforcement and even coordination of regulations. The commissions in the USA and Europe are currently focusing those efforts at cooperation and coordination in the International Organization of Securities Commissions ("IOSCO").

Finally, the EU has taken initiatives to develop a common framework for securities regulations and some of the world's largest exchanges are located in London, Frankfurt and other European financial capitals.

14

Relationships with Regulators

Internal controls

INTRODUCTION

In general, corporations should pursue effective and efficient operation throughout a foreseeable future, while complying with applicable ethical and legal standards and reporting reliably on their financial condition. "Internal controls" refer to administrative arrangements within corporations intended to provide reasonable assurances that corporations appropriately balance their three objectives: effective and efficient operation, legal compliance and reliable reporting.

There are many different approaches to internal controls, most of which are similar. Taken together, they are – unfortunately – somewhat confusing. Rather than reviewing all of these approaches, this chapter attempts to provide a single approach to establishing and maintaining a system of internal controls. For this purpose, I have focused on authoritative guidance provided from sources within the United States.

In the United States, an independent panel of finance industry associations has proposed a system of internal controls in respect of all corporate objectives, including effective and efficient operation. Sentencing guidelines established by US courts have addressed issues of internal control in respect of legal compliance, i.e., establishing and maintaining systems within corporations to provide reasonable assurances that the corporation's business is conducted in "compliance with applicable government regulations." US securities regulations require that publicly-traded corporations establish and maintain a system of internal controls to provide reasonable

assurances of "reliable financial reporting." Finally and most recently, US securities regulations have even begun to require that corporations establish and maintain systems of internal controls in respect of "ethical behavior."

Internal controls are intended to assure that employees implement senior officers' decisions in a manner consistent with all three corporate objectives. While internal controls cannot completely ensure that employees implement decisions properly, failing to establish and maintain systems of internal controls is clearly a breach of senior officers' duty of care. As outlined in this chapter, internal controls do not include the corporate arrangements ensuring that senior officers make decisions which appropriately balance all three corporate objectives.

Directors are charged with maintaining supervisory arrangements, sometimes called a "corporate governance system," to ensure that senior officers' decisions appropriately balance corporations' sometimes conflicting objectives. Those supervisory arrangements will be examined in Chapter 15.

THE THREE GOALS OF EVERY CORPORATION

Both "natural persons," i.e., individuals, and "fictional persons," e.g., corporations, have the status of "legal persons." In other words, their individuality is recognized under the law. Corporations differ legally from individuals, however, in important respects. Most importantly in this context, the "purpose" for individuals is not legally defined, while corporate purposes are typically limited, for legal purposes, to the conduct of legal businesses – generally, the production and distribution of goods and services.

In 1992, the Committee of Sponsoring Organizations of the Treadway Commission ("COSO"), an authoritative, independent body sponsored by five major associations of US financial professionals, took a further step in defining the purposes for all corporations. COSO identified the following three objectives for all corporations. For more information on COSO, go to www.coso.org:

1 effective and efficient operations;
2 compliance with applicable laws and regulations; and
3 reliable financial reporting.

COSO also underlined the importance of corporations establishing and maintaining systems of internal controls, i.e., "a process ... designed to provide reasonable assurance regarding the achievement of [the three] objectives." From the perspective of corporate law, establishing and maintaining systems of internal controls is an important part of senior officers' duty of care in their conduct of corporate business.

PROVIDING ASSURANCES OF EFFECTIVE AND EFFICIENT OPERATION

In accordance with COSO, there are at least five parameters for establishing an effective system of internal controls:

1 "Tone at the top": Prioritizing conflicts among businesses' three objectives by establishing clear corporate programs set out in corporate directives such as business plans and codes of conduct.
2 Risk assessment: Reducing threats to successful implementation of corporate programs by anticipating threats during program design.
3 Control activities: Implementing corporate programs, including the use of written "policies and procedures" intended to enhance the likelihood of achieving business objectives as set forth in plans and codes. Appointing the right persons to assume the various responsibilities within the organization is a vital part of control activities.
4 Information and communication: Providing the right information to the right persons at the right time to enable them to achieve their internal control objectives.
5 Monitoring: Assessing the performance of the internal control system and modifying it as necessary.

These five framework considerations are applicable to all three fundamental corporate purposes: effective and efficient operation, legal compliance and reliable reporting. As discussed below, internal control frameworks have been legally mandated for the second and third corporate purposes, i.e., legal compliance and reliable reporting. COSO's framework will be expressly discussed exclusively in the context of effective and efficient operation.

EFFECTIVE AND EFFICIENT OPERATION

The tone at the top

Conflicts are inevitable whenever a person or organization pursues more than one goal. The tone at the top involves a clear communication of priorities for the purpose of resolving those conflicts. Obviously, before senior officers can communicate clear priorities for resolving conflicts amongst multiple objectives, they must establish those clear priorities amongst themselves. The tone at the top involves senior officers establishing clear priorities.

"Effective and efficient operation" refers to operations which maximize revenues and minimize costs – with "effectiveness" referring to maximum revenue and "efficiency" referring to minimum cost. As with the broader goals of legal compliance and reliable reporting, conflicting priorities can arise between maximizing revenue and minimizing costs. For example, operations intended to minimize costs over a short period of time – such as one or three years – might not maximize revenues over longer periods of time, such as five or ten years.

A "tone at the top" in respect of effective and efficient operation requires clear business goals, i.e., a program for realizing effective and efficient operation as set forth in a business plan. Of course, senior officers must resolve the conflict between eventual revenues and current costs in order to have a clear business plan. In order to resolve that conflict rationally, senior management must define an applicable time frame. Most corporations are established to operate independently for an indefinite duration. Accordingly, in order to resolve rationally the conflict between costs and revenues, senior management should examine its business goals and plan from various points in time throughout the foreseeable future.

Just as a "tone at the top" in respect of effective and efficient operation requires clear business goals set forth in a plan, so a tone at the top in respect of a corporation's broader objectives requires:

1 effective and efficient operation;
2 legal compliance; and
3 reliable reporting

requires clear corporate values, as set forth in a code of conduct. Of course, senior officers must resolve the conflicts inherent in those three objectives in order to have a clear code of conduct.

As with the conflict between current costs and eventual revenue, senior management must define the applicable time frame in order to develop clear corporate values. Again, since corporations are intended to operate independently for at least an indefinite period, in order to develop clear corporate values, senior officers should examine its values from various points in time throughout the foreseeable future.

As suggested above, a reasonable resolution of the potential conflicts amongst the broadest objectives of all corporations would be as follows: pursuing effective and efficient operation throughout a foreseeable future, while at all times complying with applicable legal and ethical standards and reporting reliably on financial condition.

Risk assessment

Business risks are conditions or events which threaten the realization of business objectives such as effective and efficient operation or compliance with law. Business risks are inevitable whenever corporations pursue objectives. Successfully managing risks – from sources both internal and external to the organization – is essential to achieving objectives. Since internal control systems are the corporate arrangements intended to assure that businesses achieve their objectives, internal control systems necessarily include risk assessment.

Assessing risks involves:

1 identifying them;
2 understanding the likelihood and significance of their occurrence;
3 determining whether the likelihood and significance can be controlled by corporate measures; and
4 deciding whether the residual risk is acceptable.

For acceptable residual risks, risk assessment includes managing the risk – to the extent reasonably possible – by adapting the design of business programs – e.g., business plans and codes of conduct – either:

1 to avoid or minimize risks; or
2 to avoid or minimize their impact on achieving your objectives.

Since business conditions are constantly evolving, the risks to which business objectives are exposed continue to evolve. As a result, risk management, including program design, is a continuing corporate process.

Of course, risk management, including an assessment of the likelihood and the significance, cannot only affect program design. In some cases, the residual risk – the risk which cannot be controlled by corporate measures – can affect the corporation's evaluation of that objective. In other words, risk assessment can affect the priorities ascribed by senior management to conflicting objectives. Obviously, an objective's value is enhanced when achieving it lies well within a corporation's control, while another objective's value is undermined if achieving it seems to be unavoidably uncertain.

At the same time, the business objectives of reliable reporting and legal compliance, as articulated in codes of conduct, generally seem to be well within most corporations' control – and therefore more likely – than the business objective of efficient and effective operation as articulated in business plans. Indeed, businesses often fail to achieve specific business plans because of intervening events beyond their control. Accordingly, at least from the perspective of risk assessment, it seems that the goals of legal compliance and reliable reporting deserve a high priority among senior officers in planning their corporate programs.

Control activities

As stated by COSO, "[c]ontrol activities are the policies and procedures that help to ensure management directives are carried out." Management directives are the business plans and codes of conduct used to prioritize objectives and manage risks.

Policies and procedures translate into practice the broad principles set forth in senior officers' directives. Having in principle:

(a) set objectives;
(b) resolved conflicting priorities;
(c) avoided unacceptable risks; and
(d) managed other risks, with a clear "tone at the top" and program design, the purpose of "control activities" is to ensure that in practice:
    (i)   objectives are pursued loyally and diligently;
    (ii)   conflicting priorities are resolved;
    (iii) unacceptable risks are avoided; and
    (iv) acceptable risks are managed.

In COSO's scheme, policies establish prior arrangements for:

1 authorization of certain activities by individual employees;
2 approval of employee activities beyond authorization levels;
3 verification of all or some employee actions, at the very least in terms of authorizations and approvals, before they are implemented as corporate actions;
4 documentation of employee authorizations, approvals, actions and verifications by keeping corporate records, books and accounts; and
5 periodic reconciliation of corporate documentation and assets with individual and corporate authorizations, approvals, actions and verifications.

In COSO's scheme, procedures are the arrangements whereby policies are implemented. Obviously, it is difficult to draw a clear distinction between policies and procedures as defined by COSO and, indeed, such distinction is not necessary for all purposes because both policies and procedures are "control activities." COSO distinguishes policies and procedures to emphasize two points. First, control activities need to be carefully considered before they are implemented. This careful consideration is embodied in written or, sometimes, oral policies. Second, implementation of control activities necessarily involves the application of policies to specific circumstances. Such implementation is embodied in

individual employee actions pursuant to specific policy elements.

For all control activities, i.e., policies and procedures, it is important that objectives set, priorities resolved, risks avoided and risks managed in principle in senior management's directives are referred to the proper person within the organization for the purpose of translating those principles into practices. Different objectives, conflicts and risks should be entrusted to different persons within the organization. Accordingly, an important element of control activities, both policies and procedures, is to designate the correct office for assuring that each of those principles is translated into practice, to appoint the correct person to that office and to provide that person with the resources necessary to fulfill his or her responsibilities effectively.

Finally, an important consideration in establishing and implementing control activities, i.e., policies and procedures, is "cost and benefit." A cost-benefit analysis is important to determining whether control activities provide "reasonable" assurances that principles are translated into practice. As previously noted, internal controls cannot provide complete assurances that all corporate objectives are achieved or even universally pursued loyally and diligently. In determining an appropriate level of assurance, the projected cost of establishing and implementing specific control activities needs to be balanced against the benefit probably obtained.

Information and communication

The entire system of internal controls presumes that senior management will establish and maintain channels for capturing and communicating information adequate to provide reasonable assurances that corporations achieve their three fundamental objectives.

Within the corporation, such information should be captured and communicated:

1 from those officers and other employees who design plans and programs ("designers") to those who implement them ("implementers");
2 from implementers to designers;
3 at all levels, among designer and implementers whose responsibilities complement each other.

Information from designers to implementers tends to be definitions of corporate "objectives":

(a) goals in business plans;
(b) principles for codes of conduct;
(c) values for resolving conflicts between goals and principles;
(d) techniques for avoiding or managing risks; and
(e) policies and procedures to assure implementation of those goals, principles, values and techniques.

Information from implementers to designers tends to be facts, i.e., reports of events and conditions relevant to a specific plan, code, policy or procedure.

In each case, it is important that all relevant information is captured and, as necessary, communicated to the person responsible for its implications. For example, implementers need to communicate facts creating a conflict between corporate goals and principles to the person(s) responsible for resolving that conflict. Implementers need to communicate facts indicating an unacceptable or manageable risk to the person(s) responsible for avoiding or managing that risk. All officers and employees need training to recognize the implications of various facts within the context of their corporations' objectives.

On the other hand, planners need to ensure that the plans and codes embody corporate goals and principles accurately and completely. Planners also need to ensure that, pursuant to policies and procedures:

1 implementers understand plans and codes so that implementers can recognize facts relevant to corporate objectives; and
2 implementers understand policies and procedures so that they can communicate relevant information to the person(s) responsible for conflicts and risks.

In COSO's opinion, the quality of information should be assessed according to five characteristics:

1 appropriate (Is the information communicated to the proper persons(s)?);
2 timely (Is the information communicated when it is required?);
3 current (Is the information communicated the most current available?);
4 accurate (Is the information accurate and sufficiently detailed?); and
5 accessible (Is the information easily accessible by the proper persons?).

Effective information systems, including training programs for those who implement corporate plans and codes, are obviously important for effective internal control systems. As with policies and procedures in general, costs and benefits are an important consideration. In this context, corporations should carefully consider the extent to which those implementers who capture information relevant for corporate plans and codes can be made responsible for the conflicts and risks inherent in that information. Allowing implementers to resolve conflicts and manage risks eliminates communications of facts but necessitates clear communication of plans and codes.

Between the corporation and its external constituencies (e.g., customers, suppliers, regulators and investors), information adequate for internal control purposes should be captured and communicated:

1 from those constituencies by officers and other employees responsible for the corporate relationship with each specific constituencies; and
2 from those responsible officers and employees to the constituencies for which they are responsible.

Such communications are needed to integrate external parties (such as suppliers, agents and distributors) into corporate control systems and, in addition, to make those control systems responsive to the changing needs of external parties (such as customers, regulators and investors).

It can even be appropriate, on occasion, for corporations to facilitate direct communications amongst external constituencies. Even where such communication is not facilitated by corporations, corporations should not assume:

1 that its various constituencies have no information about each other; or
2 that constituencies are not communicating directly amongst themselves in respect of any such information.

Monitoring

Monitoring is already built into COSO's policies and procedures as:

(a) verification of all or some employee actions, at least in terms of authorizations and approvals, before they are implemented as corporate actions; and

(b) periodic reconciliation of corporate documentation and assets with individual and corporate authorizations, approvals, actions and verifications.

In addition, COSO recommends that the internal control system be subject periodically to separate evaluation on the basis of:

(a) experience with existing internal controls;

(b) changes within the corporation (such as personnel and business); and

(c) changes within the external environment (employees, suppliers, regulators and investors).

Such evaluations involve a review of the entire system of plans, codes, policies and procedures, including arrangements for authorizations, approvals, actions, verifications, reconciliations and gathering and communicating information.

PROVIDING ASSURANCES OF COMPLIANCE WITH GOVERNMENT REGULATIONS

COSO intends its approach to internal control generally to provide reasonable assurances that corporations can achieve their objectives of:

1 pursuing effective and efficient operation throughout the foreseeable future; while at all times

2 complying with applicable legal and ethical standards; and

3 reporting reliably on financial condition.

COSO recognizes that each corporation needs to adapt the COSO system to its specific needs.

The preceding discussion focused on the application of COSO's approach to achieving the objective of effective and efficient operation, with only occasional references to the objectives of legal compliance and reliable reporting.

This section focuses on the minimal steps necessary for a corporation to have an "effective compliance and ethics program" (an "Effective Program") in the Federal Organizational Sentencing Guidelines adopted by US courts. The minimal steps outline a

system of internal controls for corporations intent on providing reasonable assurances that they achieve their goal of legal compliance (see Subsection (b) of Chapter 8, Part B, Section 8B2.1("Effective Compliance and Ethics Program") of the "2004 Federal Sentencing Guideline Manual," as amended effective 1 November 2004 (hereinafter referred to as the "Minimal Steps").

The US courts developed the Minimal Steps as part of the criminal justice system. In an effort to induce corporations to adopt the preventive measures they embody, most government regulations carry possible criminal sanctions. Within the US criminal justice system, maintaining an Effective Program will reduce the criminal sanctions imposed on a corporation for violations of government sanctions. An Effective Program is accepted as evidence that the corporation violated a government regulation even though it made a good faith effort to comply with the law. In the context of an Effective Program, a violation of government regulations appears to be the action of a single "rogue" employee as opposed to a corporation's systematic violation of government regulation.

It is quite possible and often appropriate to adopt separate systems of internal control in respect of each of the three fundamental corporate objectives. At the same time, the systems proposed for general purposes by COSO are surprisingly similar to the systems proposed specifically for legal compliance and reliable reporting. After all, each of these systems of internal controls is intended to assist senior corporate officers in complying with their duty of care in respect of specific corporate responsibilities. I suggest that you review each framework for elements of internal control appropriate for your purposes (for example, by adopting one approach as the unifying thread for developing an internal control system and reviewing the second approach for additional elements to enhance the system you develop on the basis of the first approach.)

Finally, it is important to note that, beginning in November 2004, the goal of an Effective Program was expanded beyond the scope of compliance with government regulations to include "promot[ing] an organizational culture that encourages ethical conduct" (Subpart (a) of Chapter 8, Part B, Section 8B2.1 ("Effective Compliance and Ethics Program") of the "2004 Federal Sentencing Guideline Manual," as amended effective 1 November 2004). Accordingly, the federal judiciary in the United States has joined the Securities and Exchange Commission and the New York Stock Exchange to address the apparent need for codes of ethics among corporations publicly-traded in the United States.

LEGAL COMPLIANCE

Company "code of conduct"

(1) The organization shall establish standards and procedures to prevent and detect criminal conduct.
(Subpart (1) of the Minimal Steps (as defined above))

A code of conduct is, of course, part of COSO's "tone at the top." For the US courts, this first step in their Effective Program includes both drafting a written "code of conduct" and the procedures necessary to implement the code.

In other words, a code of conduct includes:

1 a restatement of applicable government regulations; and
2 procedures for providing reasonable assurances that the regulations are applied consistently throughout the organization.

Both restatements and procedures should be brief and clear. Restatements and procedures which are not both brief and clear are ineffective and costly.

At the same time, most government regulations are relatively complex. In order to have brief and clear restatements and procedures, it is best to capture the underlying principle of each government regulatory system in a few sentences – omitting exceptions which might exist to the corporation's benefit – and to provide a simple procedure in which exceptions can be applied on a case-by-case by the right person, usually a lawyer but sometimes a person trained in a specific regulatory system. For example, competition laws can probably be captured, in my opinion effectively, with the following words:

Summary: Do not enter into exclusive arrangements with distributors or suppliers. Do not communicate or cooperate with competitors. If there is no effective competition in your business (requiring you to treat your customers fairly), be

certain that you are treating your customers in a manner they perceive as fair.
Procedure: Please contact the Legal Group before engaging in any activities in violation of this summary of competition law.
(A model policy and procedure)

Support of high level personnel

(2)(A) The organization's governing authority [i.e., its board of directors] shall be knowledgeable about the content and operation of the compliance and ethics program and shall exercise reasonable oversight with respect to the implementation and effectiveness of the compliance and ethics program.
(B) High-level personnel of the organization [i.e., senior management] shall ensure that the organization has an effective compliance and ethics program … Specific individual(s) within high level personnel shall be assigned overall responsibility for the compliance and ethics program.
(C) Specific individuals within the organization shall be delegated day-to-day operational responsibility for the compliance and ethics program.
(Subpart (2) of the Minimal Steps (as defined above))

This element of an Effective Program is obviously part of COSO's "tone at the top." Both COSO and the US courts realize that internal controls are expensive in at least two ways. First, establishing and maintaining internal controls is undeniably an expense for the corporation. Second, legal compliance can compromise revenues, at least in the short-term.

Indeed, avoiding the costs of implementing preventive measures prescribed by government regulations results in immediate cost savings, helping to maximize a company's results from operations in the short-term. At the same time, it is rarely possible to maximize long-term results in this way. The immediate savings realized by ignoring government regulations can lead to a threefold increase in costs in the long run:

1 paying compensation for the harm the regulation was intended to prevent;

2 paying penalties for violating the regulation; and
3 in the end, having to implement the preventative measures prescribed by government regulations.

For the same reasons, even though reported earnings might be maximized in the short run, the quality of earnings is always immediately eroded – even in the short run – by undisclosed violations of law.

For all of these reasons, it is important to have the support of the board of directors and senior management for the purpose of designing and implementing an effective compliance and ethics program. For all of these reasons, in the absence of a high level mandate, there will be no impetus to incur the expenses and forgo the short term returns sometimes available through illegal and unethical conduct.

Proper delegation

The organization shall use reasonable efforts not to include within the substantial authority personnel of the organization any individual whom the organization knew, or should have known through the exercise of due diligence, has engaged in illegal activities or other conduct inconsistent with an effective compliance and ethics program.

(Subpart (3) of the Minimal Steps (as defined above))

This provision goes beyond the previous versions of the Minimal Steps. In the past versions, corporations were urged to exclude any person previously engaged in illegal activity from a significant role in their Compliance Program. Since November 2004, corporations have been urged to exclude such persons from all significant roles in the corporation. (To understand this point, it is useful to know that: "substantial authority personnel" is defined to include all "individuals who exercise a substantial measure of discretion in acting on behalf of the corporation." It includes all high-level personnel and other employees such as plant managers and sales managers (Commentary 3 to Chapter 8, Part A, Section 8A1.2 ("General Application Principles") of the "2004 Federal Sentencing Guideline Manual," as amended effective 1 November 2004 (hereinafter referred to as the "General Application Principles")).

Effective communication

The organization must have taken steps to communicate periodically and in a practical manner its standards and procedures, and other aspects of the compliance and ethics program, to … the governing authority [i.e., the board of directors], high level personnel [i.e., senior management], substantial authority personnel [as defined above], the organization's employees, and, as appropriate, the organization's agents.

(Subpart (4) of the Minimal Steps (as defined above))

As with COSO, the US courts emphasize the importance of effective communication. In fact, US courts are more concrete in prescribing the use of training programs and publications, presumably restatements of government regulations in simple terms explaining the practical significance of those regulations for corporate operations. The types of communication envisioned include periodic training and publications.

As with COSO, the US courts recognize the importance of including corporate agents other than officers and other employees in communications efforts. It is usually prudent to include external agents, such as commercial agents, distributors and even contract manufacturers and construction contractors, as appropriate within the scope of Effective Programs because corporations can incur criminal penalties for their violations of law in discharging their obligations to corporations.

It is also usually prudent to include provisions in contracts with external agents obligating them:

1 to comply with government regulations applicable to corporations as and to the extent that the agents' actions can be attributed to the corporations pursuant to those regulations; and
2 to cooperate and participate in programs intended to assure that the agents are in compliance with such regulations.

Reasonable steps to ensure compliance

The organization shall take reasonable steps – (A) to ensure that the organization's compliance and ethics program is followed, including monitoring and auditing to detect criminal conduct; (B) to evaluate periodically the effectiveness of the organization's compliance and ethics program; and (C) to have and publicize a system, which may include mechanisms that allow for anonymity and confidentiality, whereby the organization's employees and agents may report or seek guidance regarding potential or actual criminal conduct without fear of retaliation.

(Subpart (5) of the Minimal Steps (as defined above))

As with COSO, the US courts recognize the importance of monitoring and auditing as part of an effective system of internal controls. Very briefly, "monitoring" can be understood as reviews of ongoing operations, i.e., a discussion of decisions as they are being made and implemented. Monitoring can be conducted effectively by immediate supervisors, i.e., individuals in the normal "chain-of-command" responsible for effective and efficient operation (i.e., profit or budget responsibility). In other words, monitoring is a continuous process, integrated into ongoing operations, such that individual employees' actions are not implemented as corporate actions until the legality of those actions has been previously approved or reviewed by at least one person, i.e., the employees' immediate supervisor. A failure of a monitoring system results in a failure to prevent a violation of government regulation.

While monitoring focuses on integrating law and ethics into planned and ongoing operations, "auditing" reviews completed operations to determine whether law and ethics have been effectively integrated. In other words, "auditing" is conducted after operations are completed, i.e., after all relevant decisions have been made and substantially implemented. While monitoring is a continuous process, auditing is an episodic process – conducted either regularly or occasionally, depending on the risk of a legal violation. While monitoring is integrated into the chain-of-command, auditing cannot be conducted effectively by immediate supervisors or, indeed, by anyone who reports to persons in the normal "chain-of-command" (except at the level of senior management). Auditing should be conducted by individuals who are accountable to those officers, employees and other agents whom they audit. While a failure of a monitoring system results in a failure to prevent a violation of government regulation, a failure of the auditing system results in failure to detect a violation of government regulation.

This Minimal Step also provides, in effect, that a "hot line" is a necessary part of an Effective Program.

A hot line is a telephone number which any officer, employee or other agent can call for the purpose of anonymously reporting suspected violations of law. Of course, as part of a hot line, the corporation should keep records of the reports received and investigate diligently the credible ones. Hot lines are usually managed by a corporation's internal legal or auditing department.

Finally, the Compliance Program should be reviewed periodically, i.e., the entire program (not just specific operations) should be audited to ensure that it is "generally effective in preventing and detecting criminal conduct."

Consistent enforcement

The organization's compliance and ethics program shall be promoted and enforced consistently throughout the organization (A) through appropriate incentives to perform in accordance with the compliance and ethics program; and (B) appropriate disciplinary measures for engaging in criminal conduct or for failing to take reasonable steps to prevent or detect criminal conduct.

(Subpart (6) of the Minimal Steps (as defined above))

COSO does not include enforcement among the five elements of its internal control system. It also does not emphasize disciplinary actions against individual officers and employees who, either intentionally or unintentionally, fail to fulfill their obligations under COSO's internal control system.

This element of an Effective Program is, therefore, an important addition, especially regarding those employees who intentionally fail to fulfill their internal control obligations. The role of "monitoring" is emphasized in this element of an Effective Program because it provides for disciplinary actions against both the employee violating a government regulation applicable to the corporation and the person, presumably a supervisor, who fails to detect the violation.

The "enforcement" element also leaves much unsaid. The US courts do not mention procedures for internal investigations, hearings and rulings – all necessary considerations. Generally, corporations would be well advised to adopt elements of "due process," as used in courts but adapted to the circumstances of a corporate proceeding.

Another important element of corporate enforcement of its Effective Program is the relationship of that enforcement with governments' enforcement of the violation of their regulations. Coordinating corporate investigations with ongoing government investigations is usually difficult. Once a government investigation is initiated, it is usually best for the corporation to defer to and cooperate entirely with the government investigation.

Finally, most government regulations do not impose additional penalties for failure to self-report violations of their regulations. At the same time, self-reporting can be an important factor considered by corporations in imposing reduced sanctions.

Continuous improvement

After criminal conduct has been detected, the organization shall take reasonable steps to respond appropriately to the criminal conduct and to prevent further similar criminal conduct, including making any necessary modifications to the organization's compliance and ethics program.

(Subpart (7) of the Minimal Steps (as defined above))

As with COSO, the US courts take the view that any violation of government regulations involves two failures. One is the failure of an individual employee – or group of employees – to comply with the law. The other is the failure of the corporation's system of internal controls, especially the monitoring system, to prevent the violation before it occurs.

Both COSO and the US courts recommend a review of the internal control system whenever there is a violation of government regulations, with corrective measures taken to avoid such violations in the future. COSO goes even further, suggesting that the internal control system is subject to regular review to reflect changes both inside and outside the corporation.

Effective programs are adapted to circumstances

(A) Each of the requirements set forth in this guideline shall be met by an organization; however, in determining what specific actions are necessary to meet those requirements, factors

that should be considered include: (i) applicable industry practice or the standards called for by any applicable government regulation, (ii) the size of the organization, and (iii) similar misconduct [at the organization in the past].

(B) Applicable Government Regulation and Industry Practice – An organization's failure to incorporate or follow applicable industry practice or standards called for by any applicable governmental regulation weighs against a finding of an effective compliance and ethics program.

(Application Note #2 for Chapter 8, Part B, Section B2.1 ("Effective Compliance and Ethics Program") of the "2004 Federal Sentencing Guideline Manual," as amended effective 1 November 2004)

Both COSO and the US courts recognize that the internal control system must be adapted to the specific needs of the corporation. "Risk assessment," including a cost-benefit analysis, is one of COSO's five elements. Past misconduct raises the same issues in the context of the Federal Sentencing Guidelines.

A corporation's industry is, obviously, a very important factor in terms of assessing its risks and implementing a cost-effective internal control system. Turning to industry associations and their guidelines can, in fact, be a very effective method for establishing at least discrete elements of an Effective Program. Competitors are allowed to cooperate on a broad range of matters within the scope of their industry associations without violating applicable competition or antitrust regulations. Those matters can include the assessment of non-commercial risks common to the industry and implementing a cost-effective internal control system.

Certain businesses are subject to specific government regulations and their internal control systems should focus on that specific regulation. A corporation in the food industry should have an organization in place to pay special attention to food regulations, such as the Food and Drug Administration in the USA. At the same time, government agencies have also frequently developed their own guidelines on compliance programs for businesses subject to their regulations. Some of those governmental guidelines are mandatory (i.e., giving rise to a violation of regulations for failure to adopt them), while other governmental guidelines are similar in effect to the Federal Sentencing Guidelines. In other words, they only can be used to reduce penalties in the event that they are adopted by businesses.

A corporation's size is the final factor specifically mentioned by US courts in determining whether a compliance and ethics program is an "Effective Program." A formal program may be appropriate for large corporations, including written codes, policies and procedures, detailed delegations of responsibility, employee orientation, regular training and periodic compliance reviews. Such programs are expensive and may not be appropriate for smaller companies. A smaller company may be able to maintain an Effective Program with more informal arrangements for one or more of the elements of an internal control system.

INTERNAL ACCOUNTING CONTROLS

Reasonable assurances of reliable financial reporting

COSO outlines a system of internal controls to provide reasonable assurances that corporate officers, employees and other agents loyally and diligently pursue all three fundamental corporate objectives: effective and efficient operation, legal compliance and reliable reporting. Maintaining such a system of internal controls is an element of senior officers' duty of care in respect of their corporate responsibilities.

Just as the US courts in the "Federal Sentencing Guidelines" have provided guidance on the internal control system they consider appropriate for assuring compliance with government regulations generally, so the US Congress has stipulated the internal control system it considers appropriate for assuring compliance with federal securities disclosure requirements ("Internal Accounting Controls") (Section 13(b)-2 of the Securities Exchange Act of 1934, as quoted extensively below).

For a corporation, following the guidance of the US courts concerning an "Effective Program" can lead to reduced sentences in the event of the corporation violating any US federal government regulations. Failure to follow the Internal Accounting Controls provisions can give rise to administrative, civil and criminal proceedings. In other words, unlike a failure to follow the guidance from COSO and the US courts, a corporation's failure to follow the Congressional guidance on Internal Account Controls is – in and of itself – a violation of law. In addition, like the guidance from COSO and the US federal courts, failure to follow the Internal

Accounting Control provisions is arguably a violation of senior officer's duty of care under corporate law.

Generally, the SEC's Internal Accounting Controls require the following steps:

1 due authorization of all corporate transactions, without regard to size;
2 execution of transactions in accordance with authorization;
3 recording authorizations and executions of transactions accurately, completely and in reasonable detail;
4 reasonable assurances that records are accurate, complete and reasonably detailed;
5 financial accounts prepared in accordance with generally accepted accounting principles; and
6 reliable public disclosures, with no intentional or material misstatements or omissions.

Accurate and complete books and records

[Every corporation with shares publicly-traded on a securities exchange in the United States] shall … make and keep books, records, and accounts which, in reasonable detail, accurately and fairly reflect the transactions and dispositions of [the corporation's] assets.

(Section 13(b)-2(A) of the 1934 Act)

Books, records and accounts must be absolutely accurate and absolutely complete. The standard of "materiality," as explained in the chapter on securities regulation, does not apply to maintenance of corporate books, records and accounts. Indeed, it would be impossible to judge the materiality of public disclosures pursuant to securities regulations if books, records and accounts were not absolutely accurate and absolutely complete.

Moreover, books, records and accounts must be kept "in reasonable detail." Vague generalities can be "accurate and complete." Accordingly, it is necessary that, in addition to being accurate and complete, books, records and accounts be kept "in reasonable detail." The statute states only that "'reasonable detail' … mean[s] such … degree of detail as would satisfy prudent officials in the conduct of their own affairs" (Section 13(b)-7 of the 1934 Act).

In general, books, records and accounts must be kept in such detail as to make them meaningful. In the context of Internal Accounting Controls, recording transactions in "meaningful" detail means that transactions are recorded in such detail as is necessary:

(a) to permit verification that all transactions were authorized in accordance with the corporation's authorizations and executed in accordance with the authorizations; and

(b) to permit verification that financial statements are prepared and presented in conformity with generally accepted accounting principles (or any other criteria applicable to such statements) (Section 13(b)-2(ii) of the 1934 Act (paraphrased)).

Controls shall reasonably assure due authorization

[Every corporation with shares publicly-traded on a securities exchange in the United States] shall devise and maintain a system of internal accounting controls sufficient to provide reasonable assurances that – (i) transactions are executed in accordance with management's general or specific authorization, [and] (iii) access to assets is permitted only in accordance with management's general or specific authorization. .

(Section 13(b)-2(B) (i) and (iii) of the 1934 Act)

In other words, corporate assets should be used and transferred only in accordance with due authorizations. Authorizations can be general or specific but must always precede the use or transfer of all corporate assets – without regard to the size of the transaction. Of course, transactions in the normal course of business are typically executed pursuant to broad delegations to specific officers within the corporation. Such broad delegations are acceptable. The most important element of authorization is establishing personal responsibility. Due authorizations are authorizations granted by individuals or groups of individuals in accordance with a corporation's constitutional documents (i.e., charter documents such as articles of incorporation and by-laws).

The statute states that "'reasonable assurances'… mean such … degree of assurance as would satisfy prudent officials in the conduct of their own affairs" (Section 13(b)-7 of the 1934 Act). Other pronouncements by the SEC have clarified that the level of "reasonable assurances" can be determined using a

cost-benefit analysis, as with the internal control systems recommended by COSO and the US courts. The standard of "reasonable assurances" does not apply to making and keeping accurate books and records, but it does apply to all other elements of the Internal Accounting Control provisions.

Controls shall reasonably assure reliable financial reports

[Every corporation with shares publicly-traded on a securities exchange in the United States] shall devise and maintain a system of internal accounting controls sufficient to provide reasonable assurances that … (ii) transactions are recorded as necessary (I) to permit preparation of financial statements in conformity with generally accepted accounting principles or any other criteria applicable to such statements, and (II) to maintain accountability for assets.

(Section 13(b)-2(B)(ii) of the 1934 Act)

In other words, corporations with shares publicly-traded in the United States must establish and maintain a system of internal controls to provide reasonable assurances that financial reports are prepared in accordance with GAAP. Again, reasonable assurances determined on the basis of cost-benefit analysis. The SEC's Internal Accounting Control provisions concretely prescribe only that such controls include physical inventories "at reasonable intervals" (see Section 13(b)-2(iv) of the 1934 Act).

Make no material or intentional misstatements or omissions

In general, the SEC's Internal Accounting Control provisions are intended to support its system of periodic public disclosures by corporations whose shares are traded on securities exchanges in the United States. Of course, such periodic public disclosures are subject to standards of "intentionality" and, in addition, "materiality": in other words, periodic disclosures pursuant to US securities regulations should not include any intentional or material misstatements or omissions. In practice, the adequacy of Internal Accounting Controls has been an issue only when public disclosures pursuant to securities regulations have been intentionally or materially misleading, either because of a misstatement or because of an omission.

Possible personal criminal liability

No person shall knowingly circumvent or knowingly fail to implement a system of internal accounting controls or knowingly falsify any book, record, or account.

(Section 13(b)(5) of the 1934 Act)

The statute also provides that any knowing failure, circumvention or falsification potentially subjects corporations and their officers to criminal violations. In practice, violations of the Internal Accounting Control provisions have not subjected corporations or their officers to criminal liability, even if the failure, circumvention or falsification is intentional, unless the failure or circumvention is committed in connection with another, independent violation of securities regulations.

Pursuant to the Internal Accounting Controls, no corporate director or officer of an issuer shall, directly or indirectly, make or cause to be made a materially false or misleading statement or omission to an accountant in connection with:

1 any audit, review or examination of the corporation's financial statements in connection with public disclosures; or
2 the preparation or filing of any document or report required to be filed with the Commission in connection with a public disclosure (Rule 13b2–2(a) of the 1934 Act).

There is no similar protection for statements to lawyers in connection with the SEC's Internal Accounting Controls. Accordingly, all audits, reviews and examinations in connection with a US corporation's compliance with applicable securities regulations probably should be conducted by accountants, with lawyers acting pursuant to accountants' instructions.

PROVIDING ASSURANCES OF COMPLIANCE WITH GENERAL OBLIGATIONS

As explained above, COSO's system of internal controls is intended to apply generally to all of a corporation's three fundamental objectives. The US courts have provided further guidance concerning an internal control system intended for compliance with government regulations. The US Congress has imposed specific requirements for internal accounting controls intended to provide reasonable assurances that publicly-traded corporations comply with its disclosure requirements.

COMPLIANCE WITH GENERAL OBLIGATIONS

Look to industry guidelines for duties of care

Just as US courts and the SEC have provided further guidance for internal controls in respect of specific corporate objectives, so industry associations often in effect provide guidance for internal control systems in respect of compliance with the law of general obligations.

As explained in the chapter on the law of general obligations, corporations can be liable for acts or omissions causing harm to others or to their property, if the act or omission breaches an applicable "duty of care." Plaintiffs, judges and juries often look to industry guidelines for standards to determine the "duty of care" applicable to specific corporate acts and omissions – and they often find applicable standards in those guidelines.

Accordingly, corporations' operations should be reviewed to provide reasonable assurances that employees conduct corporate activities in accordance with applicable industry guidelines. In other words, operating policies and procedures set forth in industry guidelines should probably be incorporated into business practices – and corporate internal control systems should review business practices to ensure compliance with those guidelines.

PROVIDING ASSURANCES OF CONTRACT COMPLIANCE AND ENFORCEMENT

In dealing with contracts, it is important to remember that they are both tangible and intangible corporate assets. The corporation might not be able to enforce its contract rights unless it can produce a signed original of the contract.

COMPLIANCE AND ENFORCEMENT OF CONTRACTS

Contracts are tangible corporate assets

Contracts are tangible corporate assets. As once stated, verbal contracts are not worth the paper on which they are written. In the absence of documentary evidence of specific contractual undertakings, it is very difficult to prove that a corporation benefits from certain contract rights – or that its contract obligations are limited in some agreed fashion.

Accordingly, just as senior corporate officers have a duty to establish and maintain internal arrangements to preserve other tangible corporate assets, senior officers have a duty to establish and maintain internal arrangements for maintaining signed originals of corporate contracts in such a manner that those signed originals can be accessed as necessary to determine and evidence contractual obligations benefiting and burdening a corporation. Verification of those arrangements is an important part of a system of internal controls.

Contract rights are intangible corporate assets

As indicated in the foregoing discussion of internal controls concerning contracts, contracts rights can benefit a corporation as well as burden it. Accordingly, unlike the Effective Program recommended by US courts and the Internal Accounting Controls prescribed by the SEC, internal arrangements to record corporate contracts are essential to preserving corporate assets.

PROVIDING ASSURANCES OF COMPLIANCE WITH COMMUNITY ETHICAL NORMS

Writing a corporate code of conduct is an important initial step to establishing and maintaining internal control systems for COSO pursuant to its Enterprise Risk Management–Integrated Framework and for the US courts for the purpose of having an effective compliance and ethics program. In addition, Section 406 of the Sarbanes-Oxley Act of 2002 requires that corporations adopt a "code of ethics" applicable to their senior officers or disclose their reasons for not doing so.

Each of these authorities makes clear that writing a code of conduct, in and of itself, is not sufficient to provide assurances of compliance with ethical norms contained in those codes. Each authority recognizes that implementation of the code of ethical conduct requires support from senior management, communication of the code throughout the organization, effective monitoring, reporting and auditing, consistent enforcement and continuous improvement.

COMPLIANCE WITH COMMUNITY ETHICAL NORMS

Ethics should be included in codes of conduct

None of the authorities requiring or rewarding the adoption of a code of ethics actually defines the terms "ethical conduct," "ethical values" or "ethics." Accordingly, each corporation is left to develop its own understanding of the ethical principles and policies to be included in its code of conduct. As discussed in this book, one good approach is to ensure that codes of conduct reflect due consideration for community ethical norms. The codes of conduct for a few corporations even reflect a sense of social responsibility beyond relevant community ethical norms. In any event, corporations should clearly indicate that undertakings set forth in a code of conduct can exceed their obligations under applicable law.

Ethics should be applied by and to principal officers

Traditionally corporate codes of conduct have been developed by chief executive officers with, at most, director approval. Since such codes of conduct were in practically all instances enforced by chief executive officers, the codes of conduct were not, as a practical matter, applicable to chief executive and other senior corporate officers.

As discussed in Chapter 15 ("Board supervision") Sarbanes-Oxley has recently mandated that all publicly-traded companies post a written code of conduct to their websites or explain their reasons for not having a code of conduct. Sarbanes-Oxley expressly indicates that such codes of conduct should be applicable to a corporation's principal officers.

15

Relationships with Directors

Board supervision

INTRODUCTION

Corporate governance has recently been extensively discussed, intensely debated and variously defined. For the purposes of this book, corporate governance shall mean the internal arrangements within a corporation intended to provide reasonable assurances that corporate directors, officers and employees make and implement decisions in accordance with their duties of care and loyalty to their corporations. In the past, corporate governance has been viewed to include two elements: board supervision and internal controls.

Comparing board supervision and internal controls

In the past, most directors understood internal controls to be structures and procedures within a corporation designed and implemented by senior management to provide reasonable assurances that other corporate officers and employees were faithfully and diligently pursuing every corporation's three fundamental objectives of effective and efficient operation, compliance with law and reliable reporting (the three fundamental objectives which, as discussed in the preceding chapter, COSO included within the scope of internal controls since 1992).

In effect, directors understood internal controls to be systems for senior management to ensure that other corporate officers and employees were faithfully and diligently implementing decisions made by senior management in the ordinary course of busi-

ness. In other words, in the past, some directors – indeed, probably many directors – did not understand or agree that board supervision includes a review of decisions made and implemented by the corporation's most senior corporate officers in the ordinary course of business. In other words, board supervision did not determine whether senior management was making decisions faithfully and diligently in pursuit of effective and efficient operation, compliance with law and reliable reporting. In fact, it appears that board supervision in the past too often did not include an investigation of whether senior management was setting goals in accordance with corporate missions and values (the fourth fundamental objective which was discussed in the preceding chapter and included within the scope of COSO's internal controls in 2004).

As a result, internal controls were considered to be only part of a corporation's governance arrangements – and, more importantly, board supervision was not considered to be part of internal controls. As explained in detail in this chapter, the intention of most legal initiatives in the area of corporate governance has been:

1 to expand the scope of board supervision over senior corporate officers to provide reasonable assurances that senior corporate officers are faithfully and diligently pursuing their corporation's fundamental objectives; and

2 to include boards of directors in internal control structures and procedures applicable to corporate officers and employees below senior management.

In other words, the intention of recent corporate governance initiatives is to eliminate the distinction between board supervision and internal control.

More concretely, the intention of most legal initiatives in the area of corporate governance has been:

1 to integrate boards of directors into internal control systems for all four of COSO's fundamental corporate objectives; and
2 to subject senior management to the rigors of such internal control systems.

It remains to be seen whether these legal initiatives will have their intended effect. Again, as of September 2004, COSO's four fundamental objectives for all corporations are:

1 strategic goals, i.e., goals in line with corporate missions and values;
2 effective and efficient operation;
3 legal compliance; and
4 reliable financial reporting.

Focusing on recent authoritative measures is most useful

This chapter does not review the many corporate governance studies and recommendations made by various panels of prominent individuals around the world even though those individuals have demonstrated a commitment to investors and the public because those studies and recommendations are not authoritative. In addition, those studies and recommendations are not included because they tend to focus on substantive guidelines for use in corporate policies rather than the structures and procedures to be used in developing those policies. As a result, only one such recent study (9 January 2003) is referenced in the notes to this chapter.[1]

This chapter does not review European Union laws regarding board supervision because there is still no directive or regulation on issues of board supervision over senior management in the ordinary course of business. On the contrary, a special commission convened by the Commission of the European Union has determined that the Union is not currently prepared to address such issues of corporate governance on a European level.

At the same time, some national corporate governance systems of long standing in Europe offer viable alternatives to the recent proposals presented in this chapter. Those national corporate laws offer alternatives to the materials presented in this chapter. First, unlike the situation in the United States, there is a national corporate law in most European countries. Second, under those national corporate laws and unlike the situation in the United States, there are national corporate laws specifically applicable to publicly-traded companies. Third, pursuant to requirements of at least some of those national corporate laws, the boards of some publicly-traded European companies have adopted the committee approach recently embraced by the NYSE. Fourth, the boards of some European companies, as permitted by national regulations, have bank representatives on their boards. Such bank representation might help to ensure that directors as a group are independent from senior management. Fifth and most controversial, the boards of some European companies, again pursuant to national legal requirements, have worker representatives on their boards. As with bank representation, such worker representation may help to ensure that directors as a group are independent from senior management.

Recent measures in the USA are authoritative

The US Congress and the New York Stock Exchange ("NYSE") have both recently adopted authoritative measures in respect of board supervision over senior corporate management. (The US Congress remained within the scope of regulatory authority previously granted to US Securities and Exchange Commission (the "SEC"), i.e., reliable financial reporting.)

These two organizations, one a private association and the other a governmental body, have acted in concert – but separately – because the United States does not have a single or comprehensive system for regulating board supervision of senior management. The United States does not have such a system:

1 because there is no federal corporate law in the United States (only the various laws of the various states);
2 because there is no corporate law in the United States specifically intended to apply to publicly-traded corporations; and

3 because there is no government agency in the United States responsible for enforcing any corporate law in the United States (not even at the state level).

The four fundamental objectives of all corporations

This chapter focuses on arrangements for board supervision in terms of the four fundamental objectives announced by COSO and discussed in this book's first chapter:

1 strategic goals, i.e., goals in line with corporate missions and values;
2 effective and efficient operation;
3 legal compliance; and
4 reliable financial reporting.

Focusing on internal control systems (as that term has been understood in the past), the US court system's effective "compliance and ethics program," as outlined in the preceding chapter, is intended to provide reasonable assurances concerning the third goal, i.e., that officers and employees comply with applicable government regulations. The "internal accounting controls" included by the US Congress in the Securities Exchange Act of 1934 are intended to provide reasonable assurances concerning the fourth goal, i.e., that corporations report reliably on their financial performance and condition. Only COSO's system of enterprise risk management addresses the first two goals, i.e., reasonable assurances:

1 that senior management sets goals in line with corporate missions and values; and
2 that corporations operate effectively and efficiently in pursuit of those goals.

Focusing on board supervision, the intent of the Sarbanes-Oxley Act of 2002 ("Sarbanes-Oxley") is limited to providing reasonable assurances that senior management prepares and presents financial reports and other public disclosures in compliance with applicable federal regulations. In other words, Sarbanes-Oxley seeks to incorporate directors into internal controls in respect of the fourth fundamental corporate objective. As you will see, the new NYSE listing requirements concerning board supervision are reasonably intended to ensure that board supervision of senior managements includes all of a corporation's four fundamental objectives.

A BIT OF HISTORY AND CURRENT CORPORATE LAW

With the spread of the industrial revolution, individuals gained the right to conduct any legal business in corporate form (with limited exceptions for professional activities and businesses with significant capital adequacy requirements like banking and insurance). Before the beginning of the twentieth century, the right to conduct business in corporate form was often based on specific charters granted by governments. During the twentieth century, the right to conduct business in corporate form was more and more based on contracts between shareholders. With the introduction of modern corporate law, governments in effect extended "freedom of contract" from isolated commercial transactions to on-going corporate associations.

Corporations differ from individuals in that more than one person is involved in making economic decisions. As a result, constitutional questions arose in the connection of the modern corporation: Who should be involved in making and implementing decisions in the name and on behalf of corporations? How should those decisions be made and implemented? In response, modern corporate law established a bare framework for corporate constitutions. Indeed, the lack of a prescribed framework, i.e., the deference to founding shareholders – both to engage in any legal business as they see fit and to arrange their corporate constitutions as they see fit – is an essential characteristic of modern corporate law.

With the growth of securities exchanges, founding shareholders had the ability to realize a return from their corporations not only in the form of dividends from operations but also by selling their shares to the public. Individual minority investors – including practically all public shareholders – typically did not want to direct their corporations. Typically, they wanted to share in the ownership without becoming involved in its direction and control. Accordingly, participating in the ownership of a publicly-traded corporation has practically always been separated from participating in the management of the corporation's affairs. Some founding shareholders of publicly-traded companies became their directors, but not all shareholders became directors – or even wanted to become directors. Gradually, some directors were not shareholders. Eventually, many and even most directors were not shareholders.

Some directors of publicly-traded companies became officers, but not all became officers – or even wanted to become officers. Over time, many and even most officers were not directors. By the end of the twentieth century, shareholders of publicly-traded companies largely defer to boards of non-shareholder directors to manage corporate affairs. In turn, directors – as permitted by corporate law – delegate to senior corporate officers the management of all corporate affairs, at least affairs in the ordinary course of the corporation's business. In other words, senior corporate officers decide what goods and services corporations will produce and sell, how to produce and sell them and even how to dispose of the income from those sales.

Having decided to delegate to senior corporate officers the management of all corporate affairs in the ordinary course of business, directors have a duty to shareholders to implement that delegation of authority loyally and diligently. Directors' supervisory obligation is, quite simply, the loyal and diligent implementation of their decision to delegate corporate management to senior corporate officers. Consistent with the rights of all "principals" under agency law, directors have the right to receive reports from senior management with respect to senior management's performance of the authority delegated to them by the board of directors. The right to receive reports is, however, merely an instrumental right, enabling directors to discharge their supervisory obligation.

Separating ownership, supervision (sometimes called "direction") and management of publicly-traded corporations has had many positive effects, but the separation has also revealed some weaknesses in corporate constitutions. As regards the role of directors, those weaknesses have returned to the fundamental questions of:

1 who should serve as directors; and
2 how should directors make decisions?

CURRENT CORPORATE LAW

Shareholders delegate corporate management to directors

Under modern corporate constitutions, achieving a corporation's objectives is delegated completely to

directors. The corporate law of the State of Delaware (the corporate law used most commonly by publicly-traded companies incorporated in the United States) provides quite simply as follows:

> The business and affairs of every corporation … shall be managed by or under the direction of a board of directors.
> (Delaware General Corporation Law § 141 (a))

Directors delegate all management to senior corporate officers

Directors universally exercise their right to delegate the power to manage corporate business and affairs to senior corporate officers, typically a single corporate president. In larger corporations, the president is usually called a "chief executive officer." In the end, the president (or CEO) both makes and implements decisions (either personally or through delegation), subject only to supervision by the corporation's directors.

Senior corporate officers have very broad discretion

Corporate law gives the individuals with the power to manage a corporation's business, i.e., its senior corporate officers, wide latitude to make and implement decisions in their corporations' names. The decisions they make and implement are subject to legal challenge by the corporation – usually at a shareholder's initiative – only to the extent that senior corporate officers violate their duty of care and duty of loyalty in making and implementing their decisions.

Senior corporate officers can generally satisfy their "duty of loyalty" with confidence by following the simple procedure in making full disclosure of conflicts-of-interest to independent directors and negotiating directly with them – or their designee. In the absence of a violation of law (including federal securities regulations), senior corporate officers are rarely found to have breached their "duty of care."

Such findings are rare because courts' review of senior officers' decisions is subject to the "business judgment rule," i.e., senior corporate officers' decisions are not reviewed on the basis of the actual facts at the time of the decision or on the basis of the results obtained. Their decisions are reviewed only on the basis of the facts available to them or which, through due diligence, could have been available to them at the time that they made their decisions – and without regard to the results obtained.

Directors reserve only supervisory rights

Because of the broad authority directors delegate to senior corporate officers, directors in effect typically reserve only three powers for themselves: the power to appoint senior corporate officers, the power to regulate compensation and the power to dismiss them. For practical and sometimes contractual reasons, directors frequently have limited discretion in reducing senior corporate officers' remuneration. Accordingly, once senior corporate officers are appointed, directors' ability to supervise them is effectively limited to the power to dismiss them.

NEW YORK STOCK EXCHANGE LISTING REQUIREMENTS

Supervising for all four fundamental corporate objectives

Recent corporate scandals suggest that directors may have abused their right to regulate compensation and, in appropriate cases, neglected their right to dismiss senior corporate officers. Compensation of senior corporate officers at some US corporations – already very high by international standards – has increased geometrically in recent years, even without a corresponding increase in corporate results.

Too frequently, it even appears that directors have not dismissed senior corporate officers even though, on the basis of facts eventually disclosed to the public, at least a few senior corporate officers may well have egregiously breached their duties of care and loyalty over long periods of time. It even appears that, too often, directors have not obtained fair results for their corporations in those instances where senior corporate officers have disclosed conflicts-of-interest and negotiated corporate contracts directly with directors.

In the absence of US corporate law applicable to publicly-traded companies, the NYSE – at the prompting of the SEC – has taken some initiatives in an attempt to correct the recent apparent abuses and

neglect by directors. More specifically, the new "corporate governance" guidelines require that companies traded on the NYSE have committees of independent directors for the purpose of:

1 determining executive compensation;
2 nominating senior corporate officers and directors; and
3 auditing information provided by senior corporate officers to boards of directors.

By addressing the corporate constitutional issues of

1 who should be corporate directors; and
2 how they should make their decisions,

the NYSE is attempting to ensure that directors discharge their supervisory obligations faithfully and diligently. More precisely, by providing that directors be "independent" (answering at least in part the question: who should be corporate directors?), the NYSE is attempting to provide reasonable assurances that directors faithfully supervise senior corporate officers. By providing reasonable assurances that directors have necessary information (answering at least in part the question: how should directors make their decisions?), NYSE corporate governance requirements also attempt to provide reasonable assurances that directors diligently supervise senior corporate officers.

Brief background

The NYSE is a private association subject to regulation by the SEC. The SEC imposes many requirements for corporate securities listed on the NYSE, most of which relate to the size of the issuer and the nature of the securities. Traditionally, the NYSE has deferred to the General Corporation Law of the State of Delaware for determining corporate governance requirements and to the SEC for determining disclosure requirements for companies listed on the NYSE.

On 13 February 2002, the SEC asked the NYSE to review its corporate governance requirements for companies listed on the NYSE. Beginning on 16 August 2002, after receiving extensive public comment, the NYSE filed its Corporate Governance Proposals with the SEC. The NYSE's corporate governance listing requirements are set forth in the new

F
O
U
R

section 303A of the NYSE's "Listed Company Manual." All of them are outlined below. Prior rules are briefly summarized for the purpose of highlighting changes.

Independent directors should supervise senior officers

"Independent directors"

As evidenced by the following specific requirements, it is most important for the NYSE listing requirements that directors be independent.

For a director to be deemed independent, the board must affirmatively determine that the director has "no material relationship with the listed company."

In the past, independence was defined as having no "relationship with the company that may interfere with the exercise of the director's independence from management and the company." It appears that the acceptance of "immaterial" fees from the listed company – in addition to directors' fees – will not jeopardize the "independence" of directors.

Neither former employees of a listed company nor any employees or partners of its independent auditors – including the immediate families of any such employees or partners – may be classified as "independent" directors for a period of five years after the end of their engagement with the listed company, called a "cooling-off" period. In the past, the cooling-off period was three years.

A majority of all directors must be independent

Unless a listed company has a controlling shareholder, corporate boards must have a majority of independent directors. This is a new requirement.

Compensation and nomination committees must be entirely independent

Compensation and nomination committees are particularly important because, as explained above, the rights to hire, fire and compensate senior corporate officers are the only "leverage" retained by directors for the purpose of discharging their supervisory obligations. The new rules provide that companies listed on the NYSE must have compensation and nominating committees and that those committees must be composed entirely of independent directors. This is a completely new requirement. In the past, neither separate compensation nor nomination committees were required.

Audit committees must be entirely independent

Audit committees are particularly important because, as explained above, the quality of the information received by directors obviously affects their ability to discharge their supervisory obligations. In the past, listed companies were required to have an audit committee and the audit committee was to be composed of at least three independent directors. Now, audit committees must be composed entirely of independent directors, as defined above. In addition to the rules for "independence" applicable to all directors, audit committee members must limit their compensation from the company to the fees they receive as directors.

Directors should supervise with clear policies and procedures

Board committees must have and disclose charters

In the past, there was no obligation for listed companies to have nomination or compensation committees or for audit committees to adopt charters, i.e., rules for procedures and decisions. Now, the boards of listed companies must adopt charters for each of their nomination, compensation and audit committees. In addition, the charters must be published. Having published charters is intended to provide reasonable assurances that the directors are diligent in discharging their supervisory obligations.

Companies must have and disclose codes of conduct.

Listed companies must adopt and disclose governance guidelines and codes of business conduct applicable to the senior corporate officers, including the chief executive officer and the chief financial officer. This is an entirely new requirement which follows an identical new requirement from the SEC. Again, it is intended to ensure that board supervision is effective.

Non-management directors must regularly hold separate meetings

The independent directors of listed companies, now sometimes called the "executive committee" or "executive session," are required to meet regularly without members of senior management for the purpose of reviewing corporate business and affairs. This is a completely new requirement.

Shareholders must approve most stock-option plans

In the past, shareholder approval was not required for many stock-option plans. Now, shareholder approval is required for all such plans, other than employment-inducement options, option plans acquired through mergers, and tax-qualified plans such as 401(k)s.

Internal auditors are required

In the past, listed companies were not required to have an internal audit function. In other words, audit committees received all information from senior corporate officers or external auditors. Now, all listed companies must have an internal audit function, available to the audit committee for investigations and other information.

Penalties include reprimand and de-listing

Under the new corporate governance listing requirements, the NYSE is allowed to issue a public-reprimand letter to listed companies who violate requirements and, as in the past, to terminate the listing of violating companies.

While self-regulation through the NYSE listing requirements has certain advantages over government regulation, the only sanctions available to the NYSE are, in effect, punishment for corporations and their shareholders – not for corporate directors and officers.

Application to foreign companies

The NYSE has determined that it will not apply any particular corporate governance listing requirement to a foreign company with securities listed on the NYSE (a "foreign issuer") if the foreign issuer provides a written certification from legal counsel in its country of incorporation that the foreign issuer complies with the corporate governance rules:

(a) of that country; and
(b) of any security exchange in that country on which the issuer's securities are listed.

US SECURITIES REGULATIONS

Supervising reliable public disclosures

Sarbanes-Oxley has received much attention as the most important US corporate governance initiative in the wake of the recent corporate scandals in the US.

As indicated above, the NYSE's corporate governance requirements are probably more comprehensive because they are intended to provide reasonable assurances that directors diligently and loyally supervise corporate affairs in light of all four fundamental corporate objectives. In contrast, the authority of the SEC – and the scope of Sarbanes-Oxley – is largely limited to reliable financial reporting.

Sarbanes-Oxley addresses three broad issues related to public disclosures by corporations pursuant to securities regulations:

(a) the substance of those disclosures;
(b) the independence of auditors of periodic financial reports; and
(c) the procedures whereby corporations prepare and present those periodic reports. Sarbanes-Oxley also imposes
(d) increases in the potential personal criminal penalties for violations of securities regulations by corporate officers.

As with the above summaries of the NYSE listing requirements, each of the following summaries of Sarbanes-Oxley gives the state of the law prior to its adoption. The term "issuers" in the following summaries refers to corporations with securities publicly traded on US exchanges.

THE SUBSTANCE OF SECURITIES DISCLOSURES

Material changes must be disclosed rapidly and clearly

> Issuers are required to disclose on a rapid and current basis … material changes to the financial condition or operation of the issuer, in plain English.
>
> (Section 409(a) of Sarbanes-Oxley)

Since 1934, issuers have been obligated to report on Form 8-K and in press releases the occurrence of any material events or corporate changes of importance to investors.

Off-balance-sheet accounting and contractual obligations

Issuers must explain their off-balance-sheet financing arrangements in "Management's Discussion and Analysis" ("MD&A"), part of management's annual report to shareholders. The off-balance-sheet financing must be explained in a separately captioned subsection. Issuers must also provide an overview of certain known contractual obligations in a tabular format (Section 401 (a) of Sarbanes-Oxley and 27 January 2003 SEC Release No. 33–8182).

These provisions change the presentation but not the substance of certain financial disclosures. Material off-balance-sheet arrangements are already disclosed in footnotes to the financial statements. Material contracts must be described and provided as exhibits.

Use of non-GAAP financial measures

Issuers that disclose or release financial measures which are not consistent with generally accepted accounting principles ("GAAP"), i.e., non-GAAP financial measures, must include in that non-GAAP disclosure or release a presentation of the most directly comparable GAAP financial measure and a reconciliation of the disclosed non-GAAP financial measure to the most directly comparable GAAP financial measure (Section 401 (b) of Sarbanes-Oxley and 22 January 2003 SEC Release No. 33–8177).

This provision is new. It responds to issuers' recent practice of disclosing pro-forma accounting statements in press releases. Pro-forma financial statements have not been permitted as part of the regular periodic disclosures (quarterly and annual reports to shareholders), except in certain circumstances – such as acquisitions during the accounting period covered by the report – and only as an addition to mandated financial statements prepared and presented in accordance with GAAP.

Companies must disclose codes of ethics

Companies must disclose whether they have adopted codes of ethics that apply to their principal executive officers and principal financial officers. Companies without such codes must disclose this fact and explain why they have not adopted them. Companies are also required to promptly disclose amendments to, and waivers from, the code of ethics relating to any of their principal officers. A code of ethics shall require: honest and ethical conduct, reliable financial disclosures and compliance with applicable regulations, including "the ethical handling of actual or apparent conflicts of interests between personal and professional relationships" (Section 407 of Sarbanes-Oxley and 27 January 2003 SEC Release No. 33–8177).

At least some issuers have had codes of ethics, but the SEC apparently suspects that – either in principle or in practice – too many companies do not have them or that too many of such codes have not been applicable to companies' most senior officers. The new rules require disclosure of a code of ethics applicable at least in principle to senior officers and, importantly, whether any waivers from the code have been granted for any senior officers.

As previously noted, US securities regulations are concerned exclusively with reliable financial reporting and the prevention of fraud in the sale of securities on US exchanges. At the same time, as evidenced by the SEC's provisions on internal accounting controls (Section 13(b)-2 of the Securities Exchange Act of 1934), the SEC cannot overlook issues of corporate due diligence to the extent that due diligence is required in order for corporations reliably to prepare and present required financial statements and other public disclosures.

Some commentators have argued that a code of ethics is not reasonably related or even necessary to provide reasonable assurances that a company's financial reports are reliable.

AUDITOR INDEPENDENCE

Create a "public company accounting oversight board"

The SEC shall establish an independent board for the purpose of regulating accountants who audit public companies and establishing auditing standards. The board will consist of five members, only two of which shall have been certified public accountants. The board will be funded by companies with securities publicly traded on US exchanges (see Sections 101 to 109 of Sarbanes-Oxley).

There already is and – since 1933 – there has been an independent board for the purpose of regulating accountants who audit public companies and for the purpose of establishing auditing standards. It is the American Institute of Certified Public Accountants, one of the members of COSO. In addition, there already is and – since 1933 – there has been an independent board for the purpose of developing generally accepted accounting principles, the Financial Accounting Standards Board.

Limitation of auditors' non-audit services

Companies are prohibited from engaging their auditors for non-audit services except with:

1 pre-approval from the audit committee; and
2 public disclosure related to services provided.

An accountant would not be "independent" from an audit client if an audit partner received compensation based on selling engagements to that client for services other than audit, review and attest services (Section 208(a) of Sarbanes-Oxley. 28 January 2003 SEC Release No. 33–8183; 34–47265).

There has been a wide-reaching SEC rule concerning Auditor Independence. Consistent with exist-ing rules, since 5 February 2001 an auditor's independence would be impaired if the auditor has a direct or material indirect business relationship with the audit client, other than providing professional auditing services.

CORPORATE PROCEDURES FOR PERIODIC DISCLOSURES

Companies must implement "internal controls over financial reporting"

In each annual report to shareholders, issuers shall state management's responsibility for establishing and maintaining internal controls over financial reporting, together with an assessment of the effectiveness of those controls. "Internal controls over financial reporting" is defined as a process designed to provide reasonable assurance regarding the reliability of financial reporting and the preparation of financial statements for external purposes in accordance with generally accepted accounting principles (Section 404 of Sarbanes-Oxley and Rule 13a-15(f)).

Since 1976, company management has had the obligation to establish and maintain "internal accounting controls," pursuant to Section 13b of the 1934 Act. Moreover, since 1976, management has voluntarily acknowledged its responsibility for internal accounting controls in each annual report to shareholders.

The Sarbanes-Oxley provision is virtually identical to the 1976 requirement concerning internal accounting controls and, moreover, is virtually identical to the management voluntary statements concerning internal accounting controls since 1976 except that:

1 under Sarbanes-Oxley senior management must review internal controls for changes and effectiveness on a quarterly basis; and
2 senior officers and directors must be involved in design and implementation as follows: the controls must be "designed by, or under the supervision of, the issuer's [i.e., the company's] principal executive and principal financial officers, or persons performing similar functions, and effected by the issuer's board of directors, management and other personnel …" (Rule 13a-15(f) of the 1934 Act).

FOUR

Companies must implement "disclosure controls and procedures"

Publicly-traded corporations must implement controls and other procedures designed to ensure that information required for public disclosure pursuant to securities regulations is recorded, processed, summarized and reported, within the time periods specified for such disclosures (Rule 13a-15 (a) and (e) of the 1934 Act), and that the information reported is reliable (13a-15 (a) and (f) of the 1934 Act).

CEO and CFO must personally certify quarterly and annual reports

CEOs and CFOs of issuers must personally certify their companies' annual and quarterly financial reports, subject to civil and criminal penalties.

Civil and criminal penalties already exist for intentional material misstatements and omissions in financial statements. In addition, since 1976, CEOs and CFOs have voluntarily made statements confirming their responsibility for financial statements and internal controls. A copy of the confirmation stated voluntarily since 1976[2] and of the form of certification required beginning in 2003[3] is attached to the notes to this chapter. They appear to be substantially identical.

Audit committee must be composed entirely of independent directors

Issuers must have an audit committee composed entirely of independent directors and disclose the name of at least one financial expert together with whether the expert is independent of management. An issuer that does not have an audit committee financial expert must disclose this fact and explain why it has no such expert (Section 406 of Sarbanes-Oxley and 27 January 2003 SEC Release No. 33–8177).

Even prior to the most recent changes in its listing requirements, the NYSE required that at least three members of a publicly-traded corporation's audit committee be independent. In addition, pursuant to SEC regulations in place since 31 January 2000, companies have had to disclose certain matters concerning their audit committees in the proxy statement incorporated by reference with each annual report to shareholders. Those matters have included whether the audit committee has:

(a) reviewed and discussed the audited financial statements with management and independent auditors;
(b) received from the auditors disclosures regarding their independence;
(c) based on the review and discussions with management and auditors, recommended to the board that the audited financial statements be included in the annual report to shareholders.

Companies have also been required to disclose whether their board has adopted a written charter for the audit committee, and if so, include a copy of the charter as an appendix to the company's proxy statements at least once every three years (22 December 1999, SEC Release No. 34–42266).

Issuers' officers and directors shall not improperly influence auditors

Issuers' directors and officers shall not "fraudulently influence, coerce, manipulate, or mislead any independent public or certified accountant … for the purpose of rendering … financial statements misleading."
(Section 303(a) of Sarbanes-Oxley and Rule 13b2–2 under the 1934 Act)

Since the 1930s, it has been illegal, subject to potential personal criminal penalties, to engage in fraudulent or manipulative practices in connection with the issuance or trading of corporate securities in the United States. Since 1976, it has been illegal, subject to potential personal criminal penalties, to make or cause to be made a materially misleading statement or omission to an accountant in connection with the preparation of public disclosures pursuant to securities regulations in the United States.

Standards of conduct for securities lawyers

An attorney must report evidence of a material violation of securities laws or breach of fiduciary duty or similar violation by the issuer up-the-ladder within the company to the chief legal counsel ("CLO") or the chief executive officer ("CEO"). If the CLO and CEO do not respond appropriately to the evidence, the attorney is required to report the evidence to the audit committee, to a committee of independent directors or to the full board of directors (Section 307 of Sarbanes-Oxley and 29 January 2003 SEC Release 33–81851).

This provision is substantially identical to the responsibilities and procedures of external auditors in respect of consequential violations of law discovered by them in the course of their audit activities pursuant to securities regulations. The responsibilities of external auditors include reporting the consequential violation of law to the SEC on the same day that they report it to the company directors (Section 10A of the 1934 Act and Rule 10A-1 under the 1934 Act).

PENALTIES FOR CORPORATE OFFICERS AND DIRECTORS

Increased criminal penalties for destroying or falsifying audit records

Officers, directors and employees will be subject to enhanced criminal penalties – up to 20 years of imprisonment and up to $5,000,000 in fines – for destroying audit records or falsifying documents and for other knowing violations of the securities regulations (Section 1102 of Sarbanes-Oxley and the Federal Sentencing Guidelines).

In addition, the SEC may issue orders prohibiting individuals from serving as officers and directors of corporations with shares publicly traded in the United States if those individuals have been involved in fraud, deceit or other manipulative practices concerning the issuance or trading of shares on a stock exchange in the United States (Section 1105 of Sarbanes-Oxley).

In addition, CEOs and CFOs are required to forfeit bonuses, incentive compensation or gains from the sale of company securities during the 12-month period after the initial publication of financial statements that have to be reinstated as a result of misconduct (Section 304 of Sarbanes-Oxley).

There is already the possibility of criminal penalties for:

(a) those individuals who have been involved in fraud, deceit or other manipulative practices concerning the issuance or trading of shares on a stock exchange in the United States;

(b) obstruction of justice; and

(c) for "knowingly circumvent[ing] or knowingly fail[ing] to implement a system of internal accounting controls or knowingly falsify[ing] any book, record, or account required [as part of the system of internal accounting controls]" (Section 17(a) of the Securities Act of 1933 and Sections 10(b), 13(b)4 and 13(b)5 of the 1934 Act).

Acts and omissions constituting violations of securities regulations can, of course, also be violations of duties of care and loyalty under corporate law. On the other hand, it is possible to violate securities regulations without having breached the duties of care and loyalty. It is worth noting that violations of securities regulations, like violations of at least some other laws, are not subject to the business judgment rule.

More importantly, senior corporate officers have reporting responsibilities under corporate law in addition to its disclosure requirements under securities regulations.

Senior corporate officers are required to report to corporate directors to the extent that directors reasonably request such reports, without regard to whether the reports requested by directors are required disclosures under securities regulations.

NOMINATING AND ELECTING DIRECTORS

The focus on the independence of directors, both in the NYSE listing requirements and in Sarbanes-Oxley, is prompted at least in part by the current arrangement in publicly-traded US corporations whereby senior corporate officers nominate candidates for their boards of directors. In effect, senior corporate officers select their own supervisors and, in addition to paying directors' fees for director services, also commonly pay them investment banking and consulting fees. The selection of directors by senior management, together with the payments to directors from senior management, is widely perceived to compromise directors as supervisors of senior management.

Corporate law does not dictate that senior corporate officers nominate candidates for their boards of directors. On the contrary, corporate law simply provides the flexibility whereby senior officers can take the initiative in nominating candidates. Whether candidates are nominated by senior officers, other directors (e.g., the nominating committee) or by shareholders themselves, corporate law stipulates that shareholders must elect directors.

Senior officers are able to nominate practically all candidates for the boards of directors of publicly-traded US corporations largely because senior officers are responsible for preparing the proxy solicitation materials pursuant to which directors are elected. At the same time, there is no routine process for soliciting nominations from shareholders. In this context, the candidates nominated by senior officers are typically the only candidates on the ballot for election as directors.

On 15 July 2003, an SEC report recommended:

1 improved disclosure to shareholders concerning the procedures whereby directors are nominated; and
2 improved shareholder access to the director nomination process the following actions.

Among other things, the 15 July report recommends that corporations:

1 establish and disclose specific procedures by which shareholders can communicate with the directors of the corporations in which they invest; and
2 require that major, long-term shareholders (or groups of long-term shareholders) be provided access to company proxy materials to nominate directors, at least where there are objective criteria that indicate that shareholders may not have had adequate access to an effective proxy process.

16

Relationships with Creditors

Creditors' rights and bankruptcy law

INTRODUCTION

Relationships with creditors are an important part of corporate governance. Corporate governance, as it is generally understood, focuses on shareholders' control over the corporations they own. However, corporate governance can be defined more broadly to include the control that all sources of corporate funding exercised over corporations, including banks, bond holders and other sources of corporate credit.

In fact, creditors arguably exercise more control over the business conduct of their corporate creditors than the shareholders of those same corporate creditors. They exercise control through warranties and covenants in credit agreements imposing strict parameters in which corporations must conduct their business. Creditors have the right to receive reports periodically and privately on corporate compliance with those parameters, together with additional rights to monitor corporate operations. Creditors also have the ability, pursuant to bankruptcy proceedings, to take direct managerial control of a corporation not in compliance with agreed operational and financial parameters with creditors.

The most recent corporate scandals, such as Enron and WorldCom, surfaced after corporate bankruptcies became inevitable. Arguably, in the absence of corporate creditors and the exercise of their rights, the violations of shareholders' rights in at least some publicly-traded corporations might never have surfaced.

SOURCES OF CORPORATE FUNDING GENERALLY

Corporate operations are funded from a variety of sources. Typically, the initial source is contributions to capital by a corporation's shareholders. Ideally, after the initial contribution to capital, corporate operations are funded entirely from operating revenues. To the extent that operating revenues are insufficient to fund corporate operations, further funds are obtained through additional shareholder contributions to capital and through credit.

For example, every time a seller delivers products or services to a corporation before receiving payment, the seller is effectively providing credit to the corporation. A corporation also obtains credit every time a buyer pays it for products or services before the corporation delivers those products or services. More often, corporations obtain credit in transactions separate and apart from their purchase and sales operations. Such transactions are often called "credit facilities."

Corporate executives are usually most familiar with funded credit facilities, such as term loans and revolving credits (sometimes also called "lines of credit"). In fact, many different types of credit facilities are available to corporations, including bank loans, letters of credit, commercial paper programs, bond issuances and equipment leases. Generally, corporate credit facilities can provide either "funded" or "unfunded" credit to corporations, as explained below. In addition, different types of credits can even be combined in the same facility to provide both funded and unfunded credit.

Lenders can agree to provide credit facilities for a corporation's general purposes, for specifically designated purposes or simultaneously for both types of purposes. Specific purposes include financing current inventories of raw materials and final product, financing fixed assets such as buildings or equipment, and financing acquisitions. From the borrower's perspective, it is most important to match the timing of principal payments under credit facilities with revenues obtained from assets acquired with the financing. For example, it might make sense for a corporation to obtain short-term credit for the purpose of financing inventories because the corporation can typically convert the inventories obtained from the short-term credit into cash before the short-term credit needs to be repaid. On the other hand, it usually does not make sense for a corporation to obtain a short-term credit facility for the purpose of financing the construction of a plant. Short-term financing for plant construction usually does not make sense because the borrower will be obligated to repay the short-term credit before the plant could be used to generate operating revenue.

ELEMENTS OF A CREDIT FACILITY

Whether a credit facility takes the form of a bank loan, letter of credit, commercial paper program, bond issuance or equipment lease, the elements of a credit facility tend to be the same. They include:

1 the bank's commitment;
2 the borrower's promise to repay fundings, together with interest;
3 conditions to the bank's commitment and fundings;
4 the borrower's warranties;
5 the borrower's positive and negative covenants;
6 default and remedy provisions; and
7 provisions for amendments and waivers.

Banks typically provide the forms of agreements to be used in corporate credit facilities. In fact, the documentation prepared by banks in connection with their credit facilities constitutes an integral part of their operations. Their credit documentation reflects their risk assessments and business methods. As a result, banks often view the terms of their credit facilities as routine – and subject to only limited negotia-

tion. Interestingly, banks are frequently more rigid as regards the wording of borrowers' contractual obligations than the substance of those undertakings. For example, it might be easier to change the ratio of free cash flow to total debt payments than to change the terms used by the banks to express that ratio.

THE BANK'S COMMITMENT

A borrower's promise to make payments to the bank in exchange for a bank's commitment to provide funding or other credit is the fundamental element of a credit facility. (Credit can be provided by many sources other than banks. For the sake of simplicity, I will refer to all sources of corporate credit as "banks" throughout this chapter.)

A credit facility is considered to be "funded," if the bank and borrower agree that the bank will sooner or later certainly provide funds under the facility. A credit facility is considered to be "unfunded," if the bank and borrower understand and agree that the bank might never need to provide funds under the facility or, in other words, will need to provide funding only in certain circumstances.

The distinction between funded and unfunded credits is important because it is essential to understanding the intention of banks and borrowers. The distinction is also important for banks because most of their capital adequacy requirements tend to be determined on the basis of their funded credits and funded credit obligations. A bank's funding commitment can be most usefully categorized according to the duration of the funding commitment.

Unfunded bank commitments

In the United States, unfunded credit facilities often take the form of a stand-by letter of credit. In most other countries, unfunded credit facilities can take the form of a stand-by letter of credit or, more commonly, a bank guaranty. Around the world, it is also possible that an unfunded credit facility takes the form of a commitment letter. In the following discussion, I will refer to an unfunded bank commitment as a stand-by letter of credit.

A stand-by letter of credit is identical in form to a letter of credit used in international trade. In an international trade letter of credit, a bank agrees to a request from one of its customers – in exchange for a fee paid by the customer to the bank – to make payment to a seller in another country. The foreign seller agrees to ship goods to its purchaser, i.e., the bank's customer, on the basis of the bank's promise to make payment under the letter of credit, not on the basis of the purchaser's promise to pay for the goods.

Similarly, in a stand-by letter of credit, a bank agrees to a customer's request, in exchange for a fee, to make payment to a third party, but the third party is not a seller and the customer making the request is not obtaining the letter of credit to support a purchase transaction. Instead, the bank's customer is typically obtaining credit from some lender other than its bank and the lender will reduce its interest and fees if the bank's customer, i.e., the lender's borrower, obtains a letter of credit from its bank to support its repayment obligation.

Such a letter of credit is called a stand-by letter of credit because, unlike a trade credit, the bank does not necessarily make payment under the stand-by letter of credit. The bank makes payment under a stand-by letter of credit only if its customer fails to make payments to its lender. Stand-by letters of credit make sense only if the fee charged by the bank issuing the letter of credit is less than the savings obtained by its customer from the lender.

Funded bank commitments

First, a bank can commit to provide a set amount of money (e.g., a total of $US1,000,000) in a single funding all at one time, with no continuing obligation to provide additional money. Such credit facilities are typically called "term loans."

Second, a bank can commit to provide a maximum amount of money (e.g., $US1,000,000) in one or more fundings over a set period of time (e.g., one year). Such credit facilities are called "lines of credit." The aggregate amount of money a bank agrees to make available pursuant to such a line of credit is limited to a set amount (e.g., $US1,000,000) even if the borrower repays part of the moneys made available while the bank still has a commitment to provide further fundings.

Third, a bank can commit to provide up to a maximum amount of outstanding money (e.g., up to an outstanding total of $US1,000,000) in one or more fundings over a set period of time, typically one year.

Such credit facilities are called "revolving lines of credit" or "revolving credits." If the borrower repays part of the moneys made available while the bank still has a commitment to provide further fundings (e.g., within one year from the initial funding), then the borrower can borrow more money provided that the amount of borrowings outstanding at any one time does not exceed the bank's maximum funding commitment (e.g., $US1,000,000).

Conditions precedent to funding

Banks usually do not commit to credits or provide fundings unless borrowers fulfill certain "conditions precedent" prior to the commitment or funding. Conditions precedent are usually tasks borrowers must accomplish.

For example, a bank will not provide funding for the purpose of acquiring a company until the borrower has executed and delivered a final agreement for the company's acquisition on terms and conditions acceptable to the bank. In construction loans, a bank typically provides agreed funding in several stages, as each of the prior construction stages is successfully completed. As a condition for the funding of each stage, banks typically require a certificate from an architect or engineer or both that the previous stages have been successfully completed.

Other conditions precedent tend to apply to all credits. For example, the borrower must be duly incorporated and have duly authorized the credit before the bank makes the commitment or funding. Moreover, all of the warranties and covenants to which borrowers agree for the periods of time that principal and interest remain unpaid in full must also be true at the time that the bank makes its initial commitment or funding.

Generally, all conditions precedent must be true both at the time of the banks' initial commitments or fundings and at the time of any subsequent commitments or fundings, even if those subsequent commitments or fundings are agreed in principle at the time of the initial commitment or funding.

BORROWER'S PROMISE TO PAY

The borrower's promise to repay the amount of money advanced to it by the bank is actually a covenant. A "covenant" is simply a borrower's promise to perform a certain act or to refrain from performing a certain act. The borrower's promise to make payments to the bank is the borrower's most fundamental covenant. All of the borrower's other covenants are intended to provide a bank with assurances that the borrower will make agreed payments to the bank. Payment covenants can usually be expressed very simply. The important parameters of a borrower's payment obligations are:

1   the amounts of the payments;
2   the times of the payments; and
3   in the manner for making the payments.

Borrower's interest payments

The amount of the payment is divided into at least two parts. The first part is the repayment of principal, i.e., the amount of money advanced by the bank to the borrower. The second part is the payment of interest, i.e., amounts in addition to the outstanding principal, due and owing for the use of the bank's money over a specified period of time. Interest is usually expressed, on a percentage basis, as the amount which would be due and owing if the principal were outstanding for one calendar year (e.g., 6 per cent per annum for $US1,000,000 = $US60,000 interest per year). Sometimes banks compute interest on the basis of a year having 360 days, which results in higher interest payments by the borrower.

Compounded interest

Even though interest is typically expressed as an annual rate (in effect: the banks' annual rate of return on outstanding principal amounts), interest is usually calculated and paid more than once each year, typically on a monthly or quarterly basis. It is generally acceptable to borrowers to have banks calculate accrued interest each time that an interest payment is due. Borrowers should be cautious, however, about allowing banks to calculate interest more often than the dates that interest payments are due. If banks are allowed to calculate interest more often than borrowers pay interest, then banks typically add the calculated interest to a credit's principal amount, thereby increasing the principal and "compounding" the interest due and owing on the payment date. In

effect, the banks are receiving interest on interest if permitted to calculate and add accrued interest to outstanding principals in the absence of interest payments. For the same reason, borrowers should be cautious about credit facilities allowing them to make regular payments in amounts less than the interest accrued and owing on the date of the payment. Such reduced payment schedules typically result in compounded interest.

Fixed and variable interest rates

Interest rates are expressed in many different ways but can be divided into two broad categories: fixed interest rates and variable interest rates. In each case, banks determine the types and amounts of interest rates at which they can extend credits to borrowers on the basis of the interest rates at which the banks can obtain funds from others.

For example, banks pay interest at variable rates for deposits which can be withdrawn on demand (i.e., "demand deposits") and at fixed rates for deposits with fixed durations (i.e., certificates of deposit). Accordingly, variable rate credits are funded by demand deposits while fixed rate credits are funded with certificates of deposits.

In addition, in either case, banks increase the interest charged to borrowers by a fixed percentage rate to cover their costs, including risk premiums and a return on capital. Accordingly, a bank might offer a one-year credit at the rate paid by the bank for one-year certificates of deposit, plus 3, 4 or 6 percent per annum.

Banks' sources of funds

Deposits placed in a bank at any point in time are usually insufficient for that bank to fund its credit activities. Moreover, demand deposits are subject to withdrawal on short notice. As a result, banks must turn to various other markets to source funds for their credit activities, i.e., money markets, short- and long-term bonds and, occasionally, equity markets.

The source of funds selected by a bank to finance a credit depends on the duration of the borrower's repayment obligation, i.e., the amount of time before the bank receives repayment of principal from the borrower. The source depends on the duration of the borrower's repayment obligation because banks match the timing of their sources of funds with the uses of those funds. For example, funds are available on short-term and long-term bond markets for more than 270 days, so credits extended by banks to corporations for periods of more than 270 days tend to be based on bond rates. Funds are available on money markets for periods of up to 270 days, so credits extended by banks for periods of 270 days or less tend to be based on money market rates.

It is possible to negotiate other interest rates with banks but the interest rates banks can make available to borrowers always depend on the rates available to banks from their sources of funds, their costs, their assessment of risks and their cost of capital.

Other payments from borrowers to banks

There are several other important elements of borrowers' payment obligations. Here it is sufficient to note that the payments demanded by banks from corporate borrowers can include commitment fees, transaction expenses, penalties for late payments and premiums for prepayments. In addition, borrowers are sometimes required to maintain "compensating accounts" or "compensating balances" with their banks as part of their obligations to banks. Such accounts or balances constitute, in effect, an additional form of payment while, at the same time, facilitating the collection of unpaid principal, interest and penalties in the event of a payment default by borrowers.

BORROWERS' WARRANTIES

Quite simply, warranties are statements included in a contract. Warranties are made by one contract party, e.g., a borrower, to another contract party, e.g., a bank, together with the promise that the statements are true at the time that they are made – or at another time expressly specified in the statements (e.g., "at the end of each fiscal year"). Sometimes, such statements are called "representations." Sometimes, they are called "representations and warranties." Banks make very few warranties to borrowers in credit documentation, e.g., that "the bank is licensed under applicable government regulations to engage in the business of banking." Borrowers, on the other hand, typically make many warranties to banks. The following discussion focuses on warranties given by borrowers to banks.

Timing of borrowers' warranties

In credit facilities, warranties are typically stipulated as being true at least:

(a) at the time of the signing of the credit facility;
(b) at the time of the initial funding; and
(c) at the time of any subsequent fundings.

In addition, most warranties are stipulated as being true during all periods of time that borrowers have payment obligations to banks or at important points in time such as the end of the shown fiscal quarter or the fiscal year. In this way, a bank contractually confirms the assumptions that it makes in extending a credit.

Concerning their businesses

Credit documentation typically contains several warranties concerning borrowers' business, most of which are related directly to financial statements delivered by borrowers to banks prior to the execution and delivery of the credit documentation. One such warranty is as follows: "the balance sheets, income statements and other financial statements delivered by borrowers to the banks prior to the execution and delivery of the credit documentation fairly reflect the borrower's financial performance and condition for the period or as of the date each such statement purports to represent, all in accordance with generally accepted and consistently applied accounting principles." It is typical to attach agreed copies of all such financial statements to the final version of the credit documentation.

Concerning their assets

Credit documentation usually contains several warranties concerning borrowers' assets. Examples of such warranties are:

1 that the borrower holds good title to all assets whose value is reflected on its balance sheet, i.e., that the borrower owns all of those assets;
2 that the value of all such assets is reflected in the borrower's balance sheet on the basis of historical cost with depreciation and amortization deductions in accordance with generally accepted and consistently applied accounting principles; and

3   that all such assets are in good condition and not subject to any security interests, of mortgages or other liens.

Of course, to avoid a breach of the agreement – and, in the proper case, even a claim of fraud – a borrower needs to disclose any exceptions to such warranties requested by a bank. If the exceptions are acceptable to the bank, then they are listed in a "schedule of exceptions."

Concerning legal compliance

Other important warranties include:

4   that the borrower is conducting its business in compliance with all applicable government regulations and contract obligations;
5   that there are no civil law suits or government proceedings pending against the borrower; and
6   that there are no court judgments or court orders outstanding against the borrower.

  Again, a borrower must disclose exceptions, and again certain exceptions are generally acceptable to a bank. For example, a bank will generally accept that "to the best of a borrower's knowledge" a borrower is conducting its business in "substantial" compliance with all applicable government regulations. A bank also typically accepts the existence of civil law suits and government proceedings if the amount at stake – either in each dispute or in all disputes taken together – is under a relatively low threshold. A bank can even accept outstanding court judgments and court orders if they are being disputed in good faith by the borrower or if they are both:

(a)   within relatively low thresholds; and
(b)   outstanding for short periods of time.

"Catch-all" warranties

As final examples, two more warranties are very important to banks:

7   that the warranties do not fail to disclose any facts important to the bank; and

8   that there is no material adverse change in the borrower's business or its assets.

The first of these warranties is typically stipulated as being true both at the time of the signing of the credit documentation, and at the time of the initial and any subsequent funding. The second warranty is typically stipulated as being true during all periods of time that the borrower has a payment obligation to the bank.

  Of course, warranties involve costs for the borrower because the borrower is under an obligation to investigate and report breaches of warranties to the bank. A borrower's warranties benefit both the borrower and bank by giving the bank an early warning of the borrower's inability to pay principal and interest as they become due. A breach of a warranty typically does not result in a bank "declaring default" under the credit documentation, as explained below. Instead, breaches of warranties are typically occasions for a borrower and bank to meet and discuss an important event's significance for their relationship.

BORROWERS' AFFIRMATIVE COVENANTS

As noted above, a warranty is a promise that certain statements are and will be true at the time that they are made – or at some future time expressly specified in the statements (e.g., "at the end of each fiscal year"). A covenant is a promise that the person making the statement will do an act or refrain from doing an act in the future. Banks usually make only one covenant in credit facilities, i.e., that they will provide funding under the terms and conditions set forth in the credit documentation.

  Borrowers, on the other hand, make many covenants to banks in connection with credit facilities. The borrowers' covenants, together with their warranties, constitute an early warning system for banks and borrowers to anticipate borrowers' possible future difficulty in making payments of principal, interest, fees and other agreed amounts to banks. Any covenant requested by banks is probably justified if the requested covenant, when viewed together with all other agreed covenants and warranties, meaningfully improves that early warning system. Any covenant requested by a bank probably is not justified if it does not improve that early warning system. In determining whether a covenant is justified, additional considerations include the measure of restraint imposed on the business (usually relevant in terms of lost revenues or lost opportunities) and the burdens of complying with the covenant (usually relevant in terms of the cost of the arrangements for monitoring and reporting compliance).

A borrower's covenants constitute an important element of corporate governance giving a bank, in some ways, more control over a borrower's operations and other business affairs than the control exercised by the borrower's shareholders.

Affirmative covenants are promises by a borrower to perform certain acts in the future. As stated above, a borrower's most important covenant is always its promise to make payments to the bank in accordance with the terms of the credit documentation, typically to repay principal, to repay interest and to pay other agreed costs, fees, premiums and penalties.

Borrowers' financial covenants

After the payment covenants, "financial covenants" are probably a borrower's most important covenant. In general, financial covenants are intended to provide continuing assurances to banks that borrowers will be able to make all current and future payments due and owing under credit facilities. The financial covenants appropriate for each credit depend upon the type of credit, the borrower's industry, specific circumstances and conditions of the borrower's business and, of course, the bank's credit policies.

Concerning future balance sheets

Of course, a borrower's balance sheet is important to a bank. Changes in a borrower's balance sheet enable a bank to anticipate the borrower's ability to continue to make agreed payments to the bank. Financial covenants based on balance sheet items include "minimum tangible net worth" and "minimum working capital." Other financial covenants are expressed as ratios. A common financial covenant based on balance sheet items and expressed as a ratio is the "minimum current ratio," i.e., the ratio of current assets to current liabilities at the end of an accounting period. Another financial statement

based on a borrower's balance sheet is the "total debt ratio," i.e., the ratio of total funded debt to the book value of the borrower's net assets.

Concerning future income statements

Financial covenants based on a borrower's income statement are equally important to a bank. For example, one financial ratio based on income statement items requires the borrower to compute its "interest coverage ratio," defined in various ways including:

(a) some measurement of the borrower's earnings, income or cash flow in the current period divided by
(b) the total interest payments due on bank debt in the current period.

One common measurement used in connection with interest coverage ratios is "EBITDA," i.e., a borrower's earnings before interest, taxes, depreciation and amortization. A ratio of less than 1.0 indicates that a borrower is not able to make its interest payments as they become due in the normal course of business. Ideally, the interest coverage ratio should be 1.5 or higher.

Concerning future books, records, reports and inspections

Together with financial covenants, credit facilities typically include various additional informational covenants enabling banks to enforce financial covenants effectively. Such covenants include the borrower's covenants:

1 to maintenance books, records and accounts in accordance with applicable law and generally accepted and consistently applied accounting principles and practices;
2 to deliver to banks periodic financial statements in form and detail reasonably satisfactory to the banks, together with reports from the borrower's accountants;
3 to permit banks to inspect facilities and to perform audits of books, records and accounts;
4 to deliver to banks all accountants' letters to management issued in accordance with applicable law,

generally accepted accounting principles and generally accepted auditing standards; and

5 to deliver to the banks compliance certificates from the borrower's senior management and from the borrower's accountants.

Borrowers' other affirmative covenants

In addition to financial covenants, credit documentation invariably includes other types of affirmative covenants. These other affirmative covenants are intended to confirm that the character and quality of a borrower and its business do not change in any manner not agreed by a bank at the time of its commitment and funding.

Maintenance of corporate existence and business

Such affirmative covenants include the obligations to maintain the borrower's corporate existence, to maintain the borrower's licenses to do business and to pay taxes and salaries in full when due. A borrower also typically agrees to maintain insurance both covering risks and in amounts agreed by the bank. In addition, a borrower usually agrees to include the bank as a named insured on its certificate of insurance and to deliver a copy of such an insurance certificate to the bank.

Notification of important legal proceedings

Credit documentation can also include an affirmative covenant for the borrower to notify the bank of the commencement of any law suit by or against the borrower where the amount at stake is over a certain minimal amount. Such a covenant highlights the interplay of warranties and covenants. While a certain law suit might violate a warranty in the loan documentation, in the absence of an affirmative covenant on the borrower to disclose the commencement of such a law suit, the bank might not learn about it until the bank receives a certificate of the borrower's compliance in connection with a bank commitment or funding.

As with certificates of compliance in respect of warranties, borrowers and their managers are also typically required to certify compliance with all affirmative covenants at the time of each bank commitment or funding.

BORROWERS' NEGATIVE COVENANTS

In addition to the actions a borrower agrees to perform at all times or at specific times during the term of a credit facility (i.e., its affirmative covenants), a borrower also often agrees to refrain from undertaking certain actions during the term of a credit facility. The borrower's agreement to refrain from undertaking certain actions is called its "negative covenants." Negative covenants are not always expressed categorically. In negative covenants, borrowers are often allowed to engage in restricted activity below a certain threshold amount or with the bank's prior consent.

Not engaging in major corporate transactions

As with warranties and affirmative covenants, the borrower's negative covenants are intended to articulate, preserve and maintain the bank's assumptions concerning the character and quality of the borrower, its assets and business. Such negative covenants include the borrower's undertaking:

(a) not to engage in any major corporate transaction such as a merger, acquisition or change in control of the borrower;

(b) not to pursue any businesses other than the businesses pursued by the borrower at the time of the bank's initial commitment or funding;

(c) not to engage in any capital expenditures; and

(d) not to declare any dividends.

Not incurring any other debt for borrowed money

Other negative covenants are intended to preserve banks' positions relative to their borrowers' other sources of credit. Often, borrowers agree – again subject to exceptions for small transactions or banks' consent – not to:

(a) enter into any other indebtedness;

(b) grant any security interests, mortgages or other liens to other sources of credit; and

(c) prepay principal or interest on any permitted debt before it is due.

DEFAULT AND REMEDY PROVISIONS

A bank's declaration of its borrower's default, i.e., the borrower's violation of its obligations under credit documentation, gives the bank the right to exercise several remedies, as discussed below. Any occurrence giving the bank a right to declare a default is called an "event of default." Events of default are equivalent to violations of obligations under other contracts. Declarations of default are equivalent to notices of violations under other contracts. Different terminology has evolved in respect of credit documentation in part because commercial and financial communities involve very different types of entities involved in very different types of transactions.

Examples of "events of default"

Credit documentation usually provides that events of default include:

1 the borrowers' failure to make payments to the banks;
2 any material breach by borrowers of any other covenants or of any warranties;
3 the borrowers' breach of any terms in any other agreements with the same banks;
4 the borrowers' breach of any terms in any agreements with other persons, including other banks;
5 the borrowers' submission of any incorrect or incomplete information to the banks; and
6 the initiation of bankruptcy proceedings – or equivalent arrangements – voluntarily by borrowers or involuntarily against borrowers by their other sources of funding.

Remedies pursuant to a declaration of default

Credit documentation tends to give banks many different remedies upon their declaration of their borrowers' default. First, banks reserve the right to terminate all continuing commitments to provide further fundings and other support to borrowers. Second, banks impose on borrowers the obligation to pay penalties, usually calculated as a percentage of the amounts paid by borrowers after the due date. Third, banks claim the right to "accelerate" all of the payments the borrowers would eventually owe to banks in the normal course of business. In effect, the banks declare an end to their forbearance in collecting the moneys due to them and demand immediate payment in full of all amounts currently outstanding under the credit documentation. Fourth, banks can foreclose on any collateral, as explained below, given by borrowers in exchange for the banks' fundings and other commitments. Fifth, the banks can initiate bankruptcy proceedings against the borrowers.

Negotiating default provisions

Banks will often agree to limit their events of default to truly significant events. First, banks sometimes agree to qualify some covenants and warranties with requirements that the amount at stake in the breach is above a specified threshold. For example, breaches of net asset financial covenants might need to be more than 5 percent or 10 percent of the minimum required net worth. Second, if breaches can be cured (e.g., compliance with a ratio in a financial covenant), then banks usually agree to grant grace periods to borrowers for the purpose of curing breaches, often agreeing to initiate such grace periods with formal notices to borrowers. For example, banks might give borrowers five, ten or thirty days to cure failures to pay interest. Third, unless banks believe that their rights might be prejudiced, banks usually agree to give notice to borrowers if it appears that breaches have not been cured after the end of any and all applicable grace periods.

"Lenders' liability"

In addition, banks usually exercise caution in declaring borrowers' defaults under credit documentation. Most importantly, banks exercise caution because they can be held liable for the materially adverse consequences of imposing remedies on borrowers in the wake of immaterial events of default. Such liability is called "lenders' liability." (Lenders' liability is good

FOUR

evidence of the fact that banks exercise a great deal of control over their borrowers.)

Banks exercise caution in declaring borrowers' defaults also because a declaration of default for one credit facility can, in accordance with the terms of any and all other credit facilities, entail an event of default in those other credit facilities. Banks exercise caution also because exercising their remedies under credit facilities usually disrupts business, diminishing the possibility that the banks will be able to collect the money borrowers owe them.

Negotiating a restructuring with an individual bank

In fact, upon the occurrence of an event of default, a bank usually seeks meetings with its borrower to discuss alternatives to declaring default. Alternatives tend to include a restructuring of the borrower's obligations so that it can comply with all covenants, warranties and other requirements under the credit documentation without risking further breaches. In exchange for such a restructuring, the bank usually expects compensation in the form of a higher interest rate, some additional collateral or some type of payment.

If a bank concludes that a restructuring is not necessary, then the bank tends to send a formal waiver letter to the borrower previously in breach of its warranties or covenants. Waiver letters are important to banks because they establish that the banks' failure to enforce certain contract provisions in one instance does not constitute an amendment of the agreement. In effect, waiver letters maintain banks' rights to enforce all covenants, warranties and other requirements set forth in their credit documentation in all future circumstances.

SECURED LENDING

Banks are sometimes unwilling to rely solely on their borrowers' promise to repay principal and to pay interest and other amounts under credit facilities. Sometimes, banks want further assurances that borrowers will make agreed payments. Banks refer to such further assurances as "collateral." As explained below, collateral falls into two broad categories: third-party guarantees and the right to seize and sell borrowers' assets.

It is important to remember that these different forms of collateral are not mutually exclusive. It is possible and relatively common for a single bank to claim various forms of collateral from a single borrower in respect of a single credit facility.

Third-party guarantees

First, banks classify third-party guarantees of various sorts as collateral. A third-party guaranty is the promise of an individual or entity other than a borrower to make agreed payments to a bank in the event that the borrower fails to make those payments. For example, banks often insist that shareholders guaranty the payment obligations of family-owned companies. In large corporate groups, banks might request that parent corporations guaranty the payment obligations of their subsidiary corporations. guarantees can also be obtained from unrelated companies in the business of providing guarantees for a fee. Banks and insurance companies, for example, will guaranty borrowers' payment obligations to other creditors in exchange for the payment of a fee from the borrower. Letters of credit are guarantees provided by banks, while guarantees provided by insurance companies are sometimes called "sureties." Third-party guarantees from unrelated companies in the business of providing such guarantees can be a valuable form of collateral because such companies' failure to honor proper demands for payment under guaranty can have a significant adverse impact on their businesses.

Seizing and selling borrowers' assets

Second, banks also classify as collateral the right to seize and sell borrowers' assets. In fact, the right of creditors to seize and sell the assets owned by defaulting borrowers is recognized, to varying degrees, around the world. As between banks and their borrowers, the banks' right to seize and sell assets is generally recognized as a valid agreement, at least as regards certain types of assets (as discussed below), if the right is set forth in applicable credit documentation. In some countries, however, serious qualifications exist concerning the banks' ability to enforce that valid agreement, even after they have won a final court judgment confirming those rights. In most countries, banks are prohibited from using force to seize and sell assets themselves. They are generally prohibited by laws intended to preserve the peace. In fact, self-help measures – such as banks seizing their borrowers' assets – can lead to episodes of violence. Moreover, under the laws of many countries, police do not have the power to seize and sell assets on behalf of banks even after the banks have won a final judgment in a court of law confirming their contractual right to seize and sell the assets. In effect, the police cannot specifically enforce the banks' rights. In those countries where banks' rights in collateral cannot be enforced, either by themselves or by police, collateral has little value.

"Perfecting" collateral interests in various assets

An important element of banks' collateral interest in their borrowers' assets is establishing those rights not only against the borrowers – which is accomplished by having borrowers sign credit documentation – but also as against individuals and entities not party to the credit documentation, i.e., "as against all third parties." Generally, banks can establish their collateral rights in certain of their borrowers' assets, even as against all third parties, either:

1   by taking possession of those assets at the time borrowers sign credit documentation; or
2   by publicly registering their collateral interest in those assets.

Establishing a collateral interest as against all third parties, either by possession or by registration, is called "perfecting" the collateral interest. Since it is often not practical for banks to take possession of their borrowers' assets, public registration is a common method for perfecting collateral interests. In fact, the laws of many countries provide for filing notices of collateral interests in public registries. Such notices preclude third parties from claiming that they did not have notice of collateral interests in purchased assets.

Registering mortgages

Land registries are the most commonly known type of public registries for recording collateral interests. Collateral interests in land are commonly referred to as "mortgages." It is, of course, impossible for banks to take possession of land while allowing their borrowers to continue to own and use it. Instead, in the same place where borrowers publicly register their ownership of land, banks publicly register their mortgages in the land owned by their borrowers. On the basis of public registrations of mortgages, purchasers of land are, as a matter of law, considered to have received notice of those mortgages. Because of the notice of the mortgage in the land registry, the bank can seize and sell the land even after it has been sold to a third party. As a result, purchasers of land are careful to search public ownership registries to determine, among other things, that banks do not have a mortgage on land they intend to purchase. Having established that banks have the right to protect their mortgages as against all third parties by publicly registering them, governments go the next step – requiring banks to register their mortgages to the extent that the governments maintain such public registries.

Perfecting other collateral interests

It is possible to claim collateral interests in most – but not all – types of asset. It is possible to claim collateral interests in tangible assets (such as cash, inventories and other personal property), in documents (such as negotiable instruments, title documents in bearer form and stock certificates) and in intangible assets (such as patents and trade secrets).

Perfection through registration

There are registries for recording ownership of various types of assets in various countries. In general, it is necessary to register a collateral interest in an asset in countries which require registration of ownership in the same type of asset (e.g., real property and vehicles in most countries). In addition, registration is sometimes available to perfect collateral interests in assets which do not require registration of ownership (e.g., personal property such as tools or furniture in the United States and in some other countries). In each case, if registration is allowed to perfect collateral interests in certain interests, then – in the absence of taking actual possession of the asset – registration is also usually required to perfect the collateral interest in that type of asset. In the United

States, for example, it is necessary to register collateral interests in inventory even though it is generally not possible to register ownership of inventory.

Perfection through possession

In the end, it is sometimes necessary to take possession of assets in order to claim a collateral interest in them. Cash is the best example of this rule. There is generally no way to register ownership in another individual's or entity's cash. It is generally necessary to take possession of cash in order to perfect a collateral interest in it.

Of course, taking possession of physical assets is almost always a legally effective way of perfecting a collateral interest, even where registration is otherwise required. Unfortunately, taking possession of a borrower's operating assets is usually not a practical solution. In addition, it is usually impossible to take physical possession of an intangible asset. In those cases where physical possession is not possible, it is necessary to determine whether perfection through public notification is available. Perfection through registration is certainly not available in all instances where taking possession is impracticable or impossible. In other words, it is quite possible that in a particular country collateral interests in certain types of assets are effectively unenforceable.

The real value of various collateral interests

Finally, it is useful to consider whether the value of different types of collateral preserves their value for the purpose of sale after being seized by banks. Viewed from this perspective, inventories probably have relatively high value as collateral. Real property, i.e., land and buildings, has a relatively uncertain value. Free standing real property can preserve its value even after seizure, but real property incorporated or embedded into other fixed assets, e.g., a building which is part of a plant site, typically has a low value. Entire businesses, as embodied in share certificates or in a pledge of a company's entire assets, tend to preserve relatively little value after being seized by banks. The market for businesses is not as liquid as the markets for inventories because of the absence of interested qualified buyers and businesses are often surprisingly perishable items.

In fact, given the difficulty in preserving the value of collateral after it is seized, banks often claim collateral interests in their borrowers' various assets primarily to prevent other banks from claiming collateral. Holding collateral to the exclusion of other banks is particularly valuable in the context of bankruptcy proceedings.

BANKRUPTCY PROTECTION

In general, bankruptcy does not give creditors additional rights. Instead, bankruptcy provides borrowers with protection from their creditors. Under the protection of the bankruptcy court, a borrower and its creditors can either:

(a) propose a plan and enter into an agreement for restructuring the borrower's debt and continuing its operations; or
(b) arrange for the orderly sale of the borrower and its assets, distributing the proceeds from the sale among the borrowers' creditors.

"Automatic stays" preserve value

Bankruptcy protects borrowers from their creditors because, for as long as bankruptcy proceedings are pending, creditors are precluded from individually exercising contractual remedies set forth in their credit documentation. In the USA, such protection is called an "automatic stay." Rather than each bank individually seeking to exercise its rights in a disorganized fashion – based on some principle such as "the first bank to file a law suit is the first to enforce its contractual rights" – under bankruptcy, the court first establishes a list of all creditors and all of their claims. In this way, the law hopes to preserve the borrowers' aggregate ability to pay their obligations to their many creditors to the greatest extent possible. While one or two individual creditors might be disadvantaged from bankruptcy's orderly approach to borrowers' defaults, the creditors as a group will benefit from the attempt to preserve the borrowers' ability to pay.

Establishing creditors' relative priorities

After establishing the list of creditors' claims in a definitive fashion, courts supervise negotiations among borrowers and their many creditors as they attempt to make the best available arrangements for satisfying, at least in part, the borrowers' payment obligations to its various creditors. The courts supervise the negotiations and approve the final arrangement because the arrangement must not be inconsistent with the relative contractual and other legal rights of the borrowers' various creditors, including its employees and others who might not be properly represented in the bankruptcy proceedings. Such relative rights are called "priorities" in bankruptcy proceedings.

Restructuring the borrower's debt and business

If it appears that restructuring the borrower's debt and continuing its operations is likely to provide the greatest return for the greatest number of creditors at the time bankruptcy is initiated, then the borrower's debt is restructured. Restructuring debt typically involves reducing, delaying or both reducing and delaying payments by a borrower to the various creditors at the time bankruptcy is initiated. The goal of restructuring is to enable the borrower to make timely payments in full of principal, interests and other amounts due to its creditors in the ordinary course of business. Of course, delaying payments of principal or interest always creates risk for creditors, so the exact amount payable to each creditor or to each class of creditor pursuant to a plan of reorganization is always subject to careful negotiation and review.

Liquidating the borrower or its assets

Generally, a borrower and each of its various creditors or classes of creditors have the right to propose plans for restructuring the borrower's debt. The probable returns from each restructuring plan are compared both with each other and with the probable returns from completely liquidating the borrower or its assets, i.e., simply selling the borrower in whole or in parts to the highest bidder(s). Sometimes, liquidation is most likely to provide the greatest return for the greatest number of creditors and so is adopted. In the event of a liquidation, the court appoints a person or entity, typically called a "trustee," to arrange for the orderly sale of the borrower and its assets and, thereafter, for the distribution of the proceeds from the sale to the borrowers' various creditors in accordance with their priorities.

Adequate protection for "secured creditors"

Secured creditors, i.e., creditors with the right to seize and sell a borrower's assets, have a special right under bankruptcy proceedings. In the USA, those special rights are called "adequate protection." Pursuant to the doctrine of "adequate protection," each secured creditor has the right to receive possession of and title to the asset in which it holds a collateral interest or, if the asset is needed for the borrower's restructured operations, the secured creditor is entitled to receive cash payments, additional or replacement collateral interests of equal value or some other relief with a value clearly equivalent to the value of the original collateral.

PART FIVE

Other Legal Facilities

17

Dispute Resolution

Litigation, arbitration and mediation

INTRODUCTION

As used in this chapter, the term "litigation" refers to activities involved in obtaining the binding resolution of disputes by government order, i.e., "judgments." The term "court" refers to the places where governments issue judgments. The term "court" can also refer to the times, or "sessions," when governments issue orders resolving disputes. For example, the House of Lords in England sometimes sits as a legislative body, adopting substantive rules of law, and sometimes it sits as the supreme court of England, resolving disputes.

Since the advent of law, disputes have been resolved in accordance with "substantive law," i.e., principles existing at the time that disputes arise, generally available to the public and applied by courts to relevant facts for the purpose of resolving disputes. Substantive rules for resolving disputes are generally accepted as legitimate by faith, by custom, by reason, by the general will or by some combination of faith, custom, reason and the general will.

In addition to substantive law, litigation also involves "procedural law," i.e., principles existing at the time that disputes arise, generally available to the public and used by courts to establish the facts to which the substantive law is applied for the purpose of resolving disputes. The procedural rules are generally accepted as legitimate to the extent they bring all relevant facts to a court's attention for the purpose of applying substantive law in resolving disputes.

IMPORTANT PRELIMINARY CONSIDERATIONS

Courts of law are legal institutions of equal significance to property rights and contracts in the conduct of business. In fact, property rights and contracts rights are legal rights because they can be enforced, at the request of the individuals holding them, by court judgments.

At the same time, this book focuses on integrating law and ethics into business decisions and corporate organizations. Accordingly, this book focuses on substantive law because substantive law, the law directly applicable to the conduct of business, is clearly a more important consideration than procedural law, the law directly applicable to the conduct of litigation, in making business decisions and ensuring a corporation's legal compliance.

Substantive law is more important than procedural law in making business decisions

Viewed from the perspective of business decisions and legal compliance, the only proper assumption corporate leaders can make is that courts will apply procedural law to the conduct of litigations:

1 to provide appropriate remedies for violations of general legal obligations, contracts and government regulations; and

2 for the purpose of determining whether and which remedies are appropriate – bringing all relevant facts to the courts' attention.

In fact, corporate leaders can properly only make the same assumptions about mediators and arbitrators in respect of their conduct of mediations and arbitrations.

The possibility of legal disputes requires managers to exercise diligence and foresight

Indeed, as regards awareness of relevant facts, at the time of litigation, courts are typically aware of more facts than those known to managers at the time they make their decisions. First, potentially, courts learn all relevant facts existing at the moment in time when managers made their decisions – even the facts not known to managers at that time. Second, of course, courts potentially learn all relevant facts arising after managers made and implemented their decisions – which cannot be known with certainty by managers when they make their decisions. Since both categories of facts unknown to managers can be relevant in resolving legal disputes, the possibility of litigation, arbitration and mediation imposes a discipline on managers to exercise, within the limits of practicability, diligence and foresight in making their decisions. Diligence and foresight enable managers to limit the scope of legally relevant facts unknown to them.

Dispute resolution involves effort, expense, delay, uncertainty, distraction and emotions

Obtaining a court judgment inevitably involves substantial effort, expense, delay, uncertainty, distraction and, usually, emotions. Considerable effort and expense are typically involved in bringing disputes and facts into court. Obtaining judgments from courts necessarily involves delay and uncertainty. In the context of an ongoing business, the distractions and emotions entailed by litigation often result in additional losses and costs for the businesses involved.

Some businesses include the effort, expense, delay, uncertainty, distraction and emotion of possible dispute resolution rightly in making decisions about the conduct of dispute resolution – and even in

making decisions about business operations. For example, after a dispute has arisen, a business might consider both of the following factors in deciding whether to proceed with litigation or pursue mediation and arbitration:

1 the relative burdens possible litigation imposes on the parties involved in the dispute; and
2 each party's ability to bear those burdens.

Similarly, some businesses consider those two factors in evaluating the risks of violating other persons' legal rights in the conduct of business operations. Since some businesses take those factors into account in making decisions about business operations, all businesses ignore them at their own peril.

Litigation involves a failure of self-regulation

Finally, court judgments are not a part of business self-regulation. Businesses engage in litigation after a failure of various other facilities in place for business self-regulation, including property, contract rights and mediation. Mediations are attempts by parties involved in business disputes to negotiate contracts to settle disputes before turning to arbitration or litigation. In an arbitration, parties involved in a business dispute agree to accept as binding upon them the resolution of their dispute by another private individual or association. Arbitration is based on a contract, but it does not constitute self-regulation to the extent that businesses defer to third persons to resolve their disputes.

CIVIL LITIGATION

The statements in the introduction to this chapter are intended specially to apply especially to civil litigation. The term "civil litigation" refers to activities involved in obtaining a court judgment to resolve a dispute between two or more businesses or other persons not acting in a governmental capacity, such as private individuals. The term "civil litigation" also applies to the resolution of disputes involving the government acting in a civil capacity, such as a purchaser of goods and services.

The terms "administrative proceedings" and "criminal litigations" refer to disputes initiated against businesses by governments in their regulatory capacity. The distinction between administrative proceedings and criminal litigation depends in part upon the sanctions sought by the government and will be discussed later in the chapter.

Complaints, summonses and answers

A civil litigation begins with a written statement by one or more persons who believe their legal rights have been violated. Such persons are called "plaintiffs." A plaintiff's written statement is called a "complaint." The complaint contains a recitation of facts the plaintiffs believe to be true and a recitation of the legal rights violated by such facts. Such recitations are called the plaintiff's "allegations" or "claims." Depending on the applicable procedural law, the allegations must be more or less detailed. More importantly, depending on the applicable procedural law, the complaint must contain "evidence" of the alleged facts, i.e., proof acceptable in court that the alleged facts are true. Complaints must contain such evidence, or indicate that plaintiffs possess such evidence, especially in courts where discovery (as defined below) is not permitted.

Again depending on applicable procedural law, plaintiffs send their complaints to either or both of:

1 the court from which plaintiffs are seeking a resolution of the dispute; and
2 the person or persons who, plaintiffs believe, violated their legal rights. Such persons are called "defendants."

If the plaintiffs send the complaint only to the court, then the court sends a copy of the complaint to defendants. At the same time, the court issues a "summons," asking defendants to respond to the complaint within a specific time frame.

The defendants' response is generally called an "answer." In answers, generally defendants must:

1 admit or deny the alleged facts, either generally or individually;
2 agree or disagree with the legal conclusions drawn by plaintiffs from the facts; and, if applicable,
3 state any additional facts defendants consider relevant to resolving the dispute, together with the legal conclusions drawn by defendants from those additional facts (called "affirmative defenses").

For example, defendants might state in their answers:

1 none of the facts alleged by plaintiffs are true;
2 even if all of the facts alleged by plaintiffs were true, the alleged facts would not constitute a violation of plaintiffs' legal rights; and
3 even if all of the facts alleged by plaintiffs were true, there are additional facts exonerating defendants from legal liability.

Motions to dismiss complaints

In fact, defendants might make a motion (i.e., "file written statements in the court") that the court should dismiss the plaintiffs' complaint for "failure to state a cause of action," i.e., that the second type of defense outlined above is true. If the court agreed with defendants' motion, then the court would dismiss the plaintiffs' complaint even without holding a hearing to determine the truth of the facts alleged by plaintiffs. Such a dismissal would be dismissal "with prejudice," i.e., the court's final judgment precluding plaintiffs from filing the same claims in any other court which recognizes its final judgment.

All of the types of allegations and claims in defendants' answer as set forth in the above answer deal with substantive law. In addition, defendants can make various motions raising legal issues under procedural law – at least for the purpose of ending the trial in the particular court selected by plaintiffs for filing their complaint. For example, defendants can make a motion (also called "move") that:

1 the court selected by plaintiffs is not a proper court for resolving a dispute involving the facts alleged by plaintiffs; or
2 the court does not have the power to issue a judgment against defendants.

Such motions are called "motions to dismiss" for, respectively, the court's lack of jurisdiction in the subject matter (i.e., in the dispute) and the court's lack of jurisdiction in the person (i.e., in the defendants). Defendants can also move that, even though the court selected by plaintiffs is a proper court, there is a better court for resolving the dispute between plaintiffs and defendants and that continuing the litigation in the court selected by plaintiffs would result in an unfair burden on defendants or an unfair advantage to plaintiffs. Such motions are called "motions to dismiss from an inconvenient forum."

If the court agreed with one or more of the defendants' procedural motions, then the court could dismiss the plaintiffs' complaint, again without holding a hearing to determine the truth of the facts alleged by plaintiffs. Such a dismissal would, however, be dismissal "without prejudice," i.e., meaning that plaintiffs could file the same complaint in any other court where the procedural defenses would not apply.

Counterclaims, cross claims and joinders

Each defendant may also typically assert claims against the plaintiffs (called "counterclaims"), against other defendants (called "cross claims") or against persons not named in the plaintiff's original complaint as either a plaintiff or defendant (called "joinder"). Counterclaims and cross claims do not need to arise out of the dispute giving rise to the initial complaint because there is no inconvenience for courts or the parties to the initial complaint to resolve all disputes between the same plaintiffs and defendants. In other words, it is usually better to decide in a single lawsuit rather than in multiple lawsuits all of the disputes between the same parties.

Joinders, however, must arise out of the dispute giving rise to the initial complaint because it would be an inconvenience for both courts and the parties to the initial complaint to resolve all disputes which any of the parties to the initial complaint has against any and all other persons. In fact, there are two types of joinder: "necessary joinder" and "permissive joinder." In "permissive joinders," one or more of the defendants to the initial complaint requests the court to allow it to name another defendant to the initial complaint. In "necessary joinder", one or more defendants to the initial complaint insists that the court must allow it to name another defendant or the trial would not be fair for the initial defendants.

Class actions

Class actions are litigations where several (usually innumerable) complaints are consolidated into a single complaint for administrative efficiency. Consolidating complaints risks jeopardizing the interests of individual plaintiffs, so individual complaints are consolidated into class actions only where the same dispute, i.e., the same alleged harm arising out of the same facts, gives rise to the various individual complaints.

The purpose of most other procedural law is to ensure that all parties involved in a dispute are given notice and an opportunity to be heard. "Necessary joinder," as explained above, is a good example of this intent. Again, pursuant to necessary joinder, if courts cannot include in litigations all defendants involved in underlying disputes, then the courts cannot proceed with the litigations. In class actions, however, courts proceed with litigations even though they cannot include all potential plaintiffs involved in the underlying dispute. Class actions are allowed, even over the objections of defendants, if it would be practically impossible for a court to join all potential plaintiffs.

DUE PROCESS

As you can see from the very incomplete summary of procedural law presented above, procedural law can become very complicated and, with some important exceptions, somewhat remotely connected to making business decisions. If a business violates a person's general or contract rights or a government regulation, then – subject to the effort, expense, delay, uncertainty, distraction and emotion of litigation – corporate executives should assume that the person harmed or the government, as the case may be, will have access to a court for the purpose of seeking, as appropriate, compensatory damages, punitive damages, criminal penalties (such as fines and imprisonment) and other available sanctions. In addition, managers should assume that courts will become aware of all legally relevant facts for the purpose of determining whether and which remedies are appropriate for violations of general legal obligations, contracts and government regulations.

Court systems usually do not afford litigants all of the elements of due process, as outlined below. Court systems also frequently accommodate each element only to a limited extent, subjecting availability to qualifications and conditions. Some limitations on due process are probably inevitable. As once stated by Louis Brandeis, a judge of the United States Supreme Court in the early 1900s: at some point, it is more important that a case is finally decided than that it is correctly decided. Other limitations are obviously not inevitable. Whether as plaintiffs or defendants, businesses can judge their ability to obtain court judgments based in part by assessing the extent to which various elements of due process are available in respect of various litigations.

Notice and hearing

"Due process" is the method generally used by courts to become aware of those legally relevant facts. There are at least two elements of due process:

1 a notice of the dispute to parties involved in the litigation (commonly called "notice"); and
2 an opportunity for each of those parties to present the facts it considers relevant to the court (commonly called a "hearing" or "trial").

Notice of the dispute is accomplished with the delivery of a complaint and summons from plaintiffs to defendants and delivery of the answer from the defendants to plaintiffs, together with deliveries of any counterclaims, cross claims and joinders. Of course, for trials to be effective, parties involved in litigations must receive their notices a reasonable time before the trial is conducted. In the absence of an opportunity to prepare for hearings, persons receiving notices may not have the opportunity to understand the dispute (including relevant substantive law), obtain all of the legally relevant facts and present them to the court.

Due process gives rise to an "adversarial process," in which all plaintiffs and defendants involved in a dispute present at trial all of the facts they consider relevant. By giving all of the disputants an opportunity to present the facts they consider relevant, courts hope to obtain all of the facts relevant to deciding the dispute in accordance with applicable substantive law. Due process embraces the adversarial system because it is considered to be the best available method for obtaining an accurate and complete understanding of relevant facts. The adversarial system does not require that any single plaintiff or defendant be completely aware of all relevant facts. The adversarial system does require, however, that plaintiffs and defendants present accurately all of the relevant facts of which they are aware. Accordingly, due process requires that courts enforce measures to ensure that plaintiffs and defendants are honest in their presentations in court.

Other elements of due process

Viewed more broadly, there are other elements to "due process." They include:

3 the prior publication of applicable substantive law and procedural law;
4 hearings and trials held in public;
5 final judgments by persons who are impartial and competent in both procedural and substantive law;
6 remedies measured in proportion to the rights or regulations violated and the harm caused or potentially caused by the violation; and
7 the opportunity to appeal judgments and other court decisions, i.e., the opportunity to obtain reviews by a superior court of whether a trial court's procedures and judgments comply with applicable procedural and substantive laws.

The right to representation by a lawyer

All businesses are charged with knowing the substantive laws applicable to their operations, just as other subjects, citizens and comrades are charged with knowing the substantive laws applicable to their activities. Businesses are not charged, however, with knowing the procedural laws applicable to litigations of possible disputes. Accordingly, as part of due process, businesses – as well as other plaintiffs and defendants – are given the right to use lawyers in litigations. Lawyers are "officers of the court" charged with knowing applicable procedural laws and representing their clients, whether plaintiffs or defendants, in accordance with those laws.

The right to competent judges

Meeting the standard of having judges competent in procedural law is relatively easy to meet. Judges serving in courts interpret and apply the same procedural law every day and, in so doing, become expert. Sometimes, it is difficult to meet the standard of having judges in substantive law. Indeed, businesses sometimes agree to arbitration, as explained below, in part because businesses consider the appointment of an arbitrator as the best way to obtain a judge competent in the substance of the dispute, i.e., someone experienced in the business giving rise to the dispute. In both civil law countries and common law countries, governments sometimes attempt to increase their judges' competence in substantive law by establishing specialized courts: such as labor law courts, patent law courts, maritime courts and commercial courts. By specializing in a specific type of dispute, the judges in these courts can increase their expertise in applicable substantive law.

The right to impartial judges

In both civil law and common law countries, judges are charged, subject to both professional and criminal sanctions, to decide disputes impartially, i.e., to issue judgments based solely on the application of substantive law to relevant facts. Administratively, impartiality is enforced by allowing judges to withdraw from cases where they have prior knowledge of the person or facts involved in the dispute. In common law courts, defendants can seek impartiality also by having a jury make final judgments. Originally, jurors were individuals – people without any governmental office – who knew the parties to the dispute and, preferably, knew the facts of the case, both even before the trial began.

Today, jurors in common law countries are individuals without any governmental office who, prior to the trial, know neither:

(a) the persons involved in the dispute; nor
(b) the facts surrounding the dispute.

To achieve this purpose, plaintiffs and defendants are permitted to question potential jurors and to exclude them from juries on the basis of their prior knowledge of the persons and facts involved in a dispute – as well as on the basis of other opinions adversely affecting their impartiality. In an attempt to make jurors competent judges, after jurors hear all of the relevant facts presented at trial, judges explain to jurors the law they are supposed to apply to the relevant facts to reach their judgments.

Jurors' decisions and verdicts are not, in fact, subject to review by judges unless jurors' decisions are "manifestly opposed to the overwhelming weight of the evidence." In such cases, judges will issue a "directed verdict," a judgment in accordance with weight of the evidence.

Appeals

The availability of appeals is another important part of due process. The term "appeals" refers to requests addressed to superior courts by litigants who do not prevail in trials (either plaintiffs or defendants). The parties making appeals (called "appellants") ask superior courts to review trial courts' interpretation of applicable law and, as appropriate, the trial courts' application of law to the facts of a case. The term "superior courts" refers to courts established for the purpose of reviewing decisions by trial courts. Accordingly, superior courts are often called "appellate courts." Some court systems maintain at least two levels of appellate courts, with the second and subsequent levels reviewing decisions by lower appellate courts. The highest court of appeal in a court system is often called a "supreme court." While litigants usually have the right to appeal trial courts' decisions to the first level of appellate courts, further appeals tend to be discretionary. In other words, appellate courts beyond the first level can refuse to hear appeals, making rulings by lower-level appellate courts effectively final and conclusive.

Appeals are almost universally limited to a review of the manner in which trial courts identify applicable law, interpret that law and apply it to facts. In other words, appellate courts almost universally do not review findings of facts by judges and juries at trial courts. There simply is no mechanism for appellate courts to hold evidentiary hearings. Instead, appellate courts simply defer completely to trial courts, either by judges or by juries, as regards fact finding. At the same time, appeals can raise issues of procedural law, including rules of evidence and burdens of proof, which constitute a review of the manner in which judges and juries conducted their fact finding. Accordingly, appellate courts frequently return (sometimes called "remand") cases to trial courts with instructions to conduct new hearings in accordance with rules of evidence or other procedural law clarified by the appellate court.

In addition to deferring completely to trial courts as regards fact finding, appellate courts also extend some deference to trial courts in their interpretation and application of substantive law.

EVIDENCE

Obtaining a remedy in court requires more than filing a complaint. It is also necessary to offer "evidence," i.e., statements and objects tending to establish the existence of a relevant fact. Unfortunately, some types of statements and objects only appear to establish the truth of a relevant fact but are unreliable for such purpose. "Hearsay" is a good example of a type of statement which is generally not admissible in court because it is unreliable. "Hearsay" evidence is one person's statement in court based on a second person's report of an event or condition to that first person. The first person is not allowed to repeat the report in court in part because no one is able to question, i.e., challenge, the second person about the factual basis for the report.

The purpose of the law of evidence is to prevent plaintiffs and defendants from presenting unreliable evidence. Judges – as trained professionals – presumably are able to assess the reliability of evidence. Accordingly, the law of evidence is most important in trials decided by juries. The main reason for preventing plaintiffs and defendants from introducing certain evidence is that juries would ascribe an inordinate importance to the evidence in reaching their verdict. For example, judges understand that documents offered as evidence have little significance in resolving disputes unless the litigants offering the documents can also explain both the way the document was generated and how it was preserved for presentation in court. Jurors may not understand the importance of such considerations, so the law of evidence requires that documents be duly "authenticated" before they can be presented to jurors as evidence.

Rules of evidence can be a part of procedural law even in the absence of jury trials. Rules of evidence in the context of litigations decided by judges tend to serve as a form of "quality control," imposing a consistent standard on all judges in their consideration of various evidence. Rules of evidence also serve for clearly establishing the facts presented in court for the purpose of appeals.

Burdens of proof

In addition, it is not sufficient for plaintiffs to offer negligible evidence to obtain judicial remedies, or for defendants to avoid such remedies. Obtaining favorable judgments requires that litigants satisfy their burdens of proof, i.e., that they present evidence necessary to establish with the requisite probability that a relevant fact exists or does not exist.

For example, in order to prevail in claims for personal injury (such as product liability), plaintiffs must satisfy their burdens of proof in respect of all four facts relevant for such a claim:

1 that plaintiffs suffered an injury;
2 that acts or omissions by defendants were one of the foreseeable causes of the injury;
3 that the plaintiffs' injuries were foreseeable at the time of defendants' acts or omissions; and
4 that defendants' acts or omissions constitute a breach of their general obligations to plaintiffs.

Once plaintiffs satisfy their burden of proof in respect of those four elements, defendants can avoid a judicial remedy for breach of their general obligations to plaintiffs only if they can satisfy their burden of proof in respect of an affirmative defense, i.e., that there are other facts – such as plaintiffs' negligence – which contributed significantly to causing plaintiffs' injuries.

Plaintiffs' burden of proceeding

The first burden of proof is plaintiffs' "burden of proceeding." In order to satisfy this burden, plaintiffs must convince judges that ordinary persons could reasonably conclude that all of the facts relevant to establishing their complaints probably exist. The burden of proceeding is sometimes quantified as a 20 percent probability that all relevant facts actually exist. Using the example of personal injury, plaintiffs satisfy their "burden of proceeding" by offering evidence sufficient for judges to conclude that ordinary persons could reasonably conclude that all four facts relevant for a complaint based on personal injury actually exist. Alternatively, plaintiffs satisfy their burden of proceeding by offering evidence sufficient to establish to a judge's satisfaction that there is a 20 percent probability that all of the facts relevant to such a complaint actually exist.

Plaintiffs' burden of proof

The second burden of proof is plaintiffs' "burden of proof," sometimes called the "burden of prevailing." In order to satisfy this burden, plaintiffs must convince the fact finders, i.e., either the judge or jury hearing the case, by a preponderance of the evidence, that all of the facts relevant to establishing their claims actually exist. The burden of proceeding in a civil action is sometimes quantified as a 51 percent probability that all relevant facts actually exist. Again using the example of personal injury, plaintiffs satisfy their "burden of prevailing" by offering evidence sufficient for the finders of fact (either judge or jury) to conclude that all four facts relevant for a complaint based on personal injury actually exist.

Defendants' burden for affirmative defenses

As indicated above in respect of the example concerning personal injury claims, even if plaintiffs satisfy their burden of prevailing in respect of all facts relevant to establishing their claims actually exist, defendants can avoid judicial remedies if they can introduce additional facts sufficient to exonerate them from legal liability. Such additional facts are called "affirmative defenses." The burden of proceeding does not apply to affirmative defenses because litigations proceed on the basis of plaintiffs satisfying their initial burden of proof.

Other burdens of proof

The preceding descriptions of burdens of proof apply generally to civil litigations. Famously, there are higher burdens of proof for governments to proceed and prevail in criminal litigations, e.g., proving "beyond a reasonable doubt" that all facts relevant for defendants' guilt actually exist for the purpose of imposing a criminal sentence. Other burdens of proof apply to other types of legal proceedings. For example, administrative agencies sometimes must establish "by clear and convincing evidence" all of the facts relevant to impose an administrative sanction such as the suspension of a business's operations. In each case, the relevant burdens of proof are established in a manner considered appropriate – in part on the basis of the severity of possible remedies in the event of findings against defendants.

Discovery

Discovery is a potentially important part of litigation. Discovery refers to the ability of each party to a litigation (i.e., each plaintiff and defendant) to compel all other parties to the litigation (i.e., every other plaintiff and defendant) to disclose all of the evidence and other relevant facts in their possession. Disclosures pursuant to discovery are made to all of the parties to a litigation, even if only one of the parties requested the disclosure.

Discovery can include:

(a) the right to obtain copies of all documents;
(b) the right to conduct "depositions," i.e., sessions where a plaintiff or defendant questions, verbally and face-to-face, persons with information relevant to resolving the dispute; and
(c) the right to obtain written answers to "interrogatories," i.e., written questions submitted by a plaintiff or defendant to any other party to the litigation.

The right of discovery can be very broad. It can include the right to obtain all relevant evidence and other facts and, in addition, the right to obtain all "probative information," i.e., information which could lead to the discovery of any evidence or other relevant facts.

Discovery significantly affects the nature of litigation

The availability and scope of discovery can significantly affect the nature of any litigation contemplated by a business or asserted against it. For example, one of the purposes of discovery is to avoid surprises at trials. As a result, pursuant to a request for discovery, plaintiffs and defendants are required to disclose both information tending to undermine their position in litigations and information supporting their position in litigations. Without this second element of the disclosure obligation, parties to litigations could withhold decisive information in their favor before trial with the intention of revealing it during the trial in court. The element of surprise would have precluded other litigants from preparing themselves against it. Indeed, allowing litigants to surprise each other with new evidence during trials arguably defeats due process, at least in respect of the surprise evidence, by denying other litigants effective notice.

Discovery improves the plaintiffs' odds of prevailing

The availability and scope of discovery can also significantly affect the relative probability of plaintiffs or defendants prevailing in litigations. In litigations where no discovery is available, plaintiffs must depend on the evidence in their own possession before they file their complaints in order to prevail in their complaints. In such litigations, defendants are allowed to introduce evidence in their own defense without the obligation to provide any evidence tending to support complaints against them. In litigations where discovery is available, defendants must provide plaintiffs with all evidence in defendants' possession, even if providing that evidence assists plaintiffs in prevailing in their complaints against defendants.

Discovery reveals many business secrets

For businesses allegedly violating general legal obligations, contracts and government regulations, there are no secrets in any resulting litigation subject to discovery. If the persons harmed – or the government agency responsible for prosecuting violations – have discovery rights, then the businesses subject to the allegations can be required to disclose all facts and circumstances surrounding the business decisions and operations allegedly giving rise to the violations. Even if a business ultimately prevails in its defense, complying with the requests for discovery will have probably resulted in considerable expense and some disruption of business.

GOVERNMENT ACTIONS

Government agencies initiate various administrative proceedings for the purpose of enforcing business regulations. These actions consist primarily of inquiries, investigations, administrative proceedings, administrative rulings, settlement decrees, administrative sanctions and criminal accusations. In most countries criminal allegations are referred to the office of the public prosecutor or attorney general, who makes a final determination concerning whether criminal prosecution is appropriate.

Limitations on agency powers

Government agencies are authorized to initiate various administrative procedures within the scope of statutory grants of power from national legislatures or executives. Accordingly, the first limitation on agencies' power is inherent in the grants of power establishing them. At the same time, some government agencies have been granted very broad powers. The Securities and Exchange Commission and the Food and Drug Administration in the United States are good examples of agencies with very broad powers.

The second limitation imposed on agencies' powers is set forth in "administrative law," i.e., statutes generally applicable to all actions by government agencies. Generally, administrative laws impose varying degrees of due process on agency actions. Finally, each country's constitution prescribes limits concerning all government action. Constitutional articles such as individual rights, generally applicable to all government action, are also applicable to administrative proceedings. Within the broad outlines of each country's administrative law and constitution, different agencies have invariably developed very different policies, procedures and practices.

Applying principles of due process to agency actions

As with civil litigation, the prospects of having administrative proceedings decided in accordance with all relevant facts can be anticipated by the extent to which due process applies to those proceedings. Obviously, it is very difficult to draw any conclusions in this vast area. At the same time, it is possible to identify recurring issues when administrative proceedings are assessed from the perspective of due process.

Understandable substantive law

First as regards administrative regulations, they are almost invariably published but are often quite extensive and difficult to understand. Understanding some of them is rendered even more difficult by frequent changes. The difficulty inherent in understanding government regulations could theoretically violate principles of due process, but such arguments rarely prevail in practice. In addition, the due process issues are often more apparent than real. While understanding extensive regulations would be impracticable for the general population, extensive government regulations tend to apply only to businesses within a specific industry. Understanding government regulations sometimes entails heavy expenses on the businesses subject to them, i.e., expenses in addition to the expense of complying with the regulations after businesses understand them. At the same time, the expense of understanding regulations – as opposed to the impracticability of understanding them – does not constitute an issue under principles of due process.

Adequate notice

Second, as regards administrative investigations, government agencies are often empowered – often subject to specific prior authorizations from courts – without warning to seize documents and demand other assets and information. As explained elsewhere, government regulations are usually intended to prevent personal injury and property damage, including systematic violations of economic rights. Preventing such injuries and damages is often classified as "police powers" under national constitutions. As a result, agencies can and sometimes do take actions unilaterally and without notice, exactly in the manner of other police services.

Competent and impartial judges

Third, if government agencies decide to pursue specific investigations, then businesses – or any other persons – who are the object of those investigations eventually receive a "hearing." Granting such hearings, of course, accords with principles of due process. At the same time, one or more officials from within the government agency pursuing the investigation usually conducts the hearing and, after the hearing, makes a ruling and, as appropriate, imposes sanctions. While such officials are likely to be competent judges – in that they know applicable substantive

and procedural regulations – their impartiality is sometimes subject to challenge. Indeed, administrative laws allow for court review of administrative sanctions in part because of concerns about the objectivity of administrative officials.

Appeals

Finally, administrative law and national constitutions usually give businesses – as well as other individuals subject to administrative sanctions – the opportunity to appeal administrative rulings. Such reviews are, of course, an important part of due process. At the same time, the reversal upon appeal of administrative rulings and sanctions does not necessarily compensate businesses – or other individuals – for the expenses, losses and other costs incurred as a result of administrative investigations, hearings, rulings or sanctions conducted or imposed in violation of the principles of due process. At the same time, judicial review of administrative proceedings is often limited in scope. In furtherance of legislative arrangements intended to delegate to administrative agencies the exercise of governmental police powers, courts will often decline to reverse administrative proceedings in the absence, for example, of "clear and manifest error" by the agency.

ALTERNATIVE DISPUTE RESOLUTION

"Alternative dispute resolution" or "ADR" refers to both arbitration and mediation. These are called alternatives because they are alternatives to civil litigation – but not alternatives to government actions.

Arbitrations are proceedings pursuant to which parties to a dispute agree to be bound to a third person's resolution of that dispute. In arbitrations, the parties to a dispute agree to be bound by a third person's resolution of their dispute even before that third person (i.e., the arbitrator) hears the dispute and announces the resolution. An arbitrator's binding resolution of a dispute is typically called an "arbitral award."

In mediations, the parties to a dispute agree to engage in certain proceedings in respect of their dispute – sometimes involving a hearing by a third person – but, in mediations, the parties to the dispute do not agree to be bound by the outcome of those proceedings. Mediation proceedings in their various forms can be best described as "discussions."

Pronouncements by third persons who preside over mediations can best be described as "proposals" – not resolutions binding on the parties to the dispute. If the parties to a mediation resolve their dispute pursuant to the mediation, then any such resolution will be embodied in a settlement agreement signed by those parties after the mediation has been conducted.

Disadvantages to litigation

Civil litigations have certain advantages over both arbitrations and mediations. First, arbitrators and mediators often resort to compromises rather than principles to resolve disputes. While the willingness to compromise can be attractive to some disputants, those who believe they have a strong position based on principles might prefer to litigate before a court.

Second, judgments issued by courts pursuant to civil litigations are generally binding on all third parties, while arbitral awards and settlement agreements are binding only on the parties to the arbitration or agreement. For example, patent holders sometimes prefer litigating patent infringements rather than arbitrating or mediating infringements if the patent holders want to establish their rights in a manner effective against all possible infringers. As another example, insurance companies sometimes prefer to litigate dispute about the scope of coverage provided by standard insurance provisions rather than arbitrating or mediating with innumerable policy holders.

Third, pursuing arbitration or mediation can prejudice or, at least, complicate subsequent litigation. For example, applicable statutes of limitations – or prescription periods – continue to run and can lapse during the course of arbitration or mediation proceedings. As another example, arbitrators and mediators – unlike courts – typically have little or no power, during the course of the proceedings over which they preside, to issue the interim and provisional remedies sometimes necessary to maintain the disputants' relative positions or effective remedies.

Finally, if one of the disputants believes that it is better able to bear the burdens of litigation (i.e., effort, expense, delay, uncertainty, distraction and emotions) than the second party to the dispute, then the first disputant might prefer to pursue litigation because of the relative advantage it provides. For example, a business deriving income from a disputed operation or transaction might prefer to litigate rather than arbitrate or mediate in spite of the overall benefits provided by alternative dispute resolution.

Advantages over litigation

Even though litigation offers certain advantages over the alternatives of arbitration and mediation, many businesses prefer to avoid litigation because of the advantages offered by those alternatives. The most important consideration tends to be lighter burdens imposed by arbitration and mediation. Arbitration and mediation proceedings are more flexible and informal and thus tend to involve less effort, expense and delay.

Second, arbitrators and mediators are selected personally by the disputants or by a private association pursuant to procedures agreed by the disputants. In either case, arbitrators tend to be selected from a pool of candidates considered to be competent judges of the underlying dispute. Businesses are often concerned that court judges are not competent in substantive law or familiar with industry and business practices.

Third, arbitration and mediation can, by agreement of the disputants, be entirely confidential proceedings. With exceptions for certain information disclosed in the course of litigations, proceedings in courts and judgments by courts are always public. As a result, it is sometimes possible for disputants to avoid risks to their reputation by pursuing alternatives to litigation. Because of the confidentiality available with arbitration and mediation, it is sometimes even possible to preserve future commercial relationships between disputants by pursuing alternatives to litigation.

Most importantly, at least as regards disputes between businesses from different countries, arbitration is often preferred over litigation because, as explained below, pursuant to the 1958 New York Convention, arbitral awards granted pursuant to an arbitration conducted in one country are generally recognizable and enforceable in other countries. In contrast, most countries are under no treaty obligation to recognize judicial remedies ordered pursuant to litigations conducted in other countries.

ARBITRATION

Commercial arbitrations are binding proceedings leading to binding resolutions of business disputes. Commercial arbitrations are conducted by one or more private individuals, i.e., the arbitrator(s), who are appointed directly by the businesses involved in the dispute or pursuant to a method agreed by the disputants at the time they agree to the arbitration.

In this context, the term "binding" means that the businesses involved in a dispute have even agreed, before the proceedings begin, to be bound by the arbitrators' decisions – both as regards the proceedings and as regards the resolution of their dispute. Depending on the arbitral agreement between the disputants, arbitrator(s) decide only the specific questions presented to them in their appointment.

In arbitrations, representatives of each side (usually trial lawyers) present their best cases to the arbitrator(s). As part of their appointment, the arbitrator(s) agree to conduct the proceedings and to resolve the dispute in accordance with, respectively, the procedural rules and the substantive law designated by the disputants at the time of their arbitration agreement. At the same time, arbitrators have broad discretion in conducting proceedings and granting awards.

There are three important bodies of law affecting arbitration:

1 the 1958 New York Convention;
2 the UNCITRAL Model Law on International Commercial Arbitration; and
3 the procedures and facilities available from various private arbitration associations.

1958 New York Treaty

Since it was adopted on 10 June 1958, the "New York Convention for the Recognition and Enforcement of Foreign Arbitral Awards" has been ratified and adopted by most of the commercial countries around the world. One other treaty needs to be mentioned, the "1975 Panama Convention." It is substantially identical to the 1958 New York Convention for our purposes and applies among the countries in the Americas.

Enforcing foreign commercial arbitral awards

Pursuant to the terms of the New York Convention, each signatory country agrees to recognize and enforce in its courts commercial arbitral awards granted in each of the other signatory countries. In other words, if a business in one signatory country fails to make a payment required by an arbitral award granted in another signatory country, then the business entitled to receive the payment can simply present the arbitral award in the courts of the first signatory country. Upon presentation of the arbitral award, the courts of the first signatory country will require the recalcitrant business to make payment in accordance with the terms of the foreign arbitral award. (Of course, there are many, sometimes significant procedural issues involved in collecting payment pursuant to the 1958 New York Convention. One point is clear, however: if the treaty applies, then the business entitled to receive payment does not have to conduct a trial in the first signatory country on any issues decided in the initial arbitration.)

Conditions for enforcing foreign commercial arbitral awards

In addition to causing potentially significant procedural delays, businesses subject to foreign commercial arbitral awards can raise certain defenses to enforcement of an arbitral award pursuant to the 1958 New York Convention. Basically, the business subject to the award can claim that:

1 the award was granted without adequate notice or hearing;
2 the award is still subject to appeal in the country where it was granted; or
3 the award was granted in violation of the underlying arbitration agreement.

As regards the underlying agreement, the business subject to the award can claim, either:

(a) that arbitration procedure was not in accordance with the arbitration agreement; or
(b) the arbitrators were not selected in the manner agreed by the parties, or in the manner provided by the law of the country where the arbitration took place.

Limited international enforcement of foreign court judgments

Within Europe, European Union Council Regulation 44/2001 (adopted 22 December 2000) provides for the mutual recognition and enforcement of judgments in civil and commercial matters. (Prior to 2001, the countries of Europe relied on the 1968 Brussels Convention and on the 1988 Lugano Convention.)

Outside of Europe, there is no equivalent treaty for the recognition and enforcement of foreign court judgments – as opposed to foreign arbitral awards. Each country recognizes foreign court judgments as it sees fit in accordance with its own domestic laws.

1985 UNCITRAL Model Law on International Commercial Arbitration

The right to impose binding resolutions of disputes concerning legal rights is, of course, one of the natural functions of government. In the absence of statutes whereby governments recognized arbitration proceedings conducted within their borders, disputants could avoid, suspend and annul arbitral proceedings and awards at will by appealing to national courts to intervene. At the same time, private arbitrations serve the useful public purpose of easing the burdens on court systems (and therefore on taxpayers).

More and more countries have adopted public policies favoring commercial arbitration. Those policies are embodied in statutes recognizing arbitration agreements and arbitration proceedings conducted within their borders. Many countries have adopted national statutes based upon a model statute issued by the United Nations in 1985: the Model Law on International Commercial Arbitration of the United Nations Commission on International Trade Law (UNCITRAL). The Model Law was restricted to international commercial arbitration in part because allowing international arbitration is less of a restriction on governmental powers than allowing all commercial arbitration. (Also, a model law on international arbitration is more clearly within the scope of the United Nations.)

The Model Law, national statutes adopted pursuant to it and other national laws allowing arbitration proceedings do not strictly define the procedures arbitrators must use in conducting their proceedings. The arbitration statutes do, however, tend to provide procedures in the event that the parties to the arbitration fail to designate procedural rules for the conduct of the arbitrations. In addition, most importantly, national statutes tend to grant arbitrators the power:

(a) to decide on their own scope of authority concerning disputes; and
(b) to provide for interim and provisional remedies intended to preserve the disputants' relative positions during the arbitration proceedings or to preserve their ability to enforce arbitral awards.

Such interim and provisional remedies include requirements that the parties post performance bonds or even deposit funds in escrow accounts.

The national statutes permitting arbitration do dictate the "rule for decision" as regards the dispute. The rule for decision is either selected by the parties or determined by the arbitrator. In other words, the parties to the arbitration agreement can decide to use a substantive law other than the substantive law of the country where the arbitration is conducted, i.e., the law of United Kingdom can be designated as the substantive law for arbitration conducted in France. The substantive law used to decide disputes does not need to come from the same country as the procedural rules used to conduct the proceedings.

Private arbitration associations

Disputants frequently designate a private association (some called an "institution") to provide services and facilities for arbitration proceedings. Services include maintaining lists of persons who are trained or experienced as arbitrators generally or in specific industries. Private arbitration institutions also maintain lists of experts in various fields to conduct investigations and to serve as witnesses in arbitrations. Facilities include conference centers with support services. If the disputants cannot agree on a procedure for selecting arbitrators or for conducting proceedings, then the private associations typically have their own procedural rules. These rules typically have the advantage of conforming to requirements under applicable national arbitration statutes and under the 1958 New York Convention.

There are many private arbitration associations located around the world, some of them specializing in specific industries or regions. Cities favored for arbitration proceedings include Stockholm, Zurich, London, New York and Miami. Each of these cities has locally-based arbitration associations. Two well-known private associations providing arbitration facilities and services are the International Chamber of

Commerce (headquartered in Paris, France) and the American Arbitration Association (with operations in most large cities in the USA).

Industry association arbitrations

Some industry associations now provide arbitration services similar to those provided by other private arbitration associations. Industry associations claim to provide better assurances of confidentiality and more competent arbitrators. "Blanket agreements" are sometimes available in connection with industry association membership. These agreements provide that a member agrees to arbitrate at the industry association with every other member who similarly agrees to arbitrate with members at the industry association.

MEDIATION

Mediations are explained generally above, under the heading of "Alternative dispute resolution." There are various forms of mediation, including negotiation, management panels, mediation, conciliation and mini-trials. Most importantly, these various forms of mediation are not mutually exclusive. In fact, they can be and frequently are attempted sequentially in the order they are presented below.

Negotiation

In negotiations, individuals involved in events leading to disputes seek to find a solution. A good strategy in such negotiations is to change the zero-sum game to a win-win game, usually by maintaining the commercial relationship giving rise to the dispute which takes into account a resolution of the dispute (e.g., discounts or rebates on future sales to a buyer with a legitimate warranty claim).

Management panels

With management panels, individuals involved in events leading to disputes seek solutions with the assistance of their senior management. At this step in mediations, respective senior management might engage in direct negotiations, either with or without the participation of the individuals directly involved in the underlying events. Such management panels are sometimes arranged in advance, for example: as the boards of directors of joint ventures or as "standing committees" amongst owners and contractors on construction projects.

Mediation (as traditionally understood)

As traditionally defined, "mediation" is a process whereby the businesses involved in a dispute seek to negotiate a settlement agreement with the assistance of a trained, neutral facilitator. Mediators attempt to facilitate settlement negotiations by helping each disputant to assess its position. Again as traditionally defined, mediators do not propose their own solutions.

Mediations are often conducted at the mediator's office. One procedure adopted by mediators is to begin the mediation with a general meeting. During the general meeting, each disputant presents its position on the dispute to the mediator with the other disputant in attendance. Each disputant then withdraws to a separate room while the mediator moves back and forth between them, discussing the dispute with each disputant in an alternating fashion. During this phase of the mediation, mediators offer their confidential assessment of each disputant's position to that disputant – not to the other parties to the dispute. In the next phase, the mediator might help one or both disputants formulate a proposed settlement and present the possible resolution to the other disputant. The mediator then moves between the disputants discussing hopefully progressive proposals for settlement agreements.

If the mediation leads to a settlement agreement, the final phase – before the parties adjourn – is to document the resolution agreed by the parties. If necessary, a final, more formal settlement agreement can be prepared and signed within the next few days.

Conciliation

As with mediation, the disputants seek to negotiate a settlement agreement with the assistance of a trained, neutral facilitator. Conciliation is identical to mediation except that, in addition to helping each disputant assess its position, the conciliator offers his own assessment of the disputants' relative positions. In practice, mediation often evolves into conciliation.

Mini-trials

Mini-trials are also sometimes called "executive tribunals." They are similar to management panels except they typically involve the most senior officers of each of the businesses involved in the dispute (or, at least, the most senior officers with an announced intention of becoming involved in the dispute). No mediators or conciliators are involved.

In the final phase of mini-trials, managers from each of the disputants meet face-to-face in an attempt to negotiate a settlement agreement – exactly like a management panel. Unlike management panels, negotiations in mini-trials are preceded by formal presentations by each of the disputants. During the formal presentations – at which senior management from both (or all) disputants are present – each disputant outlines its best arguments concerning the dispute for the benefit of the other disputant(s), as if the disputants were making their final arguments before a judge in a civil litigation. The presentations are supposed to be well researched, prepared and presented. Trial lawyers for each disputant are often involved in each step of the mini-trial presentation.

Disputants usually agree to mini-trials with the understanding that they are the last step in the mediation process. If the disputants fail to reach a settlement agreement at the mini-trial, then the next step is either litigation or arbitration.

F
I
V
E

18

Intellectual Property Rights

Patents, copyrights, trademarks and trade secrets

INTRODUCTION

Faced with the pressures of today's increasingly competitive business environment, it is more important than ever that each and every employee help with the preservation and efficient use of corporate intangible assets, especially its intellectual property rights.

"Intellectual property rights" is a term used to refer generally to legal rights such as those created by patents, which protect inventions and discoveries from exploitation by others for a period of twenty years from filing utility patent applications (excluding design patents); trademarks, which protect names and other designations of origin for goods and services from confusingly similar use by others; copyrights, which protect original works of authorship fixed in tangible mediums of expression; and trade secrets, which protect confidential information used in one's business and which give one the opportunity to obtain an advantage over competitors who do not know or use it.

PATENTS

In general, a *United States* patent may be obtained on an invention or discovery made in the United States if it:

1 is new;
2 is useful;
3 was first invented by the applicant for the patent;
4 was not patented or described in a printed publication more than one year prior to the date the application for the patent is filed;

5 was not on sale or in public use in the United States more than one year prior to filing of the application; and
6 would not have been obvious to a person of ordinary skill in the art at the time the invention was made.

Although there are other statutory requirements, these are the most important statutory requirements for patentability of an invention, and failure to meet any of the requirements precludes the issuance of a valid patent.

Many *foreign* countries operate on what is known as an *absolute* novelty requirement for patentability. As a result, in many important industrial countries, *any* sale of an item incorporating an invention *or any* publication describing the invention, e.g., promotional handouts or advertisements, *or any* public display or access that makes the invention available to the public can prevent issuance of a valid patent. Accordingly, *before* making any public disclosures of an invention, sales or offer for sale of products using or made by the invention, or issuing publications describing the invention, *disclosures should be submitted to patent counsel in sufficient time to consider whether patent protection should be sought*. In general, patent lawyers, patent agents, and liaisons are to assist in the legal issues associated with patent protection, and are not to be listed as inventors. The following procedures should be followed:

1 Whenever an employee makes an improvement or an invention the employee believes to be significant, a written description of the idea and any sketches,

if appropriate, should be drawn up and submitted to the employee's superior for transmittal to patent counsel, or other designated recipient, together with a completed invention disclosure form.

2   All records and drawings should bear the date and signatures of the person(s) doing the work and of at least one witness (who is not an inventor) who has read and understood these written materials, or who has witnessed the tests or demonstrations throughout all experimental stages of work. This witnessing corroborates the date of conception of the invention and its reduction to practice – i.e., the date of the first successful testing of the invention. Persons performing research or other tasks which may lead to inventions should keep accurate, contemporaneous, dated records of their work in a bound notebook with numbered pages. Such books, when filled, should be kept in an appropriate long-term storage file for later reference.

3   If determination is made that a patent application should be filed, all pertinent prior publications and patents of which the inventor[s] is[are] aware should be brought to the attention of the patent attorney preparing the case. In addition, if affidavits of experiments are submitted during prosecution of the patent application, such affidavits should be complete and should include unfavorable as well as favorable data. Failure to include all data, whether favorable or not, may later result in a court holding the patent unenforceable.

4   No disclosure of an invention should be made to any person not employed by the corporation, at least until a patent application has been filed. Where a joint development program exists, an agreement governing inventions should be entered into *well before* commencement of work under the program. The opinion of patent counsel should be sought to work out the appropriate agreement for the circumstances.

5   Even after a patent application has been filed, it may be decided to abandon the application and retain the invention as a trade secret. (Patent applications are held secret by the US Patent and Trademark Office for a period of eighteen (18) months from the priority date.) Therefore, care should be taken not to publish information regarding the invention until such a determination is made. Premature publications may put the disclosed invention in the public domain and thus preempt trade secret protection.

COPYRIGHTS

Scientific articles, technical manuals, lectures, drawings of a scientific or technical nature, tape recordings, videos, computer programs, and similar works, whether written or prepared for oral presentation by corporate employees, may be subject to copyright protection. In the United States, for works created after 1977 copyrights are usually granted for a term equal to the life of the author plus 70 years. This conforms with Canada and most other countries. However, in certain circumstances, such as where the work is created by an employee in the scope of his or her employment, the term is 95 years from publication – generally achieved by the general sale or distribution of the work – or 120 years from creation, whichever is less. It is advisable to affix an appropriate copyright notice to the work and on all subsequent copies of the work on or before the first date of publication. The following are guidelines to ensure appropriate form and use of a copyright notice:

1   The copyright notice should be affixed to the work in the following form: "Copyright © ['2XXX,' i.e., year of first publication] ['author or assignee'] – All Rights Reserved."

2   The date provided in the copyright notice should be the date of the first publication of the work in which the notice appears. This date should not be changed when the work is reprinted, although the notice should be changed when the material is revised and reprinted. If a copyrighted work is revised, counsel should be consulted to determine the form of the copyright notice required.

3   A copyright notice in a book should ordinarily be placed either on the title page or on the page next following the title page.

4   All copyright notices should be of a size which can be easily read with the naked eye.

A corporation and its employees should adhere to the following procedures, to assure that copyright protection is maximized. First, employment agreements should contain a clause ensuring corporate ownership of copyright rights. For independent contractors, a separate assignment of copyright must be prepared. Second, if the work is experimental in nature and no publication is intended, the following legend should be prominently displayed on the work (including computer programs):

Finally, ultimately, but preferably within three months of publication, copies of the copyrighted material should be registered with the Register of Copyrights in Washington, DC. Copyright registration is not necessary to obtain copyright protection in a work. However, registration does provide many useful benefits, especially if registered within three months of publication. Thus, any published material should be forwarded to corporate legal counsel as promptly as possible.

TRADEMARKS

Trademarks are an important and valuable business asset. They help identify the goods and services provided by companies. A trademark is any word, name, symbol or device, or any combination thereof, adopted and used to identify a company's goods and services and distinguish them from those of others. Unlike patents and copyrights, trademark rights do not arise by grant of the government. Trademark rights accrue to a company as a result of *actual use* of the mark in connection with the sale of goods or services to identify the source or origin of the goods or services.

Selection of an appropriate trademark, one that identifies and distinguishes a product in the marketplace, is most important. A coined word with no dictionary meaning or an arbitrary word with a dictionary meaning unrelated to the product best serves this purpose (e.g., KODAK, XEROX, CAMEL for cigarettes, APPLE for computers, etc.).

Although it is not necessary to register a trademark to obtain trademark rights, certain advantages accrue from federal registration. It is recommended that federal registration be obtained for all trademarks used in interstate or foreign commerce. The US federal government sets up minimum standards which must be met by the trademark owner if the trademark is to be registered. It is therefore important that these standards are complied with when a trademark is first selected for use and that the trademark be consistently used in connection with the goods by adopting

a standard format for the trademark. The following comments relate to the standards of trademark registrability imposed under the law.

In selecting a mark, it must be kept in mind that the mark must be one which the public can use to identify the goods as goods from a single source of origin and it should not be possible for this meaning to be confused. It follows, therefore, that the mark selected must be one which can be monopolized and used exclusively for the purpose of identification without interfering with the rights of others to accurately describe their own products.

In general, when choosing a mark, the following factors should be considered. First, purely descriptive or laudatory terms such as tough, strong, shiny, transparent, etc., or misspellings thereof will have to be disclaimed. Second, deceptive terms will not be sustained as valid marks. For example, the following mark has been found to be deceptively misleading: "OLD COUNTRY" soap, for soap manufactured in the United States. Third, words that geographically describe products or businesses are sometimes difficult to protect. However, protection for such geographic terms may be obtained upon achieving secondary meaning in the mark or when the mark is used in conjunction with other non-descriptive terms. Secondary meaning exists when, after extensive use, the general public comes to exclusively associate the producer or the product with the mark. Fourth, family names should be avoided. Although there are a great many family name trademarks, these types of marks often prove to be troublesome since a showing of secondary meaning is required prior to enforcement or registration of the mark, and because individuals with the same name may have the right to use their name on their products in competition with you.

Once a proposed trademark is selected, counsel can be asked to perform a "search" to determine whether the mark is available for adoption and use, whether it is confusingly similar to another's mark or name, or whether it might infringe another's existing rights in a trademark or trade name. Undertaking this analysis prior to making any investment in advertising and packaging materials can avoid substantial losses to the company by limiting the chance of a conflict.

It may be necessary to search several proposed marks before finding one that does not conflict with an existing trademark or name of a business. The more descriptive the mark, the greater the likelihood that conflicting marks may exist.

F
I
V
E

Even when a proposed mark appears to be available for adoption and use, a search cannot guarantee the uncovering of all possible conflicts. For example, occasionally there are local users of a conflicting but unregistered trademark who operate small-scale businesses who have rights that may come to your attention only after the new mark is used and promoted. It is difficult to protect against this latter situation.

After approval of the selected mark, the question of whether an application for US federal registration of the mark is warranted should be considered. An application can be filed if a mark has been used in interstate commerce or in commerce between the United States and a foreign country. In addition, a trademark the company intends to adopt, but has not yet used, can be applied for under the intent-to-use provisions of the trademark law, although a registration will not issue until the mark is in actual commercial use. State trademark registrations are also available.

To maintain a trademark registration, the mark must be used essentially continuously. A trademark will be deemed abandoned when the owner ceases use with intent not to resume use. A lack of use for three consecutive years constitutes *prima facie* evidence of abandonment. Abandonment of a mark through nonuse constitutes grounds for cancellation of the mark's registration. Further, an affidavit must be filed in the Patent and Trademark Office between the fifth and sixth year after registration stating that the mark is in actual commercial use on the goods or services set out in the registration, and evidence of such use must be submitted.

Once a registered mark has been used continuously for five years, the owner's rights in the registered mark become "incontestable." After five years from registration, the mark cannot be canceled except for a few limited grounds on which the validity of the registration may be challenged. This incontestability extends only to the goods or services named in the registration upon which the mark is being used.

Use of a registered trademark again becomes a factor at ten-year intervals when the registration must be renewed. The mark must be in actual commercial use at the time of the renewal application (or nonuse at that time must be due to "special circumstances"). The registration will be renewed only for those goods in connection with which the mark continues to be used in commerce. If the mark is no longer in use, there is no need to renew the registration.

To protect and preserve a trademark, the following guidelines should be observed. First, always use the mark as an adjective and followed by the common, generic term for the product or service ("I will make a XEROX copy"), never as a noun or verb (not "I will make a xerox," nor "I will xerox it"). Second, always attach the appropriate trademark symbol to provide notice that the mark is protected. The symbol "®" may be used only with a federally registered mark, and the symbols "TM" or "SM" are used with an unregistered mark. Third, always print the mark in a distinctive fashion (using, for example, Initial Capital Letters, ALL CAPITAL LETTERS or **bold face fonts**).

As to trademarks used outside the United States, most foreign countries accord rights in a mark to the first person to obtain a registration and most do not require use of the mark as a prerequisite to obtaining a registration as in the United States. However, in most of these countries, the mark must eventually be used within a certain time period in order to maintain rights in the mark.

A foreign filing program can be expensive, with initial costs of filing trademark applications, costs of prosecuting the applications and additional costs for maintenance and renewal of registrations. As a result, registrations usually are sought only in those countries where use of the mark is, or is expected to be, of sufficient magnitude to justify the expense of registration and maintenance. Generally speaking, both in the United States and foreign countries, proper use of a trademark, whether registered or unregistered, is necessary to preserve rights in the mark. Nonuse of a mark, particularly nonuse of the mark with an intention not to resume its use, will result in abandonment of the mark.

TRADE SECRETS

The importance of confidentiality

Valuable intellectual property rights can be forfeited by failing to adhere to adequate standards of confidentiality with respect to a corporation's processes used and products produced. Such rights attach not only to current processes and products, but also to technology developed for use in the future.

Patent rights can be lost by premature disclosure or publication of new ideas, discoveries or inventions to persons not employed by the corporation. In the absence of patent protection, the company runs the risk that it will not be able to prevent a competitor from appropriating its commercial developments. This reduces any return on investment in research and development.

Even if an invention cannot be protected by the patent laws, unauthorized use or disclosure of technical information relating to such inventions may be protected as a trade secret if such information is kept confidential and is disclosed only to those persons who expressly agree (preferably in writing) to keep the information confidential.

Confidential or proprietary information can be described as any knowledge, information or facts concerning any processes, methods, inventions, formulas or devices used by a corporation. An employee should keep confidential any information disclosed to or discovered by the employee through his/her employment with a company, which is not generally known in the industry, about the company's processes, products, and services, including information relating to research, development, inventions, production, purchasing, accounting, engineering, marketing, merchandising and selling.

Protecting information having potential commercial value

Generally speaking, trade secrets comprise information about formulas, business processes, computer programs, methods, machines, manufactures, compositions, inventions, discoveries or the like which a corporation keeps secret or confidential. A corporation should strictly prohibit unauthorized use or disclosure of its trade secrets by anyone. Although trade secret protection is subject to a state's individual laws, to assure that a corporation's trade secrets can be protected from such unauthorized use or disclosure, a corporation and its employees should adhere to at least the following procedures:

1 Employees should execute an agreement binding them not to disclose a corporation's trade secrets to persons not employed by the corporation.
2 Persons not employed by a corporation should not be permitted to have unrestricted access to a corporation's facilities. Consultants should execute a consulting agreement.
3 Information relating to trade secrets should never be divulged to any person not employed by a cor-

poration without careful review by management and counsel. In those circumstances in which information will be revealed, it is of paramount importance that written agreements restricting the receiving party's use and further disclosure of a corporation's trade secrets be signed *before* any information is divulged. Moreover, a corporation's trade secrets should only be disclosed to those employees of the receiving party who have a "need to know," and who are obligated to the receiving party in writing not to use or disclose the trade secrets.
4 All drawings and other materials which include corporate trade secrets should be kept in a secure place and prominently marked:

"CONFIDENTIAL / PROPRIETARY INFORMATION"

Strict adherence to the above procedures, as well as the specific state laws where the technology is used or kept, by all employees will ensure that valuable intellectual property rights resulting from the company's research and development will be protected to the fullest extent possible.

Company policy statement

In the ordinary course of business, it is often necessary for corporate employees to reveal certain types of information to persons outside the corporation. At various times, disclosures must be made to outside contractors or consultants, customers, or design firms. Similarly, disclosures may be made to other corporations or to universities to further mutual interests in joint projects. A corporation's personnel may also participate in seminars, conferences, or trade shows, write technical articles or give speeches to trade or other scientific and business groups.

The release of such information is part of doing business, but extreme care is required to make sure that all such disclosures are properly authorized within the corporation, i.e., by someone who understands the nature and consequences of such a disclosure. Sound judgment is also necessary in determining whether or not such releases may reveal trade secrets or otherwise jeopardize new developments and their protection. The release of all such information should be approved in advance by a designated person who has sufficient knowledge of the technology and legalities involved so that an informed decision can be made as to how the information should be treated.

A corporation should make arrangements intended to provide reasonable assurances that its intellectual property rights are protected. Those reasonable assurances should include measures to prevent the unintended disclosure or publication of confidential information that could prevent a corporation from obtaining legal protection for that information.

To this end, employees should be provided with a company policy statement similar to the statement set forth below. Furthermore, they should be supported and encouraged in their efforts to comply with implementing procedures such as those in the following policy statement. Here is an acceptable form of company policy concerning trade secrets:

> Protecting a company's proprietary information and other intellectual property rights is essential in fulfilling the company's obligations to its employees, stockholders and customers. Each employee is responsible for safeguarding the company's proprietary information and other intellectual property rights, and for preventing any detrimental loss or misuse. The company has adopted general instructions and operating procedures for the purpose of assisting the employees in discharging this responsibility.

Implementing procedures

To aid in implementing a corporation's policy of protecting proprietary information, the following operating instructions can be used.

Prospective employees

1   Screen prospective employees who are being considered for positions in which they will be privy to proprietary information.
2   Require prospective employees to disclose to a corporation any obligations to former employers regarding proprietary information and apprise the prospective employees that information regarding such obligations may be elicited from their former employers.
3   Apprise prospective employees that proprietary information of former employers must remain confidential.
4   Contact former employers of prospective employees to determine if a previous proprietary information agreement may engender conflicts.
5   Place new employees having confidential information of others in positions precluding use of such information for a reasonable period.

Employment agreements

Require employees to sign an agreement with a corporation regarding both disclosure and use of proprietary information in which they agree that during their employment with a corporation and for a reasonable period thereafter they will forgo participating with someone else in activities similar to those they pursued at the corporation.

Training

Provide training programs and presentations informing employees about proprietary information, its value, and its protection.

Departing employees

Impress upon departing employees, in an exit interview, their obligations regarding the corporation's proprietary information and supply them with a departure or exit letter.

Identification and distribution of proprietary information

Recognize proprietary information as it is created, and clearly mark it as such. Declassify proprietary information when no longer confidential. Restrict access to and distribution of proprietary information to those who require it and have undertaken to maintain its confidentiality. Require outsiders to whom proprietary information is submitted to sign an agreement in advance of the disclosure which obligates them to maintain the information in confidence. The advice of legal counsel should be obtained as to an appropriate agreement for the circumstances. When proprietary information is disclosed (pursuant to agreement, of course), make and retain a written record of the information disclosed.

Storage and disposal of proprietary information

Store proprietary information in a secure place, accessible only to designated personnel, and dispose of proprietary information, e.g., documents, carefully to preclude its being salvaged or reconstructed. Consider installing security devices or similar systems for safeguarding proprietary information.

Treatment of proprietary information of others

When a corporation has entered into a confidentiality agreement with a third party to receive proprietary information from the third party, employees to whom the information is disclosed should be advised of the terms of the confidentiality agreement and that they are bound by them. Proprietary information received from others should be treated with the same care as a corporation's own proprietary information.

General guidelines for protecting proprietary information

Employment agreements and assignment of inventions

At the very least, designated employees should be required to sign an agreement with the company regarding confidential information, inventions, and trade secrets. It is wise to have *all employees* execute such agreements prior to commencing employment.

Designated employees should be primarily technically trained individuals who are most likely to invent, e.g., key operating personnel, research and development department technical employees, graduate engineers, chemists, and managerial personnel, etc., involved in technical areas.

Invention disclosure forms

Employees should be encouraged to advise their supervisors of their new ideas and developments. If the supervisor believes that the new idea or development may be worthwhile, an invention disclosure form should be completed and submitted to a designated recipient who determines whether patent protection should be sought. Failure to do so promptly can lead to a waiver of both domestic and foreign patent rights. A positive review should be conducted by supervisors on a periodic basis to determine whether any potentially patentable products, machines, or processes have been created. Alternatively, if no supervisors are part of the corporate structure, these forms may be directly submitted to the designated patent individual.

Preclude access to proprietary information

Plant visits by non-employees should be carefully controlled, and access by visitors to restricted areas or restricted information should be governed by a written agreement with the visitor. Valuable papers should not be left unprotected where others may see them. Desks and files should be kept locked when not in use, particularly at night.

Prevent inadvertent disclosure of proprietary information

Employees should be instructed to eliminate careless chatter and idle shop talk, particularly outside of the office or in the presence of non-employees.

Conversations and negotiations with non-employees, particularly sales representatives, should not reveal company processes or developments. Outsiders should not have access to company files or company documents that could or would reveal trade secrets or other confidential information. It is only under special circumstances, upon advice of counsel and approval of management, that any such information should be revealed to non-employees. In such circumstances, a written agreement should be obtained from each non-employee whereby he or she agrees to hold such information confidential and never use it or reveal it to third persons without the prior written approval of the corporation. It is important that such agreements carefully define the information not to be revealed in order to gain maximum protection.

Corporations disclose and receive valuable proprietary information in many different contexts, including its dealings with consultants, customers, suppliers and joint venture partners. The appropriate agreement for use in each case should be obtained from legal counsel. For example, technical consultants, independent contractors and the like should be required to sign secrecy agreements to restrict their use and revelation of confidential corporate information and trade secrets and to limit their retention of any documentation containing such information. Outside consultants should also be required to sign an agreement insuring that inventions, discoveries, and trade secrets made by such consultants while performing the work for which they are retained become the property of the corporation. Any disclosure of technical information (including the delivery of samples) to a customer should also be preceded by a signed secrecy agreement. The ownership of discoveries made by a customer while testing samples from a corporation should usually be addressed in a signed secrecy agreement. Again, advice of legal counsel should be obtained for an appropriate agreement under the particular circumstances.

Of course, all agreements should be signed by all the parties *prior to disclosure* of any confidential corporate information.

Competition

A format should be created for reviewing the purchase orders of companies which contract to have research and/or development work performed by a corporation to ensure that such work remains the property of the corporation

Competitors should be monitored by a person designated to keep abreast of technological advances in areas of interest to a corporation. This could entail a review of the Official Gazette of the US Patent Office on a weekly basis to review summaries of patents issued in technologies of interest to a corporation.

A policy should be maintained to ensure that a corporation's patent numbers are marked on any patented products. This will place potential infringers on notice of the patent. Failure to do so may result in waiver of the ability to collect damages from an infringer.

Any existing licenses of proprietary information should be reviewed and revised, if necessary, to police their performance and ensure compliance with current laws.

Patent rights should be reviewed periodically. A cost/benefit analysis of such patents should be carried out in view of the periodic patent maintenance taxes required in most countries and the future prospects of the invention.

Develop procedures for unsolicited outside submissions

It is advisable *not* to accept non-public information from outside a corporation under any circumstances without prior approval by management and legal counsel. Therefore, managers should be made aware and kept aware that unsolicited ideas can be a source of litigation regardless of their merit or value. Receipt of an unsolicited idea should be treated in accordance with the following procedures.

It is frequently the case that outside "inventors" greatly overvalue the merit of their ideas. Ideas may come in many forms, such as technical ideas, marketing plans, accounting methods, etc. Any unsolicited idea received should be forwarded to a designated supervisor who should forward it to legal counsel, *without prior review or consideration of the idea by the recipient.* Under *no* circumstances should a copy of the submitted materials be retained in any files other than those of legal counsel. Legal counsel should forward the original materials to a manager with appropriate responsibility with an unsolicited idea form letter. A copy of the submitted idea should be kept in a file in legal counsel's office, inaccessible to corporate employees.

The unsolicited idea letter should designate the manager to whom the idea should be resubmitted by the submitter. If the idea is resubmitted with a signed unsolicited idea letter, distribution of the submitted materials should be kept to a minimum number of persons consistent with obtaining appropriate evaluation of the idea. Persons reviewing the idea should be aware that distribution of this material must be kept to a minimum. Copies of these materials should not be kept in the reviewers' files unless it is determined that the company will use the idea.

Limited distribution of the idea material will assist an "independent discovery" or "public domain" defense, if a rejected idea or similar idea is later independently discovered by a corporation or comes into the public domain and the corporation subsequently determines the idea to be useful. If the idea or a similar idea is already known to the corporation, the reviewer should, if possible, record where the information related to this idea is documented [e.g., laboratory notebook number and pages] and return this information to legal counsel. Likewise, if the reviewer believes the idea is in the public domain, the reviewer should record the basis of his/her belief. All materials related to rejected ideas should be returned to legal counsel for filing. Originals of submitted materials for rejected ideas should, if possible, be returned to the submitter.

Export of technical data

US federal law and the national laws of European and other countries prohibit the export of certain categories of technical data, unless the export is authorized by a license. A license usually can be easily obtained within a short period of time. Employees should be advised that legal counsel should be consulted before the export of any technical data to any foreign country.

DETECTING AND PROTECTING AGAINST INFRINGEMENT OF OTHERS' RIGHTS

The following procedures can be implemented to help ensure that a corporation avoids transgressing or infringing upon the rights of others:

1 No new product or process should be commercially made, used or sold without ensuring that it does not infringe upon the rights of others, or without obtaining the appropriate rights therefor. Patent counsel should be consulted to perform such clearances.

2 The Official Gazette of the US Patent Office should be monitored to help avoid any infringement problem, or to obtain early notice of activities of others in which a corporation is interested. (As previously explained, a designated person can perform this function in the first instance with guidance from the corporation's patent counsel.)

3 Language in routine agreements, such as purchase orders, should ensure that a corporation owns any proprietary rights in anything developed in the course of fulfilling the order, and one individual should be assigned responsibility for monitoring such agreements.

4 A corporation should establish a policy to ensure that purchase orders of others are reviewed to protect against infringing upon the rights of third parties.

5 A corporation should seek indemnification from suppliers of products, where those products are not manufactured according to a corporation's own specifications, to protect a corporation from liability for any infringement of the rights of others.

International and European Patents

INTRODUCTION

As civilization developed from hunting, to agriculture, to specialization and trade, there also developed the artisan or tradesman whose skill and tool-making or weaving, for example, caused him to devote more time to his trade than to the hunting or growing of food. He would obtain food in barter but at the same time he did not find it advantageous to teach his trade to all comers. He would perhaps pass it on to his son or other members of his family.

Regardless of any "natural" rights that artisans or tradesmen had in their own ideas, skills and inventions, these rights could not be profitably used without some means of protection and enforcement due to the "natural" right of others to copy what they observed. Thus, a little later in history, we find these artisans grouped together and organized in guilds for mutual aid and protection. Protecting their skills by secrecy and improving and maintaining the quality of workmanship were the chief functions of the guilds which also regulated hours of labor and terms of admission to the guild, including apprenticeship.

This organized effort of the guilds to protect and promote the skills and knowledge of master artisans is the first known attempt to provide trade secret protection. The guilds also developed and enforced rules for the fair conduct of commerce and trade which were the genesis of the law of unfair competition.

The guilds used pictures or symbols on the goods produced by their members to identify the goods and their producer, provide a check on qual-ity, identify imitations, and discourage competition by non-members. Incidentally, the guilds virtually never used words on goods because most consumers were illiterate. Thus, trademarks were a part of the organized efforts of the artisans and guilds in Europe.

The restrictive power of the organized guilds of artisans was felt to be inimical to the state and, hence, some means was sought to encourage the disclosure of the skills of the artisans, as well as to foster the creation and importation of new ideas and devices for the benefit of the general economy.

Thus, kings, emperors and organized states began to encourage the creation and disclosure of new ideas and devices by providing rewards and the right to exclude others from using the new ideas and devices for a limited time. These early efforts to reward and encourage the disclosure of the intellectual and artistic creations and discoveries of authors and inventors are the beginning of copyrights and patents. From these early efforts of encouraging and protecting intellectual property the distinct areas of legal protection of trade secrets, unfair competition, trademarks, patents and copyrights have evolved.

TYPES OF INTELLECTUAL PROPERTY RIGHTS

"Utility patents" protect technical inventions which are new, useful, and non-obvious *vis-à-vis* the prior art. Articles of manufacture, compositions of matter, processes and, in Europe, uses can all be inventions qualifying for registration as a patent. Utility patents have a duration of twenty years from the date of filing.

"Utility models" protect technical inventions which are new, useful and non-obvious *vis-à-vis* the prior art. Articles of manufacture and compositions of matter can all be inventions qualifying for registrations as utility models, but *neither* inventions of processes nor inventions of uses can qualify as utility models. Utility models have a duration of a maximum of ten years from the date of filing in Germany and a maximum of fifteen years from the date of filing in Japan.

"Design Patents" (also "Design Models") protect ornamental features of articles of manufacture (industrial designs) which are new, ornamental, and non-obvious. Design of fabrics, furniture, cars and kitchen appliances are examples of designs qualifying for protection as design patents. Design patents have a duration of fourteen years from the date of grant in the United States and a maximum of fifteen years from date of filing (DE, JP).

"Trademarks" protect identification symbols and features which are distinctive (and do not have to be kept free for the competitors.) Names such as "Coca-Cola" or "Kellogg's" and signs such as the "Mercedes star" are all examples of symbols qualifying for trademark protection. Trademarks have a duration of initially ten years (with unlimited renewal possibilities) and, in most countries, requirements concerning use of the trademark.

"Copyrights" are expressions in tangible media. Literary works, musical works, dramatic works, choreographic works, graphics, sculptures and motion pictures are all expressions in tangible media protected as copyrights. Copyrights have a duration of a maximum of seventy-five years from date of filing in the United States and seventy years after death of creator in Germany.

"Trade Secrets" are information and know-how. Inventions qualifying for protection as patents also qualify for protection as trade secrets, but only for such time as information concerning the invention meets certain secrecy requirements. For example, as soon as an invention application is published, the invention no longer qualifies for protection as a trade secret. The manufacturing process for Coca-Cola is probably one of the most famous trade secrets. Trade secrets have an indefinite, potentially unlimited duration – as long as the information qualifies for statutory protection.

REGISTRATION REQUIREMENTS IN GENERAL

The requirement and, in the absence of a requirement, the availability of registration with government authorities for each of the various types of intellectual property rights is summarized in Tables 19.1 and 19.2.

The requirement of a government examination in respect of registrations is also summarized below.

REGISTRATION REQUIREMENTS FOR UTILITY PATENTS

As noted before, a secret is information which the possessor has entrusted to nobody. While trust of fellow human beings has not completely deteriorated, nevertheless, the statement illustrates that as a number of persons taken into confidence increases, and as the value of the information increases, the difficulty of maintaining secrecy increases. Without casting aspersions on the general level of morality, it may be observed that in an increasingly mobile society, certain kinds of loyalty often do not have a chance to develop.

In contrast, the patent system encourages disclosure to achieve its primary purpose of advancing the

Required	Available
Trademarks (except US and UK)	Trademarks (US and UK)
Copyrights (except US and UK)	Copyrights (US and UK)
Utility patents	
Design patents	
Utility models	

Table 19.1 Registration of intellectual property rights.

Examination	No examination
Utility patents	Utility models (DE, JP)
Design patents (US, JP)	Design patents (DE)
Trademarks	Copyrights (US)
	Trade secrets

Table 19.2 Examination before grant of registrations (US, DE, EU, JP).

practical parts by increasing public knowledge. It allows free use by the public of a new invention or idea after the inventor has enjoyed exclusive protection for a limited time.

In the case of a utility patent, the grant shall include "the right to exclude others for making, using, offering to sell or selling the invention." The protection is limited to the territory of the state which granted the patent. Thus, single patent applications will have to be filed in each of the countries of interest. If an invention is of worldwide interest, e.g., certain medicaments, a high financial investment is required to obtain world-wide patent protection.

Some procedures have been created to simplify and render more economical the obtaining of protection for inventions where protection is sought in several countries, and to facilitate and accelerate access by the public to the technical information contained in documents describing new inventions.

Internationally

The Patent Corporation Treaty (PCT) is an international agreement that provides for the filing of patent applications on the same invention in a number of member countries. The members include numerous manufacturing-countries around the world, such as the United States, Japan, and all Western European countries. The international patent application must be filed in a receiving office, such as the United States Patent and Trademark Office (for US citizens) or the European Patent Office (for EU citizens). At the time of filing, the international patent application must designate the member countries where patent protection is desired.

An international searching authority, such as the United States Patent and Trademark Office or the European Patent Office, conducts a prior art search relating to the invention claimed in the international application. An international search report is issued listing relevant prior art documents. Within a certain term, the applicant must send to each designated Office of a member country any required translation and the required filing fee. Each designated Office determines patentability based on its own patent laws.

Most countries in Western and Eastern Europe – not just members of the European Union – are members of the European Patent Convention.[1] To secure patent rights, an applicant files a European patent application at the European Patent Office, located in Munich, Germany, designating some or all of the countries under the Convention. The patent is examined and granted on the basis of a uniform body of substantive patent law. If the European patent application is allowed, it is forwarded to the designated European countries where it becomes a national patent without further examination.

In Europe

European patents are granted for any inventions which can be used for industrial application, which are new and which involve an inventive step (are non-obvious).

Invention

The EPC does not define "invention" but contains a list of items which cannot be regarded as inventions, or as inventions which can be used for industrial application. Particular attention should be paid to the following three fields:

1 Programs for computers are not regarded as inventions insofar as they are claimed as such. However, if the subject matter claimed adds a contribution of a technical character to the known art, a patent should not be refused simply because a computer program is involved. This means that, e.g., machine processes of manufacture or control processes controlled by a computer program may be patented.
2 Methods for treatment of the human or animal body by surgery or therapy and diagnostic methods practiced on the human or animal body are not regarded as inventions which can be used for industrial application.
3 Plant or animal varieties or essentially biological processes for the production of plants or animals are expressly excluded from patentability. The exclusion does not apply to microbiological processes or the products thereof.

Novelty

An invention is considered to be "new" or novel if it does not form part of the state of the art. The definition of the state of the art in the EPC amounts to "absolute novelty," i.e. the state of the art is held to comprise everything made available to the public by means of written or oral description, by use, or in any other way, before the date of filing or the priority date.

Additionally, the content of European patent applications filed prior to the date of filing or priority date and published on or after that date is considered in determining the state of the art for the later application, but only insofar as a Contracting State designated in respect to the later application was also designated in the earlier application as published (first-to-file principle). The whole content of the earlier application as filed is prejudicial to novelty.

Finally, within the period of twelve months from the date of filing an application for a patent in or for any country party to the "Paris Convention for the protection of Industrial Property," an applicant for a European patent or utility model *for the same invention* may claim the "priority" of that patent application, i.e., the applicant for a European patent may claim the date of the earlier application as the date of filing of the European patent application for the purposes of novelty and inventive step.

Inventive step

An invention will be considered as involving an "inventive step" if, having regard to the state of the art (not including priority rights as explained in the previous paragraph), the invention is "not obvious to a person skilled in the art." The inventive step requirement is intended to prevent exclusive rights forming barriers to normal and routine developments.

For determining whether or not the invention involves an inventive step various factors are taken into account, such as unforeseen technical effects produced by a new combination of known elements or by selection of particular operating conditions within a known range, the degree of difficulty the person skilled in the art must overcome, and secondary considerations such as the fact that the invention solves a long-standing technical problem which there have been many attempts to solve.

THE PROCEDURE UNDER THE PATENT COOPERATION TREATY

For international applications under the PCT the EPO may be the *Receiving Office*, *International Searching*

Authority (ISA) and *International Preliminary Examining Authority* (IPEA). During this phase the designated or elected (national or regional) Office is not allowed to process the application.

The EPO as a PCT receiving office

The international application has to be filed with the national office of the PCT contracting state of which the applicant is resident or national. Applicants from the EPC contracting states may also file international applications directly with the EPO acting as a receiving Office, provided the law of the contracting state in question does not prescribe that such applications be filed with the national office. If the EPO is the receiving Office, the international application must be filed either in English, French or German.

The EPO as an international searching authority

The international search report is established and transmitted to the applicant and the International Bureau within three months of the receipt of the search copy.

The EPO's competence as an ISA is not restricted to international applications from the EPC contracting states or to Euro-PCT applications. The EPO also acts as an ISA for other international applications if the relevant receiving Office has designated the EPO as ISA. For example, US applicants may choose between the USPTO and the EPO as ISA.

The EPO as an international preliminary examining authority

It is not the aim of the international preliminary examination to grant or refuse a patent, but to issue a preliminary and non-binding opinion on whether the invention appears to be novel, to involve an inventive step and to be industrially applicable. The PCT criteria applied correspond to those of the EPC.

The EPO's competence as an IPEA is not restricted to international applications from the EPC contracting states or to Euro-PCT applications. The EPO also acts as an IPEA for other international applications if the relevant receiving Office has desig-

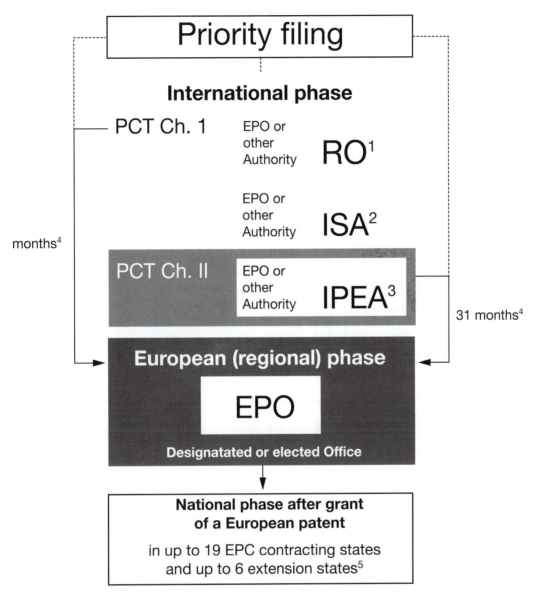

Priority filing

International phase

PCT Ch. 1   EPO or other Authority RO^1

EPO or other Authority ISA^2

PCT Ch. II   EPO or other Authority $IPEA^3$

months[4]

31 months[4]

European (regional) phase

EPO

Designatated or elected Office

National phase after grant of a European patent

in up to 19 EPC contracting states and up to 6 extension states[5]

[1] RO   = Receiving Office.
[2] ISA = International Searching Authority
     (to be designated by the RO or chosen by the applicant).
[3] IPEA = International Preliminary Examining Authority
     (as for ISA; EPO only when ISA = EPO or AT, ES, SE Patent Office).
[4] As from the date of filing or earliest date of priority. The 21-month time limit applies entry into the regional phase before the EPO as designated Office (Ch. I). the 31-month time limit applies before the EPO as elected Office (Ch. II).
[5] Based on bilateral agreements with the EPO.

Figure 19.1 The Euro–PCT phases

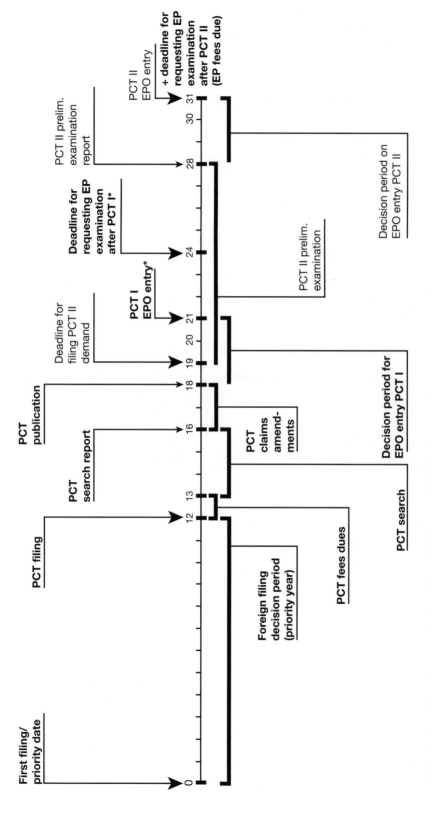

* The designation dees are due together with the examination fee.

Figure 19.2 Utility Patents. Timeline for PCT/Euro-PCT applications at end of priority year.

nated the EPO as IPEA. For example, US applicants may choose between the USPTO and the EPO as IPEA in connection with the choice of ISA.

The international preliminary examination procedure

Every applicant must indicate in the demand for international preliminary examination whether it is to be based on the international application as originally filed or whether it should take account of amendments to claims filed after receipt of the International Search Report. If there are no objections to the international application on the grounds of lack of novelty, inventive step or industrial applicability, or on any other grounds, the international preliminary examination report is established immediately. If there are objections the EPO issues a written opinion. This sets for the applicant a time limit within which to reply. The time limit for the reply is usually two months but may be extended to a maximum of three months at the applicant's request.

The international preliminary examination report is then established and transmitted to the applicant and the International Bureau. The applicant then has no further opportunity to submit comments to the IPEA (but may do so in the national or regional phase). Applicants who filed the demand for international preliminary examination in due time (i.e., within nineteen months from the first priority date) thereby obtain an extension of the time limit for entry into the regional phase. They may decide on the basis of the results of the international preliminary examination report whether and where they wish to pursue their international application further and take the national/regional route.

The procedure for the grant of patents is an examination procedure beginning with a formalities examination and a mandatory search report.

Regional phase of international patent applications

An international application, for which the EPO acts as *designated Office* subsequent to PCT Chapter I proceedings or *elected Office* subsequent to PCT Chapter II proceedings is deemed to be a European patent application. If the international search report was not drawn up by the EPO itself (or by the Austrian, Spanish or Swedish Patent Office) a supplementary European search report is drawn up; otherwise the application is passed on for substantive examination.

Where the international preliminary examination report has been drawn up by the EPO and contains objections, and the applicant does not file any amended documents on entry into the European phase, the first communication will generally only refer to this report. If new facts relevant to assessing patentability are in evidence (from a supplementary European search report, for example), it is possible that the EPO may depart from the opinion expressed in its international preliminary examination report.

The remaining procedure corresponds to the grant procedure for European patents. After grant of a European patent, it must be transferred into national patents in the designated states to become valid there. In many instances this requires the translation of the patent into the official language of the designated state.

PROCEDURE AT THE EUROPEAN PATENT OFFICE

The examination of the filing

The first part of the procedure is carried out by the EPO branch at The Hague and Berlin sub-office. It comprises the examination on filing, the formalities examination, the preparation of the European search report and the publication of the application and the search report.

During the examination on filing the EPO examines whether the application contains: an indication that a European patent is sought, the designation of at least one Contracting State, particulars identifying the applicant, a description and one or more claims.

If a date of filing has been accorded, the Receiving Section will check for compliance with other formal requirements such as filing of the abstract, contents of the request for grant of a European patent, priority, designation of inventor. Where the receiving Section notes that there are deficiencies which may be corrected it will give the applicant the opportunity to do so. The search is performed at the same time as the formalities examination.

The European search report is drawn up on the basis of the claims with due regard to the description

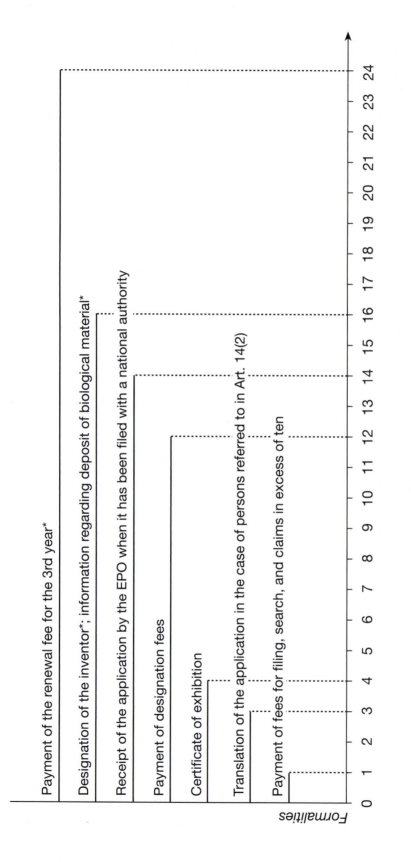

Figure 19.3 Time limits laid down by the EPC computed from the date of filing a European patent application for which no priority is claimed

0 – Filing of the European patent application

* – The time limit is computed from the date of filing, which can be later than the date on which the application was actually filed

and any drawings. It mentions those documents available to the EPO at the time of drawing up the report which may be taken into consideration in assessing novelty and inventive step. The European search report does not contain reasons and expresses no opinion whatever as to the patentability of the invention covered by the application. Immediately after it has been drawn up the European search report is transmitted to the applicant together with a copy of any cited documents. The European search report is published in the European Patent Bulletin, usually together with the application.

Substantive examination and possible grant

The second part of the procedure, handled by the Examining Divisions in Munich, comprises substantive examination and grant. An Examining Division consists of three technical examiners, who may be joined by a legally qualified examiner if necessary. Nevertheless, the processing of the application prior to a final decision is normally entrusted entirely to one technical examiner, who issues the necessary communications and keeps in touch with the applicant, normally in writing, but also by telephone and in informal interviews.

The request for examination can be filed by the applicant up to the end of a period of six months after the date on which the European Patent Bulletin mentions the publication of the European search report. After the request for examination has been made, the EPO examines in the light of the search report whether the European patent application and the invention to which it relates meet the requirements of the EPC, and in particular whether the invention meets the criteria of novelty and inventive step.

Following the receipt of the search report and prior to the examiner's first communication with the applicant, the latter may file substantive comments on the search report and amendments to the description, claims or drawings. If there are any objections to the application, the examiner responsible within the Examining Division invites the applicant, in a first reasoned communication, to file observations and, where appropriate, to amend the description, the claims and the drawings. The applicant must endeavor to reply fully to the examiner's objections. The guiding principle of the examination procedure is that a decision

on whether to grant a patent or refuse the application should be reached in as few actions as possible. If the applicant fails to reply to this or further communications within the specified time limit, the application is deemed to be withdrawn.

If, after examining the applicant's response, the examiner still considers that the application is not yet ready for grant, he continues with the examination procedure by dispatching a further communication or holding a telephone conversation or interview with the applicant, according to the circumstances. The applicant may at any time request oral proceedings.

If the Examining Division considers that a European patent cannot be granted, it will refuse the application. The decision is issued by the Examining Division as a whole and must contain the reasons for refusal. These reasons may only be based on grounds in respect of which the applicant has had an opportunity to put forward comments.

If the Examining Division considers that the application and the invention to which it relates meet the requirements of the EPC it will decide to grant a European patent, provided that the applicant approves the text in which it is intended to grant the patent, that the fees due (fees for grant and printing and, where applicable, renewal fees and claims) have been paid in time and that a translation of the claims in the other two official languages of the EPO has been filed in time.

The Examining Division first informs the applicant of the text in which it intends to grant the European patent, requesting him to indicate his approval within a specified period (currently set at four months).

Only when the applicant has approved the text communicated to him, or the Examining Division has agreed to allow further amendments, does the Examining Division set the applicant a non-extendible period of (currently) three months within which to pay the fees for grant and printing and any claims fees due, and to file a translation of the claims intended to serve as the basis for grant in the two EPO official languages (English, French, German) other than the language of the proceedings.

The opposition period

The third part of the procedure consists of the opposition proceedings in which, for the first time during the procedure, third parties (competitors) take part.

The examination of oppositions is handled by the Opposition Divisions in Munich, which are composed on the same basis as the Examining Divisions.

Within nine months from the publication of the mention of the grant of the European patent. any person may give notice to the EPO of opposition to the European patent granted. However, a European patent cannot be opposed by its own proprietor.

Opposition can only be filed on the grounds that: the subject-matter of the patent is not patentable (not novel or not based on an inventive step); the European patent does not disclose the invention in a manner sufficiently clear and complete for it to be carried out by a person skilled in the art; the subject-matter of the European patent extends beyond the content of the application as filed.

The notice of opposition must be filed in a written reasoned statement within the time allowed. This means that the opponent must give at least one ground for opposition under Article 100 EPC and indicate the facts, evidence and arguments presented in support of the ground(s). Otherwise the notice of opposition is rejected as inadmissible.

As soon as the EPO receives the notice of opposition it is communicated to the proprietor of the patent and the opposition is examined for admissibility. Deficiencies in the notice of opposition are communicated to the opponent. If the deficiencies thus notified are not corrected in due time, the opposition will be rejected as inadmissible.

Immediately after expiry of the opposition period or the period laid down for remedying deficiencies or for presentation of evidence, the proprietor of the patent will be invited to file his observations and to file amendments, where appropriate, within a period to be fixed by the EPO (normally four months). Amendments to European patents are admissible only if they are occasioned by grounds for opposition.

Once these preparatory steps have been completed the Opposition Division will examine whether the grounds for opposition prejudice the maintenance of the European patent. If it sees fit, it will invite the parties to file observations, within a period fixed by it, on communications from another party or issued by itself.

At the request of either one party or EPO (where it sees a need), oral proceedings may take place. Together with the summons the Opposition Division will draw attention to and explain in an annexed note the points which in its opinion need to be discussed for the purposes of the decision to be taken.

Normally, the annex will also contain the provisional and non-binding opinion of the Opposition Division on the positions adopted by the parties and in particular on amendments filed by the proprietor of the patent. At the same time a final date will be fixed for making written submissions or filing amendments in preparation for the oral proceedings. New facts and evidence presented after that date need not be considered, unless admitted on the grounds that the subject of the proceedings has changed.

If the Opposition Division concludes that the grounds for opposition prejudice the maintenance of the European patent, it will revoke the patent. If it concludes that the grounds for opposition do not prejudice the maintenance of the patent as granted, it will reject the opposition.

If the Opposition Division is of the opinion that the patent can be maintained in amended form, the Opposition Division immediately issues an interlocutory decision stating that, taking into consideration the amendments made by the proprietor of the patent, the patent and the invention to which it relates meet the requirements of the EPC. An interlocutory decision of this nature, against which separate appeal is allowed, is issued in all cases where a patent is maintained in amended form.

The appeals period

The appeals procedure constitutes a special procedural phase. Appeals can be filed during the three aforementioned parts of the procedure against decisions of the Receiving Section, the Examining Divisions, the Opposition Divisions and the Legal Division. Decisions regarding appeals are taken by the Boards of Appeal, also situated in Munich. Notice of appeal must be filed in writing within two months after the date of notification of the decision appealed from. Within four months after the date of notification of the decision, a written statement setting out the grounds of appeal must be filed.

The Boards of Appeal deal with appeals as the second and final instance. After the statement of grounds and any observations by opponents have been examined, the Board of Appeal will give the appellant any necessary directions for the filing of further observations. Oral proceedings take place either at the instance of the European Patent Office or at the request of any party to the proceedings.

When the Board decides on the appeal, it may either exercise any power within the competence of the department which was responsible for the decision appealed or remit the case to that department for further prosecution. In the latter case, that department is bound by the decision of the Board of Appeal.

MAINTENANCE

Renewal fees must be paid to the EPO in respect of European patent applications. These fees are due in respect of the third year and each subsequent year, calculated from the date of filing of the application. The last renewal fee payable in respect of a European patent application is that for the year in which the mention of the grant of the patent is published. Renewal fees for subsequent years during the term of the European patent must be paid to the national industrial property office of each designated State. Current renewal fees for the European patent applications in euros: €383 for the third year, €409 for the fourth year, €434 for the fifth year, €715 for the sixth year, €741 for the seventh year, €766 for the eighth year, €971 for the ninth year and €1,022 for the tenth year and each subsequent year.

INFRINGEMENT

Litigation procedures

Generally European patents must be enforced separately in each contracting state. Pan European deci-sions may be obtained only in particular cases. As indicated in Table 19.3, the different European states have different procedural laws. Accordingly, forum shopping becomes very important.

Remedies

There are various remedies available from national courts in Europe in respect of patent infringement. Those remedies include:

1 injunction, i.e., a final judgement that the infringer must stop the infringement indefinitely;
2 preliminary injunction, i.e., the infringer must stop the infringement in anticipation of, and until, a final judgement.

Infringement is assessed in speeded procedures:

3 damages, i.e., lost revenues minus costs or a reasonable royalty;
4 trial costs, i.e., the losing party must reimburse the trial costs of the winning party; and
5 destruction, i.e., the infringing goods are destroyed (Table 19.4).

INTELLECTUAL PROPERTY STRATEGIES

Patents enable companies to stake out and defend a proprietary market advantage. That is their most powerful benefit. Properly deployed, patents can translate into category-leading products, enhanced market share, and high margins. In some cases, they

EU State	Specialized court	Preservation of evidence (discovery)	Time from writ to trial	Trial costs
Denmark	No	No	1–4 years	8,000–150,000
United Kingdom	Yes	Yes	0.5–3 years	150,000–1,800,000
France	Yes	Yes	2–3 years	180,00–55,000
Germany	Yes	No	about 12 months	30,000–500,000
The Netherlands	Yes	No	Few weeks up to 18 months	up to 55,000
Italy	No	Yes	2–4 years	20,000–50,000
Spain	No	Yes	1.5–3 years	15,000-30,000
Sweden	No	No	2–3 years	$ 2,000-65,000

Table 19.3 Litigation procedures

EU State	Injunction	Damages	Trial costs	Decision published
Denmark	Yes	Yes	Yes	No
United Kingdom	Yes	Yes	Yes	No
France	Yes	Yes	Yes	Yes
Germany	Yes	Yes	Yes	No
The Netherlands	Yes	Yes	Yes	No
Italy	Yes	Yes	Yes (partially)	Yes
Spain	Yes	Yes	Yes	Yes
Sweden	Yes	Yes	Yes	No

Table 19.4 Patent infringement remedies

can even serve as the foundations for a new industry (as the original xerography patent).

But they can do more. They can serve as an income source since they can be subject to licenses or they can serve as "currency" for exploiting new market opportunities. Bill Gates, the co-founder of Microsoft, once told *The Washington Post* that patents are "the new gold rush." Indeed, Microsoft, with formerly only a handful patents, is rushing to establish a huge IP portfolio. The software company was issued 199 US patents in 1997. A patent portfolio needs to be carefully managed to serve all these purposes.

The Dow experience

Out-licensing

By the early 1990s, Dow Chemical Corporation had evolved into a $20 billion plastics and chemicals powerhouse owning some 10,000 (global) patents and more than 120 process technologies.

Deeply embedded in the company's culture were beliefs that Dow must protect its technologies solely for Dow use, and that out-licensing to third parties represented a threat to Dow's integrity. In 1994, Dow Chemical Company was generating $25 million in licensing income from its portfolio, without putting any focused effort on licensing.

By early 1994, a handful of Dow managers had begun to believe that a licensing component could be woven into a new strategic initiative. An early key to the change came when individual Dow businesses were asked to manage their own IP portfolios and become accountable for IP as a part of their asset base. Each business took inventory of its intellectual property and then established structures and processes to manage it.

In May 1995, the Dow Technology Licensing and Catalyst Business formed, with a staff of four, and key legal, R&D, and manufacturing support. Its assignment was to create a new business platform focused on extracting value from intellectual property. It was the corporation's goal to earn $125 million in annual licensing fees by the year 2000. The company reached and surpassed that goal in 1997.

On the other hand, the Dow Chemical Company estimates that from 1986 to 1996, it reduced its patent maintenance fees by $40 million by reviewing its portfolio and eliminating patents that were no longer useful.

In-licensing

Further, Dow research and manufacturing were not able to optimize the cost of fabrication of the chlorine cell which Dow developed, while competitors continued to optimize their technology and cost position. A license agreement with Asahi made it possible for Dow to achieve cutting edge chlor alkali art quickly and at a lower initial construction cost. This also gave Dow researchers a leg up in integrating this technology into traditional Dow strengths. This scenario has since been successfully repeated in polypropylene, ethylbenzene and hydrocarbon resins.

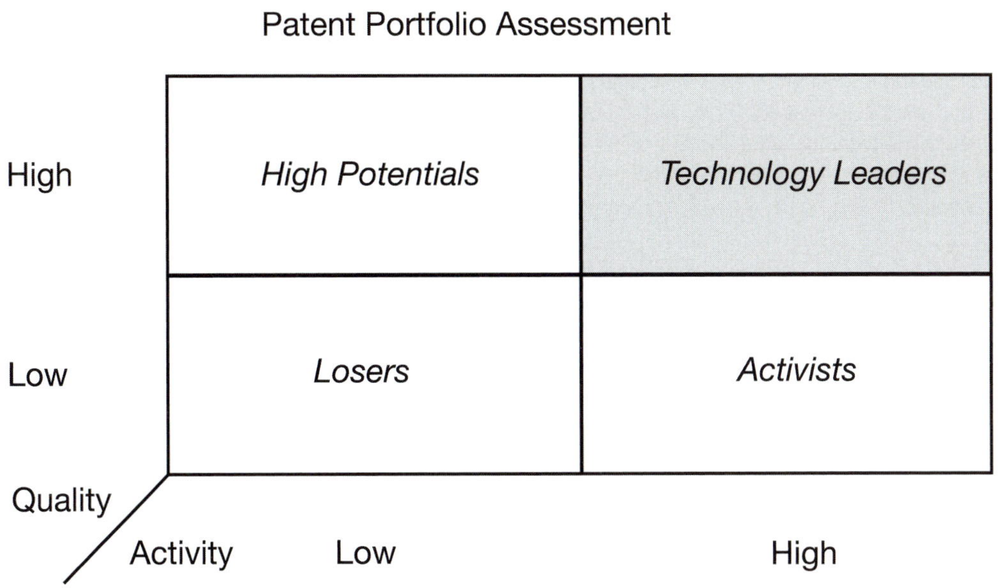

Patent Portfolio Assessment

	Low	High
High	*High Potentials*	*Technology Leaders*
Low	*Losers*	*Activists*

Quality / Activity   Low   High

Figure 19.4 Patent Portfolio Assessment

There were seven key building blocks of early success: a clear strategy focused on creating value from advantaged technology, the development of a formal licensing process and standardized technology valuation tools, the realization that in-licensing could also be a powerful value creator, the decision to take a broad intellectual property managing approach, top management support and commitment, access to essential resources and expertise (the right people), bottom-line accountability through a licensing profit and loss statement.

Patents can be subject to licenses. Licenses can be: exclusive, non-exclusive, limited to a specific technical field or use and limited to a specific territory. Patents can also be sold and assigned to others. In this case all rights are transferred to the buyer. Other forms of agreements are cooperation agreements, development contracts, settlement agreements following infringement and know-how transfer agreements. Anti-trust regulations may apply.

MANAGEMENT TOOLS

There are, generally speaking, five tools for managing patents: patent portfolio evaluation, draft and file patent applications, manage and coordinate patent prosecution, EPO opposition procedures and IP Committees.

Patent portfolio management

Patent portfolio management involves three steps. The first step is assessing how many patents your firm owns and to which classes of the international patent classification they belong. Most of the patents probably belong to a small number of classes only.

The second step involves identifying the companies having the highest number of patent applications in these classes. Competitors, including new and potential competitors, can be identified in this way.

The third step is comparing patent activities and patent quality with your competitors and creating a graph showing the patent activities and patent quality of each competitor (Figure 19.4).

Technology leaders

Companies in the upper right corner have at the same time high patent activity and high patent quality. They determine the technological progress in the technical area and are price-setters.

Activists

Companies in the lower right corner have high patent activity, but low patent quality. They just follow the technology in the technical area and are price-takers. They often spend much money on patents they do not really need.

High potentials

Companies in the upper left corner have low patent activity but own patents of high quality. Mostly these companies are more successful than "activists."

Losers

Companies in the lower left corner can often not follow the technology. In these companies R&D is not sufficient or not sufficiently productive. R&D investments should be increased and R&D processes should be checked.

Internal controls

Structures need to be created within which engineers, scientists and software programmers can create and are motivated to communicate their ideas to the company.

Ideas can exist everywhere in the corporation. Accordingly, reward programs help to motivate employees to communicate their ideas to the company.

Patent applications are necessarily filed with the help of the inventor(s). Structures (forms) are important which enable the inventor to communicate their ideas to the management or patent department and which ensures a standard evaluation of the ideas.

It must be decided where to file. It does not make sense to file a patent application in countries where neither the company nor the competitors are active. PCT and EPC procedures help to postpone that decision up to the entry of the national or regional phase or the validation of the patent, respectively. At the same time, with these procedures also an opinion on the validity of the patent is obtained. The patent offices of many countries follow the decision of the European Patent Office. It should be ensured, for example, that the wording of the claims is similar throughout the world. Otherwise, problems may occur when licensing said patent. Therefore, it is necessary to coordinate prosecution.

Anticipating European patent oppositions

Opposition procedures are a good opportunity to find out about the validity of competitors' patents. The costs of opposition proceedings are reasonable, and low in comparison to infringement procedures in the USA. Usually, the parties bear their own costs.

Intellectual property committees

This is a coordinated effort to focus on maximum commercialization for corporate R&D efforts (inventions) and their legal protection (patents, trade secrets, etc.). IP committees are composed of patent counsels, inventors and managers of the respective business units. They regularly review the following: filing of patents, maintenance of patents, filing of oppositions and licensing-in and licensing-out.

20

Insuring Business Risks

INTRODUCTION

In the absence of insurance, three possible individuals bear the burden of an economic loss: the individual suffering the loss; the individual causing the loss via negligence or unlawful conduct; or lastly, a particular party who has been allocated the burden by the legislature.

While types of insurance vary widely, their primary goal is to allocate the risks of a loss from the individual to a great number of people. Each individual pays a "premium" into a pool, from which losses are paid out. Regardless of whether the particular individual suffers the loss or not, the premium is not returnable. Thus, when a building burns down, the loss is spread to the people contributing to the pool. In general, insurance companies are the safekeepers of the premiums. Because of its importance in maintaining economic stability, the government and the courts use a heavy hand in ensuring these companies are regulated and fair to the consumer.

THE INSURANCE CONTRACT

Insurance is a contract by which one party for a stipulated consideration promises to pay another party a sum of money on the destruction of, loss of, or injury to something in which the other party has an interest or to indemnify that party for any loss or liability to which that party is subjected.

The parties

The parties to an insurance contract are the *insurer* (the insurance company) and the *insured* (the person

covered by the insurer's provisions or the holder of the policy). Insurance contracts are usually obtained through an *agent*, who ordinarily works for the insurance company, or through a *broker*, who is ordinarily an *independent contractor*. When a broker deals with an applicant for insurance, the broker is, in effect, the applicant's agent. In contrast, an insurance agent is an agent of the insurance company, not of the applicant. As a general rule, the insurance company is bound by the acts of its agent when they act within the agency relationship. A broker, however, normally has no relationship with the insurance company and is an agent of the insurance applicant.

Insurable interest

A person can insure anything in which he or she has an insurable interest. Without this insurable interest, there is no enforceable contract, and a transaction to insure would have to be treated as a wager. In regard to real and personal property, an insurable interest exists when the insured derives a pecuniary benefit from the preservation and continued existence of the property. With regard to life insurance, a person must have a reasonable expectation of benefit from the continued life of another in order to have an insurable interest in that person's life. The benefit may be pecuniary (for example in the case of key-person insurance, which insures the lives of important employees, usually in small companies), or it may be founded on the relationship between the parties (by blood or affinity).

For property insurance, the insurable interest must exist at the time the loss occurs but need not exist when the policy is purchased. In contrast, for life insurance, the insurable interest must exist at the time the policy is obtained. The existence of an insurable interest is a primary concern in determining liability under an insurance policy.

The contract

The formation of a contract of insurance is governed by the general principles applicable to contracts. By statute, it is now commonly provided that an insurance policy must be written. To avoid deception, many statutes also specify the content of certain policies, in whole or in part. Some statutes specify the size and style of type to be used in printing the policies. Provisions in a policy that conflict with statutory requirements are generally void.

The application as part of the contract

The application for insurance is generally attached to the policy when issued and is made part of the contract of insurance by express stipulation of the policy. The insured is bound by all statements in the attached application.

Statutory provisions as part of the contract

When a statute requires that insurance contracts contain certain provisions or cover certain specified losses, a contract of insurance that does not comply with the statute will be interpreted as though it contained all the provisions required by the statute. When a statute requires that all terms of the insurance contract be included in the written contract, the insurance company cannot claim that a provision not stated in the written contract was binding on the insured.

Cancellation statutes and provisions

The contract of insurance may expressly declare that it may or may not be canceled by the insurer's unilateral act. By statute or policy provision, the insurer is commonly required to give a specific number of days' written notice of cancellation.

Modification of contract

A contract of insurance can be modified if both insurer and insured agree to the change. The insurer cannot modify the contract without the consent of the insured when the right to do so is not reserved in the insurance contract. To make changes or corrections to the policy, it is not necessary to issue a new policy.

An endorsement on the policy or the execution of a separate rider[1] is effective for the purpose of changing the policy. When a provision of an endorsement conflicts with a provision of the policy, the endorsement controls because it is the later document.

Interpretation of contract

A contract of insurance is interpreted by the same rules that govern the interpretation of ordinary contracts. Words are to be given their ordinary meaning and interpreted in light of the nature of the coverage intended.

The contract of insurance is to be read as it would be understood by the average person or by the average person in business rather than by one with technical knowledge of the law or of insurance. If there is an ambiguity in the policy, the provision is interpreted against the insurer.

Burden of proof

When an insurance claim is disputed by the insurer, the person bringing the suit has the burden of providing that there was a loss, that it occurred while the policy was in force, and that the loss was of a kind that was within the coverage or scope of the policy. The insured must comply with a number of time limitations in making a claim.

A policy will contain exceptions to the coverage. Exceptions to coverage are generally strictly interpreted against the insurer. The insurer has the burden of providing that the facts were such that there was no coverage because an exception applied. Under state cancellation statutes, insurers must produce proof that each cancellation notice was mailed to the address of record.

Insurer bad faith

An insurer must act in good faith in processing and paying claims under its policy. When it is a liability insurer's duty to defend the insured and the insurer wrongfully refuses to do so, the insurer is guilty of breach of contract and is liable for all consequential damages resulting from the breach.

If there is a reasonable basis for the insurer's belief that a claim is not covered by its policy, its refusal to pay the claim does not subject it to liability for a breach of good faith or for statutory penalty.

In the case of a bad-faith breach of an insurance claim, the insurer is exposed not only to compensatory damages but also may be liable for exemplary or punitive damages.

Reinsurance

Reinsurance is basically an insurance bought by insurers. It effectively increases an insurer's capital and therefore its capacity to sell more coverage. The business is global and some of the largest reinsurers are based abroad. A reinsurer assumes part of the risk and part of the premium originally taken by the insurer, known as the primary company. It also has its own reinsurers, called retrocessionaires. One main difference with insurers is that reinsurers do not pay policyholders' claims. Instead, they reimburse insurers for claims paid.

DIRECTORS AND OFFICERS (D&O) INSURANCE

Corporations are not required by their corporate or state charters to provide indemnification and a few prefer not to do so. In addition, corporations are prohibited from providing indemnification to the directors and their officers for certain, self-serving and knowingly criminal activity. In those instances where corporations do not or may not indemnify their directors and officers, insurance coverage might still be available. The following materials lay out the general outline of most policies for directors and officers (D&O) insurance. Basic provisions deal with general coverage, defense issues, definition of claim, definition of loss, exclusions, and specialized coverages.

DIRECTORS AND OFFICERS (D&O) INSURANCE COVERAGE

General coverage

The insurance covers directors and officers of a company for negligent acts or omissions, and for misleading statements that result in suits against the company, often by shareholders. Directors and officers insurance policies usually contain three coverages.

First, personal coverage is available for individual directors and officers not indemnified by their corporations for their legal expenses or judgments against them. Second, coverage is available to reimburse corporations for indemnifying directors and officers. Third, entity coverage for claims made specifically against the company may also be available.

Directors and officers (D&O) insurance protects directors and officers from liability arising from actions connected to their corporate positions. The individual coverages discussed below typically are subject to distinct terms, conditions and deductibles, and even may be subject to distinct policy limits or sublimits. However, some common threads run through the various coverages offered in a D&O policy. For example, D&O insuring agreements generally specify that coverage is limited to claims first made during the policy period. In addition, the insurer typically does not have a duty to defend but is required to cover the costs of the insured's defense.

Insuring Agreement A

Insuring Agreement A, often referred to as "A-Side Coverage," typically provides coverage directly to the directors and officers for loss – including defense costs – resulting from claims made against them for their wrongful acts. A-Side Coverage applies where the corporation does not indemnify its directors and officers.

A corporation may not indemnify its directors or officers because it:

(a) is prohibited by law from doing so;
(b) is permitted to do so by law and the company's bylaws but chooses not to do so; or
(c) is financially incapable of doing so, due to bankruptcy, liquidation, or lack of funds.

The laws regarding indemnification differ from jurisdiction to jurisdiction. Insuring Agreement A additionally may specify that coverage is limited to those claims connected to an insured's capacity as an insured director or officer of the company.

The limiting language may appear in the insuring clause, in the definitions of "wrongful act" or "insured" found elsewhere in the policy, or in all three clauses. Although a claim sometimes implicates an insured in a single and clear capacity, a claim may well arise out of an individual's multiple capacities. For example, an individual may be sued as a director and a shareholder of a company (perhaps as a purchaser or seller of company stock), or an officer of a homeowner's association may also be a homeowner and it may not be clear whether his or her actions were taken as one or the other – or both. Similarly, a corporation's lawyer may also sit on the board of directors. In each case, it is important to determine the capacity in which the insured is acting.

Insuring Agreement B (corporate reimbursement)

A typical Insuring Agreement B, or "B-side coverage," reimburses a corporation for its loss where the corporation indemnifies its directors and officers for claims against them. B-side coverage does not provide coverage for the corporation for its own liability. The language and conditions of Insuring Clause B typically mirror Insuring Clause A.

Insuring Agreement C (entity securities coverage)

Many D&O policies offer an optional coverage to protect the corporation against securities claims. Such coverage provides protection for the corporation for its own liability. Many policies today provide such coverage to the corporation whether or not its directors and officers are also sued; other policies, however, provide such coverage only where the corporation is a co-defendant with its directors and officers. Entity coverage may be part of the policy form as "Insuring Agreement C" or may be added as an endorsement.

Defense issues

Most D&O policies do not impose a duty to defend on the insurer. They do, however, provide coverage for defense costs and give the insurer the right to associate with the defense and approve defense strategies, expenditures and settlements.

Right to select counsel

A D&O insurer cannot impose its choice of counsel on an insured – the insured generally has the right to select counsel, subject to the insurer's consent. D&O policies typically provide that an insurer may not unreasonably withhold approval of an insured's choice of counsel. This feature is important to the insured corporation, which typically has developed ongoing relations with corporate and litigation counsel that it would want to use in high-stakes litigation against the company.

Reimbursement and advancement of defense costs

Although D&O insurers generally do not have a duty to defend, D&O policies do cover defense costs. The primary questions that arise in connection with the payment of defense costs regard:

(a) control over the costs incurred; and
(b) when the insurer must make defense payments.

In connection with the first question, although insurers do not control an insured's defense, under D&O policies they are required to reimburse only reasonable defense costs arising out of covered claims. Thus, an insured or his chosen counsel does not get a blank check.

Whether a D&O insurer must, or should, advance defense costs – that is, pay them as they are incurred – is a common question. Many of the issues affecting coverage cannot be resolved until the claim has been resolved. Specifically, certain exclusions only apply after a finding of fact has been made. For example, as discussed below, policies generally exclude coverage for losses arising out of fraud. The exclusion only applies, however, where there is a final judgment finding fraud. Thus, where fraud is alleged, coverage is uncertain until the completion of the claim. In such situations, insurers may have an interest in not advancing defense costs until coverage is certain. However, insurers have an interest in seeing their insured vigorously defend claims against them. A vigorous defense can be a costly endeavor that may be well beyond the means of an insured. Thus, many policies provide that insurers advance defense costs under the condition that, should the facts ultimately demonstrate a lack of coverage, the insured will reimburse the advanced monies.

Definition of a "claim"

Common to all coverages in a D&O policy is that each insuring clause generally provides coverage on a "claims-made" basis. In other words, it provides the coverage described for claims made during the period for which the coverage is purchased. Additionally, the insured typically must report the claim to the insurer during the policy period or within a reasonable time.

D&O policies generally define claim as any:

(a) civil, criminal or administrative proceeding; or
(b) written demand for damages against an insured.

Who is included as an insured will depend on which coverages are implicated and how the term is defined in the policy.

That is, if it is a securities claim, and the policy so provides, a claim may be made against the company or against a director or officer. If it is an employment claim, and the policy so provides, a claim may be made against the company, a director or officer, or an employee.

Some policies offer more detailed definitions of claim. For example, a policy may state that a civil proceeding includes arbitration, mediation or other alternative dispute resolution. A policy may also explain that an administrative proceedings includes a formal investigation.

Many policies also include limiting a claim to those proceedings or demands made against an insured in his or her capacity as an insured. The capacity issue may be stated directly in the definition of claim, or may be stated in the definitions of "insured" or "wrongful act," either of which may be part of the definition of claim.

Definition of loss

Loss generally includes damages, judgments, awards, settlements and defense costs. Loss usually excludes fines or penalties, taxes, treble (or other multiplied) damages, and matters uninsurable under law. Where treble or multiplied damages are assessed, a D&O policy generally will cover the base amount, but not the multiplied portion of the loss. Some policies include punitive and exemplary damages in the definition of loss. Where included, coverage of punitive and exemplary damages explicitly is effective only where permitted by applicable law.

Punitive or exemplary damages

Some states do not permit punitive or exemplary damages to be assessed at all. Those states that do permit punitive damages to be assessed may not permit insurance against them. Those states prohibiting coverage of punitive damages generally base the prohibition on public policy concerns. The longstanding reasoning is that the assessment of punitive damages is intended to set an example or punish the wrongdoer, and permitting insurance against such punishment would render such punishment ineffective.

Matters uninsurable under applicable law

Matters deemed uninsurable under law also may be the basis of explicit exclusions elsewhere in a policy. For example, coverage for liability for fraud may be barred by law, as well as by a dishonesty exclusion. As discussed above, coverage for punitive damages also may be barred by law.

Exclusions

Dishonesty exclusion

Dishonesty exclusions bar coverage for claims made in connection with an insured's dishonesty, fraud or willful violation of laws or statutes. The dishonesty exclusion also may be coupled with a personal profit exclusion, barring coverage in connection with an insured's illicit gain. These exclusions typically are followed by a severability clause – that is, a caveat providing that the acts or knowledge of one insured will not be imputed to any other insured for the purposes of applying the exclusion. In other words, the exclusion only bars coverage for the insured(s) whose acts or knowledge are the basis of the claim at issue.

Insured versus insured exclusion

This exclusion bars coverage for claims made by an insured (e.g., a director, officer or corporate insured) against another insured. In addition, the exclusion may bar coverage for claims brought:

(a) by anyone directly or indirectly affiliated with an insured;
(b) by a shareholder unless the shareholder is acting independently and without input from any insured; or
(c) at the behest of an insured.

The exclusion essentially prevents a company from suing or orchestrating a suit against its directors and officers in order to collect insurance proceeds. Questions regarding the application of the exclusion arise in the context of derivative lawsuits, bankruptcies and receiverships.

Professional liability exclusion

As a general matter, D&O policies do not provide coverage for liability associated with the provision of professional services. Thus, where a bank officer is liable for acts as a banker rather than an officer of the bank, a D&O policy with a professional liability exclusion would not provide coverage. Similarly, where a doctor is the president of a professional corporation, the D&O policy would only protect him or her against liability from acts as president of the corporation, and would not provide coverage for professional malpractice claims.

Prior acts exclusion

Prior acts exclusions bar coverage for claims arising out of an insured's wrongful acts prior to a specified date. The date may coincide with the termination of coverage under a previous policy. The date may also coincide with a change in corporate status – such as a merger or acquisition. For example, where a subsidiary is acquired, the prior acts exclusion may

exclude coverage for the subsidiary prior to the time it became a subsidiary. In such situations, the subsidiary may have run-off coverage from a previous policy to protect against liability arising from those excluded acts.

Prior and pending litigation exclusion

Prior and pending litigation exclusions generally exclude coverage for:

(a) claims pending prior to the inception of the policy, or another agreed upon date; and
(b) subsequent claims based on the same facts or circumstances.

Conflicts primarily arise regarding the second component of this exclusion. Specifically, the question arises as to when a subsequent claim is based on sufficiently overlapping facts and circumstances to fall within the scope of the exclusion.

Specialized coverages

"Underwriting" is the task of deciding what risks to insure. It allows insurers to discriminate between good and bad risks. Differences in prices for insurance must reflect expected differences in losses and expenses. When the risk of future losses increases or when rates are inadequate, insurers become more selective about the degree of risk they will assume in an effort to preserve their profit margin.

Underwriters offer specialized policies for the specific risks to which various industries are exposed. In this way, D&O insurance has expanded to include policies covering special risks. For example, directors and officers of non-profit organizations or condominium associations require different protections to directors and officers of banking and financial institutions or health care systems.

Allocation

Allocation is required where a policy does not provide entity coverage and a lawsuit – often a securities or antitrust action – is brought both against directors and officers and also against the corporate entity.

Under such circumstances, a policy would cover the defense and settlement expenses attributable to the directors and officers, but not those attributable to the entity. Where allocation is indicated, the parties attempt to reach an agreement as early as possible.

Combined risk policies

The combined policies often include D&O coverage (A-Side, B-Side and Entity Securities coverage), employment practices liability insurance coverage, fiduciary liability coverage, professional liability errors and omissions coverage (for financial institutions), and fidelity or crime bonds (for employee dishonesty and related losses). Combining these risks presents challenging issues for both insurers and insureds, since the risks insured are quite varied, often subject to different terms, and involve significant limits of liability and premium dollars.

OTHER TYPES OF BUSINESS INSURANCE

Businesses today are exposed to innumerable risks in their daily operations. Therefore, there is a broad range of insurance that applies to every imaginable risk. Furthermore, policies differ in the persons and interests that they protect. Below is a short explanation of the most common insurance policies.

Commercial General Liability Insurance (CGLI)

Commercial General Liability Insurance (CGLI) policies provide comprehensive coverage for businesses or other organizations with respect to liabilities that are not covered under other more specialized types of policies. Among the kinds of liability insurance that are not usually encompassed within general liability are:

1 automobile, navigation, and aircraft risks;
2 workers' compensation and employers' liability; and
3 liquor liability, which is applicable primarily to sellers of liquor, such as taverns and restaurants.

In addition, CGLI does not offer insurance for directors' and officers' potential personal liability; nor

for various kinds of professional liability insurance such as medical, dental, legal, and accountants' liability insurance, which protects practitioners from the consequences of their professional errors and omissions. Such coverage is available, as noted above, under directors and officers' insurance or under policies covering professional acts and omissions.

The standard CGLI policy contains three basic parts:

(a) a general grant of coverage, also called 'insuring agreement';
(b) exclusions from the grant of coverage; and
(c) policy conditions and miscellaneous provisions.

The major categories of coverage under the basic CGLI form are for an entity's premises-based risk and its business products-completed operations risk. Under the portion of the policy often referred to as Coverage A, bodily injury and property damage are insured against. Under Coverage B, the standard CGLI policy insures for personal injury and advertising injury. Coverage C covers medical payments caused by an accident on the insured's premises, regardless of fault.

Employment Practices Liability Insurance (EPLI)

Employment Practices Liability (EPL) is an insurance against employment lawsuits. EPLI covers businesses against claims by workers that their legal rights as employees of the company have been violated.

EPLI provides protection against many kinds of employee lawsuits, including claims of:

(a) sexual harassment;
(b) discrimination;
(c) wrongful termination;
(d) breach of employment contract;
(e) negligent evaluation;
(f) failure to employ or promote;
(g) wrongful discipline;
(h) deprivation of career opportunity;
(i) wrongful infliction of emotional distress; and
(j) mismanagement of employee benefit plans.

The cost of EPLI coverage depends on the type of business, the number of employees and various risk factors such as whether the company has been sued over employment practices in the past. The policies will reimburse your company against the costs of defending a lawsuit in court and for judgments and settlements. The policy covers legal costs, whether the company wins or loses the suit. Policies also typically do not pay for punitive damages or civil and criminal penalties. Liabilities covered by other insurance policies such as workers' compensation are excluded from EPLI policies.

Environmental liability insurance (ELI)

Various environmental liability insurance (ELI) policies have been created that facilitate the development of brownfields. These protect landowners and banks and others financing real estate deals from the costs of unexpected pollution cleanups that could cause an agreement to fall apart or lead to a foreclosure later on.

ELI policies can also be used to facilitate merger and acquisition transactions, to remove fears of the unknown now that companies must report financial impact of environmental exposures and to fund clean-up cost overruns. Coverage can now include first party pollution clean-up and bodily injury costs (for the owner) as well as third party property damage and bodily injury risks that have traditionally been part of the policy. ELI policies may also be designed to protect companies against lawsuits filed by local communities where pollution has become a problem. These liability policies may include coverage for loss of income due to business interruption and property value diminution where homeowners believe their homes have lost value because of the presence of toxic waste.

Product liability insurance

As we discussed in a previous chapter, product liability is a section of tort law that determines who may sue and who may be sued for damages when a defective product injures someone. No uniform US federal law guides manufacturer's liability, but under strict liability, the injured party can hold the manufacturer responsible for damages without the need to prove negligence or fault. Thus, it is important for a manufacturer to purchase this kind of insurance.

Product liability insurance protects manufacturers' and distributors' exposure to lawsuits by people who have sustained bodily injury or property damage through the use of the product. A "product" is anything that is tangibly used, touched or consumed. This type of insurance is recommended for every business that manufactures a product, but is especially important for companies that produce food, clothing, toys or anything else that could conceivably cause harm to someone.

Workers' compensation insurance

As we have mentioned in a previous chapter, workers' compensation is designed to ensure that employees who are injured or disabled on the job are provided with fixed monetary awards, eliminating the need for litigation. Workers' compensation insurance protects employers from claims resulting from injuries to employees. On-the-job injured employees have the right under tort law to claim compensatory and punitive damages from their employers.

Basic workers' compensation coverage includes medical treatment, rehabilitation costs, and lost-wage replacement, covering up to two-thirds of an employee's regular salary while he or she is out of work. Most workers' compensation policies also include liability coverage, which applies if a worker's family sues the employer for damages stemming from a worker's compensation claim.

Failure to carry this insurance exposes the employer to pay what the insurer would have paid, plus severe fines, and possibly jail time for violating the law. The benefits may amount to hundreds of thousands of dollars. The employer has a legal duty to ensure that employees get the legally mandated benefits without delay.

Intellectual property insurance

We discuss briefly two of the most important types of intellectual property insurance: patent infringement litigation and patent enforcement litigation.

Patent infringement litigation insurance is a form of professional liability insurance for manufacturers, users and sellers accused of infringing a patent holder's rights. Coverage is provided for defense and indemnity and can include profits and royalties that must be turned over to the patent holder. Coverage is written on a claims-made basis.

Patent enforcement litigation insurance is insurance for a holder of a patent against infringement by another person. Coverage is written on a claims-made basis and includes the cost of legal defense to enforce the patent. The policy includes a co-payment provision, usually 25 percent. Excluded are liability for compensatory or consequential damages, fines, punitive damages, exemplary damages and multiple damages.

Terrorism insurance

The unprecedented events of 11 September 2001 triggered a radical reshaping of the risk landscape worldwide. Several countries have sought to develop public/private risk-shaping partnerships to handle terrorism risks over the years. For example, in the early 1990s the United Kingdom established Pool Re, a government-backed scheme providing coverage for property damage and business interruption losses arising from terrorist attacks. The Pool Re model has been followed by other countries. Recognizing the finite claims-paying ability of insurers, yet faced with virtually unlimited terrorism exposures, the US industry also requested that the federal government provide a "backstop" for terrorism risks.

Under the Terrorism Risk Insurance Act of 2002 (TRIA), only businesses that purchase optional terrorism coverage are covered for losses arising from terrorist acts. The exception is workers' compensation, which covers injuries and deaths due to acts of terrorism. It also established that insurers and the federal government share the risk of future losses for a three-year period.

It is important to mention that a report published by Swiss Re in May 2003 suggests that property and business interruption losses resulting from terrorism are still insurable, providing the following criteria are met:

(a) the additional premium for inclusion must be commensurate with the anticipated claims burden;
(b) the liability for losses caused by terrorism must be limited in normal property and business interruption policies; reinsurance cover for these types of policies must also be limited; and

(c) the risk community should be extended where the number of risks threatened by the same peril is too small to obtain a reasonable premium rate.

Self-insurance

Self-insurance is assuming a financial risk oneself, instead of paying an insurance company to take it on. Every policyholder is a self-insurer in terms of paying a deductible and co-payments. Large firms often self-insure frequent, small losses such as damage to their fleet of vehicles or minor workplace injuries. However, to protect injured employees state laws set out requirements for the assumption of workers' compensation programs. Self-insurance also refers to employers who assume all or part of the responsibility for paying the health insurance claims of their employees. Firms that self-insure for health claims are exempt from state insurance laws mandating the illnesses that group health insurers must cover. In most cases, a self-insuring employer contracts with an insurance company to administer the plan. Thus, the employee may be required to fill out the same forms that are required of others who are in fact insured by an independent company. The only difference is that when a bill is paid, it comes out of the employer's account rather than that of the insurance company.

SUBROGATION AND SURETYSHIP

Subrogation means the substitution of one person for another. If an insurance company pays a claim, it is subrogated to the rights of the insured, meaning that the company acquires whatever rights the insured had against any third parties.

Subrogation serves two purposes:

1 it prevents the insured from recovering twice – once from the insurance company and once from the person who caused the damage; and
2 it reduces the cost of insurance for everyone.

If an insurance company receives reimbursement from a third party, it can offer lower premiums.

If the insured waives his or her claim against the third parties, then the insurance company also loses any right it might have against them.

FIVE

It is important to mention that the principle of subrogation applies to property and fire insurance, but not to life insurance.

In subrogation, the insurance company succeeds to the rights of the insured. In suretyship, the insurance company succeeds to the obligations of the insured. A suretyship contract protects one party to a contract against default by another. For example, federal contractors are often required to post surety bonds to ensure completion of their job. If they fail to finish the contract, the surety pays the cost of hiring someone else. For large contracts, sureties are almost always insurance companies, but individuals and others can also serve as sureties.

Notes

CHAPTER 3: BUSINESS REGULATION IN GENERAL

1   In fact, in order to understand the significance of interests conflicting with a business's interests and of community ethical norms differing from a business's ethical perspective, it is typically necessary to assess the potential impact of those conflicting interests and differing norms on a business's own self-interests. Just as intended results are often quantified after they have been identified, so it is also often possible to quantify the impact of conflicting interests and differing ethical perspectives. While such impacts cannot always be calculated with certainty, they can often be estimated with sufficient certainty to enhance the decision-making process.

2   These limitations on private property rights are referred to as "general obligations" in France and other civil law countries. Such limitations are referred to as "general obligations" because they are obligations each person owes to everyone, even in the absence of prior consent. In common law countries, "general obligations" are referred to as torts. "Torts" are, quite simply, violations of general obligations. The law of general obligations, or torts, is explored in more detail in Chapter 7 ("Non-contractual Relationships").

3   "General obligations" are obligations which governments enforce against one individual on another individual's behalf even without the consent of that first person. In this way, general obligations are different from "contract obligations," which governments enforce against one individual on another individual's behalf because of prior consent given by the first person to the second person.

4   Of course, intentionally injuring other persons and damaging their property are also acts against those persons and so, in addition to being crimes, can also be torts (i.e., breaches of general obligations).

5   Intentional violations of contracts raise slightly different questions. If a person intended to breach a contract at the time that he entered into it, then the act of entering into the contract constitutes a "fraud," which can be a tort and, sometimes, a crime. In other words, entering into a contract with the intention of breaching it constitutes breach of one person's "general obligations" to another person (and sometimes a crime). If a person does not intend to breach a contract at the time that he or she entered into the contract, then that person breaches his or her "contract obligation" by subsequently failing to perform his or her contract duties. In so doing, the person in breach of the contract does not breach any "general obligation," even if the person intentionally breaches his or her contract obligations.

6   Violations of individual rights are not limited to personal injury and property. Property and contract rights can also be enforced by recourse to courts. In fact, granting individuals the ability to seek compensation in court for harm to any personal interest elevates that interest to the status of a legal right.

7   In some countries, such as the USA, punitive damages against businesses are relatively common, quite large and paid to the victims. In other countries, punitive damages are relatively uncommon, very low and paid to the court or government.

8   In each case, however, an important element in determining whether punitive damages are necessary to act as a deterrent is whether a business intended to violate its general or contract obligations at the time that the business incurred the obligation. In the case of general obligations, such moment is the moment at which the business took the action causing the harm.

In the case of contract obligations, such moment is the time at which the business entered into its contract.

9   Given real choices (i.e., choices subject to the same transaction, contingent and collateral costs), individuals participating in market transactions – both businesses and consumers – can transfer their assets when and as they see fit to maximize their own welfare. In order to maximize individual welfare, however, it is not enough to have real choices. It is also important for all market participants, both sellers and buyers, to have all relevant information about those choices. In the absence of all relevant information, sellers and buyers cannot maximize their individual welfare and markets cannot allocate resources efficiently.

Unfortunately, sellers and buyers are not in a reciprocal situation regarding their need for relevant information. In market transactions, buyers typically offer to transfer money. Assuming that money is real, sellers do not need information to ascertain its value. Sellers in market transactions, on the other hand, offer to transfer goods or services. Buyers typically need information to ascertain the value of those goods and services. Even though the availability of real choices for the buyer (i.e., effective competition between two or more sellers) imposes a certain discipline on all sellers to disclose information about their goods or services, sellers generally prefer to give information only to the extent necessary to make a sale.

10   Enforcing competition is not sufficient to ensure the disclosure of adequate information generally in two circumstances. First of all, competition law is not always applicable. For example, historically, competition law has usually been considered inapplicable for public utilities (such as water, electricity and gas) and other networks with significant initial capital investments (e.g., railroads and telephone services). Providing choice for buyers in such markets implies creating a second network, but creating a second network entails high costs – costs not warranted by the benefit obtainable through consumer choice. Second, even in competitive markets, buyers are not always able to obtain the information necessary to protect their interests. For example, buyers can have difficulty obtaining adequate information in mass markets (where face-to-face negotiation is not possible) or in connection with the purchase of goods and services whose incidental costs or inherent value is not readily apparent (such as synthetic chemicals, financial services or electronic appliances).

11   Expressed in terms of private property and contract rights, there is another difference between, on the one hand, these more intrusive regulations and, on the other hand, the competition and disclosure regulations described earlier. While competition and disclosure regulations generally restrict the freedom of contract, these regulations restrict the right to use private property freely. Limiting the free use of private property is not usually considered to be "expropriation" in part because the owner's right to use private property freely is arguably only an implied right: implied from the owners' right to exclude the use of their property by others. Government protection of property from use by others does not necessarily preclude restrictions on the owners' use by the government.

12   Such general principles are set forth in the "case law" of countries following the English tradition of common law and in the "codes" of countries following the Roman and French traditions of civil law.

13   Class actions are legal proceedings in courts where several (usually innumerable) law suits are consolidated into a single cause of action for administrative efficiency. Consolidating law suits risks jeopardizing the interests of harmed individuals, so several individual law suits are consolidated into class actions only where: (1) the same conduct gives rise to the various individual claims; and (2) the same harm has been caused to each of the various individuals.

14   Punitive damages and class actions are available in courts pursuant to breaches of general and contract obligations. Such actions can and do increase the measure of damages for such breaches to amounts equal to and even in excess of the amount of government penalties. However, punitive damages and class actions are available only in special circumstances. Special circumstances sufficient to initiate a class action exist where a single business has allegedly caused similar personal injuries, similar property damage or similar contract breaches to a relatively large number of individuals in similar circumstances. Punitive damages are available for breaches of general or contract obligations where monetary judgments above and beyond compensation for actual injuries and damages are deemed necessary to deter similar breaches in the future. It is difficult to maintain a case for punitive damages unless it can be shown that the business intended to breach a general obligation or a contract obligation at the time that it was incurred.

15   Damages awarded by courts pursuant to violations of general obligations constitute a form of "compensatory justice," reallocating the cost for past business conduct away from those persons who suffer the losses and costs on to the businesses causing the losses and costs. Business regulation constitutes a form of "distributive justice" as companies pass on to customers and shareholders the costs of implementing the regulatory requirements.

16   The amount of penalties for violating government regulations, in many cases, can reasonably be limited

to an amount in excess of the amount the business would have incurred had it voluntarily taken the precautionary actions necessary to avoid the harm the regulation is intended to prevent. Viewed in this way, penalties for violations of government regulations are effective if they provide incentive for businesses to adopt measures inspired by "distributive justice," i.e., taking the actions necessary to avoid harm and spreading the cover to all of those who benefit from avoiding the harm.

17   The amount of harm needed to prompt individual court actions usually needs to be significant in part because pursuing court actions involves lawyers' fees, court costs, effort, delay, uncertainty and emotions.

18   The "economic hurdles" for agency enforcement actions tend to be: (1) budgetary limitations; and (2) within those limitations, "prosecutorial discretion," i.e., decisions by agencies whether they could, in the aggregate, prevent greater harm by taking other actions.

19   Self-regulation has become increasingly important in light of expanding globalization and rapid technological innovation. Globalization has increased the importance of self-regulation because global business organizations, products, services and practices, together with their incidental consequences, extend beyond the borders of single nations, encompassing the globe. The rapid pace of recent innovation has also increased the importance of self-regulation because today's business products, services and practices, together with their incidental consequences, evolve faster than regulators can react. This does not mean that self-regulation is new. Many current self-regulatory practices have their origins in practices which have evolved into customary conventions. In fact, many of today's commercial codes have their origins as customs, conventions and other market-based practices amongst medieval merchants – practices essentially "international" in nature. Modern commercial codes in Europe and the Americas, for example, are based on such practices. To formulate their commercial codes, nation-states simply adopted long-standing, widely-accepted commercial practices. For this reason, the commercial codes of different countries are surprisingly similar. Since the inceptions of national commercial codes in the nineteenth century, innovations in transportation and communication have been the main reason for the most important modifications.

20   For example: two criminals rob a bank at gunpoint. They are arrested the evening of the same day as they sleep in a local motel. They are in possession of the stolen money so both are clearly guilty of simple bank robbery, with a possible maximum sentence of ten years. At the same time, the police cannot find the hand gun the criminals used to rob the bank. Without the actual gun in evidence, the police cannot convict the criminals of armed bank robbery, with a mandatory twenty-five-year sentence. The police adopt the following strategy: They separate the two prisoners and offer to free the first prisoner who reveals the location of the hand gun. This creates a dilemma for each of the prisoners: If neither reveals the gun's location (effectively cooperating with each other), neither can be convicted of the armed robbery, so each will go to prison for no more than ten years. On the other hand, the one who first reveals the location of the hand gun (effectively betraying the other) will be completely free – and at a safe distance from his comrade for the following twenty-five years.

21   One example of unfair dealing is the failure of one contract party (e.g., the seller) to disclose to the other party (e.g., the buyer) during the negotiation of a contract facts which risk becoming detrimental to the second party (i.e., the buyer) after the negotiation of the contract.

22   Following my example: while the arguably unfair business conduct is the sale, at list price and with only a standard warranty, of dining chairs with an undisclosed defect. Based on complaints from its customers, SP will most probably discover in the normal course of business that the joints in the dining-room chairs are defective. SP will be concerned because the defects will increase SP's repairs on the furniture it sells. In fact, even with successful warranty repair, the defects in the dining chairs well could undermine SP's relationships with its customers. In the absence of an ongoing relationship, SP could only seek judicial remedy for MH's failure to disclose a known defect. Since SP has an ongoing relationship with Miraculous Hardwood (MH), SP can both: (1) seek a judicial remedy; and (2) threaten to terminate its relationship with MH. Given the legal fees, court costs, uncertainties, delays, effort and emotion involved in seeking judicial remedies, the threat of terminating an ongoing commercial relationship is an important deterrent to MH's unfair dealing.

23   Remember, in the absence of a specific government regulation, sellers do not breach any obligations under general principles of commercial law by keeping secrets such as defects. The availability of a judicial remedy in this case would depend on the terms of the contract between MH and SP.

24   Governments should be viewed as a separate constituency because governments have the ability to react in powerful ways not available to other groups, i.e., governments can adopt regulations.

25   Again using my example of Miraculous Hardwoods, Inc. ("MH"), Sitting Pretty & Co. ("SP") is directly involved in the arguably unfair treatment proposed by Mr Oakes. There is a good chance that furniture chain

stores other than SP would learn about its unfair treatment by MH, e.g., through discussions with SP, litigation initiated by SP, securities law disclosures and/or press reports. Even though the other stores would not be able to initiate litigation, the unfair treatment might prompt them to re-evaluate their relationship with MH, diversifying away from MH or even possibly terminating all purchases. Obviously, MH shareholders, MH employees and the communities where MH operates would be concerned about the potential litigation and drop in sales. Even the government might become involved by adopting legislation requiring full disclosure of all defects or mandatory replacements of all defective furniture.

26   Business dealings with embargoed countries are probably the best example. In the absence of an applicable government regulation, there is no widely recognized community ethical norm against delivery goods and services to any country around the world. As soon as the USA or any other government adopts regulations prohibiting business dealings in certain countries, e.g., Cuba, North Korea or Iraq, it becomes a violation of both government regulations and widely accepted community ethical norms to deliver goods or services to those countries.

27   In Chapter Two, I listed and described five prevalent community ethical norms: (1) the purely self-interested approach; (2) utilitarianism; (3) individual rights; (4) trust; and (5) justice. I also mentioned (6) social contracts and (7) "survival of the fittest" as two other widely recognized community ethical norms often applicable to business practices.

28   As a rough rule of thumb, I suggest that management carefully consider any business decision which is not consistent with: (1) individual legal rights; (2) government regulations; (3) community ethical norms; or (4) management's own ethical perspectives.

29   The lawyers' fees, court costs, effort, delays, uncertainties and emotions involved in pursuing judicial remedies detract from this deterrent effect.

30   Government agencies also often have the power to impose sanctions in addition to penalties. Plant closures and product seizures are also clearly intended to prevent future personal injury and property damage.

31   Lax or sporadic enforcement of government regulations undermines this reasoning.

32   Most commentators agree that, with the fall of communism, there are three legal systems in the world: common law, civil law and Islamic law. As regards the three major legal systems, it is useful to note that most business objectives and transactions can be accommodated within the framework of each system. European colonization has also contributed to the ease with which business can be conducted globally.

Through colonization, English and continental European legal concepts have been spread to the Americas (e.g., the United States), Africa (e.g., South Africa) and commercial centers in the Far East (e.g., Singapore and Hong Kong). In the Middle East, many English, French and Portuguese outposts have accommodated – within the context of Islamic law – the largely European legal principles and practices used in international commerce. With the decline of communism as an economic system, private property and freedom of contract have become the basic legal institutions for the conduct of business around the world. In addition to private property and freedom of contract, other fundamental legal principles (such as competition and disclosure requirements, as discussed above) are becoming more generally accepted as the basis for the conduct of business around the world.

33   Defined in this way, industrial enterprises are either typically "artisanal enterprises" or "capitalist enterprises." An industrial enterprise is "artisanal" to the extent that the person who supplies the raw materials and fixed assets (i.e., plant, fixed equipment and tools) applies his or her labor to the fixed assets to convert the raw materials into final products and services. An industrial enterprise is "capitalist" to the extent that the person who supplies the raw materials and fixed assets (i.e., plant, fixed equipment and tools) does not apply his or her labor to the fixed assets to convert the raw materials into final product. In other words, the industrial enterprise is a capitalist enterprise to the extent that the labor is provided by persons who do not own the raw materials and fixed assets.

34   We have already encountered private property and freedom of contract as "natural rights" and important elements of the 1789 French Declaration of the Rights of Man and Citizen. Viewed from another perspective, these rights have been referred to as "laissez-faire." In English, this term means that individuals should be "allowed to do" as they please concerning the use and transfer of property they own. In the English world, this concept was popularized – again with an economic focus – by Adam Smith with the term "invisible hand." With this term, Adam Smith was making the point that if individuals within each nation are allowed freely to use and transfer their property as they see fit for the purpose of increasing their individual material welfare (the political), then the wealth of that nation (measured in aggregate material terms) will also increase (the economic issue).

35   Consistently breaching other persons' legal rights (including the rights of shareholders based on the trust they place in management), neglecting those persons' commercial interests and offending commu-

nity ethical norms can, however, have adverse consequences of different sorts for corporations.

36   This second point might require more explanation; as explained earlier in this chapter, the compensation available in court for breaches of contract rights is the difference between, on the one hand, the value of the complaining party's reasonable expectations and, on the other hand, the value of the goods, services or money actually received. At the same time, obtaining compensation in court usually involves legal fees, court costs, delay, uncertainty and emotions. Even in those cases where complaining parties can recover their legal fees and court costs, seeking compensation in court typically still involves delay, uncertainty and emotion.

37   Yes, there are limitations to the amount of cooperation permitted within an industry under competition laws, but those limitations typically apply only to commercial forces: such as product offerings and pricing.

38   Again, national competition laws can theoretically limit the scope of such international collaborations, but in practice the international confederations restrict their collaborations to areas not in violation of competition laws.

CHAPTER 4: PRIVATE PROPERTY RIGHTS

1   In fact, the law defines the groups affected by corporate business activity in terms of their relationships to the private property used and transferred by corporations in the conduct of their businesses. Those groups involved in the use of corporate assets can be viewed as the corporations' typical "internal relationships," i.e., corporate officers, directors and shareholders. The groups involved in transferring assets to and from corporations can be viewed as the corporations' typical "external relationships," i.e., purchasers of corporations' final products, users of their final products and the communities where corporations operate.

Accordingly, as indicated by the chapter titles in this book, it is organized roughly around those external and internal corporate relationships, all arising out of private property rights and obligations as defined by law and contract. Specific "external relationships" are the topics for this book's entire section on government regulations (Chapters 3 through 7) and for the chapters on general obligations and on contracts (Chapters 9 and 10). Specific "internal relationships" are the chapter topics for the section on corporate governance (Chapters 11 to 15). Employees and competitors do not fall clearly within the dichotomy of internal and external relationships, but their relationships to a corporation can also certainly be defined in terms of property rights. Employees sell their services to their employers. Under competition law, businesses have not only the right to use their assets to deliver goods and services without the involvement of others – as exists under the law of private property. Under competition law, businesses also have the obligation to do so, especially without the involvement of their competitors.

2   Copyrights are another good example of an intangible asset. Copyrights consist of the right to reproduce for profit a work of art or other creative expression. Copyrights are an excellent example of intangible assets because they can be clearly distinguished from the tangible assets to which they apply. For example, a book is a tangible asset. More precisely, it is personal property. As with other personal property, "ownership" of a book is presumptively evidenced and transferred by possession. However, a person does not own the copyright to the book simply by virtue of his ownership of a copy of the book – even the original manuscript. In other words, a person does not have the right to reproduce a book and sell it commercially simply because that person purchases a copy of the book. In fact, only the creator of a creative expression, such as a book, can own the copyright to the creative expression. In this case, only the book's author can own the exclusive right to reproduce and sell the book for profit. The author owns the copyright by virtue of the fact that the author wrote the book. No person can own the copyright unless the author transfers the copyright to that person, quite separate and apart from a transfer of the book. In summary, a copyright is an asset quite separate and apart from the tangible creative expression covered by the copyright. Since copyrights are not embodied in tangible assets, they are intangible assets.

3   Lease transactions provide a related example. Lease transactions create a relationship involving elements of trust owed by the tenant to the landlord. In lease transactions, landlords temporarily transfer to tenants certain ownership rights in land and fixtures, i.e., the rights to possess, use and profit from that land and those fixtures. To the extent that landlords retain present or future private property rights pursuant to the lease transaction, the transaction imposes certain trust obligations on the tenant. The "trust" involved in the lease arrangement consists of the tenants' obligations to respect the present and future private property rights not transferred by the landlord pursuant to the lease arrangement. The tenants' obligations of trust exist under law, in addition to the tenants' contract obligations, because the trust obligations are a necessary incident to the landlords' retained property rights, enforceable by landlords without the tenants' consent. (Landlords can, however, effectively waive those rights in lease agreements.) The tenants' legal

obligations also exist in addition to the legal obligations of other persons to respect the landlords' retained property rights because the trust obligations are a necessary incident to the private property rights transferred exclusively to the tenants.

CHAPTER 6: CONTRACT RIGHTS AND OBLIGATIONS

1   INCOTERMS 2000. The following summary is taken from Ray August, *International Business Law*, Fourth Edition, © 2004 by Pearson Education, Inc., pages 598–9.

"Ex works…"
The seller fulfills his obligations to deliver when he has made the goods available at his premises.

"Free Carrier…"
The seller fulfills his obligations to deliver when he has handed over the goods, cleared for export, into the charge of the carrier named by the buyer at the named place or point.

"Free alongside Ship…"
The seller fulfills his obligations to deliver when the goods have been placed alongside the vessel on the quay at the named port of shipment

"Free on Board…"
The seller fulfills his obligations to deliver when the goods have passed over the ship's rail at the named port of shipment.

"Cost and Freight…"
The seller must pay the costs of freight necessary to bring the goods to the named port of destination, but the risk of loss of or damage to the goods, as well as any additional costs due to events occurring after the time the goods have been delivered on board the vessel, is transferred from this seller to the buyer when the goods pass the ship's rail in the port of shipment.

"Cost, insurance and Freight…"
The seller has the same obligations as under the cost and freight term but with the addition that he has to procure marine insurance against the buyer's risk of loss of and damage to the goods during the carriage.

"Carriage Paid to…"
The seller pays the freight for the carriage of the goods to the named destination. The risk of loss of or damage to the goods, as well as any additional costs due to events occurring after the time the goods have been delivered to the carrier, is transferred from the seller to the buyer when the goods have been delivered into the custody of the carrier.

"Carriage and Insurance Paid to…"
The seller has the same obligations as under the carriage and freight term but with the addition that he has to procure cargo insurance against the risk of loss of or damage to the goods during the carriage.

"Delivered at Frontier…"
The seller fulfills his obligation to deliver when the goods have been made available, cleared for export, at the named point and place at the Frontier, but before the Customs border of the adjoining country.

"Delivered ex ship…"
The seller fulfills his obligation to deliver when the goods have been made available to the buyer on board the ship, but is cleared for import, at the named port of destination. This seller has to bear all the costs and risks involved in bringing the goods to the named port of destination.

"Delivered at quay (duty paid)…"
The seller fulfills his obligation to deliver when the goods have been made available to the buyer on the quay at the named port of destination cleared for importation. This seller has to bear all risks and costs including duties, taxes, and other charges of delivering the goods to the point of delivery.

"Delivered duty unpaid…"
This seller fulfills his obligation to deliver when the goods have been made available at the named place in the country of the importation. This seller has to bear the costs and risks involved in bringing the goods thereto (excluding duties, taxes and other official charges payable upon importation) as well as the costs and risks of carrying out Customs formalities. The buyer has to pay any additional costs and to bear any risks caused by his failure to clear the goods for importation in time.

"Delivered duty paid…"
This seller fulfills his obligation to deliver when the goods have been made available at the named place in the country of importation. This seller has to bear the costs and risks, including duties taxes and other charges of delivering the goods cleared for importation.

2   Summary of procedure for issuing and confirming letters of credit. The following summary based on ICC,

Guide to Documentary Credit Operations (© 1978 by ICC, Paris France), pages 36–37.

1 The buyer and the seller conclude a sales contract providing for payment by letter of credit.
2 The buyer instructs his bank, the issuing bank, to issue a credit in favor of the seller (the beneficiary).
3 The issuing bank asks another bank, usually in the country of the seller, to advise or confirm credit.
4 The advising or confirming bank informs the seller that the credit has been issued.
5 As soon as the seller receives the credit and is satisfied that he can meet its terms and conditions he is in a position to load the goods and dispatch them.
6 The seller then sends the documents evidencing the shipment to the bank where the credit is available (the bank). (This may be the issuing bank, or the confirming bank.)
7 The bank checks the documents against the credit if the documents meet the requirements of the credit. The bank will pay according to the terms of the credit.
8 The bank, if a confirming bank, sends the documents to the issuing bank.
9 The issuing bank checks the documents and, if they meet the credit requirements, either a) effects payment in accordance with the terms of the credit, either to the seller if he has sent the documents directly to the issuing bank or to confirming bank, or b) reimburses the confirming bank in the prearranged manner.
10 When the documents have been checked by the issuing bank and found to meet the credit requirements, they are released to the buyer upon payment of the amount due, or upon other terms agreed between him and the issuing bank.
11 The buyer sends the shipping document to the carrier who will then proceed to deliver the goods.

3   STANDARD TERMS AND CONDITIONS OF SALE

Quantities. It is understood that the quantity of materials (the "Products") to be delivered under this Invoice may vary by ten percent (10%) more or less than the quantity ordered. In the absence of manifest error, Seller's weights and measures shall govern.

Delivery, title and risk of loss. All sales and prices are ex works (the place of manufacture) (INCOTERMS 2000) unless otherwise specified on the front of this Invoice. Title and risk of loss shall pass from Seller to Buyer at the time and place of delivery.

Taxes included in the price. At Seller's option, Seller shall have the right to add to the price herein specified any tax, government charge, carrier's fee, insurance premium or other third party expense to the extent that: (i) it increases the cost to Seller of manufacturing and delivering the Product; or, (ii) Seller is required by law to collect such amounts.

CHAPTER 7: RELATIONSHIPS WITH COMPETITORS

1   Of course, competition amongst sellers enables buyers not only to protect their legal rights, such as freedom from personal injury and property damage. Competition amongst sellers also enables buyers to promote their many interests in addition to their legal rights.
2   The following quote from the US Department of Justice reveals the market purpose served by US antitrust law:

> The historic goal of the competition laws is to protect economic freedom [i.e., choice for consumers] and opportunity [for new and small competitors] by promoting competition in the marketplace. Competition in a free market benefits American consumers through lower prices, better quality and greater choice. Competition provides [new and small] businesses the opportunity [and requires the big ones] to compete on price and quality, in an open market and on a level playing field, unhampered by anticompetitive restraints.
>
> "Overview," Competition Division of the U.S. Department of Justice Internet Website. (Bracketed material added by Professor Nelson)

Moreover, historically, when there has been a conflict between the interests of consumers and the interests of small competitors, the US Department of Justice sides with consumers even if their position favors larger competitors at the expense of small competitors.

3   In other words, free markets cannot sustain themselves without government intervention. In this way, markets are the third fundamental legal principle facilitating the conduct of business. While all sellers benefit from free markets at some point in their careers, each seller – if left to its own devises – would eventually work to eliminate the market. At the very least, each seller would like to eliminate entry into the market after it has established itself. It is interesting to note that the principle of the "invisible hand" – each person unintentionally but effectively serves other persons and the common good by pursuing his or her own best interest – is arguably valid assuming that there are free markets; but that the principle of the "invisible hand" is not adequate for maintaining free markets. The

"invisible hand" is not an adequate principle for maintaining markets because established sellers pursuing their own best interests would harm the interests of other sellers and all buyers by cooperating rather than competing. This difficulty was evidenced by the opposition of the *chambres de commerce* to Baron Turgot's attempts to introduce competition into pre-revolutionary France.

4   Quesnay advocated a natural order ("*l'ordre naturel*") in French political economy as an alternative to the mercantilist system established by Jean Baptiste Colbert (1619–83), French Controller General of Finances under Louis XIV (the "sun King"). *La Tableau Economique*, 1758, was Quesnay's most important work. It was translated into English in 1766.

5   Adam Smith had this to say of the physiocrats:

> This system, however, with all its imperfections, is, perhaps, the nearest approximation to the truth that has yet been published upon the subject of political economy, and is upon that account well worth the consideration of every man who wishes to examine with attention the principles of that very important science.
>
> (*An Inquiry Into the Nature and Causes of the Wealth of Nations*)

Smith initially intended to dedicate *Wealth of Nations* to Baron Turgot. Neither Smith nor the physiocrats thought that "service providers," such as teachers and lawyers, added any value to the economy. Quesnay and many physiocrats believed that manufacture and commerce also added no value to the economy. Smith, Gournay and some other physiocrats believed that manufacture and commerce did indeed add value, provided they were concerned with tangible objects.

6   The United States law was enacted at a time when technical innovation and capital concentrations made it possible for individual companies (organized as "trusts") to attempt to restrain trade throughout the United States (railroads, steel and oil).

7   There is another reason for considering competition rules to be fundamental for the European Union. The EEC was initially formed as, and continues to qualify as "customs union," as defined by the World Trade Organization and its predecessors, GATT and Bretton-Woods. It is important for the EU to qualify as a customs union because from its inception an essential element of the commercial union in Europe has been a common customs tariff. i.e., a single tariff rate imposed by all nations within the EU on products from all nations outside of the EU. In order to continue as a member of WTO, it is necessary that there be no tariff or non-tariff barriers to trade within the customs union. This rule, called the "single market" rule, is the basis for four important legal principles within the EU. Those important legal principles are that, with in the European Union, there should be free movement of: (1) goods; (2) services; (3) people; and (4) capital. Competition law is considered to be an important corollary to the four principles of free movement. In other words, the EU has adopted the position that, without free competition, there cannot be free movement of: (1) goods; (2) services; (3) people; and (4) capital.

8   In the United States, the prohibition against applying dissimilar conditions to similar transactions is set forth in The Robinson-Patman Act (1914). The Robinson-Patman Act is part of the Clayton Act, but it is commonly referred to as though it were a separate statute. The most important provision of the Robinson-Patman Act is Section 2(a), which prohibits a seller from discriminating in prices charged to different purchasers on sales of goods of like grade and quality, where such discrimination may cause injury to competition either between competing customers of the seller, or between the customers of the direct customers of the seller engaging in price discrimination. Price "discrimination" means simply offering a different price to two customers and covers all conditions of sale, including preferential pick-up allowances, discounts and credit terms. There are two important defenses to a charge of price discrimination under the Robinson-Patman Act. Price differences among customers are lawful if they are "cost justified"; that is, if the price difference does no more than reflect actual differences to the seller in the cost of manufacturing, selling or delivering goods to different customers. A seller also has a complete defense against a price discrimination claim if the lower prices offered to a customer were offered in good faith to meet an offer of a competitor. Several conditions attach to the "good faith meeting competition" defense. The defense is available only if the seller reasonably believes it is *meeting* a competitor's price, not if it intentionally *beats* that price. However, a seller will be allowed to "beat" a competitor's price if the undercutting was done unknowingly and in good faith. The "good faith" element is critical to successful use of the meeting competition defense. To demonstrate good faith, the seller must show that it took reasonable steps to verify its belief that the granting of a lower price would in fact meet a price being offered by a competitor; however, you should never attempt to "verify" the competitive price through direct discussions with our competitors as this verification could, in and of itself, raise substantial antitrust issues. Another important limitation on use of the meeting competition defense is that a seller

9   cannot lower its price to meet the price of a competitor if the seller knows or has reason to know that the competitor's price is itself unlawfully discriminatory.

9   In the United States, the prohibition against "tying arrangements" is set forth in Section 3 of the Clayton Act (1914). Section 3 of the Clayton Act prohibits a seller from dealing with a customer on the condition that the customer not deal in the goods of a competitor, but only where the effect of such an agreement may be substantially to lessen competition or to tend to create a monopoly. The three principal types of arrangements which could potentially violate this section are: (a) exclusive dealing contracts (requiring a customer not to handle the products of a competitor of the seller); (b) requirements contracts (in which a buyer agrees to purchase all of its requirements of a certain product from the seller); and, (c) tying arrangements (which force a customer to purchase a product it does not want or would prefer to purchase from another source, i.e., the "tied" product, in order to purchase a desired product i.e., the "tying" product). These practices also may violate Section 1 of the Sherman Act. The legality of the above arrangements often depends on the circumstances surrounding the particular transaction, including, among other elements, the seller's market power and the impact on competition of the particular arrangement.

10   Of course, the same can be true for buyers who cooperate in their dealings with sellers. These aspects of competition law will be discussed below under the headings of "Restraints on Suppliers" and "Monopolies." Combinations of buyers who dominate the markets in which they purchase goods and services are referred to as "monopsonies" and are also illegal under competition law.

11   For the moment, we will disregard the possibility of joint ventures amongst buyers, i.e., purchasing cooperatives.

12   In fact, marketing joint ventures are clearly permissible only in geographic markets where one or both of the joint venturers are not active and where there are substantial distribution costs (such that the joint venturer(s) inactive in that geographic market is (are) likely to remain inactive).

13   Another important limitation on the formation of joint ventures by actual or potential competitors is the ability of the joint venture to prevent further competition. If the joint venture is able to obtain a dominant position, then its geographic scope or its duration might be limited to promote competition.

14   The issue of enforceability can arise when consumers seek to be excused from long-term purchase obligations, often after a drop in market price.

15   For example, prohibiting distributors (or other customers) from reselling products between EEA countries (i.e., requiring a distributor to promise to sell a particular product only in one national market) is almost always illegal under EU competition rules. Often this "ban" takes the form of a restriction on parallel importing, which is where someone buys a product legally available in one EEA country and then exports it into another EEA country. As explained above in Note 7, bans in parallel imports strike at the very heart of the European Union. The EC Commission has consistently required that export bans between EEA Member States be removed from distributor agreements and conditions and terms of sale.

16   Imposing a maximum resale price on distributors and other customers is not acceptable, for example, if the manufacturer – or one of its subsidiaries – competes with the distributor or customer for sales of the products or services subject to the maximum resale prices. In those cases where customers and distributors are also competitors with the manufacturer or one of its subsidiaries, suggested resale prices, retail price lists or pricing plans of any kind for the competing products should not be discussed or agreed with distributors and customers.

17   Accordingly, one business should never become involved in any conversations, meetings or arrangements that could be interpreted as agreements with another company on the price you would pay a supplier for its goods or services. Choosing one supplier should never be based on an agreement with another company or person to foreclose (or freeze) certain other supplier(s) from the market. Similarly, discussing the termination of a particular supplier with a competitor, or with the competitors of that supplier, can lead competition authorities to conclude that the termination is part of a concerted action amongst competitors.

18   The following activities may be viewed as evidence of unlawful reciprocity: Communicating to suppliers that a business will give preferences to those suppliers that purchase from it; communicating to suppliers or customers that a business expects its suppliers to buy some or all of their requirements for other products from Demeter.

19   The prohibition against reciprocity agreements does not preclude simultaneous agreements for the purchase and sale of goods and services, i.e., agreements whereby the purchase by one party is not conditioned on a purchase by the other party. Such simultaneous arrangements, including product swaps and barter, are permissible as long as they are not "coercive" in nature, i.e., "in order to sell me your product you must purchase my product."

20   Here is a sampling of impermissible topics: (1) *on pricing*: prices, pricing procedures, past, present or future prices, prices for a particular product, prices to a

particular customer, prices for geographic market, planned price increases or planned price decreases, (2) *on other terms and conditions of sale*: cash discounts, discount schedules, credit terms and warranty terms, return policies; and (3) *on profit margins*: past, present or future profit margins, "fair" or "reasonable" margins.

21   In the words of the European Court of Justice, Article 81(1) prohibits "any direct or indirect contact between [competitors], the object or effect of which is *either* to influence conduct on the market of an actual or potential competitor *or* to disclose to a [competitor] the course of conduct which they themselves have decided to adopt or contemplate adopting on the market." *Suiker Unie v. Commission* [1975] ECR 1663.

22   In 1776, Adam Smith wrote:

> People of the same trade seldom meet together, even for merriment and diversion, but the conversation ends in a conspiracy against the public, or in some contrivance to raise prices. ... It is impossible indeed to prevent such meetings by any law which either could be executed or would be consistent with liberty and justice. But though the law cannot hinder people of the same trade from sometimes assembling together, it ought to do nothing to facilitate such assemblies, much less to render them necessary.
>
> (*An Inquiry into the Nature and Causes of the Wealth of Nations*, Book One, Chapter X, Part Two)

In this famous quote, Adam Smith – often considered to be one of the patron saints of capitalism – recognizes that, left to their own devises, competitors would prefer the comforts of cooperation over the disciplines of the free market. He also indicates that such cooperation can easily exist on an informal basis. He disagrees with modern competition regulators only on the feasibility of enacting a law which prohibits informal cooperation amongst competitors. Modern competition regulation can be and indeed often is applied to meetings, conversations and other informal cooperation amongst competitors.

23   The statutory term in the EU is "dominant position." The statutory term in the USA is "market power." For our purposes, unless otherwise noted, these terms are synonymous.

24   The European Court of Justice has defined a dominant position as follows:

> a position of economic strength enjoyed by an undertaking which enables it to prevent effective competition [from] being maintained on the relevant market by giving it the power to behave to an appreciable extent independently of its competitors, customers and ultimately of its consumers.
>
> (*United Brands* [1978] 1 CMLR at 486–7)

25   A "relevant market "is a geographic area from which substitute products are available to a single consumer from alternate suppliers.

26   In fact, "extending" a dominant position is nothing other than obtaining a dominant position in one market on the basis of a monopoly maintained in another market.

27   There is slight difference in the scope of these two concepts between the USA and EU. As suggested by the terms, the concept in the EU does not literally refer to obtaining a dominant position by means other than competition. The difference will be disregarded for the purpose of this presentation, in part: (1) because, as evidenced by Article 82 itself, the same actions which constitute "abuse of a dominant position" (i.e., maintaining a dominant position) can also constitute actions tending to obtain a dominant position by means other than competition; (2) because obtaining a dominant position by means other than competition is covered under Article 81 as well as 82 of the Treaty; and (3) because in practice there is frequently no clear distinction between obtaining and maintaining a dominant position.

28   The Treaty goes on to provide that:

> Such abuse may, in particular, consist in: (a) directly or indirectly imposing unfair purchase and selling prices or other unfair trading conditions; (b) limiting production, markets or technical development to the prejudice of consumers; (c) applying dissimilar conditions to equivalent transactions with other trading parties, thereby placing them in a competitive disadvantage; (d) making the conclusion of contracts the subject to acceptance by the other parties of supplementary obligations which, by their nature or according to commercial useage have no connection with the subject of the contracts.
>
> (Article 82 of the Treaty (originally Article 86 of the Treaty of Rome))

Subparts (a) through (d) of Article 82 are effectively identical to subparts (a), (b), (d) and (e) of Article 81. The repetition is deemed necessary because Article 82 applies to practices tending to *maintain* a dominant position through improper means, while Article 81 applies to anti-competitive practices, i.e., practices tending to *obtain* a dominant position through improper means. To the extent that practices are used to obtain but not to maintain a dominant position, they are subject to the rule of reason in the EU. There is no rule of reason for these practices to the extent that they tend to maintain a dominant position.

29   Another abuse of a dominant position consists in tying and full-line forcing, already discussed under the heading of "Vertical Restraints on Customers." As with price discrimination, it is unlikely that a supplier can impose tying or full-line forcing without having a dominant position. If the supplier did not have some degree of dominance, then the customer would simply refuse the supplier's attempt by contracting with another supplier.

30   "Price discrimination" is another common abuse of a dominant position. Price discrimination consists of charging different prices – or imposing other differing terms – on different customers. Such a practice can amount to charging monopoly prices to some, rather than all, of the customers in a market dominated by one or a few suppliers. Price discrimination raises other legal issues where it creates a competitive advantage for one customer over another.

31   Of course, the larger the market segment subject to predatory pricing, the more expensive it is for a dominant supplier to sustain predatory pricing over a long period of time. If the market segment subject to predatory pricing is relatively small, it is conceivable that a dominant supplier can continue predatory pricing for an indefinite period. "Anti-dumping regulation" addresses exactly the same abuse in the arena of international trade. In "dumping" practices, the market segment benefiting from (and subject to) the pricing based on marginal costs is the foreign segment.

32   Markets with only a few suppliers are referred to as "oligopolies." It certainly is possible for the dominant supplier in an oligopoly to be guilty of abusing its dominant position. It is also quite possible for there to be more than one supplier in a dominant position in an oligopolistic market.

33   The longest-standing such national review is the review in Germany by the *Bundeskartellamt*. As in many other countries, Germany claims the right to review an acquisition even if the acquired business has no assets located in Germany. It is enough if buyer, seller or the acquired company has sales into Germany. Unlike some other countries, Germany has relatively high thresholds for the amount of sales or assets located in Germany before notification is required. Other countries, such as Ireland, Greece and Belgium, have very low thresholds on sales for acquisitions requiring notification.

34   In the event that more than two EU member states are so affected by the proposed acquisition, then EU notification is required if the notification is required in respect of any two of the member states or if: (1) the

buying and selling groups have a combined worldwide sales revenues of more than 2.5 billion Euros, (2) combined sales revenues exceeds 100 million in each affected EU member state, and (3) the individual sales revenues of any two businesses exceed 25 million Euros in all affected EU member states and there is more than 100 million Euros sales revenues for any two businesses in the entire EU.

35   There are different aspects to each of these industries, networks and monopolies. From an economic perspective, each can be viewed from the perspective of fixed assets (e.g., wires, towers and switches for telephones and ports for shipping), equipment used to render services (e.g., headsets for telephones and ships for shipping) and the services rendered (e.g., communication for telephones and transportation for shipping).

36   It is important to realize, however, that such monopolies have a value even in the absence of high start-up costs. Even if there were no cost to starting a new airline, its value as a natural monopoly would depend at least in part on its ability to tie into existing airlines, i.e., at airports. (Each airport, by the way, is another natural monopoly – a place where airlines "network.")

37   This paragraph is subject to important qualifications. In general, advantages to consumers are not diminished if the monopolies network with each other. Indeed, creating compatible networks is a good way to limit the power of monopolies to their natural scope. In one new industry, wireless communication, monopolies are restricted in part by the fact that service providers have created technologically compatible networks of facilities, with each providing access to the others through its facilities. Competition authorities have attempted to create the possibility for more competition in established industries by using similar techniques. In telecommunications, for example, AT&T's monopoly in the USA on land-based (i.e., wired) communication facilities, equipment and services has been broken into different monopolies on facilities, equipment and services. Railroads in Britain, utilities in the United States and airlines in Europe are all examples of efforts to create competition in existing monopolistic industries by: (1) separating ownership of facilities, equipment and services; and (2) promoting competition in those segments where monopolies are not necessarily natural (e.g., equipment and services) even if another segment is a natural monopoly (e.g., facilities).

38   Others might argue that fundamental technologies such as computer operating systems should be viewed as natural monopolies and, therefore, subject to regulation of their availability and pricing. Indeed, fundamental technologies arguably are natural monopolies

once they establish themselves as industry standards. Most industry standards are established by governments and industry associations and so do not typically raise issues under competition law. Such standards do not typically raise issues because all competitors have free and equal access to them. Industry standards raise monopoly issues under competition law if they are privately owned by one or more businesses because, in such circumstances, all competitors do not have a free and equal access to them. In addition to operating systems for personal computers, some argue the operating systems for mobile telephones (e.g., GSM) constitute natural monopolies. Actual compatibility of competing technologies and the benefits of identity over compatibility are important issues as regards privately owned technologies considered to be industry standards.

Payment. Deliveries shall be subject to Buyer's prior cash payment in full or prior credit arrangements with Seller on a delivery-by-delivery basis. If payment is not made in accordance with the terms hereof, or if Seller has any doubt at any time as to Buyer's financial condition, Seller shall have the right, at its option, to withhold delivery of Products.

LIMITED WARRANTY AND EXPRESS DIS-CLAIMER. Seller makes no warranty of any kind express or implied, except that Seller owns the Product and that the Products conform to Seller's or manufacturer's standard specifications. SELLER MAKES NO OTHER REPRESENTATION OR WARRANTY OF ANY KIND, EXPRESS OR IMPLIED, AS TO MERCHANTABILITY, FITNESS FOR A PARTICULAR PURPOSE, OR ANY OTHER MATTER WITH RESPECT TO THE PRODUCTS, INCLUDING WITHOUT LIMITATION THE ABSENCE OF CONTAMINANTS. The warranties set forth herein are made only to Buyer and are not transferable by Buyer to its customers or any other party.

SOLE AND EXCLUSIVE REMEDY. In the event that Buyer notifies Seller of a failure of the Product to conform with the limited warranty set forth in the preceding paragraph with ten (10) calendar days after receipt by Seller of the Product in question, then Seller shall, at its sole option, replace non-conforming Product or refund the purchase price thereof to Buyer. Any transportation charges incurred by Buyer in returning of the Products shall not be reimbursed unless authorized in advance by Seller. SUCH REPLACEMENT OR REFUND SHALL BE BUYER'S SOLE AND EXCLUSIVE REMEDY FOR BREACH OF THE LIMITED WARRANTY PROVIDED BY THIS SECTION.

LIMITATION OF SELLER'S LIABILITY. SELLER'S TOTAL LIABILITY TO BUYER FOR ANY AND ALL LOSSES AND DAMAGES ARISING OUT OF ANY CAUSE WHATSOEVER (WHETHER IN CONTRACT OR TORT, INCLUDING NEGLIGENCE AND STRICT LIABILITY) SHALL IN NO EVENT EXCEED THE PURCHASE PRICE OF THE PRODUCTS. SELLER SHALL NOT UNDER ANY CIRCUMSTANCES BE LIABLE FOR ANY (AND BUYER SHALL INDEMNIFY SELLER FROM AND AGAINST ALL) INCIDENTAL, INDIRECT, SPECIAL, CONSEQUENTIAL, EXEMPLARY OR PUNITIVE DAMAGES INCURRED, SUFFERED OR PAID BY BUYER AND ALL OTHER PERSONS. THIS LIMITATION OF LIABILITY SHALL SURVIVE THE FAILURE OF THE EXCLUSIVE REMEDY PROVIDED HEREINABOVE. If Seller furnishes technical or other advice to Buyer, whether or not at Buyer's request, in connection with the Product, Seller shall not be liable therefor (whether in contract or tort, including negligence and strict liability), and Buyer assumes all risk of such advice and the results thereof. The limitations of Seller's liability in this paragraph are without prejudice to any other limitation or restriction available to Seller under contract, statute, other law or equity.

Buyer's Claims Procedure. Buyer specifically acknowledges that Seller manufactures the Products for sale to customers for use in a wide range of applications. Buyer specifically assumes all responsibility for determining whether or not the Products sold hereunder are suitable for the applications for which Buyer will use such Products, and Buyer specifically assumes all responsibility for testing said Products to determine whether or not said Products as delivered are appropriate for the intended applications. Buyer shall examine and test each delivery of Products pursuant to this Agreement upon receipt hereof. Before such Products are used and within ten (10) days from each such delivery, Buyer shall notify Seller in writing of any claims on account of weight, quality, loss of or damage to the Products so delivered. Failure to so notify Seller shall constitute a waiver by Buyer of all claims with respect to all of the Products so delivered. Use of Products shall be deemed to mean Seller's satisfactory performance of this Agreement in respect of such Products.

BUYER INDEMNIFIES SELLER. UPON DEMAND FROM SELLER TO BUYER, BUYER SHALL INDEMNIFY SELLER FROM AND AGAINST ANY AND ALL COSTS (INCLUDING COURT COSTS AND ATTORNEYS' FEES), JUDGMENTS (INCLUDING PUNITIVE DAMAGES) AND OTHER PAYMENTS IN CONNECTION WITH ANY AND ALL CLAIMS, LAW SUITS, COURT ORDERS AND SETTLEMENTS MADE, BROUGHT, ISSUED

OR AGREED BY OR WITH ANY AND ALL PER-SONS OTHER THAN BUYER (INCLUDING WITH-OUT LIMITATION BUYER'S EMPLOYEES, AGENTS AND CUSTOMERS) AND ARISING OUT OF SELLER'S EXECUTION, DELIVERY AND PERFOR-MANCE OF THIS CONTRACT, INCLUDING WITH-OUT LIMITATION CLAIMS, LAW SUITS, COURT ORDERS AND SETTLEMENTS ON THE BASIS OF ANY AND ALL DIRECT, INDIRECT, INCIDENTAL, SPECIAL, CONSEQUENTIAL, EXEMPLARY, PUNI-TIVE OR OTHER DAMAGES INCURRED, SUF-FERED OR PAID BY ANY OR ALL SUCH PERSONS OTHER THAN BUYER (INCLUDING WITH LIMI-TATION BUYER'S EMPLOYEES, AGENTS AND CUSTOMERS).

Interpretation. These terms and conditions, together with the invoice to which they are attached (the "Invoice"), constitute the entire agreement between the parties in connection with the Products described in the Invoice. Any inconsistencies between the Invoice and any purchase and sales agreement which applies to the Products described in the Invoice (a "Purchase Agreement") shall be decided in favor of the Purchase Agreement. Each partial delivery of the total quantity of Products specified in the Invoice shall be a separate sale. The manufacture and delivery of Products by Seller shall be excused as and to the extent affected by *force majeure*. The validity, interpretation and performance hereof and any dispute connected herewith shall be governed and construed in accordance with the substantive laws of Switzerland, without regard to its choice of law rules. The Convention on the International Sale of Goods is expressly excluded.

Arbitration All disputes arising out of or in connection with these terms and conditions, including disputes on its conclusion, binding effect, amendment and termination, shall be resolved to the exclusion of ordinary courts by a Sole Arbitrator in accordance with the International Rules of the Zurich Chamber of Commerce.

CHAPTER 8: RELATIONSHIPS WITH CONSUMERS

1   Markets are based primarily on individual choice. The aggregate effect of buyers' individual choices, all made more or less independently one from the other, constitute the discipline markets impose on sellers. Certain weaknesses are inherent in the market as a mechanism for regulation. Communication and coordination amongst buyers are not an inherent part of market transactions, just as communication and coordination are not an accepted part of market transactions. As we will see, regulatory agencies and consumer protection groups attempt to address this shortcoming in mass consumer markets.

2   It undoubtedly would have been commercially impracticable for Ford Motor Company to disclose the potentially lethal defect in the Pinto gas tank. This does not imply that Ford Motor Company was morally justified in manufacturing the Pinto with the undisclosed potentially lethal defect. Instead, the impracticability of such a disclosure simply highlights the limitations of disclosure obligations as a mechanism for protecting consumer interests.

3   Immanuel Kant is sometimes cited as providing, with his second formulation of the "categorical imperative," a sound philosophical justification for the right to know. Immanuel Kant's second formulation of the "categorical imperative" can be paraphrased as follows: "never treat others only as means, but also always as ends." At the same time, Kant assumes that treating persons "as ends" entails allowing each of them to exercise fully his or her nature as an independent individual, i.e., allowing them to make their own decisions. In other words, no one should tell lies or keep secrets about relevant information in their dealings with others. Kant's second formulation is certainly consistent with the efficiency theories in market economics. Efficient allocation under market conditions assumes that all participants in the market have complete information. Kant's categorical imperative goes further than the contract and commercial law. In the absence of government regulations, merchants are not permitted to tell each other lies in their business dealings but they are permitted to keep secrets from each other. Pursuant to government regulation, companies are more and more required to disclose all relevant facts known to them at the time they make decisions, especially in their dealings with consumers. In other words, under government regulation, companies are increasingly prohibited from keeping secrets.

4   Other interesting issues are raised when decision-makers take action knowing that they do not have all relevant information. Can they be found to have assumed the risk inherent in their ignorance, so as to exonerate in whole or in part others who may have misrepresented or concealed information?

5   There are other assumptions made in establishing that market transactions are economically efficient. Some of those assumptions are (1) the availability of alternatives, (2) no transaction costs, and (3) no third party costs.

6   Some persons argue that, other than price and other information consumers negotiate, sellers should have

no obligation to make any disclosures regarding the goods and services they offer. It is interesting to note that such persons are sometimes referred to as "market fundamentalists." In fact, markets do not function efficiently unless consumers have complete information. Moreover, consumers theoretically have complete information in completely competitive markets. The fact that sellers are not compelled by market conditions to disclose all information concerning their products and services is arguably evidence of the fact that their markets are not completely competitive and therefore not completely efficient.

7   Research on the asymmetrical availability of information in various markets has received significant attention lately. James A. Mirrlees and William Vickrey shared the 1996 Nobel Prize in economics for their work in this area. And again in 2001, three economists shared the Nobel Prize in economics for their work in the area of asymmetrical information. (George A. Akerlof, A. Michael Spence and Joseph E. Stiglitz).

8   The exceptions to this general rule are the "warranties" implied by law in connection with the purchase and sale of goods in market transactions. Those implied warranties include: (1) the promise that the seller owns the goods offered for sale; and (2) the promise that the goods are suitable for their common usage. Warranties implied by law are discussed in the chapter on contract and commercial law.

9   Ford Motor Company was, of course, eventually held legally liable for the persons killed and injured as a result of the defective Pinto gas tank. It was held liable for "product liability," a tort (i.e., a violation of its general obligation to avoid personal injury or property damage).

10   "It is abundantly clear that any general framework on fair trading must spell out the concept of competition for which the European Community stands. So far, *competition law*, [the] law on *fair trading* and *consumer protection law* co-exist but are not inter-linked. ... These findings should be read as a plea for basing the general framework on fair trading on a coherent concept of competition which enshrines *consumer protection as the explicit aim of the regulation of market practices* [both competition and fair trading]." Taken from *The Feasibility of a General Legislative Framework on Fair Trading* (November 2000, Executive Summary, page 8) by the Institut für Europaisches Wirtschaft und Verbraucherrecht e. V. for the Director General on Consumer Protection for the European Commission.

11   The FTC Act also empowers the FTC to prohibit "unfair methods of competition." This additional power is similar to the powers of the US Justice Department to enforce the criminal provisions of the Sherman Act, discussed in Chapter 7.

12   The Treaty goes on to state that: "Consumer protection requirements shall be taken into account in defining and implementing other Community policies and activities." Treaty of Rome. Title XIV Consumer Protection Article 153 (1).

13   For example, see Decision No 283/1999/EC of the European Parliament and of the Council of 25 January 1999 establishing a general framework for Community activities in favor of consumers. Official Journal L 034 , 09/02/1999 P. 0001 – 0007.

14   FTC Policy Statement on Deception (14 October 1983), FTC letter to The Honorable John D. Dingell, Chairman, Committee on Energy and Commerce, US House of Representatives, Washington, DC 20515 USA.

15   The promotion and guarantee of "fair business practices" is essential to the relationship between consumers and suppliers. In this context they relate to the economic interests of consumers, as opposed to their health and safety which are regulated elsewhere. The aim is to promote a fair, transparent and competitive internal market, where consumers and suppliers can conduct business with confidence. Consumers and businesses benefit from the prevention of misleading, deceptive or otherwise unfair trading practices that exploit consumers and damage competitors. Consumers can enjoy better quality goods and services, lower prices and increased innovation as a result of a more competitive and efficient internal market.

      (The Mission Statement of the Health and Consumer Protection Directorate General)

16   There are several related, but different, concepts of fair trading in countries of Europe: "fault" in France; "bonos mores" in Germany, Austria, Greece and Portugal; "fair commercial practices" in Belgium, Italy, Luxembourg and Spain; "good marketing practices" in Denmark, Finland and Sweden; "unlawfulness" in The Netherlands. There are several concepts applied in England, Ireland: "truthful advertisement," "clear, helpful and adequate pre-contractual information" and "clear and fair contracts." *The Feasibility of a General Legislative Framework on Fair Trading*, (November 2000, Executive Summary, page 5) by the Institut für Europaisches Wirtschaft und Verbraucherrecht e. V. for the Director General on Consumer Protection for the European Commission.

17   See 2 October 2001 "Green Paper on European Union Consumer Protection," Commission of the European Communities, COM (2001) 531 final.

18   As an alternative to [having consumer protection] based upon [the various European nations'] com-

mercial practices, the framework directive could be based on the more restrictive concept of misleading and deceptive practices. It would probably be easier to reach agreement on such framework directed at this concept [i.e., of misleading and deceptive practices] is in many ways the common core of unfair trading concepts across the EU.

(2 October 2001 "Green Paper on European Union Consumer Protection," Commission of the European Communities. COM (2001) 531 final, Section 4.2, page 13)

19 In the European Union, advertising is regulated by The Council Directive concerning Misleading Advertising (84/450/EEC 10 September 1984); The EP & Council Directive dealing with Comparative Advertising, amending the previous one (97/55/EC 6 October 1997); The "Television Without Frontiers" directive (89/552/EEC), revised by the European Parliament & Council Directive (97/36/EC 30 June 1997); and The Commission Report to the Council and the European Parliament on Consumer Complaints in respect of Distance Selling and Comparative Advertising (COM 2000 127 final).

20 The Council Directive concerning Misleading Advertising (84/450/EEC 10 September 1984). The last term used in the Directive concerning Misleading Advertising is "competitor." However, as indicated in Chapter 7, there has been an active, long-standing debate over the individuals intended to benefit from "unfair competition" regulations. See generally *The Feasibility of a General Legislative Framework on Fair Trading* (November 2000) by the Institut für Europaisches Wirtschaft und Verbraucherrecht e. V. for the Director General on Consumer Protection for the European Commission, already cited above in Note 16.

21   The [FTC's] determination of what constitutes a reasonable basis depends on a number of factors relevant to the benefits and costs of substantiating a particular claim. These factors include: the type of claim, the product, the consequences of a false claim, the benefits of a truthful claim, the cost of developing substantiation for the claim, and the amount of substantiation experts in the field believe is reasonable. Extrinsic evidence, such as expert testimony or consumer surveys, is useful to determine what level of substantiation consumers expect to support a particular product claim and the adequacy of evidence an advertiser possesses.
(FTC Policy Statement Regarding Advertisement Substantiation, published pursuant to 11 March 1983 request for comments (48 FR 10471, 11 March 1983))

22 In the European Union: comparative advertising is permissible if: (a) it is not misleading; (b) it compares goods or services meeting the same needs or intended for the same purpose; (c) it objectively compares one or more material, relevant, verifiable and representative features of those goods and services, which may include price; (d) it does not create confusion in the market place between the advertiser and a competitor or between the advertiser's trade marks, trade names, other distinguishing marks, goods or services and those of a competitor; (e) it does not discredit or denigrate the trade marks, trade names, other distinguishing marks, goods, services, activities, or circumstances of a competitor; (f) for products with designation of origin, it relates in each case to products with the same designation; (g) it does not take unfair advantage of the reputation of a trade mark, trade name or other distinguishing marks of a competitor or of the designation of origin of competing products; (h) it does not present goods or services as imitations or replicas of goods or services bearing a protected trade mark or trade name. Article 4 of The European Parliament and The Council Directive 97/55/EC of 6 October 1997 amending Directive 84/450/EEC concerning misleading advertising so as to include comparative advertising.

23 Comparative advertising in the USA can also raise issues under trademark law: "Any person who … in commercial advertising or promotion, misrepresents the nature, characteristics, qualities, or geographic origin of his or her or another person's goods, services, or commercial activities, shall be liable in a civil action by any person who believes that he or she is or is likely to be damaged by such act" (15 USCA 1125(a)(2). The Lanham Act, Section 43(a)(2), enacted in 1945 and amended in 1988.)

24 The classification of "franchising arrangements" as a consumer transaction requires some clarification. Franchise arrangements are classified as consumer transactions because the franchisee is entering into several long-term exclusive purchasing arrangements from the franchisor, including supplies of raw materials, final products, supplies and equipment, trademark licenses and, often, business consulting services. These long-term arrangements, taken individually and together, constitute franchisees as significant "outlets" for franchisors' goods and services.

25 See Article 3(2) of Council Directive 93/13/EEC of 5 April 1993 on unfair terms in consumer contracts. In this fundamental regulation, a consumer contract is equated with a contract which has not been negotiated, and a contract which has not been negotiated is equated with a potentially unfair contract.

26   In contrast, disclosure requirements, including disclosure requirements for franchising, mortgage lending and other consumer financial services, apply to the most essential contract terms: the goods and services to be provided and the price to be paid for those services.

27   The European Union even provides an extensive list of such potentially "unfair" (i.e., unreasonable) contract terms in consumer transactions. The EU list is set forth as an Annex to this chapter. It is important to note that the annexed EU list is considered to be an indicative, not exhaustive, list of unfair contract provisions in consumer transactions.

28   The Commission has identified three factors in applying the prohibition against consumer "unfairness." These were: (1) whether the practice injures consumers; (2) whether it violates established public policy; (3) whether it is unethical or unscrupulous (17 December 1980 FTC Policy Statement on Unfairness).

29   Emotional impact and other more subjective types of harm, on the other hand, will not ordinarily make a practice unfair (17 December 1980 FTC Policy Statement on Unfairness).

30   The principles in this paragraph should not be confused with the principles of agency and corporate law applicable to management's relationship with shareholders. Under agency law and corporate law, even if managers make accurate and complete disclosures as required under the securities law, managers are not exonerated from legal liability for losses suffered by shareholders as a result of managers' breaches of their duties of care and loyalty to shareholders. Shareholders are not deemed to have "assumed the risk" for management's conduct by virtue of the accurate and complete disclosures. This is true in part because managers' disclosures follow their actions on behalf of shareholders.

CHAPTER 9: RELATIONSHIPS WITH LOCAL COMMUNITIES

1   It is difficult to develop an all-encompassing definition of environmental pollution. The "physical assets" referenced in my definition include assets in addition to personal property, such as national parks, rivers, lakes, oceans and the atmosphere. The value derived from "use" includes recreational and aesthetic value. In addition to environmental pollution, there are other sorts of environmental degradation. For example, the depletion of natural resources – such as deforestation – raises issues of environmental degradation quite separate from issues of environmental pollution. In general, this chapter does not address broader issues such

as depletion or biodiversity. It also does not deal with narrower issues outside the scope of this text, such as collecting and disposing of solid waste and processing human waste from residential areas, which is handled by municipalities or waste management businesses.

2   The personal injuries typically caused by environmental contamination are illnesses of various sorts, including cancer. Property damage typically caused by environmental contamination takes the form of polluted soil or water which, in turn, results in reduced use values for real estate, reduced transfer values for real estate and a heightened risk of various illnesses for those persons who have occasion to occupy the real property.

3   As a practical matter, businesses never intend to cause environmental contamination; they simply intend to manufacture a product or provide a service. The environmental contamination is an unintended, incidental effect of businesses' productive activity.

4   Interestingly, businesses may not contribute the most to the "wealth of nations," as postulated by Adam Smith in 1776, if the social costs of economic transactions – such as soil, water and air pollution – are not included in the calculation of national wealth, i.e., used to reduce the calculation of national wealth. In other words, the wealth of a nation may not be maximized to the extent that the costs of a transaction are not borne by the parties to the transaction. (Such costs are often referred to as "externalities.") From another perspective: historically, clean air, clean water in rivers and lakes – and, in some places at some times, even land – have been considered to be practically limitless and therefore to have no economic value. Accordingly, a nation's wealth was maximized even if some of its air, water and land were contaminated by economic activity. More recently: as population and industrial activity have increased, clean air, water and land are no longer considered to be practically limitless. To the extent that governments impose preventative environmental regulations, they have begun to place a value on clean air, water and land.

5   For a general introduction of this topic, please read my discussion in Chapter 3 (Business Regulation in General) under the heading "Government regulation", page 35.

6   Precipitation is another method for soil remediation. Precipitation is a remediation method similar to incineration. Rather than exposing the contaminated soil to heat, the contaminated soil is exposed to a liquid, which soaks through the soil, washing the contaminants into a tank. Sometimes the precipitates react chemically with the contaminants, rendering them harmless.

7   For example, under a brown field standard, a former lead refinery – usually a very polluted facility – may

not require any remediation if it is sold to a developer for the construction and use of a shopping center. Of course, the developer will probably pay a lower price for the former lead refinery because the continuing soil contamination will inevitably restrict future uses and sales of the land. At the same time, the seller is not obligated to remediate the former lead refinery for the purpose of selling it to the developer for use as a shopping center. In fact, the regulators give the developer a promise that the developer will not need to remediate the soil for as long as the land is used as a shopping center. The issues of migration and ingestion can be handled, for example, simply by demolishing the lead refinery and covering the site with asphalt.

8   For this reason, businesses which lease land from another business or individual are usually prohibited by the owner under the lease agreement from conducting environmental tests on the land they occupy.

9   A final regulatory issue concerning remediation, of less immediate importance to most businesses, is the clean up of locations where hazardous wastes from various industrial operations have been collected for the purpose of disposal, e.g., land fills. Government environmental authorities issue licenses to land fills permitting them to accumulate and store certain types of hazardous wastes, provided that it remains isolated from humans, animals and the surrounding environment. Land fills can be subject to remediation if they do not benefit from such licenses, if the substances found at the site exceed the types and quantities of substances covered by the license, or if the hazardous substances are not effectively isolated with the land fill, i.e., there is some migration. Remediation of landfills is very expensive. At the same time, land fills typically have only one or a few owners, who typically are not able to pay for the remediation. At the same time, innumerable operators of other industrial and agricultural sites have used the location to varying extents. Each has paid for the right to dispose of hazardous waste in the land fill and most probably is not responsible for the failure to operate the site in compliance with permits. As a result, the remediation of such sites is often covered by government trust, endowed with funds specifically intended to accomplish such remediations of land fills. In the United States, the federal government's fund is called the "Super Fund," and such sites are called "Super Fund" sites.

10   In the United States, each such person is referred to as a "potentially responsible party" or "PRP." Each PRP, beginning with the current owner and operator, is required to pay the entire amount for remediation. In this way, regulators have the greatest assurance that past pollution will in fact be remediated. It becomes the responsibility of the PRPs who actually pay for

remediation to obtain a monetary contribution from the other PRPs. If the entire group of PRPs cannot supply the funds for the remediation, then the government will provide the funds, sometimes from a trust especially established for the purpose of paying such remediations.

11   Relying on remediation also creates broader public policy issues. If pollution from a technology can be addressed (i.e., prevented) before the technology is commercialized, pollution regulations usually reflect a policy balance of: (i) environmental costs for local communities; against (ii) economic benefits to businesses and consumers. If pollution from a technology is addressed (i.e., remediated) after the technology is commercialized, pollution regulation needs to strike a more complicated balance of: (i) environmental costs against both; (ii) economic benefits to businesses and consumers; and (iii) employment issues for local communities. Employment issues obviously moderate local communities' environmental concerns and complicate their efforts to address environmental issues.

Remediation requirements also typically raise policy issues concerning the opportunity costs for business which are more difficult than similar issues raised by preventive environmental regulations. If environmental regulations are introduced before a technology is commercialized (i.e., preventive measures), then the issue presented to business is whether there is a better application for its money. If environmental regulations are introduced after a technology is commercialized (i.e., including remediation), then the issue presented to business is whether there is a better application for its fixed investment in plant and equipment. Since it is usually easier to find an alternative application for money than for fixed assets, alterations of planned economic activity in anticipation of preventive environmental regulation are arguably not as potentially distortive as the modifications to existing businesses caused by reaction to remedial environmental regulation.

12   See Chapter 12 ("The Environment") in *Global Business Regulation*, by John Braithwaite and Peter Drahos (© 2000) ("Braithwaite and Drahos"), published by Cambridge University Press (UK), especially pages 269, 279–85.

13   Forms of international coordination useful in other regulatory areas are not effective in preventing air and water pollution. "Mutual recognition," for example, is sometimes a useful form of international coordination in terms of product safety (e.g., electrical equipment). Pursuant to this principle, if a product is made in one country (e.g., Germany) and complies with its product safety regulations (i.e., with the German regulations), then another country (e.g., France) deems the product

to be safe for sale and use within its borders. Mutual recognition is not typically useful for coordinating environmental prevention because of the cumulative, cross-border effect of air and water pollution.

14   This discussion of the permissive and precautionary approaches focuses primarily on preventative environmental regulation. Policy decisions between precautionary and permissive principles can also apply to remediation regulations. More commonly, however, remediation regulations are the result of the application of the permissive principle to preventive regulation. If remediation is mandated, then a government has usually determined that remediation is required, even pursuant to a permissive principle. In other words, the remediation is mandated because the government has determined that the product has proven to be unsafe.

15   For such scientists, the only realistic standard for stating scientific conclusions is to state that they are a "consensus" based: (1) in the first instance, on individual scientists' personal observations; and (2) in the second instance, on a consensus among those scientists who have made such personal observations. Furthermore, the level of confidence in any consensus among scientists – and, thus, in any given scientific conclusion – depends upon the conditions in which each scientist individually makes his own observations. For example: Were the conditions controlled? Were the results measured? Have the results been independently verified by anther scientist obtaining the same results in the same conditions?

16   The Organization for Economic Cooperation and Development has developed a framework of laboratory procedures for testing chemicals. If the chemicals are tested anywhere in the world using these guidelines, then the results of that test are binding everywhere in the world. See Braithwaite and Drahos, page 258. The OECD guidelines do not, however, mandate testing of chemicals before commercialization. Such mandates are left to national environmental authorities.

17   The greater risk probably exists when available evidence is insufficient to assess environmental risks. At the current time, for example, there are tens of thousands of synthetic chemicals available for sale around the world. Only a small portion has been tested individually for toxicity, with practically no testing of the interactions of toxic chemicals. The regime for testing synthetic chemicals obviously differs dramatically from the regime for testing pharmaceuticals, primarily because pharmaceuticals are intended for human ingestion while other synthetic chemicals are not intended for human consumption (any consumption occurs only incidentally as a result of exposure in the work place or in the greater environment). This issue was addressed

in the United States, arguably with limited success, by the federal Toxic Substances Control Act (TOSCA). The European Union is currently addressing the same issues of testing before commercialization with its proposed REACH program ("Registration, Evaluation and Authorization of Chemicals").

18   Such a distinction might account, at least in part, for the different regulatory stance toward bio-engineered organisms in the European Union, depending on whether they are used in medicine or agriculture. The EU is certainly more permissive regarding bio-engineered medications than bio-engineered food crops even though bio-engineered materials both for medicine and for agriculture are subject, each in its own way, to extensive testing on humans. Still, in the EU, the commercialization of many bio-engineered medicines is currently permitted (evidencing a permissive approach – at least as regards environmental matters) while the commercialization of most bio-engineered crops is not currently permitted (evidencing a precautionary approach – prompted to a great extent by environmental concerns). One important reason for the difference might be found in the assessment that bio-engineered medicines deliver a clear and significant benefit to consumers (i.e., individual health as opposed to illness) with releases into the environment occurring in relatively controlled conditions on a relatively small scale and therefore presenting a limited risk. The important benefits derived from bio-engineered medicines, together with limited environmental risks, lead to a permissive attitude. Bio-engineered foods, on the other hand, do not deliver a clear and significant benefit to consumers (i.e., Europe already has abundant food supplies) with releases into the environment (i.e., seeding fields) occurring in relatively uncontrolled conditions on a relatively large scale and therefore presenting a significant risk.

19   For example, even though it may have been appropriate to take a permissive attitude toward the commercialization of the first synthetic chemicals in the 1950s (i.e., fertilizers, pesticides, herbicides and plastics), it might be appropriate today to take a precautionary attitude toward the commercialization of new synthetic chemicals (with tens of thousands of such chemicals registered for sale in some or all of the countries around the world). Such a change in regulatory attitude can be justified not only by the regulatory experience and improvements in scientific methods useful in detecting potential harm. Such a change can be justified by the diminishing marginal returns obtained from adding more synthetic chemicals to the commerce.

20   An important factor in weighing these risks might be the assessment by regulators and the general public

about the adequacy of monetary compensation pursuant to judicial remedies in the absence of precautionary government regulation

CHAPTER 11: RELATIONSHIPS WITH TAXING AUTHORITIES

1   As with the application of other areas of business law to specific situations, the application of international corporate income taxation can be a very difficult task, with the exact outcome depending on authoritative precedent, specific regulations, administrative practice, the details of specific transactions and a taxpayer's overall position in respect of the regulatory authorities. At the same time, there is probably no area of international law where the rules are more detailed and change more continuously, more rapidly and more dramatically (except for international economic sanctions). In no other area of international law is the outcome so determined by the interplay of detailed substantive rules in various countries, none of which is willing to defer to any other country's legislative authority. In addition:

> One of the reasons the topic [i.e., international corporate income taxation] is so important in the real world and yet so little loved by scholars is that international tax law is both excruciatingly complex and fundamentally arbitrary.
> (Lebovitz, M. S. and Seto, T. P. (2001) The fundamental problem of international taxation, *Loyola of Los Angeles International and Comparative Law Review*, 23(4), 529–36)

2   For example, the tax consequences arising from any individual transaction usually depend on a taxpayer's broader tax position and exposures, e.g., the existence of profits or losses from the current and prior tax periods.

3   August, R. (2004) *International Business Law* (Fourth Edition), Upper Saddle River, NJ: Pearson Education, Inc., page 715.

4   August, R. (2004) *International Business Law* (Fourth Edition), Upper Saddle River, NJ: Pearson Education, Inc., page 724.

5   There is another model treaty addressing issues of international corporate taxation. It is the United Nations' Model Double Taxation Convention between Developed and Developing Countries. This chapter will focus exclusively on the OECD Model Convention.

6   There are usually very few differences between priority based on a nationality principle or on a residency principle because the nationality and residency of most companies is the same for the purpose of the OECD Model Convention. In other words, the nation in which a company is incorporated is also the nation in which it has its central management and control. For example, a company incorporated in Germany tends to have its central management in Germany. If, however, a company's central management is located outside of its nation of incorporation, then priority will be given to the nation from which it exercises "effective management":

> Where by reason of the provisions of paragraph 1 a [corporation] is a resident of [two] Contracting States, then it shall be deemed to be a resident only of the State in which its place of effective management is situated.
> (OECD Model Convention. Article 4(3))

7   As with many other conclusions in this chapter, this conclusion is limited to the situation where the exporting company and its customers are located in the countries with a bilateral income tax treaty following the OECD Model Convention.

A discussion of the taxation of export sales is a good occasion to remind you that examples in this chapter are given simply for the purpose of illustrating principles: In this case, the general principle that under the OECD Model Convention resident nations have priority over source nations as regards the taxation of business profits.

A closer examination of the taxation of export sales by nations where exporters are resident illustrates the difficulties that can arise out of apparently straightforward issues of international corporate taxation. For decades, the US taxation of export sales by US corporations has been the source of international trade tensions with Europe. Of course, all nations want to promote their resident companies' exports. Many European nations, for example, tax their resident corporations only on the "territorial" principle, effectively promoting export sales. In other words, income derived from exports by corporations resident in some European countries is not subject to income taxation there – even in the absence of an exemption, deduction or credit. European countries rely on broader legal principles unilaterally to limit their right to tax residents in accordance with the "territorial" principle. Accordingly, this self-imposed limitation preventing the taxation of residents on their income from extra-territorial sources is not specifically intended to pro-mote exports. At the same time, the "territorial" lim-itation makes it possible for corporations from some European countries to engage in tax-free export sales.

In contrast to European countries, the United States claims the right to tax the worldwide income of all of its residents, including resident corpora-tions. Accordingly, if the USA wants to provide a tax incentive for its resident corporations to engage in exports, then the US needs to provide a total or par-tial exemption, deduction or credit from its income taxes specifically intended to favor export income. From time to time over the years, the US has offered exemptions, deductions and credits for its resident corporations' export income, relying most recently on exemptions. Each time, European countries have objected to these arrangements – and each time pre-vailed before the WTO and its predecessor organiza-tions. The EU announced that it intended to begin retaliatory procedures against $4 billion of US exports if, by January 2004, the US failed to elimi-nate its current "exemption" scheme. For further dis-cussion of these issues – from the US perspective – please see the 14 May 2003 testimony of Gary Clyde Hufbauer before the US House Committee on Small Businesses.

8   As previously noted, there are always two levels of analysis in international corporate tax issues. The first is the taxes imposed by nations and the second is the effect of a bilateral tax treaty to limit that taxing power. This analysis is important, for example, as regards export operations. Importing nations often claim the right to tax an import operation into their country if that operation is continuous and substantial enough to constitute a "trade or business" within the importing nation. In this context, the OECD Model Convention provisions concerning "permanent estab-lishments" imposes a limit on the ability of the import-ing nation to tax the importer (resident in another country). If the exporting and importing nations have entered into a bilateral income tax treaty consistent with the OECD Model Convention, then the importing nation can tax the trade or business within its borders only if that trade or business constitutes a "permanent establishment."

9   To the extent that such a trade or business imposes taxes on income from sources within the country, e.g., domestic sales, then the national claim is based on principles of both residency and source. If the national claim to tax the trade or business extends to export sales by the non-resident corporation's trade or business, then the national claim is based on principles of residency alone.

10   OECD Model Convention. Article 5 (1). Also consider: "such a presence [i.e., a permanent establishment] especially includes a) a place of management; b) branch; c) an office; d) a factory; e) a workshop; and f) a mine, an oil or gas well, a quarry or any other place of extraction of natural resources" (OECD Model Convention. Article 5 (2)).

11   OECD Model Convention. Article 5 (5).

12   OECD Model Convention. Article 5 (6).

13   OECD Model Convention. Article 5 (4).

14   OECD Model Convention. Article 5 (4).

15   The OECD Model Convention provides further guid-ance concerning the expenses properly allocated to a permanent establishment:

> In determining the profits of a permanent estab-lishment, there shall be allowed as deductions expenses which are incurred for the purposes of the permanent establishment, including executive and general administrative expenses so incurred, whether in the State in which the permanent estab-lishment is situated or elsewhere.
> (OECD Model Convention. Article 7(3))

16   OECD Model Convention. Article 7(4).

17   Withholdings at the source are also permitted for cap-ital gains from the sale of real estate and some other types of sources not treated here. See OECD Model Convention, Chapter III (Taxation of Income).

18   If a nation subjects a non-resident corporation more generally to income taxes (e.g., on the basis of busi-ness profits derived from a trade or business con-ducted there by the non-resident corporation's permanent establishment), then the nation can – pur-suant to its own domestic tax rules, in the appropriate case – assimilate any interest, royalties or dividend payments to the business profits received and reported by the non-resident corporation, and collect taxes from the non-resident corporation, either on the basis of gross revenues or net income.

19   OECD Model Convention. Article 10(2).

20   OECD Model Convention. Article 11(2).

21   OECD Model Convention. Article 12.

22   The use of income tax incentives to attract desirable types of business operations from abroad is an important cause of "tax competition," discussed later in this chapter. Nations could also adopt domestic tax rules reducing or eliminating taxes for all foreign corporations, without regard to the nationality or residency of the foreign corporation. Tax havens often adopt this approach. Other coun-tries prefer to negotiate reductions in withholding rates in the context of tax treaties to insure recipro-cal treatment for their resident corporations receiv-

ing interest, royalty and dividend payments from abroad.

23 "The profits of an enterprise of a Contracting State shall be taxable only in that State … " (OECD Model Convention. Article 7(1)).

24 Please see my discussion of the trade issues raised by the US system at Note 7.

25 Limiting the reach of a nation's income taxes on its resident corporations to the income they derive from within the nation's territory (i.e., the "territorial" principle) should not be confused with the 'source" principle, which nations apply to non-resident corporations.

26 In fact, a nation can grant exemptions for taxes imposed by another nation even in the absence of a tax treaty requiring it to do so. If such an exemption exists in Canada on the basis of taxes imposed in Chile, such an exemption would in fact be granted on the basis of internal Canadian law without any treaty requirement because, at the present time, there is no bilateral income tax treaty between Canada and Chile. Finally, an exemption granted by Canada for taxes imposed by Chile on trades and businesses located there would be different from the exemptions currently granted by the United States for export transactions of its resident corporations because the US grants those exemptions without regard to foreign taxes imposed on those transactions.

27 Of course, the exemption principle would not lead to the payment of less tax if Chile used a lower tax rate than Canada. In my example, if Chile imposed tax at a rate of 30 percent and Canada imposed tax at a rate of 15 percent, then the Canadian corporation would pay $300,000 to the Chilean government even though the applicable Canadian tax rate would result in only $150,000 in corporate income tax.

28 There is a third mechanism for avoiding double income taxation: the "deduction." While the credit is used more than the exemption by national taxing authorities to defer to other countries' income taxation, the deduction system is used only rarely. Pursuant to a deduction, the nation where a corporation is resident defers to taxes imposed by another nation by subtracting from the income otherwise taxable in the resident nation the amount of income tax paid to the other nation. For example, pursuant to the "deduction" mechanism, Canada would allow Canadian corporations to deduct from their worldwide income – otherwise taxable in Canada – the amount of taxes paid in Chile or in any other country on business profits realized abroad. The deduction mechanism is least preferred by corporations because it never provides complete relief from double taxation. For example, if Chile used its 12 per cent tax rate to impose taxes of $120,000 on $1,000,000 of business profits of a Canadian corporation, and if Canada used the "deduction" mechanism to avoid double taxation in respect of its 30 per cent tax rate on business profits, then the Canadian corporation would pay (a) $120,000 to Chilean taxing authorities, plus (b) another $264,000 to the Canadian taxing authorities. The Canadian corporation would pay $264,000 in Canada because it would still be subject to Canada's 30 percent tax rate on the business profits taxed in Chile. Rather than receiving an exemption or credit, the Canadian corporation would only receive a "deduction" for the taxes it paid in Chile. In other words, the Canadian corporation could only subtract from the $1,000,000 of income taxable in Canada the $120,000 in income taxes paid to Chile. As a result, the Canadian corporation pays $384,000 in combined income tax on the Chilean income, more than the $300,000 required to be paid under the higher of the two applicable national tax rates.

29 This list of examples for both tax evasion and avoidance was developed by the United Nations International Cooperation in Tax Matters: Guidelines for International Cooperation Against the Evasion and Avoidance of Taxes (with special reference to taxes on income, profits, capital and capital gains) (UN Doc. ST/ESA/142, 1984). The distinction between tax evasion and avoidance is not authoritatively established by the United Nations. As noted in my text, it is quite possible that cases of intentional thin capitalization and intentional transfer pricing abuse can give rise to criminal sanctions in at least some countries.

30 A parent and subsidiary are unlikely to shift profits to the subsidiary unless the subsidiary has a foreseeable use for the funds or the overall tax burden of repatriating the profits from the subsidiary to the parent is less than the parent's tax burden for its business profits.

31 Under the OECD Model Convention: "If an enterprise in one nation controls an enterprise in another state or if those enterprises are under common control" and "conditions are made or imposed between the two enterprises in their commercial or financial relations which differ from those which would be made between independent enterprises, then any profits which would, but for those conditions, have accrued to one of the enterprises, but, by reason of those conditions, have not so accrued, may be included in the profits of that enterprise and taxed accordingly" (OECD Model Convention. Article 9 (1)).

32 OECD Model Convention. Article 9(2).

33 Other rules of law can also apply, requiring the subsidiary not only to recharacterize its interest payments as dividends but also to recharacterize some of its

debt as shareholders equity. If subsidiaries seek funding from banks, the banks will review the extent to which loans from a parent should be characterized as shareholders equity and impose such a recharacterization as a condition to lending.

34   In 1998, the OECD established criteria for designation as a tax haven. The OECD summarized those criteria in 2000 as follows:

> The four key factors [are:] 1) there is no or [only] nominal tax on the relevant income (from geographically mobile financial and other service activities); 2) there is no effective exchange of information with respect to the regime; 3) the jurisdiction's regimes lack transparency, e.g., the details of the regime or its application are not apparent, or there is inadequate regulatory supervision or financial disclosure; and 4) the jurisdiction facilitates the establishment of foreign-owned entities without the need for a local substantive presence or prohibits these entities from having any commercial impact on the local economy.
>
> (Towards Global Tax Cooperation – Progress in Identifying and Eliminating Harmful Tax Practices, an OECD Report (2000), page 10, note 4)

35   Since 1998, the OECD has made efforts to improve tax cooperation with the countries it designated as tax havens. As of 20 May 2003, only six countries designated as tax havens by the OECD have not agreed to cooperate in the elimination of harmful tax practices: Andorra, The Principality of Liechtenstein, Liberia, The Principality of Monaco, The Republic of the Marshall Islands and The Republic of Nauru. Most recently, on 20 May 2003, the OECD announced that Vanuatu had agreed to cooperate with OECD initiatives addressing harmful tax practices. Moreover, the OECD has announced that, on the basis of effective existing cooperation with OECD member states, three countries (Barbados, Maldives, and Tonga) are no longer considered to be un-cooperative tax havens. Prior to June 2000, six tax havens – Bermuda, Cayman Islands, Cyprus, Malta, Mauritius, San Marino – made commitments to cooperate with the OECD in addressing harmful tax practices. On 18 April 2002, the OECD reported that another twenty-five tax havens had agreed to cooperate with OECD initiatives addressing harmful tax practices: Anguilla, Antigua and Barbuda, Aruba, Bahamas, Bahrain, Belize, British Virgin Islands, Cook Islands, Dominica, Gibraltar, Grenada, Guernsey, Isle of Man, Jersey, Montserrat, Netherlands Antilles, Niue, Panama, Samoa, St Christopher (St Kitts) and Nevis, Saint Lucia, Seychelles, St Vincent and the Grenadines, Turks & Caicos and US Virgin Islands.

36   Profits from the conduct of a business or trade (i.e., active income) are typically generated by tangible assets such as plant, equipment and inventories. In contrast to the intangible assets giving rise to passive income (loans, technology and shareholdings), tangible assets are fairly difficult to relocate and are only occasionally moved out of a nation once installed there. Accordingly, the issues posed in respect of passive income, as outlined in this section, typically do not arise in the context of profits from the conduct of a trade or business.

37   "The Deferral of Income Earned Through US Controlled Foreign Corporations," US Department of Treasury, page 58, note 10. One example of such anti-tax-avoidance rules is the US rules applicable to "subpart F Income – Controlled Foreign Corporations," Sections 951–64 of the Internal Revenue Code. Another closely related example is the "Foreign Personal Holding Companies," Sections 551–6 of the US Internal Revenue Code.

38   For details, please see Note 35.

39   These nations also typically do not have exorbitant secrecy regulations (e.g., bank secrecy laws). In addition, most of these nations are large countries, are OECD members and generally cooperate with taxing authorities of other nations in the manner proposed in the OECD Model Convention: i.e., competent authority proceedings, exchanges of information and assistance in the collection of taxes.

40   In 1998, the OECD identified several features of potentially harmful competitive tax practices. In 2000, the OECD summarized those features as follows:

> In brief, there are four main factors, similar to the tax haven criteria … : 1) the regime imposes low or no taxes on the relevant income (from geographically mobile financial and other service activities); 2) the regime is ring-fenced from the domestic economy; 3) the regime that lacks transparency e.g., the details of the regime or its application or not apparent, or there is inadequate regulatory supervision or financial disclosure; and 4) there is no effective exchange of information with respect to the regime. There are also a number of other factors to be considered, including the extent of compliance with the OECD Transfer Pricing Guidelines.
>
> (Towards Global Tax Cooperation – Progress in Identifying and Eliminating Harmful Tax Practices, an OECD Report (2000), page 9, note 3)

41   According to the OECD, in 2000 twenty-one countries were engaged in potentially harmful tax competition:

Australia, Belgium, Canada, Finland, France, Germany, Greece, Hungary, Iceland, Ireland, Italy, Korea, Luxembourg, Netherlands, Norway, Portugal, Spain, Sweden, Switzerland, Turkey and the USA.

42 Holding company regimes could probably be listed as another category of potentially harmful tax competition. As of 2000, according to the OECD, such regimes existed in Austria, Belgium, Denmark, France, Germany, Greece, Ireland, Luxembourg, Netherlands, Portugal, Spain and Switzerland. Research and development activities can probably also be added to the OECD's list of business activities considered to be desirable.

43 August, R. (2004) *International Business Law* (Fourth Edition), Upper Saddle River, NJ: Pearson Education, Inc., page 742.

CHAPTER 12: RELATIONSHIPS WITH SHAREHOLDERS

1 Braithwaite, J. and Drahos, P. (2000) *Global Business Regulation*, Cambridge, UK: Cambridge University Press, pages 145–8.

2 As noted in the chapter on ownership rights, owners sometimes transfer to other persons some, but not all, of their ownership rights in certain assets, i.e., the rights of possession, usage, profit and transfer. As set forth in that chapter:

> "Agent" is a term used to describe a person who, in pursuit of a business's specific purposes, accepts to exercise some – but not all – of that business's ownership rights in specific assets. "Principal" is the term used to describe businesses who, in pursuit of their specific purposes, transfer to agents some – but not all – of their ownership rights in specific assets. Within the scope of the agency arrangement, the agent is said to act "on behalf of" the principal. Depending on the terms of the agency arrangement, the agent may additionally have the right to act "in the name of" the principal.

In other words, appointments of agents create a relationship involving trust, the principals' trust of their agents. The "trust" involved in agency arrangements consists generally of the agents' obligations (i) to exercise the transferred property rights for the principal's specific purposes, and (ii) to respect the principal's present and future private property rights not transferred to the agents. The agent's trust obligations are a necessary incident to their principals' retained property rights.

CHAPTER 13: RELATIONSHIPS WITH SHARE TRADERS

1 Selected disclosures required in a prospectus for an initial public offering

Selected provisions of SEC Form S-1

A prospectus shall contain all of the information required for shares publicly traded on a securities exchange in the United States, as provided by SEC Form 10-K (Annual Statement to Shareholders). In addition, a prospectus is required to contain certain information specific to the facts and circumstances surrounding the issuance of shares, including the information set forth below:

General terms of the offering, including class of shares, number of shares and pricing. The prospectus cover provides a summary of the general terms of the offering, including the title and number of shares being sold, a suggested price range for the shares, and a list of the underwriters. The final prospectus will list the offering price of the deal. If there is already an existing public market for this class of shares from this issuer and there is a substantial discrepancy between the public price for the outstanding shares and the offering price for the shares to be issued, then the disparity should be explained. 17 CFR §229.501 & 505. Items 501 & 505.

Prospectus "subject to completion" legend. If you use the prospectus before the effective date of the registration statement, a prominent statement follows. Please recall that the completion of the SEC registration process for any particular securities does not constitute approval of those securities by the SEC.

"The information in this prospectus is not complete and may be changed. We may not sell these securities until the registration statement filed with the Securities and Exchange Commission is effective. This prospectus is not an offer to sell these securities and it is not soliciting an offer to buy these securities in any state where the offer or sale is not permitted." 17 CFR §229.501(B)(10) Item 501(b)(10).

Dealer prospectus delivery obligation. In addition to the subject to completion legend, the prospectus shall contain the following information. The purpose of this information is to confirm that buyers receive a prospectus before they purchase newly-issued securities.

"Until (insert date), all dealers that effect transactions in these securities, whether or not participating in this offering, may be required to deliver a prospectus. This is in addition to the dealers' obligation to deliver a prospectus when acting as underwriters and with respect to their unsold allotments or subscriptions." 17 CFR §229.50. Item 502.

Risk factors. This section is meant to highlight the specific risks that an investor faces in a particular offering. This can be a good place to glean a list of concerns to consider as you read deeper into the prospectus. The risk factors may include, among other things, the company's (1) lack of an operating history; (2) lack of profitable operations in recent periods; (3) financial position; (4) business or proposed business; and (5) lack of a market for your common equity securities or securities convertible into or exercisable for common equity securities. 17 CFR §229.503. Item 503 (c).

Use of proceeds. This section states the principal purposes for which the net proceeds to the registrant from the securities to be offered are intended to be used, such as debt repayment or construction of new facilities, and the approximate amount intended to be used for each such purpose. Where registrant has no current specific plan for the proceeds, or a significant portion thereof, the registrant shall so state and discuss the principal reasons for the offering. 17 CFR §229.504. Item 504.

Selling security holders. If any of the securities to be registered are to be offered for the account of security holders, name each such security holder, indicate the nature of any position, office, or other material relationship which the selling security holder has had within the past three years with the registrant or any of its predecessors or affiliates, and state the amount of securities of the class owned by such security holder prior to the offering, the amount to be offered for the security holder's account, the amount and (if one percent or more) the percentage of the class to be owned by such security holder after completion of the offering. 17 CFR §229.507. Item 507.

Underwriting/plan of distribution. The section still lists the underwriters involved and details about the execution of the offering. 17 CFR §229.508. Item 508.

2   **Selected disclosures required in annual report to shareholders**

Selected provisions of SEC Form 10-K

General development of business. Describe the general development of the business of the registrant, its subsidiaries and any predecessor(s) during the past five years, or such shorter period as the registrant may have been engaged in business. Information shall be disclosed for earlier periods if material to an under-

standing of the general development of the business. 17 CFR §229.101. Item 101 (a).

Narrative description of business by segments. Describe the business done and intended to be done by the registrant and its subsidiaries, focusing upon the registrant's dominant segment or each reportable segment about which financial information is presented in the financial statements. 17 CFR §229.101. Item 101 (b).

Financial information about segments and geographic areas. Report for each segment, as defined by generally accepted accounting principles, revenues from external customers, a measure of profit or loss and total assets. A registrant must report this information for each of the last three fiscal years or for as long as it has been in business, whichever period is shorter. A registrant must give similar information for each geographic area in which it conducts business. 17 CFR §229.101. Item 101 (c).

Description of property. State briefly the location and general character of the principal plants, mines and other materially important physical properties of the registrant and its subsidiaries. In addition, identify the segment(s) that use the properties described. If any such property is not held in fee or is held subject to any major encumbrance, so state and describe briefly how held. 17 CFR §229.102. Item 102.

Legal proceedings. Describe briefly any material pending legal proceedings, other than ordinary routine litigation incidental to the business, to which the registrant or any of its subsidiaries is a party or of which any of their property is the subject. Include the name of the court or agency in which the proceedings are pending, the date instituted, the principal parties thereto, a description of the factual basis alleged to underlie the proceeding and the relief sought. Include similar information as to any such proceedings known to be contemplated by governmental authorities. 17 CFR §229.103. Item 103.

Market information for registrant's securities. Identify the principal United States market or markets in which each class of the registrant's common equity is being traded, the range of high and low bid information for the equity for each full quarterly period within the two most recent fiscal years and any subsequent interim period for which financial statements are included. Where there is no established public trading market for a class of common equity, furnish a statement to that effect. 17 CFR §229.201. Item 201 (a).

Number of shareholders and amounts of dividends. Set forth the approximate number of holders of each class of common equity of the registrant as of the latest practicable date. State the frequency and amount of any cash dividends declared on each class of its common equity by the registrant for the two most recent fiscal years and any subsequent interim period for which financial statements are required to be presented. 17 CFR §229.201. Item 201 (b) and (c).

Equity compensation plans. In tabular format, provide the following information as of the end of the most recently completed fiscal year with respect to compensation plans (including individual compensation arrangements) under which equity securities of the registrant are authorized for issuance: (1) Number of securities to be issued upon exercise of outstanding options, warrants and rights, Weighted average exercise price of outstanding options, warrants and rights, Number of securities remaining available for future issuance. 17 CFR §229.201. Item 201 (d).

Recent sales of unregistered securities. Furnish the following information as to all securities of the registrant sold by the registrant within the past three years which were not registered under the Securities Act. Include sales of reacquired securities, as well as new issues, securities issued in exchange for property, services, or other securities, and new securities resulting from the modification of outstanding securities. 17 CFR §229.701. Item 701.

Selected financial data. Furnish in comparative columnar form the selected financial data for the registrant referred to below, for (a) Each of the last five fiscal years of the registrant (or for the life of the registrant and its predecessors, if less), and (b) Any additional fiscal years necessary to keep the information from being misleading. The following items shall be included in the table of financial data: net sales or operating revenues; income (loss) from continuing operations; income (loss) from continuing operations per common share; total assets; long-term obligations and redeemable preferred stock (including long-term debt, capital leases, and redeemable preferred stock); and cash dividends declared per common share. 17 CFR §229.301. Item 301.

Acquisitions, divestments and changes in accounting methods. Briefly describe, or cross-reference to a discussion thereof, factors such as accounting changes, business combinations or dispositions of business operations, that materially affect the comparability of the information reflected in selected financial data. Discussion of, or reference to, any material uncertainties should also be included where such matters might cause the data reflected herein not to be indicative of the registrant's future financial condition or results of operations. 17 CFR §229.301. Item 301.

Management's discussion and analysis of financial condition and results of operations. Discuss registrant's financial condition, changes in financial condition and results of operations. The discussion shall provide specified information with respect to liquidity, capital resources and results of operations and also shall provide such other information that the registrant believes to be necessary to an understanding of its financial condition, changes in financial condition and results of operations. 17 CFR §229.303. Item 303.

Changes in and disagreements with accountants. If during the registrant's two most recent fiscal years or any subsequent interim period, an independent accountant … has resigned (or indicated it has declined to stand for re-election after the completion of the current audit) or was dismissed, then the registrant shall disclose the circumstances and procedures involved in the resignation, dismissal or refusal to stand for re-election. 17 CFR §229.304. Item 304 (a) (1).

Identification of directors. List the names and ages of all directors of the registrant and all persons nominated or chosen to become directors; indicate all positions and offices with the registrant held by each such person; state his term of office as director and any period(s) during which he has served as such; describe briefly any arrangement or understanding between him and any other person(s) (naming such person(s)) pursuant to which he was or is to be selected as a director or nominee. 17 CFR §229.401. Item 401 (a).

Executive compensation. Provide clear, concise and understandable disclosure of all plan and non-plan compensation awarded to, earned by, or paid to the CEO, any acting CEO, the five other most highly compensated executive officers and all directors. All compensation shall be reported, even if also called for by another requirement, including transactions between the registrant and a third party where the primary purpose of the transaction is to furnish compensation to any such named executive officer or director. 17 CFR §229.402. Item 402.

Employment, resignation and retirement agreements. Describe the material terms of any employment contract between the registrant and a named executive officer. Any compensatory plan or arrangement, including payments to be received from the registrant, with respect to a named executive officer, if such plan or arrangement results or will result from the resignation, retirement or any other termination of such executive officer's employment with the registrant and its subsidiaries or from a change-in-control of the registrant or a change in the named executive officer's responsibilities following a change-in-control and the amount involved, including all periodic payments or installments, exceeds $100,000. 17 CFR §229.402. Item 402 (h).

Compensation of directors. Describe any standard or other arrangements, stating amounts, pursuant to which directors of the registrant are compensated for any services provided as a director, including any additional amounts payable for committee participation or special assignments. Describe any other arrangements pursuant to which any director of the registrant was compensated during the registrant's last completed fiscal year for any service provided as a director, stating the amount paid and the name of the director. The material terms of any such arrangement shall be included. 17 CFR §229.402. Item 402.

Security ownership of 5% beneficial owners. Furnish certain information in tabular form with respect to any person or group of persons who is known to the registrant to be the beneficial owner of more than five percent of any class of the registrant's voting securities. 17 CFR §229.403. Item 403 (a).

Security ownership of officers and directors. Furnish information in tabular form as to each class of equity securities of the registrant or any of its parents or subsidiaries … beneficially owned by all directors and nominees, naming them, each of the named executive officers and directors and executive officers of the registrant as a group, without naming them. 17 CFR §229.403. Item 403 (a).

Certain relationships and related transactions. Describe briefly any transaction, or series of similar transactions, since the beginning of the registrant's last fiscal year, or any currently proposed transaction, or series of similar transactions, to which the registrant or any of its subsidiaries was or is to be a party, in which the amount involved exceeds $60,000 and in which any of the following persons had, or will have, a direct or indirect material interest: (1) Any director or executive officer of the registrant; (2) Any nominee for election as a director; (3) Any security holder who is known to the registrant to own of record or beneficially more than five percent of any class of the registrant's voting securities; and (4) Any member of the immediate family of any of the foregoing persons. Identify each such transaction or series of transactions and each such person, indicating the person's relationship to the registrant, the nature of such person's interest in the transaction(s), the amount of such transaction(s) and, where practicable, the amount of such person's interest in the transaction(s). 17 CFR §229.404. Item 404(a).

Code of ethics. Disclose whether the registrant has adopted a code of ethics that applies to the registrant's principal executive officer, principal financial officer, principal accounting officer or controller, or persons performing similar functions. If the registrant has not adopted such a code of ethics, explain why it has not done so. 17 CFR §229.406. Item 406.

Audit committee report. The audit committee of the board of directors must state the names of its members and whether the audit committee has (1) received and discussed with the corporation's auditors the required written assurances of the auditors' independence, (2) reviewed and discussed the audited financial statements with management and independent auditors, (3) recommended to the entire board of directors that the audited financial statements be included in the company's annual report on Form 10-K. 17 CFR §229.306. Item 306.

Internal controls and procedures. Disclose the conclusions of the registrant's principal executive officer or officers and principal financial officer or officers, or persons performing similar functions, about the effectiveness of the registrant's disclosure controls and procedures (as defined in §§240.13a-14(c) and 240.15d-14(c)) based on their evaluation of these controls and procedures as of a date within 90 days of the filing date of the quarterly or annual report that includes the disclosure required by this paragraph. Disclose whether or not there were significant changes in the registrant's internal controls or in other factors that could significantly affect these controls subsequent to the date of their evaluation, including any corrective actions with regard to significant deficiencies and material weaknesses. 17 CFR §229.307. Item 307(a) and (b).

CHAPTER 15: RELATIONSHIPS WITH DIRECTORS

1   An excellent summary of nineteen such reports and recommendations can be found in *International Comparison of Corporate Governance Guidelines and Codes of Best Practices – Developed Countries*, by Holly Gregory with assistance from Ira Millstein. Guidelines included within this study include: (1) the General Motors Board Guidelines, (2) OECD Principles by Ira Millstein, (3) the Bosch Report (Australia), (4) the Brussels Stock Exchange, (5) the Federation of Belgian Companies, (6) the Dey Report (Canada), Vienot Reports I and II (France), (7) Berlin Initiative Group Code (Germany), (8) Mertzanis Report

(Greece), (9) Preda Report (Italy), (10) Corporate Governance Forum Principles (Japan), (11) Peters Code (The Netherlands), (12) Securities Market Commission Recommendations (Portugal), (13) Olivencia Report (Spain), (14) Swedish Academy Report (Sweden), (15) Cadbury Report (United Kingdom), (16) Hampel Report (United Kingdom), (17) The Combined Code/Turnbull Report (United Kingdom), (18) 1996 NACD Report (USA), (19) 1997 BRT Report (USA). Since Ira Millstein was both involved in preparing the summary and in developing the OECD guidelines, the summary is probably credible. On 3 January 2003, The Conference Board issued its recommendations on corporate governance issues.

2 Voluntary Statement Confirming Management's Responsibility for Financial Statements and Internal Accounting Controls (customarily given by all CEOs and CFOs since 1976).

Example from Lucent Technologies, Inc.

1999 Annual Report to Shareholders

Management is responsible for the preparation of Lucent Technologies Inc.'s consolidated financial statements and all related information appearing in this Annual Report. The consolidated financial statements and notes have been prepared in conformity with generally accepted accounting principles and include certain amounts which are estimates based upon currently available information and management's judgment of current conditions and circumstances.

To provide reasonable assurance that assets are safeguarded against loss from unauthorized use or disposition and that accounting records are reliable for preparing financial statements, management maintains a system of accounting and other controls, including an internal audit function. Even an effective internal control system, no matter how well designed, has inherent limitations – including the possibility of circumvention or overriding of controls – and therefore can provide only reasonable assurance with respect to financial statement presentation. The system of accounting and other controls is improved and modified in response to changes in business conditions and operations and recommendations made by the independent public accountants and the internal auditors.

The Audit and Finance Committee of the Board of Directors, which is composed of directors who are not employees, meets periodically with management, the internal auditors and the independent auditors to review the manner in which these groups of individuals are performing their responsibilities and to carry out the Audit and Finance Committee's oversight role with respect to auditing, internal controls and financial reporting matters. Periodically, both the internal auditors and the independent auditors meet privately with the Audit and Finance Committee and have access to its individual members.

Lucent engaged PricewaterhouseCoopers LLP, independent public accountants, to audit the consolidated financial statements in accordance with generally accepted auditing standards, which include consideration of the internal control structure. Their report appears on this page.

Richard A. McGinn Donald K. Peterson, Chairman and Executive Vice President and Chief Executive Officer Chief Financial Officer

3 Certification of Management's Responsibility for Financial Statements and Internal Accounting Controls (required from all CEOs and CFOs since 2003)

I, [identify the certifying individual], certify that:

I have reviewed this [specify report] of [identify registrant];

Based on my knowledge, this report does not contain any untrue statement of a material fact or omit to state a material fact necessary to make the statements made, in light of the circumstances under which such statements were made, not misleading with respect to the period covered by this report;

Based on my knowledge, the financial statements, and other financial information included in this report, fairly present in all material respects the financial condition, results of operations and cash flows of the registrant as of, and for, the periods presented in this report;

The registrant's other certifying officer(s) and I are responsible for establishing and maintaining disclosure controls and procedures (as defined in Exchange Act Rules 13a-15(e) and 15d-15(e)) and internal control over financial reporting (as defined in Exchange Act Rules 13a-15(f) and 15d-15(f)) for the registrant and have:

(a) Designed such disclosure controls and procedures, or caused such disclosure controls and procedures to be designed under our supervision, to ensure that material information relating to the registrant, including its consolidated subsidiaries, is made known to us by others within those entities, particularly during the period in which this report is being prepared;

(b) Designed such internal control over financial reporting, or caused such internal control over financial reporting to be designed under our supervision, to provide reasonable assurance regarding the reliability of financial reporting and the preparation of financial statements for external purposes in accordance with generally accepted accounting principles;

(c) Evaluated the effectiveness of the registrant's disclosure controls and procedures and presented in this report our conclusions about the effectiveness of the disclosure controls and procedures, as of the end of the period covered by this report based on such evaluation; and

(d) Disclosed in this report any change in the registrant's internal control over financial reporting that occurred during the registrant's most recent fiscal quarter (the registrant's fourth fiscal quarter in the case of an annual report) that has materially affected, or is reasonably likely to materially affect, the registrant's internal control over financial reporting; and

The registrant's other certifying officer(s) and I have disclosed, based on our most recent evaluation of internal control over financial reporting, to the registrant's auditors and the audit committee of the registrant's board of directors (or persons performing the equivalent functions):

(a) All significant deficiencies and material weaknesses in the design or operation of internal control over financial reporting which are reasonably likely to adversely affect the registrant's ability to record, process, summarize and report financial information; and

(b) Any fraud, whether or not material, that involves management or other employees who have a significant role in the registrant's internal control over financial reporting.

Date: ....

_____

[Signature]

[Title]

Provide a separate certification for each principal executive officer and principal financial officer of the registrant.

CHAPTER 19: INTERNATIONAL AND EUROPEAN PATENTS

1   Member states of the EPC:

Austria
Belgium
Cyprus
Denmark
Finland
France
Germany
Greece
Ireland
Italy
Liechtenstein
Luxembourg
Monaco
The Netherlands
Portugal
Spain
Sweden
Switzerland
Turkey
United Kingdom

CHAPTER 20: INSURING BUSINESS RISKS

1   A rider is an attachment to an insurance policy that alters the policy's coverage or terms.

INDEX

17–18; probability theories 20; public information 20; putting it all together 18–19; self-interested decision-maker 18; the "right" decision? 19–21; utilitarianism 18

business ethics 10–12; enforced by civil society 11; not commercial expectations 11; societal categorical imperatives 10–11

business insurance 257–66

business law 9–10; governmental categorical imperatives 10; courts apply to past 10; executive agencies apply to ongoing 10

business profits 142

business regulation 25–38; breaches of contract obligations 26; breaches of general obligations (torts) 26; punitive damages 27; economic impact 35–6; differences from judicial remedies 28–30; establishing quality standards 28; giving choice and information to buyers 27–28; governmental 27–30; international governmental 30–1; introduction 25–6; judicial remedies 26–7; notes 267–71; self-regulation 31–7; three opportunities for self-regulation 36–7

business trusts 155

capitalization 147-8

caring and trust 15, 19

causation 55–6; "but for" or actual 55; "proximate" or foreseeable 55–6

charters 194

civil litigation 218–20; class actions 220; complaints, summons and answers 219; counterclaims, cross claims and joinders 220; motions to dismiss complaints 219–220

Civil Rights Act of 1866 123

Civil Rights Act of 1964 123–4

Civil Rights Act of 1991 125–6

Civil Service Reform Act of 1978 119

Class Actions 220

code: of ethics 196–7; of conduct 181–5, 194–5

collective bargaining: in Europe 131–4; in US 117–20; agreements, 132-3; representation process 132; third-party dispute resolution

133; union rights and recognition 131–2

collective redundancies and transfers of undertakings 134

commercial and contract law 65–76

commercial: relationships 31–3; reputations 33–4

commercial transactions: contractual modifications of 73–6; covenants 67–8; delivery 66–7; essential terms 65–7; exclusive remedies 74; incidental terms 69–73; indemnifications 75–6; letters of credit 68; limitations of liability 74–5; payment terms 67; warranties 70–2, 74

community ethical norms 13-16, 34–5; freedom of contract 15; general obligations 15; individual rights 14–15; justice 16; notes 282–5; other ethical norms 16; relationships with 103–13; private property 14-15; self-interested decision making 13; trust and caring 15-16; utilitarianism 14

compensation 59-60

competition 240

competition law 79-92

competitors: effects doctrine 91–2; Herfindahl-Hirschman Index 90, 92; history of 79–80; horizontal restraints on trade 82–3; introduction 79; notes 273–9; relationships with 79–92; restraints on trade 82–92; monopolies regulation 87–91; verbal agreements 86; vertical restraints 83–5

compliance: adaptability of effective programs 184–5; CEO's enforcement and delegation 181–2; company codes of conduct 181–5; consistent enforcement 183–4; continuous improvement 184; effective communication with employees and agents 182; enforcement of contracts 188; industry guidelines "duties of care" 187; reasonable steps to achieve 182–3; with contracts, intangible and tangible assets 188; with ethical norms 188; with general obligations 187–8; with government regulations 180–5

concerted practices 86

conciliation 230–1

concurrent ownership 47–8

confidentiality 236–7

Consolidates Omnibus Budget Reconciliation Act of 1985 (COBRA) 127

consumers: disclosure obligations 96–9; fair dealing 95–102; fundamental EU law 96, 101–2; fundamental US law 95–6; introduction 93; notes 279–82; protection 76; reasonable contracts 99–100; relationships with 93–102; quality standards, consumer health and safety 100; torts 100; unfair trading with, examples of 101–2;

contract and commercial law 65–76; essential terms in commercial transactions 65–8; incidental terms 69–73; introduction 65; contractual modifications 73–6; notes 272–3; self-regulation 76

contracting agent 142–3

contracts 17, 26, 37, 42–3, 65–76, 99–100, 160, 187–8, 258

control stock" 173

cookie jar" reserves 172

copyright 234–5, 244

corporate constituencies 19

corporate constitutions157–8; legal representatives 158; shareholders and directors 157–8

corporate funding 201–2

corporate indemnifications 161

corporate governance 4–5 7–8; COSO's Internal Control-Integrated Framework 1992 7; COSO's 2004 Enterprise Risk Management Integrated Framework 7-8; governance procedures 4–5; governance structures 4; opportunity and risk management 5-7; Sarbanes-Oxley Act of 2002 7; structures and procedures 4; workable procedures 5

corporate law 153–162, 163–6, 191–2

corporate officers 20–21, 51–2, 156–62, 163–6, 189–200, 259–63; as agents 158; bankruptcy 161; corporate indemnifications 161; delegations of authority 160; duty of care 159; duty of loyalty 160; fiduciary duties 159; obligations of trust 158–9; officers' and directors' liability insurance 161–2;

unemployment and severance: Europe 131

unfair trading with consumers: examples of 101–2

unincorporated place of business 142

US securities exchanges 173–4

US securities regulations 166-8, 195–7

utilitarianism 14, 18

utility models 244

utility patents 243–5; invention 245; inventive step 246; novelty 245–6

verbal agreements 86

visas 129

wages, working time, and leave: US 134–6; Fair Labor Standards Act of 1938 121; Family and Medical Leave Act of 1993 122; Federal unemployment taxes 122; military leave 122–3; Social Security and Medicare taxes 121–2

wages, working time, and leave: Europe 134–6; leave 135–6; wages 134–5; working time 135

warehouse receipts 51

warranties 70, 71, 74, 205–6

water, bodies of 45

withholding taxes 143–4

workers: free movement of in Europe 137

workers compensation 62–3, 126, 264

workers participation: Europe 133–4; Dutch model 133; German model 133; through a body representing company employees 133–4; through collectively agreed systems 134

WTO negotiations 113